THE

BEER

LOVER'S

RATING GUIDE

BY BOB KLEIN

WORKMAN PUBLISHING

Copyright © 1995 by Bob Klein

Library of Congress Cataloging-in-Publication Data
Klein, Bob
    The beer lover's rating guide / by Bob Klein.
        p.   cm.
    ISBN 1-56305-682-8
    1. Beer. I. Title.
TP577.K63 1994
641.2'3—dc20   94-22247
                                                          CIP

Cover photograph by Michael Harris
Book illustrations by David Cain

Workman books are available at special discount when
purchased in bulk for special sales promotions as well as
fundraising or educational use. Special book excerpts or
editions can also be created to specification. For details,
contact the Special Sales Director at the address below.

Workman Publishing Company, Inc.
708 Broadway
New York, NY 10003

Manufactured in the United States

First printing May 1995
10 9 8 7 6 5 4 3 2 1

ACKNOWLEDGMENTS

This guide of (mostly) good cheer could not have happened, of course, without the glorious multitude of beer makers out there in breweryland, especially those who consciously strive to offer pleasure and quality in every barrel. I salute them all, with a beer in my hand and a glow of satisfaction on my face.

But there are others, too, who must be acknowledged for helping to make this book the catholic collection that I hope it is. Since I no longer can be certain of regularly finding new beers during my own travels or at home in Albuquerque, I also rely on dedicated globe-trotting friends to selflessly schlep back the untried and unusual. Gayle Zieman, for example, returned from a South Pacific idyll with Western Samoan brews. On several other occasions, he heroically contended with customs officials, querulous shopkeepers, and airline weight restrictions in order to hand-deliver suitably packaged large bottles of beer from various spots in India and nearby countries.

My friend Scott Obenshain periodically brings me a bottle or two from his European and East Coast travels and Spider Johnson, my connection from Mason, Texas, has sent me beer from the land of the Lone Star.

My appreciation as well to Anne Kass and Janeanne Snow for scouring the local beer stores trying to find something I haven't had when they know I will be coming over for a visit. And, thanks, too, for the cache of ten bottles from Brazil from someone I don't even know—a bank VP in New York who got my name from my sister. I thank them all.

In New York, I always pay a visit to Alex Anastasiadis, the serious-minded proprietor of Alex's Deli in Manhattan's Greenwich Village, who is always searching for new and different beers. Alex's extensive assortment in the large glass-door cooler has got to be one of the best in the city, and I invariably come away with a dozen new brews or more. I am particularly grateful to Brad Kraus, one of only eleven certified Master Judges of beer in the country (Brad would be in a higher category, if there was one) and the extraordinarily knowledgeable and talented brewmaster at Rio Bravo Brewpub in Albuquerque, where, in my judgment, some of the country's finest stouts and ales are consistently made. Brad, and also Dan Baumann, former president of the Dukes of Ale and an experienced homebrewer in his own right, were kind enough to go through my manuscript at various stages. Both were generous with their time—between the two of them, there wasn't a brewing question I couldn't get answered.

A very special thank you to John Zonski, owner of Jubilation Fine Wine and Spirits in Albuquerque (with his wife, Carol, whose next-door restaurant offers a wonderful green chile–chicken soup). Not only does John stock his shelves with care and consideration for his customers, but he also encouraged me to write my beer newsletter (and lent me his photocopier). John was always patient and detailed with answers to my questions about the bottled beer he sold, and unfailingly went out of his way to obtain the sometimes esoteric information that I needed. Both his kindness and his inventory of quality beers were important to the completeness of this book.

To my agent Jim Levine and his stalwart crew: Thanks for your help, taste buds, and enthusiasm. My appreciation to Suzanne Rafer, my editor at Workman, who learned from me about beer while I learned from her about the sometimes subtle, sometimes arcane, but always helpful ways of a busy editor. And a special toast of thanks must be offered to Joni Miller, the Guide's intrepid and always-ebullient copy editor, who brought erudition, tact, and a sense of humor to an occasionally tedious, if not frustrating, editing process. Alas, despite this solid lineup of aid and comfort, any errors, of omission or commissions, are mine.

If gold medals were to be given out for personal attention and support, my wife, Norma, would have the world's largest collection, in all categories and every style (style, in fact, is her middle name). Endlessly supportive and resourceful, she provided me unsparingly and (usually) in good cheer all manner of assistance, from emergency scraps of paper on which to write my ratings to hour after (late) hour at the computer sorting out sometimes horrendous manuscript glitches and solving them with the aplomb and accuracy and mind-boggling tenacity of the talented professional that she is. She is also a most amiable and tolerant drinking companion (not to mention my mate and partner of 32 quite interesting years). Her help in putting this book together was enormous. It is safe as well as accurate to say, with no diminution of the generous input of those noted above, that Norma's contribution alone equals that of all the others combined. I trust that we all can drink to that.

—Bob Klein
Albuquerque, New Mexico

CONTENTS

THE RATING GUIDE

APPENDIXES

WORDS FROM A BEER LOVER

I've been called a beer nut. And, despite the pun, I guess that's accurate.

I drink beer. Lots of it.

Not just any beer, mind you. Nor in copious, indiscriminate amounts. I don't chug barrels of Coors in front of the TV or cases of Bud at family picnics.

I'm more focused than that, and I have a goal: to judiciously locate, sip, and rate at least one beer from every nook and cranny of the globe. A gargantuan task, to be sure; may everyone have a job so stressful.

Amazingly, I have succeeded—to the point where I am now asked to judge sanctioned beer competitions. (Yes, there *are* such things—many of them.) I also have written and been a guest judge for the national publication, *All About Beer.* And copies of *Jubilation News,* my monthly beer newsletter, which I published for a couple of years, are in the Anheuser-Busch library. That's what drinking and keeping a careful record of more than 1,200 beers can get you.

During the past decade-and-a-half, I have logged over 90,000 miles searching for the perfect—and, alas, also meeting up with the imperfect—beer, traveling to places like Moscow and Leningrad; Valdivia and Santiago, Chile; Quito, Ecuador; Shannon, Ireland, and Helsinki, Finland. Nearer to home, I have sampled beer made in locations as far-flung as Pottsville, Pennsylvania, and Auburndale, Florida; Victoria, B.C., Canada, and Mazatlan, Mexico. I have asked for seconds at brewpubs in Southern California and central St. Louis (where I also had, not so incidentally, the best dessert in the world; but that's another story); Albuquerque, New Mexico, and New York City; and, of course, Oregon and Washington state, where brewpubs and microbreweries flourish like hops in the Yakima valley region.

In order to keep track of my tastings, I have an assistant who logs each beer I drink into my computer. The electronic storage system allows me to sort, categorize, and rate the beers by state, city, and country; best and worst styles; lowest and highest rankings by different regions of the world and country; and a host of other breakdowns—all of which are yours for the page-turning in *The Beer Lover's Rating Guide.*

In 1987, my list showed a paltry 150 different beers rated; by 1989, it had increased to 639. As this book went to press, I had tasted and evaluated 1,298 brews from every part of the world—covering all five continents, several islands and a jungle or two. My generously supportive wife—she usually sticks to Harp and lets it go at that—urges me ever onward to reach 2,000 brews by the year 2,000.

RATING GUIDELINES

Like many others, I drink beer socially, often requesting something different or unusual whenever I eat out or purchase a couple of bottles to take home. Over time I began to have difficulty recalling whether I had already tasted a particular beer, and if so, whether I cared to have it again. I also began to go to great lengths to locate unique beers or ones that were not readily available. I started to plan trips around the locations of breweries and brewpubs, sometimes extending or modifying vacations for the sole purpose of adding even one more new find to my list.

Finally, I decided to keep a record of what I drank. At first I jotted down the pertinent information on handy scraps of paper. Now, I carry my computerized alphabetical listing with me, adding new beers to it as I find them. I also note the city in which the beer is brewed (not always, as I soon learned, the same location as the company), my impressions of what I'm paying for—taste, aroma, alcohol content, balance—and how it all goes with the food at hand. I always have beer with food.

As I drain the glass, and make a judgment about its connection to the food, I rank the brew on a scale of 0 to 5. (In a few pages, I will show you how to do that.) Over time, I have come to learn which beers to avoid, which to try again, and which to order for my friends. After awhile, I began to get requests for copies of my computer-generated, alphabetized list of ratings. I gave them out as birthday presents, holiday gifts, and just plain because I liked somebody and wanted him or her to have some guidance and pleasure when selecting a beer to drink.

IN THE FIELD WITH THE RATING GUIDE

Ten years ago, beer drinkers in the United States were limited in domestic choice to the half-dozen or so national megabreweries, a few regionals, a small handful of hard-to-find microbreweries, and hardly any brewpubs. Even finding imports, particularly from lesser-producing countries, took some effort.

Today, we can choose from almost 500 brewed-in-the U.S.A. local, regional, and national brands stretched across the landscape from Utica, New York, to Boonville, California, from New Ulm, Minnesota, to Cave Creek, Arizona—not to mention places like White River Junction, Vermont, or Strongsville, Ohio (and 80 to 100 in Canada). Mind you, each of these U.S. breweries—tiny, medium, large—has anywhere from three or four to a dozen or more styles available at any given time, plus a changing roster of seasonal and specialty offerings that pushes the total number of choices out of the barrel or the tap into the thousands. And the numbers, varieties, and sources of beers coming into the country have increased markedly—3% to 5% annually over the past half decade. All in all, there are roughly 4,800 to 5,200 breweries throughout the world, give or take a merger or closure or two.

This burgeoning largesse has served to solidify at least one ranking that has remained constant: The U.S. is by volume the world's largest brewing nation. (Germany, Great Britain, Japan, and the former Soviet Union are two to five respectively, much of their production finding its way to our taverns, package stores, and restaurants). However, we don't drink all we produce: The United States is not even in the top ten in per capita consumption, hovering around twelfth in the world (Germany, Czechoslovakia, Denmark, New Zealand, and Belgium are first to fifth).

Overall, close to 95% of American domestic producers are brewpubs (beer made in small batches and sold and consumed on the premises) and/or microbreweries (small quantities of beer bottled and distributed mostly to nearby retail outlets.) Although the accounting is always changing, the latter are defined as having a brewing capacity of no more than 20,000 to 30,000 barrels annually; by comparison, a commercial megabrewery like Anheuser-Busch, the largest in the world, regularly churns out 5 to 6 million barrels at one plant alone (in the U.S. one barrel equals 31 gallons). Still, the total output of brewpubs and micros combined doesn't add up to 2% of U.S. beer production; this, despite the fact that there are no more than approximately six national breweries and perhaps thrice that many local, regional, and contract commercial breweries remaining in the country.

In general, brewpubs and micros are small, craftsmanship-oriented outfits where quality often can vary as unpredictably as the weather outside. The mortality rate is high, and one year's favorite drinking spot may easily become next year's empty parking lot. This guide is as up-to-date as it can be, but it's always best to check the status of the brewery—pub, micro, or mega—that interests you prior to paying it a visit or searching out its product.

Riding this ever-cresting wave of malts, hops, yeast and water, *The Beer Lover's Rating Guide* will help you determine and select which are the very best beers of any type—lagers, ales, stouts, wheats, porters, fruit, specialty, whatever—from all over the United States and the world.

By providing sections on style characteristics, serving temperatures, alcohol content, color variations, taste, aroma, ingredients, and foodworthiness—even a listing of the beers with the oddest names—this field guide to beer drinking pleasure will also identify those beers less deserving of your attention.

TAKING YOUR OWN FIELD TRIP

But this is not a book portentously telling you what to drink, or what to avoid; it is instead a guide meant to encourage you to select beers that *you* will enjoy, for your own personal reasons. While the ratings and comments in *The Beer Lover's Rating Guide* reflect my standards and opinions, I have tried to present the information in a way that makes it easy for you to determine what is tasty and satisfying and what is not.

The guide is user-friendly, easy to read, and designed to be fun and informative. As my friends, and their friends, have come to rely on my list, I invite you to match your evaluations with those you find in this guide. Remember: one person's sip is another one's swallow.

What follows are the results of careful research. Hope you enjoy the tasting as much as I did. And, with the guidance of *The Beer Lover's Rating Guide,* may you Never Buy A Bad Beer Again—anywhere, anyplace, anytime.

—Bob Klein

BEER STYLES:
What's the Difference?

ALE

Ales tend to be sweet, fruity, and texturally smooth. Many ales are higher in alcohol content than lagers and have a pronounced taste and flowery aroma. Ales are top-fermented. Most are served at 50°F to 55°F.

Types of Ale

BARLEY WINE: A strong, full-bodied dark ale with malt sweetness. Medium-to-strong hop bitterness with very high alcohol presence. Almost like wine.

BITTER: Highly hopped and quite bitter. Strength varies from Ordinary to Best to Extra Special Bitter (ESB). Usually served from the tap in England.

BLOND/GOLDEN ALE: A lighter version of pale ale, this offering is closer to a lager in flavor than most ales. It has a floral aroma with a light, dry taste.

BROWN ALE: A lightly-hopped, sweet, full-bodied brew with low-to-medium alcohol content. Color ranges from reddish-brown to dark brown. Lower in alcohol than porter and not as dry.

INDIA PALE ALE IPA: High in hops with a moderate amount of malt flavor. A dry, assertively bitter brew that ranges from pale (many IPAs fall into this category) to deep copper in color. It is fruity and flowery with evident alcohol.

PALE ALE: Pale ales combine distinct bitterness with some malt-based sweetness. Distinguishing characteristics are dryness and defined hop taste. So named to separate them from the darker porters, these ales range from amber to copper-brown and may be fairly mild to quite bitter.

PORTER: Black or chocolate malt contributes significantly to the dark brown color. Well-hopped and heavily malted. Hops help mitigate what might be a heavier drink. Porters can be malty sweet and range from bitter to mild and are drier than stouts—somewhere between stout and ale.

SCOTTISH ALE: Classically strong and amber to dark brown in color with a sweet, malty character. Rich and chewy. Low in hops; however, some variations brewed outside Scotland tend to be a bit bitter. Wide range of alcohol content. Also called "wee heavy."

STRONG ALE: Powerful flavor, highly alcoholic, but without clear-cut style characteristics. Usually dark in color with medium-to-low hops, producing a dry, bitter beverage.

ALCOHOL CONTENT

*T*he alcohol content of beer is measured in the United States by percentage of alcohol by weight. The chart below shows a general guideline for alcohol levels for major beer styles. Keep in mind that many beer styles—and therefore the defining amounts of alcohol—overlap.

BEER STYLE	% ALCOHOL BY WEIGHT	BEER STYLE	% ALCOHOL BY WEIGHT
U.S. LIGHT	2.3–3.5	EUROPEAN AMBER	3.9–4.7
ALE	2.5–6.0	MÄRZEN/ OKTOBERFEST	4.4–5.0
LAGER (EUROPEAN AND U.S.)	3.1–4.3	MALT LIQUOR	4.4–6.0
PILSENER	3.2–4.4	BOCK	4.7–7.0
PORTER	3.4–5.0	DOPPELBOCK	5.2–9.0
STOUT	3.5–8.0	BARLEY WINE/ ABBEY ALE	6.5–13.0
WHEAT	3.6–4.5		

STOUT

NOTE: Stouts and porters are often visually mistaken for each other, as both are very dark in color. Unlike porter, however, stout comes in a variety of types which are described below. Highly roasted barley is the keynote of this ale style.

Types of Stout

DRY STOUT: Plenty of hops, which produce a bitter taste; the addition of roasted unmalted barley or flaked barley results in a drink that is almost like a strong cup of coffee. Also called Irish Stout.

IMPERIAL STOUT: Created as an export to the frozen climes of Czarist Russia, this is very rich and malty with fruity overtones. Somewhat dry and strongly alcoholic.

MILK STOUT (also called English Stout or Sweet Stout): Malty sweet instead of dry, milk stout has a lower alcohol content than dry stout. The name reflects the addition of lactose—milk sugar—as a sweetener.

OATMEAL STOUT: Like milk stout, this is a sweeter product. The addition of oats is the sweetener in this case.

LAGER

Meant to be aged for 6 to 8 weeks or longer at cool temperatures, lagers should be clear, crisp, and distinctly carbonated. Most are maltier, less hoppy and aromatic, lighter colored, lighter in body, and less alcoholic than other beers. Lagers are bottom-fermented. *Lagern* means "to store" in German. Drink at 40°F–45°F.

Types of Lager

AMERICAN DRY LAGER: Despite the name, this product is a Japanese development. Pale to golden in color, it is distinguished by high carbonation but is low in bitterness, malt and hop flavors, and, often, taste. Dry (not sweet), low in alcohol, and scientifically balanced light body.

AMERICAN PILSENER: Crisp and more carbonated than European pilsener, but weaker and lighter in body and flavor. Prevalent style in the United States. Corn or rice adjuncts are often added during the brewing process, giving bulk and filler. Corn also imparts some flavor.

BOCK: Bock is traditionally full-bodied, strong, and high in alcohol content. It has an obvious malt and hop presence. Color is copper to dark brown. Bocks brewed in the United States often are brown or light brown, mild, and not complex. The more full-bodied doppelbock (double bock) is even higher in alcohol content. It is often identified by "ator" at the end of the name (for example, Celebrator). Helles Bock, a lighter version, both in color and taste, is somewhat sweeter and softer.

ENGLISH LAGER: Light variant of the American-brewed version, both in color and taste.

EUROPEAN DARK/MUNCHNER DUNKEL: Malt, as opposed to

GLOSSARY OF TERMS

Beer Language

BALANCE: The subjective impression of how well the various ingredients, especially malts and hops, go with one another. Ideal balance varies from style to style.

BODY: The thin-to-thick feel in the mouth. Beers can be full-bodied, medium-bodied, or light-bodied.

BOTTLE-CONDITIONED: Yeast continues fermentation process in the bottle, resulting in unpasteurized, naturally carbonated beer.

BOTTOM-FERMENTED: Lagers are made from a type of yeast that ferments at the bottom of the liquid; the brewing process involves longer brewing

times and colder temperatures. During brewing, the beer is stored for periods ranging from weeks to months. Storing, or lagering, encourages a smoother, more settled taste in the beer.

BRUSSELS LACE: Wisps of tightly-packed small bubbles, or foam, that attach to sides of the glass, often in intricate, spiderweb-like patterns or with a delicate curtain or sheeting effect. Usually a sign of a fresh, quality-made brew.

CLOYING: A sweet, sticky taste and feel on the tongue and sides of the mouth; often results in a thickish aftertaste.

hop, taste predominates. Suggestion of caramel, although not as sweet as brown ales. Clean and crisp with nice carbonation. Roasted malts give this beer its dark amber-to-brown coloration.

EUROPEAN PILSENER: Light-bodied with high hop bitterness. Clean, dry, rich taste and restrained flowery finish. Pale color with medium alcohol content. Pilsener, the palest of all lagers, is the most widely brewed and copied beer style in the world.

EXPORT: Often, but not always, refers to Dortmund-style brew (named for that Rhineland city's classic style): smooth, pale, fuller-bodied, and higher alcoholic content. Also, as the name suggests, may indicate beer sold only outside the coun-

FERMENTATION: The process by which alcohol and carbon dioxide (carbonation) are produced as the yeast acts on sugars in the grain.

HOPS: Flowers that give beer its bitter and aromatic character. Specific hops are selected for their taste- or aroma-giving properties. They are also a natural preservative and enhance the alcohol effect. Hops slow the pulse rate and give a sense of euphoria.

MALT (MALTED BARLEY): The defining ingredient, malt gives the beer its distinctive roasted, grain, or sweet character by influencing color, flavor, aroma, and head retention.

MOUTHFEEL: Overall physical impression of the beer as it travels from the lips to the throat.

TOP-FERMENTED: Ales are made from a type of yeast that ferments at the top of the liquid; the process involves warmer brewing temperatures and a shorter brewing time, often only days. Prior to the advent of refrigeration and the introduction of hops as preservatives, ale was the only game in town.

YEAST: A single-celled organism that converts sugars to alcohol and carbon dioxide. Also contributes to the production of certain flavors (e.g., citrus) and aids in the expression of malt and hop flavors.

try of origin, usually to meet specific, or assumed, foreign taste preferences. Sometimes, it means nothing at all.

MALT LIQUOR: Generally pale in color with no particular flavor profile. Very high in alcohol (where allowed by law). Some may have a sweet finish. Essentially an American invention.

MARZEN/OKTOBERFEST: Amber to pale copper in color. Malty aroma and sweetness with lots of hops to balance the malt. Good carbonation with low-to-medium bitterness. Toasted malt flavor predominates. Originally brewed in March (*Märzen*) and stored until October.

VIENNA AMBER: Toasted malt flavor with some rich, malty sweetness. Low hop aroma. Similar in flavor to the American-made lagers but darker in color, which is amber to copper.

COMBINATION STYLES

Beers produced by a mix of ale and lager brewing techniques and/or ingredients.

ALTBIER: Well-hopped and fairly malty, alt beers are quite aromatic and bitter. These beers are a well-defined amber color to a deep brown. *Alt* is the German word for "old" or "old style" and refers to the use of the old brewing method (warm ale-like fermentation) as opposed to the age of the beer. It is basically the German equivalent of English ale, although alts are aged cold, like lagers, which puts them in the combination-style category. In southern Germany, ordering an alt will get you a dark lager.

BIERE DE PARIS/BIERE DE GARDE: Strongly hopped, high in alcohol, copper colored, vibrant palate, and bottle-conditioned, laid on its side to age. Some are top-fermented (ale), some are bottom-fermented (lager, for example, Brasseurs).

CREAM ALE: A mild, pale ale with hop aroma. Sometimes blended with a lager, or using both ale and lager yeasts, cream ale is an American term. A close cousin to "steam beer."

KOLSCH: A lighter-colored version of alt beer, Kölsch is pale gold. It is delicate, dry and almost wine-like with low hop flavor and less bitterness than the true alt beer.

STEAM: Brewed at warmer ale temperatures and made with lager yeast. Medium-bodied, amber, and tellingly hoppy, with a generous head. A beer style created in the U.S., it is generically known as California common.

WHEAT/WEISSE/WEIZEN; WEISSBIER (White Beer): Offers wheat malt concentration, high carbonation, and lower alcohol content. Yeasty tartness is a distinctive characteristic with hints of fruity/spicy overtones, especially clove and apple or banana. Belgium's *witbier* has a honey-orange character. American wheat beers are not as well-defined as European wheats. A good hot weather thirst-quencher. Wheat beers that are conditioned in the bottle, with resulting cloudiness or sediment, carry the prefix *Hefe,* which means "yeast" in German.

SPECIALTY BEERS

These beers may be ales, lagers, or combination-style beers. What distinguishes them is the addition of flavorings, such as fruits (including chile peppers), herbs and spices, smoke, honey, or the use of uncommon brewing techniques. Specialty beers may fit into more than one category. Some of the most distinctive are listed here.

ABBEY or TRAPPIST: Dark, rich ales, these brews were traditionally produced at Trappist monasteries throughout Europe. Five Belgian Trappist monasteries still make the strong concoction using centuries-old processes under the direction and supervision of monks. Only this quintet—Chimay, Orval, Rochefort, Westmalle, Westvleteren (St. Sixtus)—can use the appellation, Trappist.

FARO: A kind of lambic enhanced in sweetness by candy sugar.

GUEUZE (pronounced *gerz*): A type of lambic, blending aged and new lambics to produce a sweeter drink.

LAMBIC: Lambics are wheat beers, with fruit added. Essences or real cherries *(kriek),* raspberries *(framboise),* or peaches *(pêche)* are blended into the beer, giving it a distinct but not overpowering fruitiness. Often sour, with low carbonation. Brewers typically do not add yeast; fermentation is accomplished naturally and spontaneously by any one, or more, of hundreds of airborne wild yeast strains, resulting in an uncontrolled variation in flavor characteristics from one brewed batch to the next.

RAUCHBIER (Smoked Beer): The smoky flavor of these beers is produced by drying the malt with wood smoke. The flavor is quite intense, like some sausages and salamis.

SEASONAL/WINTER: Christmas beers are typical of this category. Cloves, coriander, ginger, cinnamon, spruce, licorice, nutmeg, and other herbs and spices are common additions. Often full-bodied ales and high in alcohol.

THE COLOR OF BEER
(Light to Dark)

Visual characteristics greatly enhance the enjoyment of a particular style of beer. The shading in the glass below will give you a general idea where within the range of beer coloring a beer style falls.

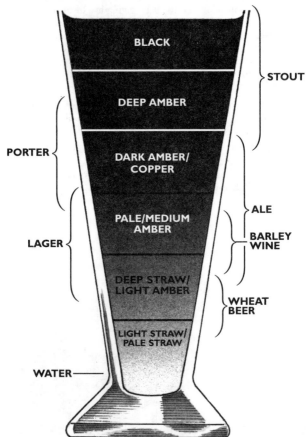

BREWERY TYPES

One hundred years ago, Americans had some 2,000 domestic breweries from which to select a favorite brew (down from 4,131 in 1873, the most ever). In the 1980s and into the 1990s, with six major brewers in the United States, the variety, if not the availability, became dramatically limited. But within the last decade or so, a resurgence of interest in quality and different styles of beer has moderated that trend. As a result, beer drinkers have become more familiar with—and appreciative of—both domestic and imported brands.

While domestic brews are still by far the cold one of choice, imported beers make up an increasingly large segment of the U.S. beer selection. Where once the focus was on readily available European brands, consumers in the United States now can find varieties from places like Russia, Ecuador, Belize, Western Samoa, and Hong Kong. Nonetheless, Europe remains the leading exporter. Number one is Holland, followed in descending order by Canada, Mexico, Germany, Great Britain, Ireland, and Japan. By brand, it's Heineken, Corona, Beck's, Molson Golden, and Labatt's Blue. Overall, beer imports went up more than 14% between 1993 and 1994. Brands and styles of imported beer currently number in the thousands and comprise almost 5% of the total beer consumed in this country. Twenty short years ago, according to one report, no more than 100 different beers arrived at our shores from elsewhere.

This imported and domestic liquid cornucopia has altered our drinking habits in still another way: American beer drinkers now can get their brews from five distinct brewery sources.

CB COMMERCIAL BREWERY:

These are the megabreweries that market their bottled and canned beers for mass consumption. Annual production is in the 50 to 90 million barrel range for individual breweries such as Anheuser-Busch and Miller. While most foreign breweries do not approach the gargantuan output of the American giants—though some do—brewers with the capacity to export their products to the United States will also be identified in this category, except as specifically noted otherwise.

NOTE: The abbreviations **CB, MB, BP, CT,** and **AB** are used throughout the guide to identify brewery types.

MB MICROBREWERY:

Producing 20,000 to 30,000 barrels or less each year (a figure constantly revised upward), these small operations offer an array of special handcrafted beers with emphasis on quality ingredients and careful attention to brewing methods. There are now 200 to 300 microbreweries in the United States and Canada, many of them also operating their own brewpubs. Distribution is usually limited and in bottles; cans are not used by these craft operations because they affect the taste, but some former micros (for example, Sierra Nevada in Chico, California, and Redhook in Seattle, Washington) have expanded local operations to reach regional and—in the case of San Francisco's legendary Anchor Brewing—national consumers.

BP BREWPUB:

With far less brewing capacity than a microbrewery, brewpub beer is produced and consumed on the premises, as specified by local and state laws. No packaged sales are allowed, though some jurisdictions do permit customers to "take out" returnable half-gallon or gallon jugs. Further, brewpubs may sell small quantities to be tapped at nearby taverns. Capacity is measured in gallons, not barrels, and variety is often limited at any given time. Most brewpubs also offer several changing styles in honor of the season or a special occasion.

CT CONTRACT BREWERY:

Individual brewers who don't have their own production facilities contract with an idle brewery, or one functioning below capacity, to make a beer to the brewer's specifications using the brewery's equipment. The brewer, not the brewery, is responsible for distribution and sales. Utica, New York; New Ulm, Minnesota; Monroe, Wisconsin; and Dubuque, Iowa, are sites of several frequently used contract breweries. Check bottle labels to determine where the beer is made versus where the company is located. For example, many of the Boston Beer Company's popular Samuel Adams brands have been brewed for years in Pittsburgh, Pennsylvania, and, more recently, in Portland, Oregon, and Utica, New York. Much smaller batches are also made at its Boston location. And Spanish-sounding Simpatico, found in the Mexican-beer section of the cooler and once made south of the border, is brewed in—Dubuque, USA.

AB ABBEY/TRAPPIST BREWERY:

Using centuries-old traditions, European monastery breweries turn out limited quantities of, usually, strong, stern stuff meant to warm the cockles of the medieval traveler's heart. Belgium is especially known for its monk-brewed ales. Today, not all abbey-style beer is made at a monastery.

BEER GLASSES ARE MORE THAN JUST CONTAINERS

ALE

Because ales often have a flowery, fruity aroma, the best glasses are tulip-shaped to capture the bouquet, or volatile odorants, thereby prolonging sensual enjoyment of the brew. Ales tend to be sweet with a smooth texture. They may also be higher in alcohol content.

Ale Glass

STOUT

Large, hefty, thick-sided glasses or tumblers with lots of clear viewing space allow depth and shades of color to be enjoyed

in a variety of stouts and other heavy brews. Enough room is also needed for head foam to settle out at its own pace or rise to the occasion as it sees fit. A wide mouth permits access to rich roasted aroma and taste as the liquid is drained to the bottom.

Stout Glasses

LAGER

Glasses with thick sides help keep cold beer cold—or at least chilled. Facets in the design help achieve that goal. Lagers in general are best served cold. Mugs with handles allow you to grasp the brew while keeping your hands off the glass, thereby minimizing the possibility of raising the beer's temperature by body warmth.

Lager Mug

**Faceted Lager Mug
(English Style)**

**Pint Lager or
Bitter Glass**

PILSENER

Pilseners, which feature an assertive carbonation, display their character best in a conical,
distinctly tapered vessel. By forcing pressure
upward within the liquid, the V shape helps to
generate a constant stream of bubbles, adding
both to the zestiness of the texture and the
appealing foamy abundance of the head.

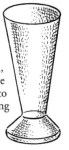

**Pilsener
Glass**

WHEAT

Because wheat beers combine the characteristics of different styles, the glass config-
uration should accommodate the variations.
Serving multi-purposes, the glass should re-
strict escaping aromas (in the upper bell-
shaped portion), while also allowing for the
relatively higher levels of carbonation (the
lower straight portion forces the bubbles

Wheat Glass   upward).

SNIFTERS, FLUTES, AND TULIPS

Because high-alcohol ales like barley wine and Christmas
beers have especially concentrated aromas and tastes, a compact, rounded glass is best for forcing the senses to pay attention. To start, take several short, quick sniffs for aroma

and enough of a brief sip to allow the liquid to touch all areas of the mouth—and then swallow. When sniffing, cup the hand around the rim of the glass to reduce the amount of escaping odors.

Brandy Snifter   **Flute Glass**   **Tulip**
(Barley Wine)   **(Lambic)**   **Champagne Glass**
                                      (Abbey/Trappist Ale)

BEST STORAGE TEMPERATURES FOR BEER

REFRIGERATED TEMPERATURE	STYLES	
45°F	Light beer American lager	Australian lager Malt liquor
47°F	Wheat beers	Bock beers
48°F	European lager Dark lager	Pilsener Kölsch
CELLAR TEMPERATURE	STYLES	
50°F–55°F	Ale (Scottish, brown, pale, etc.) Stout Lambic	India pale ale Bitter Doppelbock
ROOM TEMPERATURE	STYLES	
55°F–60°F	Barley wine Strong dark ale	Abbey/Trappist ale

PAIRING
BEER AND FOOD

W hile European beer drinkers have long known the pleasures of pairing beer and food, it is only recently that
we in this country have come to appreciate the close
connection between a good brew and a pleasurable meal.
There are several reasons for this change, but two stand out.
The increasing availability of tasty, quality beers has revolu-
tionized our attitudes and taste buds about a drink that had
come to be seen as uniformly bland and/or mainly for those
desiring an alcoholic thirst-quencher at a ballgame. Secondly,
the new willingness to sample a broader spectrum of cuisines,
coupled with their more universal accessibility, has encouraged a similar receptivity to different drink accompaniments,
including beer. Also, beer is reasonably priced, is unlikely to
spoil as easily as wine, and it's there when you want it—at
restaurants, pubs, grocery stores, and convenience stores—in
quantities and serving sizes that minimize waste and are small
enough to encourage sampling a wide enough variety to find
favorites. In short, the renewed interest in beer—for that's
what it is: the recalling of pleasures and quality hardly experienced since Prohibition—parallels our search for satisfying
ways to enjoy what we eat and drink.

There are no hard and fast guidelines for choosing the
"right" beer for particular foods. In truth, beer is so versatile
it pretty much goes well with whatever food or meal your individual taste tells you is compatible. For some, and for some
foods, that may mean, for example, a textural or flavor contrast between the beer and the food. At other times, locations,
companionship, or mood of the moment you may desire a
beer that complements or integrates smoothly with the food.
Whatever the situation, the choice is up to you. Unlike wine
drinkers, we are not constrained by proscribed food/drink
compatability—allowing us a more varied, changing range of
choices and pleasures.

The following chart lists traditional beer and food pair-
ings. But, remember, the final opinion is yours. Feel free to
experiment and explore, with one goal in mind: to enjoy what
you drink—and eat—regardless of what food may be on your
plate or any preconceived notions you may have brought with
you to the table.

Similarly, suggestions regarding the shape of the serving
glass are based on helping you get the most enjoyment from

the characteristics of a particular brew. Don't worry if you can't locate just the right container; in the end, as long as it doesn't leak (and it's not made of plastic), you've got the right one in your hand. Skol! Prost! Good cheer!

ALES

One of the four basic beer categories. Ale, top-fermented and the oldest of the brewing styles, takes only a few days to mature. Serve at cellar temperature (between 50°F and 60°F).

STYLE	GLASS/ SERVING TEMP.	FOODS
BARLEY WINE	Snifter/60°F	Strong-flavored cheeses, nuts; as a complement to Cognac, sweet whiskeys, or as an *apéritif* or *digestif.*
BITTER	Straight-sided pint/55°F	Strong-flavored cheeses and good company.
BLOND/GOLDEN ALE	Straight-sided pint/55°F	Generally, fish or fowl.
BROWN ALE	Undulating (like old Coca Cola glass)/55°F	Game, spicy foods, well-seasoned beef dishes.
DRY STOUT	Clear tumbler with wide mouth/60°F	Oysters, spiced shellfish dishes, hearty breads, game.
IMPERIAL STOUT	Goblet or snifter/60°F	Best alone, or before a meal, with snack foods.
INDIA PALE ALE	V-shaped or pint glass/55°F	Smoked meats and cheeses; foods that need sharp, pointed contrast.
MILK/CREAM STOUT	Clear, gradually tapered tumbler with wide mouth/55°F	Lighter foods and sweeter desserts, or alone.

STYLE	GLASS/ SERVING TEMP.	FOODS
OATMEAL STOUT	Clear tumbler with wide mouth/55°F	Italian foods, beef dishes, stronger-flavored seafoods.
PALE ALE	Straight-sided pint glass/55°F	Fish, shellfish, sharp cheeses; also spicy foods, beef, and well-seasoned seafoods.
PORTER	Clear tumbler/ 55°F	Shellfish, veal, lighter-flavored meats.
SCOTTISH ALE	Mug or thistle-shaped glass/ 55°F	Strong-flavored meats and cheeses; melons.
STRONG ALE	Goblet, tumbler, or snifter/50°F	Fruits, nuts, soft cheeses; rich foods in general.

LAGERS

These bottom-fermented brews require up to six weeks or more of storage at cool temperatures (*lagern* is German for "to store"). Serve them the way they came into this world— chilled (between 45°F and 50°F).

STYLE	GLASS/ SERVING TEMP.	FOODS
AMERICAN DRY LAGER	Your choice/ 45°F	Your choice of bland foods.
AMERICAN PILSENER/ EUROPEAN PILSENER	Tapering (V-shaped) glass from narrow bottom to wider top or elongated tulip-shaped glass/ 45°F-48°F	Freshwater fish, salads, fresh tart fruits.

STYLE	GLASS/ SERVING TEMP.	FOODS
BOCK	Thick-sided stoneware mug or glass tumbler/50F°-55°F	Smoked and unsmoked meats, garden salads.
DOPPELBOCK	Stemmed, rounded tumbler/50°F	Pastries, desserts, smoked meats, wild fowl.
ENGLISH LAGER	Faceted mug/ 45°F-50°F	Light summer-type foods, or drink by itself.
EUROPEAN DARK/ MUNCHNER DUNKEL	Undulating (like old Coke glass)/48°F-50°F	Well-seasoned pastas or chicken, but you decide for yourself.
EXPORT	Mug or thick-sided glass/ 45°F	Sliced cold meats, hearty meat dishes.
HELLES BOCK	Stemmed tumbler or straight-sided glass/45°F	Spicy foods, stronger-flavored meats with mustard and onions on the side.
MALT LIQUOR	Your choice/ 45°F	You name it.
MARZEN	Tall earthen-ware or glass mugs/48°F-55°F	Sausages, German-style foods, heavier but simple foods.
OKTOBERFEST	Thick-sided glass or earth-enware mug/ 48°F-55°F	Sausages, sauerkraut, and lots of oompah music.
VIENNA AMBER	Straight glass or glass mug/ 48°F-50°F	Mexican food, spicy pastas, sweet desserts.

SPECIALTY BEERS

Specialty beers usually contain some additive to give them a distinctive taste. Fruits, smoke, herbs, and spices are but some of the ingredients.

STYLE	GLASS/ SERVING TEMP.	FOODS
ABBEY/ TRAPPIST ALE	Snifter or goblet/60°F	Cheeses, breads, hard fruits, shellfish, freshwater fish, light seafoods.
FRUIT LAMBIC: CHERRY RASPBERRY PEACH	Champagne glass/45°F-50°F	Foods that are flavored with or complement the particular lambic fruit flavor. Cherry goes well with other tart fruits, such as apricots, cranberries, and cherries. Raspberry is delicious with chocolate. Peach is nice with waffles covered with peach slices.
LAMBIC (NON-FRUIT)	Tumbler/55°F	Stronger cheeses, shellfish. Use lambic as you would a dry sherry *apéritif,* or *digestif.*
RAUCHBIER (SMOKED BEER)	Rounded glass mug/55°F	Smoked meats and fish, grilled foods, apples, cheeses, and walnuts.
RED (OR GREEN) CHILE ALE	Tumbler or clear tankard/ 55°F	Mexican-style or other spicy-style foods. Pork-based meat dishes.
SEASONAL/WINTER ALE	Clear tumbler or goblet/ 55°F-60°F	Smoked meats, game, hard fruits (pears and apples).

COMBINATION-STYLE BEERS

These beers blend the features of both lager- and ale-brewing processes.

STYLE	GLASS/ SERVING TEMP.	FOODS
ALT	Thin, straight glass/55°F	Tart fruits, breads, lighter meats, tomato-based dishes.
BIERE DE PARIS/ BIERE DE GARDE	Snifter or champagne glass/50°F-55°F	Gourmet foods—make believe this is wine.
CREAM ALE	Your choice	Anything.
KOLSCH	Thin, straight glass/48°F	Vegetables, less-than-tart fruit, white chicken meat, breads, appetizers.
STEAM	Sturdy mug/ 45°F-50°F	Cheeses and moderately spicy foods.
WHEAT	Long vase-shaped glass or large tumbler with beveled top/48°F-50°F	Smoked fish, meat; heavier but not highly-spiced foods; German-style dishes; alone as good summer thirst-quencher.

THE
RATING
GUIDE

HOW I JUDGE AND
RATE A BEER

Tasting and evaluating a beer is not a complicated or sophisticated process. Basically, all I need is a clean glass (very important), the beer, and, if I am planning to have more than one brand or style without a meal, some unsalted crackers (I prefer unsalted Nabisco Saltines) or French bread (or other bread made without sugar), and water to cleanse the palate between tastings.

I rank beers from 0 to 5. In official beer competitions, judges use a 50-point scale. That range can be useful in helping the commercial brewer or serious homebrewer to pinpoint trouble spots (for example, bacterial infection or too much bitterness for a particular style). Likewise, judges using this method can confirm for the brewer the attractive qualities of the product (for example, malt and hop balance, fruit subtlety).

However, I find the 50-point scale to be too cumbersome for the ordinary beer drinker, the interested consumer who wants to enjoy a freshly-poured glass at home or at a restaurant, but who would also like to be able to sort out the various characteristics defining a good, bad, average, or exceptional beer. My five-point scale takes the important elements from the 50-point scale and makes them manageable: It is meant to add to the enjoyment of the beer as well as serve as a guide, or aid, to the understanding of what makes a satisfying (or not-so-satisfying) brew.

The following section defines the overall qualities—separated by one-point intervals—I look for in assigning a rating: from *Bad* (0 to 1) to *Outstanding* (4 to 5). A separate chart outlines the five steps I use to arrive at a rating of the beers I sample. Each beer style and its defining characteristics can be found earlier in this book. I also include a chart that suggests the shape of the glass to use with each style. Pictorial representations of the various shapes are shown as well.

BEFORE YOU TASTE

First, a few quick reminders:

• Pour the beer slowly and gently in a steady, thin cascade against the inside of the glass, gradually angling the liquid so that it becomes a vertical stream down the middle by the time the beginning of the head is about an inch from the rim of the glass. Careful pouring reduces the likelihood that you will wind up with a glass full of foam while simultaneously ensuring the presence of foam, in the form of a head, where it is desired—at the top of the glass.

• Beer should never be tasted straight from the container, whether bottle or can (cans in particular tend to impart a metallic or otherwise taste-distorting sensation). Using a glass or mug ensures that a beer's aroma components, called "volatile odorants," will be slightly jostled in their journey through the air from container to glass. The relatively brief contact with the oxygen allows for a fuller release of the ingredients into your nose and mouth, where your senses—taste, aroma, tactile—await them.

• Remember: a clean glass is an absolute must. Dirty glasses destroy the head and cause the beer to go flat. Bubbles in the liquid that adhere to the side or bottom of your glass are a sign of a dirty glass—no bubbles sticking below the beer line is a wise motto to keep in mind.

• Also, stay away from those frosty, iced mugs. They may be appealing, especially on a hot day, but they cause thermal shock to the beer, essentially obscuring the beer's flavor.

Now, begin pouring and start enjoying. You're on your way to never having to tolerate a bad beer again.

JUDGING A BEER

1. LOOK

Hold the glass up to the light; note the head shape and uniformity of color.

CHARACTERISTICS

Color: according to style.
Clarity: according to style.
Head: according to style. Quality beers have tightly packed small bubbles. Large, quickly disappearing bubbles in the foam are a sign that artificial foaming agents have been added. *Note:* Beers tend to have a bigger head at higher altitudes.

Points: 0-1_____

2. SNIFF

- Leave 1 to 2 inches between the rim of the glass and the head to allow for the collection of volatile odorants (bouquet or aroma).
- Swirl the beer to release some carbonation.
- Place your nose inside the glass, cup your hands around the rim, and inhale deeply. (Some experts suggest taking three to four short, quick sniffs.)

CHARACTERISTICS

Malt: generally clean and fresh.
Hops: generally tonic and bracing, sharp.

Points: 0-1_____

3. SIP

- A very personal process.
- Make sure the beer gets to all parts of the mouth.
- Swallow.
- Take another sip.

CHARACTERISTICS

Malt: generally sweet, clean-tasting.
Hops: generally bitter, perhaps flowery.
Balance: do the malts and hops balance or does one dominate?
Conditioning: e.g., carbonation, full- or light-bodied brewing flavors—does it adhere to beer style (flowery, fruity, for ale, for example)?
Aftertaste: is it pleasant, intrusive, nonexistent, long-lasting?

Points: 0-1_____

4. ANOTHER LOOK

Beer can change while sitting in the glass waiting for you to take another sip.

CHARACTERISTICS

Bubbles: still rising (good) or nonexistent (bad).
Brussels lace: plentiful, ringing sides of glass in more or less parallel circles (good); erratic, thin and wispy (bad).
Clarity: according to style.
Color: according to style.
Head: according to style; should be at least one-half thickness of original after one minute.

Points: 0-1_____

5. EVALUATE

This is an overall impression. Try to pay attention to the separate elements in steps 1 to 4. Better yet, pay heed to all of the senses, as suggested by Munich's Weihenstephen Brewing School: ". . . to sight it must ring clear as a bell, it must snap in the ear, feel pleasantly sticky between the fingers, smell fresh and tempting and taste heavenly." In short, does this beer you have in your hand make you want to have more— or less?

Points: 0-1_____

TOTAL POINTS: 0-5_____

RATING THE BEERS

Using the "Judging a Beer" information starting on page 27, rate each of the five components (look, sniff, sip, another look, evaluate) anywhere along the continuum from 0 to 1. Next, add the five scores to get your own individual total rating. For example, Brand X Lager receives the following: Look: 0.3; Sniff: 0.7; Sip: 0.2; Another look: 0.5; Evaluate: 0.5 (Total - 2.2). Or simply drink, enjoy, and come up with one overall rating anywhere from 0 to 5. Then, check the list on the following page to find out what your rating means. In this case, Brand X Lager is at the low end of the Average range.

One enjoyable approach is to gather several friends, give each the same beer, and rate it individually without any discussion. When everyone is finished, compare the ratings, and go on to the next bottle.

RATING	DEFINITION
4 TO 5	OUTSTANDING, with or without food. Makes you eager to share with friends and to keep stocked in your refrigerator.
3 TO 4	ABOVE AVERAGE, complementing and adding to the enjoyment of food and satisfying by itself. The choice when no 4 to 5 is available.
2 TO 3	AVERAGE, neither enhancing nor detracting from the food and hardly satisfying by itself, but serviceable in a pinch. Okay for when your attention is directed elsewhere, e.g., at TV.
1 TO 2	BELOW AVERAGE, with few redeeming qualities except for being wet and/or cold and you are very thirsty. Ingredients may be apparent, but are weak and/or of poor quality.
0 TO 1	BAD! Unfinishable under most circumstances.

AROMA AND TASTE

It always helps to know the right word to identify what your senses experience. Here are the basic terms to help convey your impressions as you sniff, taste, and swallow.

TERM/ DEFINITION	KEEP IT	SEND IT BACK	COMMENT
ASTRINGENT: dry, puckering mouthfeel, raw	✔		Too much is not a good sign.
BITTER: sharp taste • bitter hops taste • bitter non-hop taste	✔	✔	Particularly noticeable at the back of the tongue; intensity varies.
BUTTERY: • slickly smooth like butterscotch		✔	Bacteria in the pro-cessing; request another brand.
• slight suggestion of sweet butter	✔		Okay in some European beers and ales.

TERM/ DEFINITION	KEEP IT	SEND IT BACK	COMMENT
CABBAGEY: smells like cooked cabbage		✔	Improper boiling method, malting process, and in some cases, contamination.
CHEESY: smells like, well, like cheese		✔	Beer stored warm or possibly old hops used in brewing.
FRUITY: the aroma and taste of banana, apple, raspberry, etc.	✔		Okay, especially in ale; generally not appropriate in lager.
GREEN APPLE: smells and tastes like unripened apples; raw tasting		✔	Brewing process is unfinished or inappropriately high fermentation temperature.
MEDICINAL: smells like a hospital, iodine, or a chemical		✔	Due to unclean brewing container, wild yeast, sanitizing residues; get your money back.
METALLIC: may also taste tinny or blood-like		✔	Brewing error: exposed to metal.
MOLDY: smells like mold or damp earth		✔	Fungal contamination in the brewing process.
MUSKY: smells like a closed-up cellar		✔	Stale water or malt with fungal contamination.
NUTTY: similar to taste of fresh nuts	✔		Malt character; a pleasure if you can find it.
OXIDIZED/STALE: winey, or unpleasantly acidic and sour; cardboard, rotten vegetable-like odor		✔	Exposed to high temperatures in shipping/storage; old beer or air in bottle; demand another bottle.

TERM/ DEFINITION	KEEP IT	SEND IT BACK	COMMENT
SALTY: tastes as if table salt has been added to the beer; generally noticed on the sides of tongue		✔	Too much sodium chloride or magnesium sulfate (both salts) used in the brewing process.
SKUNKY/LIGHT-STRUCK: smells like a skunk		✔	Exposed to light; don't buy beer displayed in sunlight, under fluorescent bulbs, or bottled in green or clear glass.
SOUR/ACIDIC: tastes like very tart lemon or like vinegar; pungent aroma	✔ (sour)	✔ (acidic)	Good (e.g. Lambic, Berliner Weiss): citric/lactic acid. Bad: bacterial infection.
SPICY: odor should be present only if spice has been added to beer	✔		Common in Christmas beers and beers advertising the addition of spice. Should not overwhelm.
SULFUR-LIKE: taste/ odor of rotten eggs/ corn, burning matches		✔	Terrible yeast problem—demand a free bottle for you and your drinking partner.
TART: • fresh, full-bodied tartness	✔		Positive attribute in *weissbier* and some other beers. Tartness should not be present in a lager or overly present in an ale.
• dry and sour; no body		✔	Unacceptable in any beer.
TURPEY: solvent or turpentine odor/taste		✔	Results from old hops or warm-temperature storage.

PUTTING IT ALL TOGETHER

E ach of the beers in the rating guide is listed by its name as it appears on the label of the beer or as indicated in the brewery literature. (Similarly, brewery location is taken from the label, information which in some cases may change from time to time—make certain to check beforehand.) If the beer's style is capitalized, it is officially part of the beer's name. The lower case boldface type indicates that I have added the beer's style for your information (in the case of draft beer, when the beer tasted was, in fact, on tap, the word "draft" appears in parenthesis). The boldface capital letters after the name indicate the type of brewery that produces the beer (for example, **CB** for commercial breweries) and the number at the far right indicates my overall rating of the beer.

It is my preference to drink beer with food, and to keep a record of their compatibility. In order to organize my impressions so that I can accurately record them, I generally don't pour the beer until the meal has been served. (At restaurants, I make sure to ask the server not to bring my beer until the food has arrived). Then, I take a sniff and sip or two before eating anything and record my perceptions. From that point on, I jot down my impressions—aroma, texture, color, mouthfeel, aftertaste—as they occur. As a result, some food/beer characteristics may be revealed by mid-bottle, and I make note of them in the middle of the entry; others do not clearly appear until the end, and accordingly, my comments about the relationship of the beer to the food appear later in the written observations.

My tasting method is loose and flexible, although I admit that on occasion I do get carried away; but, after all, this is meant to be fun, not preparation for a final exam in Advanced Malts and Hops. Indeed, I would encourage you to freely use the pages of The Rating Guide to record your own tasting impressions and ratings.

In most entries, I offer a generalized food suggestion rather than a specific food recommendation. Each is based on food I sampled with the beer and is meant to give you an idea of what type of dish to order or prepare. The suggestions are not meant to be limiting—"Klein says try this with chicken, but I'd rather have a burger." Rather, use them as a starting point. Then, eat, drink, and enjoy.

AASS AMBER Lager   CB   3.2
(Drammen, Norway)

Oat-nut aroma; smooth and easily digestible; minimal head atop ruby-brown-peach color; malty nuttiness; moderated freshness; somewhat flat; suggestions of roasted smokiness—nice combination of style and cultural influences; well-made, as is true of all Aass brews. Accompanies pasta dishes nicely.

B E E R   F A C T

*A*ass, the country's oldest brewery, means "summit" in Norway.

AASS BOCK   CB   3.2
(Drammen, Norway)

Immediately pleasing fruity aroma followed by pleasant, round, natural, fruit taste; thin at the tip of the tongue, but more full-bodied going down; pleasant sweetness with smooth tang at the edge; basically warm, creamy, and comforting, though weak on flavor. Try it with hot dogs (and other spicier sausages) and beans.

AASS JUBILEE Lager   CB   3.9
(Drammen, Norway)

Fresh and grainy with a hint of zip; attenuated sweetness is not intrusive; honey fruitiness and hoppiness increases and lolls around the back of the tongue with some mustiness remaining for a while; mellow, light-golden hue with a shade of cloudiness; a certain textural firmness adds to the overall effect; comes together nicely by the end of the bottle; a lubricant all over the mouth. Goes well with a solid meat and potatoes meal.

AASS JULE ØL Lager   CB   4.5
(Drammen, Norway)

Very enticing initial aroma followed by burst of mild, mellow, dark nutty-caramel taste; water is clear and fresh; texture remains mellow and smooth; sweetness shades the palate nicely; calm, tasty, uncomplicated, and delicious. Accompanies deli-style foods.

AASS PILSNER   CB   2.9
(Drammen, Norway)

Smooth with an edge that fits comfortably into place; fresh and clean-tasting; moderate body somewhat manipulated by food—reflects and mirrors the ingredients; semi-dry, thickish finish. Serve with barbecued ribs, coleslaw, and onion rings.

AASS WINTER Lager   CB   2.3
(Drammen, Norway)
Very faint wine taste on the first sip with hardly any textural accompaniment; remains sour and even a little bloating; strong, with nutty ending, almost unexpected from this part of the world; finishes with a hint of complexity. Accompanies burgers, pasta, and snacks.

ABC EXTRA STOUT   CB   3.7
(Singapore)
Burnt taste becomes slowly integrated as it warms; musty and flat, food gets lost in its creamy maltiness and is ultimately enveloped by dominant richness; cherry-black color; very full-bodied, with a zest for life—watch out you don't get bowled over by this energetic brew. Goes well with Mexican food.

TAP TIP

Quenching the Fire on the Tongue

*N*o, it's not your imagination that beers high in alcohol seem to go well with hot, spicy foods. The scientific fact is, they actually do. Potent, highly alcoholic brews—typically malt liquors and strong lagers—are quicker to quiet the pain on your tongue. In spices such as chilies, certain compounds are specifically alcohol-soluble and as the concentration of alcohol increases, the fiery molecules are washed away. As a result, water is always less of a fire extinguisher than even the most minimally alcoholic beer.

ABC VERY SUPERIOR STOUT   CB   3.6
(Singapore)
Moderated bitterness turns calm as it reaches the back of the mouth; combination of ambiguous wine/burnt taste; appropriately thick and creamy without being obtrusive; onrushing bitterness significantly enhances the overall flavor, raising it above average. Appropriate with charbroiled steaks and salad.

ABITA AMBER Lager   MB/BP   2.6
(Abita Springs, Louisiana)
Thick on the tongue with a honeyed aroma; somewhat flat; maltiness predominates, as appropriate for Vienna-style lager; mild, toasted sweetness also adheres to style, though gets washed out by spicy foods; satisfying, but unexciting. Accompanies pasta carbonara and other non-tomato-sauced pasta dishes.

ABITA GOLDEN Lager   **MB/BP**   **2.8**
(Abita Springs, Louisiana)
Hardly any mouthfeel; flat with a hint of citrus taste; some slight mustiness; warming trend comes up at mid-bottle and beyond; good balance between hops and malt, though to be truthful, neither ingredient is really tangible or apparent; well-made, but not overly exciting; pleasant, affecting sweetish finish. Try it with plain grain and vegetable dishes such as rice, green beans, and corn.

ABITA IRISH RED ALE   **MB/BP**   **2.0**
(Abita Springs, Louisiana)
Slightly skunky; meager carbonation and general flatness do not bode well; some back-of-the-throat fruitiness; not zesty or alcoholic; bland; some pleasant, mild, honey taste at the finish—too bad it wasn't present earlier.

ABITA TURBO DOG Dark Ale   **MB/BP**   **3.8**
(Abita Springs, Louisiana)
Mild, rough perfuminess both in the nose and on the tongue; glimmer of fruitiness, but not sweet or alcoholish; very malty with surrounding burnt-caramel ambience; fresh water helps tie it all together; deep brown color with underlying auburn undertone is revealed in the light; softens and mellows food; smooth on the tongue, grizzled and rough on the throat; very textured and aromatic—a feast for all senses; substance and staying power. Complements All-American meals, such as roasted turkey with stuffing or grilled cheese sandwiches.

ACME LAGER   **MB**   **2.7**
(Santa Rosa, California)
Immediate, sweet, winey bouquet doesn't translate into taste; mellow, warm, and nicely bodied; soft caramel mouthfeel; surprisingly integrated and responsive; maintains heartwarming, and mouth-pleasing, subtlety throughout. Accompanies grilled beef dishes, such as London broil.

ADELSCOTT MALT LIQUOR   **CB**   **4.2**
(Schiltigheim, France)
Distinctive, mellow, smoky aroma and, particularly, taste, accompanied by fresh, yeast character; deep-seated earthy ambience with a hint of spice—perhaps cloves; smooth and whiskey-like; delicious alcoholic warmth emerges with sweet-sauced food; whiskey/tea color is solid, underpinning a steady, quarter-inch head of clean white foam; Brussels lace remains clinging to the sides of the glass after it is drained; there is a suggestion that the sweetness may accumulate and become overwhelming after more than two or three bottles; finishes with the ingredients—smoked malt, alcohol, yeast—even more integrated than at the begin-

ning; a delightful little beer, full of zip and surprise; brewed with peat-smoked malt à la whiskey distillation. Makes for a good *apéritif*, but also would go with chicken with fruited sauces.

ADLER BRAU PILSNER   MB/BP   0.9
(Appleton, Wisconsin)
Thick, bland, and no hint of complexity or ingredients; continues its crawl to nowhere although redeemed slightly when paired with food; take your business elsewhere.

ADMEERAL TYEYSKOYE Lager   CB   0.8
(Moscow, Russia)
Rough, raw graininess, with faint alcohol aroma; rough, raw graininess, with faint alcohol aroma; rough, raw graininess, with faint alcohol aroma—need anything further be said? Try at your own risk, one sip at a time.

AEGEAN HELLAS Lager   CB   4.2
(Atalanti, Greece)
Nice, sweet, barley taste lingers pleasantly on the tongue; subtly well-defined, soft and receptive; substantive and close to full-bodied, this is a quality brew. Goes well with fish and shellfish.

AFFLIGEM TRIPEL ABBEY Ale   MY   3.6
(Opwijk, Belgium)
Distinct but passing burnt taste; very soft on the upper palate and sides of the mouth; head is creamy, soft, and delicately bubbled and remains on top of cloudy, apple-cider body; enhanced by mild, fruity taste; consistent, predictable, and modest in its expectations; gets a little too winey as meal progresses; more appealing at the beginning than the end, though creamy fullness is especially tasty at the finish; rounded body and full in character. Accompanies meatballs and spaghetti.

AGUILA IMPERIAL ALE   CB   3.8
(Madrid, Spain)
Airy and light, with rice aftertaste; complex without making you pay too much attention; restrained hoppiness and maltiness make this a delightful, but not heavy-handed, beer for snacks and other light dishes. Try it with pistachio nuts, creamy dips, celery, carrots, and thinly sliced hard salami.

AKTIEN JUBILAUMS PILS   CB   2.8
(Kaufbeuren, Germany)
Slight clove mouthfeel with subdued, spritzy texture; dry and softly straightforward; soft, creamy head doesn't hang around too long, so enjoyment quickly fades; modulated crispness along with appropriate balance; faint hoppiness and enduring mild sharpness settles into fuller workmanlike pilsener with food, including appropriate golden hue; no particular distinction or distraction;

clove remains; texture could be thinner; not something you would seek out at the bar, home, or restaurant, yet there is no reason to refuse it if it's delivered to your table. Accompanies all types of poultry dishes.

AKTIEN ST. MARTIN
DUNKLER DOPPELBOCK   **CB**   **2.8**
(Kaufbeuren, Germany)
Soapy aroma and stuffy, roasted, almost burnt, taste on first sip; too much syrupy sweetness; alcohol becomes more apparent as beer is imbibed—clearly needs help from food that is strong enough to absorb and neutralize its alcoholic excesses. Spicy dishes such as chili nicely absorb the cloying sweetness and sharpness of the alcohol, turning this doppelbock into a smoother, more drinkable brew.

ALASKAN AMBER Alt   **MB**   **3.8**
(Juneau, Alaska)
Deep, attractive aroma greets your nose as full-bodied sharpness greets your mouth and upper palate; although smooth texture eventually weakens, it maintains its vitality and very pleasing balance; easy sipping and easy going down, though not particularly complex; maintains composure from start to finish; a frisky little brew. Try it with heavily sauced barbecued spareribs.

ALASKAN PALE ALE   **MB**   **1.0**
(Juneau, Alaska)
Fizzy but neutral-tasting with a faint hint of raw fruitiness; decidedly uncomplex; muddied copper color—not distinctive or defined; slight sneaker smell, as if it sat in the closet too long; no nuances. Remains neutral with food. Nonetheless, this beer clearly has its fans: It was a Bronze Medal winner at the 1993 Great American Beer Festival.

ALBORZ ALE   **CT**   **3.2**
(Seattle, Washington)
Malty roastedness comes through strongly, sweet, and inspiring; thick and smooth; fruity and yeasty, though it could be more complex; light, translucent apple-cider color adds to this ale's country-fair, easygoing ambience; unpasteurized, it is fresh and ready to drink; finishes with a flash of hops zipping through the taste of caramel malt. Provides an inviting balance to cooked prawns with zesty hot sauce.

ALFA Pilsener   **CB**   **3.1**
(Schinnen, Holland)
Crisp with a comforting tastiness; mellow, unassuming; almost an afterthought to the food, but it's appealing enough, with sharp carbonation and light texture, to succeed on its own; finishes a touch dry. Accompanies barbecued pork dishes.

ALGONQUIN SPECIAL RESERVE ALE   **CB**   2.9
(Formosa, Ontario, Canada)
Immediate surge of barley malt followed by subdued tang and
some fullness in the mouth; sort of lays back and lets the food
do its thing; sharpness remains at the bottom of the throat while
body fullness remains detached, to everyone's advantage; vague
fruitiness confirms its ale character. Accompanies home-style
meals.

ALLEGHENY PENN PILSENER   **MB/BP**   3.7
(Pittsburgh, Pennsylvania)
Tingly with warm, comforting undercurrent; nicely balanced between barley malt and hops; refined textural quality usually found
in more expensive beers; rounded body, provides rolling satisfaction along the tongue; heftier than the usual pilsener; good
for 2 to 3 bottles at a time with or without food—won't give you
any unexpected taste jolts; a very satisfying beer. Best with chiliburg-
ers, roast beef sandwiches, or a pot of baked beans.

ALMAZA PILSENER   **CB**   3.9
(Beirut, Lebanon)
Sharp, crisp, and to the point, with a faint hint of mustiness;
adds comfortable zestiness to food and gains sweetness and co-
herence as meal progresses; this surprisingly refreshing brew comes
in a minuscule 9.5-ounce bottle—not enough to let you fully enjoy its tantalizing delights; delectable and light; I liked this a lot.
Goes well with lightly flavored poultry dishes.

ALPINE VILLAGE HOFBRAU LAGER   **MB**   2.3
(Torrance, California)
Sour and vaguely oxidized on the first sip—almost like apples
about to ferment; aroma and taste disappear and settle into somewhat flat and characterless interplay with food; malt is tasted as
meal progresses, especially after a chew or two of bread; not much
head, but Brussels lace is present as glass tilts for a drink; ultimately falls somewhere between an American lager (relatively
plain and featureless) and a European one (assertive, hoppier);
less-than-solid presentation—lacks complexity, balance, and attraction. Accompanies Italian tomato-sauced dishes, such as veal
Parmesan.

ALPINE VILLAGE HOFBRAU PILSENER   **MB**   2.3
(Torrance, California)
Slight hint of malt and skunkiness on the first sip; fast, up-ris-
ing bubbles are apparent in the glass, but less so on the palate;
slight sourness and ambient sweetness; turns perfumey later on;
a chameleon of a brew; too soft and sweet at the end—not brittle enough for a pilsener; finishes malty with a sweet honey trace.
Deteriorates into thinnish ballpark beer.

ALTENMUNSTER EXPORT Lager   CB   2.0
(Marktoberdorf, Germany)
Full, creamy texture; bland, weak aroma; initial watery mouth-feel; mildly flavorful; hangs around; indeed, provides unobtrusive, occasionally fruity, background setting for food; overall, undistinguished and lightweight—especially for a German brew; honey-colored; grainy taste fades rapidly; sort of the Schaefer of Germany—not filling or exciting. Accompanies barbecue flavors well.

ALTENMUNSTER MALT LIQUOR   CB   2.4
(Marktoberdorf, Germany)
Milky appearance; quickly distinctive taste appears at first to be headed in flavorful direction but instead quickly fades into sour-stale taste; becomes appealingly neutralized with spicy food; can't stand alone; all in all, cheap-tasting and underpowered.

ALTES GOLDEN LAGER   MB   1.3
(Frankenmuth, Michigan)
Oxidation, greenness, and an obvious, but unsuccessful, attempt at draft freshness; no complexity or compelling interest, but that's okay with simple foods; easy-going, undemanding, just-drink-me-and-don't-pay-too-much-attention-to-my-taste beer; lightweight and hassle-free.

AMARIT LAGER   CB   2.0
(Bangkok, Thailand)
Smooth; slight rice presence comes through when the bottle is almost finished; additional overall flavor also appears as the end nears, especially without food; no aroma or taste markers to guide you through the bottle; some palates have detected an unlager-like fruitiness, but I couldn't find any; still, not bad-tasting, just not aggressive enough. Accompanies chicken breast covered with sharp Cheddar cheese and green chile peppers.

AMBAR DOS ESPECIAL Lager   CB   3.3
(Zaragoza, Spain)
Mini-fizziness with sharp, honey taste on tongue; tart hoppiness plays around with subdued serious malt presence; remains smart and tart with medium head (with, alas, big bubbles) on top of red-tinted, golden hue; hangs in there with strong qualities that are accommodating to food; dryness on the palate at the finish, as well as warmth in the throat; gentle sweetness gradually emerges with spicy chips and dips—beer matches dip in attraction on one-to-one basis; mellow, soft, and contented; finishes with just the perfect touch of hoppiness, letting you know that there is some bitterness hidden in there somewhere.

AMBER—VIENNA STYLE Lager   CT   3.1
(Monroe, Wisconsin)

Predictable and unprovocative; not unpleasant, cheesy smell; almost crisp; small-bubbled; quickly fills the palate; deceptively bland and Americanized at first taste, quickly followed by creamy, mildly burnt undertow; soft and mellow, with follow-through of opposing bitterness on the roof of the mouth; comforting, friendly beer; somewhat sweet in the end. Accompanies spaghetti and meat sauce.

ANCHOR LIBERTY ALE   CB   3.7
(San Francisco, California)

Sweet, mild taste with clear hop presence; not too sharp or sparkly; distinctively mellow and subtly dry; cloudy amber; natural carbonation; sips smoothly, quietly, and responsively; somewhat chewy, as if waiting for food to munch on; very pleasant, highly aromatic from mid-bottle to the bottom; nicely done; Silver Medal winner at the 1993 Great American Beer Festival. Makes for a fine combination with scallops or other mild seafood lightly sauced with butter and garlic.

B E E R   F A C T

Anchor Brewing is an old San Franscisco company resuscitated in 1965 by Fritz Maytag of appliance fame while he was a graduate student at Stanford University. One of the early microbreweries, Anchor's increased capacity, along with a full range of brews now distributed nationally, has moved it into the commercial brewery category.

ANCHOR OLD FOGHORN ALE (draft)   CB   3.4
(San Francisco, California)

Immediately cheery, spicy-sweet, and fresh-tasting; sprucy-citrus, similar to Anchor's Our Special Ale; packs a punch that creeps up on you; gets stickier and fruitier but maintains distinctive Anchor taste—all without food; subtle, continuing undertow of hops; surrounded by gummy spiciness; not a bashful brew; delicate, stenciled Brussels lace—cobwebby and long-lasting—adds to the party; well-made. Good with desserts.

ANCHOR OUR SPECIAL ALE (annual)   CB   2.5–4.0
(San Francisco, California)

Anchor's annual Christmas beer since 1974, this is indeed something special—sort of like a liquid Christmas tree. I have had several bottles of this fruity, spicy confection every holiday season since 1988, and look forward to each year's incarnation (six-packs begin reaching retail outlets in early November; supplies are often gone by mid-December); a distinctive clove presence is a perennial feature, along with a fizzy, creamy texture and a full, restrained heartiness; unfortunately, a cloying, syrupy sweetness also shows up regularly as does (less regularly) some bitterness at the back of the throat; taste and aroma are richly complex, with modifications from year to year—spruce livened up the 1991 edition, while orange pekoe tea aroma greeted 1992 consumers—articulately balanced, consistent, and predictably satisfying from bottle to bottle as well as from year to year. Goes well with pretty much any food, but I find it to be most enjoyable all by itself, slightly warmed. My average rating over the six-year period is 3.6.

ANCHOR PILSENER   **CB**   **2.5**
(Singapore)

Slight, flowery taste, along with faint clove mouthfeel; quite pale; zesty and almost tart; smoother than many pilseners; tends to weaken and flatten as you drink it; well-meaning. Best imbibed alone or with chips and mildly spicy dip.

ANCHOR PORTER   **CB**   **4.0**
(San Francisco, California)

Full-bodied, mellow, sweet, burnt taste; strong and muscular; attractive molasses chewiness; tends toward bitter; richly dark and satisfying. Accompanies corned beef and cabbage with lots of yellow mustard, or a pastrami on rye sandwich.

> **BEER FACT**
>
> *O*riginally called *entire*, porter was much preferred by eighteenth-century London porters (hence its name) who asked for a heady mixture of ale and several other beers at their local drinking spots. Only recently reclaiming interest among all types of beer drinkers, it is now a style of ale made with darker, roasted malt. Porterhouse steaks are so-called after the popular cut of meat offered up at the early porter bars, or houses.

ANCHOR STEAM   **CB**   **3.9**
(San Francisco, California)

Full, rounded, and unpretentious with a ribbon of fruitiness along the edges; distinctive bite and attenuated bitterness don't chase you away; this unique cross of ale and lager massages the sides of the mouth with a subtle tang; integrated smoothness, responsive character, and overall quality presentation suggest this is a food-friendly beer you could drink in (moderate) quantities without tiring, getting bored, or feeling unduly filled; too much heartiness and zest are lost at the bottom of the glass; sample the draft version to fully enjoy its mellow grittiness and lasting charm. Try it with egg dishes or seafood pastas.

B E E R   F A C T

*C*arbonation "steam" released from warm-temperature brewing gives Anchor Steam its unusual name, although others say it was derived from its original source of power. Whatever the case, Anchor now owns the "Steam" trademark.

ANCHOR WHEAT DRAFT CB 3.8
(San Francisco, California)
Subdued and smooth; tamped-down fruitiness, with a slight lemon nuance; sheets of full Brussels lace enhance the ambience; smooth and very swallowable; maintains mellowness and attraction with food; well-hopped, but controlled and measured; citrus flavor emerges more pointedly at the end of the meal; color is weak for this style. Good with a turkey or tuna salad sandwich.

ANDERSON VALLEY BARNEY FLATS
OATMEAL STOUT MB 4.0
(Boonville, California)
Fresh and burnt-tasting malt; magnificent deep, deep-brown color; full and creamy with ongoing well-balanced mix of caramel and chocolate malts; smooth; expresses itself very well overall and does likewise with individual nuances in taste, color, and texture; well-made; perhaps a little thin at the end; a bit chewy toward the bottom of the bottle. Blends almost seamlessly with plain foods.

ANDERSON VALLEY DEEP ENDERS
DARK PORTER MB 3.8
(Boonville, California)
Soft and gently prickly; creamy with palpable backbone; a little too thin; gentle caramel/mild roasted flavor; rich, dark-brown, opaque color with chocolate aroma, but not taste; needs a bit more integration and settling; creamy head, with a modicum of nicely patterned Brussels lace; watery richness; subdued, but appropriate bitterness; sediment on bottom of glass; in the end a little too weak for porter. Retains even-handed bite with grilled chicken breast with Cajun-style sauce.

ANDERSON VALLEY HIGH
ROLLERS WHEAT   MB   3.6
(Boonville, California)

Rounded, appealing, sweet-cider taste with just enough head to
let you know it really is a beer; some freshness bordering on green;
fruit remains in the nose, not on the palate; ripening floweriness
as it warms; cloudy, blond color as befits a wheat beer; fresh-tasting brew with hoppy strength and yeasty exuberance with little
tang. Good with dried fruit or whole-grain snack crackers.

ANDERSON VALLEY POLEEKO
GOLD LIGHT ALE   MB/BP   3.7
(Boonville, California)

Honey-gold, lightest-bodied ale; crisp, clear, and richly scented
with hops; hint of English bitter gives it a zesty flavor and some
bite; furry, citrus overtones; alcoholic with a foamy, long-lasting
head; some bitterness and snap settle into a creamy fruitiness;
perhaps a bit too fizzy; supportive and unobtrusive with food. A
light accompaniment to linguine with clam sauce or sautéed
chicken with fresh ginger.

ANDES Lager   CB   2.6
(Caracas, Venezuela)

Typical lager with more heartiness and grain flavor than most;
flavor and texture even out and become more integrated with
food; prickly sharpness also emerges; slight musty aftertaste detracts from graininess of this mid-range—but not great—South
American beer.

ANDES PILSENER   CB   1.2
(Santiago, Chile)

Visually very bubbly, but, alas, you can't taste the carbonation;
rather tasteless overall with a hint of grain to catch your attention; exudes freshness due to what the label says is "pure Mountain water"—not to any other ingredients, certainly; no real
substance; filled with adjuncts, it's sort of the Budweiser of Chile,
but with better water; has a certain soft crispness; a touch skunky
at the end.

ANKER PILSNER   CB   2.9
(Djakarta, Indonesia)

Mild, pleasant, grainy taste on the first sips; sharp and spicy itself, it exacerbates and encourages hotness of Chinese food; smooth
with a slight jolt of sharpness; nice, integrated balance of the texture and the water. Responsive to spicy or well-seasoned dishes.

ANTARCTICA Pilsener   CB   2.7
(São Paulo, Brazil)

Lightly perfumed, with sweet aftertaste; good carbonation; distant hint of cloves; thin, but nicely configured and visible Brus-

sels lace; finishes with a coffee taste on the sides of the mouth. Compatible with Southwestern–Mexican food.

ARCTIC BAY CLASSIC LAGER   **MB**   **2.0**
(Vancouver, British Columbia, Canada)
Hoppy ballpark beer, with just a hint of tanginess to keep you interested; somewhat thin and light with pallid golden color; sharpness diminishes and what little complexity it has disappears with food; okay if you want pedestrian, low-denominator brew at the local tavern; otherwise, it's not worth the trouble—or the money.

ARNOLD PILSNER   **CB**   **1.9**
(Bavaria, Germany)
Smooth and easy to swallow; slightly musty and somewhat bland, leaning toward mild; unobtrusive, tentatively sweet taste; light for a German beer; does nothing for food; slight, quickly dissipating aftertaste; definitely undistinguished.

ARTEVELDE ALE   **CB**   **4.1**
(Melle/Ghent, Belgium)
Fresh breeze aroma redolent of an equal balance of hops and malt; pours a heavy, large-bubbled head that literally hangs around when the bottle is finished; silky smooth with just a hint of grit to allow it to cling to your tongue and be savored a bit longer; nice and gentle, like a pat on the head; deep-rooted alcohol presence; remains refreshing without much fruitiness or yeastiness, but lacks a certain depth of character; full, creamy, off-white head and rich, deep-brown body make for a picture-perfect classic Belgian ale; improves with warmth; satisfying. Best with unadorned chicken or fish.

ASAHI DRAFT Pilsener   **CB**   **1.5**
(Tokyo, Japan)
Nutty and relatively tasteless; more American than Japanese; smell and taste of adjuncts, particularly rice, are in the air (and in the glass); this is the least satisfying of Asahi's long line of beers.

ASAHI SUPER DRY DRAFT Pilsener   **CB**   **2.9**
(bottle/can)
(Tokyo, Japan)
"Rigid" feel with unvarying taste; predictable; dull aftertaste is minimally apparent; unexciting, but of good quality; came in smallest commercial beer container I have ever seen: a 135-ml micro-mini can (about 4.5 ounces). Okay with plain food.

ASAHI Z DRAFT Pilsener (bottle/can)   **CB**   **3.7**
(Tokyo, Japan)
Sharp, fresh, and refreshing with a quick thickness on the tongue; light, with a tasty complexity of hops, malts, yeast, and water; touch of sweetness comes and goes; no hint of impurities; good

thirst-quenching summer beer. An almost perfect complement to just-caught rainbow trout.

ASMARA Lager   **CB**   **2.1**
(Asmara, Ethiopia)
Sweet/sour, quickly resolving to light, fruity/syrupy ambience; spritzy underlayer; evolving grain taste pushes aside initial fruitiness; holds creamy, quarter-inch-thick head throughout; in the end, too much weak, dusty off-taste with food; not complex or interesting.

ASPEN SILVER CITY ALE   **CT**   **2.4**
(Boulder, Colorado)
Fruity, as expected, and flat, as unexpected; fruitiness and honeyness emerge as it warms, but not enough to be really meaningful; even with slight, emerging fizziness, essentially remains flat and lifeless with food; at the end, honey-citrus flavor is at a modulated peak—a nice note on which to end, but not enough to recommend this beer with food; acceptable as an *apéritif.*

ASSETS BLACK CHERRY ALE   **MB**   **0.9**
(Albuquerque, New Mexico)
Tastes far more like cherry than beer; good, pleasing aroma misleads you into expecting beer with a cherry taste rather than cherry with a beer taste; curtain of Brussels lace hides faded, golden color; no feel of normal, or abnormal, brewing ingredients; no ale characteristics to speak of, e.g., alcohol, yeast, you name it; like a cherry Coke or a cough drop—either way, it's not what you paid for.

ASSETS DUKE CITY AMBER LAGER   **MB**   **1.9**
(Albuquerque, New Mexico)
Slight, fruity aroma, but weak taste and minor toastedness; generic, nondescript; tastes more like ale than amber; color approaches appropriate (but so what?); pleasant hoppy aroma doesn't translate into zesty, integrated beer; sweetish finish is a bit cloying.

ASSETS HEFE WEIZEN   **MB**   **2.2**
(Albuquerque, New Mexico)
Creamy, smooth with a slight hint of clove, as advertised; perfumey aroma with thick, foamy Brussels lace that hangs like a curtain; not as pungent or sharply defined as it should be; needs to be drier and fruitier; remains smooth with a little snap only at the end; cloves fade rapidly—as does your interest.

ASSETS RIO GRANDE WHEAT   **MB**   **1.2**
(Albuquerque, New Mexico)
Light, flat, but tasty; no carbonation; hard to detect the grains, or any other ingredients; turns sweetish; nice Brussels lace; uninteresting except as lightly flavored mouth rinse.

ASSETS ROADRUNNER ALE   MB   1.0
(Albuquerque, New Mexico)
Warm; rather weak, and less than fruity; malty, with a pleasant
hint of yeastiness; weak Brussels lace, taste, mouthfeel, and con-
sequences; where's the alcohol?

ASSETS SANDIA STOUT   MB   2.5
(Albuquerque, New Mexico)
Light in body and soul; musty on the tongue with a flattened,
roasted taste; thin; large, erratic bubbles form what passes for a
head; gives evidence of proper ingredients—and appropriate
arrangement—but not enough of them, or not enough character to make them either distinctive or enjoyable; no aroma—a
distinct loss for stout; Brussels lace is okay, while it lasts; if this
could be pumped up, it could be a decent beer.

ASTICA PREMIUM LAGER   CB   3.6
(Haskowo, Bulgaria)
Flavorful; firm head greets you with a continuing hoppy taste;
lots of grain present; rounded sharpness mellows and becomes
even more agreeable with spicy dishes; stable, firm, full-bodied
with character and aplomb. A beer to enjoy with a variety of
foods.

ATHENIAN—THE GREEK BEER Lager   CB   0.8
(Athens, Greece)
Vaguely sour; very thin and textureless; no head and no body to
speak of; minor fizziness provides the only continuous suggestion that this might be beer; light and undistinguished with a
bitter off-taste; finishes flatter than it begins; those may be hops
lamely bringing up the rear, but they're too late—and too faint—
to help.

AUGSBURGER BOCK   CB   2.5
(St. Paul, Minnesota)
Lightweight, dark beer with mild, fruity, fizziness; smooth, watery consistency with hollow innards; warm, cozy, and somewhat
insipid with food; a pleasant, easy-to-get-along-with beer of no
real consequence; lazy and unassertive; a surprising freshness at
the end.

AUGSBURGER DARK Lager   CB   2.2
(St. Paul, Minnesota)
Smooth, gentle, and tasteless; easy-going background beer; acceptable alone, with appetizer, or main dish; taste of both malt
and hops is suppressed; thin, reddish-brown color detracts from
overall ambience; in the end, uncaring and neutral; friendlier
companions are easy to find.

AUGSBURGER GOLDEN Pilsener **CB** **1.1**
(St. Paul, Minnesota)

Gritty taste with an expectation of similar texture that never occurs—so, you wait for a balance or at least a presence of an important ingredient and are left hanging; remains flat and
straight-line in taste with no variation; thin-to-nonexistent head;
light, honey-golden color; actually seems to lose taste when accompanied by food; surprisingly bland.

AUGSBURGER PILSENER **CB** **3.5**
(Monroe, Wisconsin)

Smooth taste and flavor, with an almost-crispness from start to
finish; detectable hoppiness; end is sharp and engagingly sweet,
with gentle, muted alcohol presence; agreeable, no-effort refreshment, which, after all, is what enjoyment should be all about.
Enjoy with raw bar shellfish.

AUGSBURGER ROT LAGER **CB** **2.3**
(St. Paul, Minnesota)

Basically aromaless with a non-distinctive taste and a head not
even worth discussing; somewhat spritzy, with thin texture; washed-
out amber color (*rot* means "red" in German) is the only sign of
roasted caramel malt; neutral taste and semi-solid backbone of
tangible hops; mellow, malty sweetness finally emerges (how come
it took so long to find its way out?); odd for lager, this lager appears to improve as it warms; no bad aftertaste, just no taste at
all. Try it with broiled or grilled beef dishes.

AUGUST SCHELL BOCK **CB** **2.2**
(New Ulm, Minnesota)

Fizzy, medium-light body and spritzy, highly caramelized taste;
dissolves into smoothness with heavyish sweetness at the back of
the tongue; too sweet and goes off in the wrong direction with
spicy foods; mellows out in the end, with no pizzazz to speak of;
low alcohol presence; not very bock-like.

BEER FACT

The August Schell brewery's public gardens and
lovely park grounds, listed on the National Reg-
ister of Historic Sites, compete for attention with
the company's lineup of beers. Contract brews from
across the country are a major part of this family-run
brewery's business.

AUGUST SCHELL DEER BRAND Lager   CB   3.8
(New Ulm, Minnesota)

Mild, light, and fizzy—this immediately strikes you as a good, common beer; not complicated; tasty and flavorful; easy to drink several bottles; appears to contain adjuncts, but never mind; a bit of a thick aftertaste on the tongue. Perfect accompaniment to kosher hot dogs with ballpark mustard or baked beans.

AUGUST SCHELL EXPORT Lager   CB   1.9
(New Ulm, Minnesota)

Mellow and weak, with a warming flavor and no fizziness at all; milky creaminess creeps in at the end, which is its major, perhaps only, plus.

AUGUST SCHELL PILSNER   CB   2.8
(New Ulm, Minnesota)

Nice, light-caramel sheen; golden amber color is romantic and appealing; variable sweetness winds its way through each sip; tends toward sourness in contact with spicy foods. Best with plain chicken.

AUGUST SCHELL WEISS   CB   3.2
(New Ulm, Minnesota)

Very fresh and light, with tangible body; taste remains neutral and decidedly unobtrusive with food; flavor muddies a bit at the bottom of the bottle; fruity, with a liquor-like feel; essentially mild, but tasty; smooth with a medium-dry finish; easy to handle for the novice who is interested in something different, but not too different. Accompanies pork dishes nicely.

AUGUST SCHELL WEIZEN   CB   3.3
(New Ulm, Minnesota)

Full mouthfeel with a counterpunch of delicate pinpricks on the roof of the mouth; nicely balanced and smooth with unassuming sweetness that is encouraging; tantalizing blandness complements snack foods; some yeastiness and a hint of lemon at the end bring it up to style; Silver Medal winner at the 1993 Great American Beer Festival.

AUSTRAL POLAR PILSENER   CB   2.8
(Punta Arenas, Chile)

Sharp, modulated hoppiness; soft on the tongue; astringent; fading tang makes taste linger too long on the roof of the mouth; initial aroma is strong, somewhat acrid, and uninviting; pale-yellow, airy, fluffy head remains thick and clingy; pleasant and unassuming with a tinge of fizziness to remind you that it's a pilsener; smooth; a little too weak for ballpark beer, but the overall taste and texture are there—where's the hot dog?; nicely decorated with intricate and tenacious Brussels lace; warmth in finish that is missing earlier; heavy German style with a hoppy touch finally comes together at the end; well-made, but not outstanding. Try with beef or chicken fajitas.

AUSTRALIAN PREMIUM LAGER   CB   1.9
(Brisbane, Queensland, Australia)

Blunted crispness with rounded, hoppy, winey mouthfeel on first sip; wineyness lingers on the tongue; taste in general is distracting even with simple foods; dwindles to bland at the bottom of the glass; yellow-brown color doesn't add to the attraction; medium-dry finish; a beer of less-than-average rating.

AYINGER BAVARIAN WHEAT   CB   2.9
(Aying, Germany)

Nice, light taste with fine, solid, wheat undertow; sharp and bubbly; milky color; maintains its grainy taste throughout; not enough individuality—could be any one of a number of similar Bavarian wheats. Okay with unspicy foods.

AYINGER CELEBRATOR DOPPELBOCK   CB   3.7
(Aying, Germany)

Sweet, toasted, and smooth on first contact; deep, dark, nutty taste, almost fruity; full-bodied, robust, rich and flavorful; full caramel taste wells up after several sips; just a touch too sweet on the tongue, burnt at the back of the

> NOTE: In Germany, Celebrator is known as Fortunator.

mouth; remains chewy, while richness begins to mellow into a dry finish; hearty, deeply powerful. Try it with German sausage, onion rings, and mounds of creamy coleslaw.

AYINGER DUNKLES UR-WEISSE   CB   4.0
(Aying, Germany)

Fresh-baked-bread aroma, with accompanying sweet, wheat taste; chewy, textural, malty head remains thick throughout; tasty and remarkably smooth; other than a relative coolness that lightens the burden, it doesn't react to spicy foods; nice complexity of fruitiness and maltiness; color of apple cider; a bit too thin for my taste, but very satisfying, expecially in hot weather; 40% wheat. Good at brunch with egg dishes and fresh fruit.

BEER FACT

U r means "source of" or "origin" in German; in this case it is just a way of emphasizing the style of this beer.

AYINGER JAHRHUNDERT BIER
Pale Lager   CB   2.9
(Aying, Germany)
Appealing, rounded fruitiness à la fresh Concord grapes welcomes
you on the first sip; gets a little rough around the edges with
food, essentially reflecting the ambience of the food rather than
complementing or supplementing it; tastes okay by itself, but
doesn't enhance the enjoyment of most meals; no head or Brussels lace to speak of; a better beer with snacks, such as nuts or
pretzels.

AYINGER MAIBOCK   CB   2.0
(Aying, Germany)
Medium-soft with a mildly fruity, metallic taste reflecting the
bock-increased alcohol—or, possibly, a brewing defect; slight
caramel taste flattens and mellows with food; sweetness surrounds
the alcohol at the end, but this still is an attractive beer.

AYINGER OKTOBERFEST-MARZEN
Lager   CB   3.9
(Aying, Germany)
Dusty-honey mouthfeel at the back of the throat along with honey
color and no head; remains fresh and substantive in taste; loses
some vitality and self-confidence if strong food flavors take hold;
character is probably best expressed with unassertive food or alone.

T A P   T I P

Ensuring Palate Pleasure

When sampling different beers, a bite of French
or Italian bread and sips of water between
tastings help rinse the palate. So does a piece
or two of a plain, bland cracker (many beer judges
use unsalted soda crackers) washed down with clean,
fresh water.

BAJAN BEER Lager   CB   2.7
(Bridgetown, Barbados)
Aggressive maltiness wrapped in a swirl of softly fizzing bubbles,
with just a hint of fruity, honey sweetness—a nice, if light, beginning; fluffy, big-bodied head sits quietly on straw-colored body;
malts and hops pleasantly interwoven with each other; musty, but
not unattractive, aroma; Brussels lace is sketchily patterned and
follows the liquid down to the bottom of the glass; finishes mildly
bitter; overall, a gentle, rather unusual-tasting beer. Try it with
lightly sautéed mild-tasting fish or with scrambled eggs for brunch.

BALLANTINE INDIA PALE ALE   **CB**   **3.8**
(Fort Wayne, Indiana)
Starts with sweet but not cloying fruitiness, in both aroma and taste; cool and relaxing with velvet consistency; deep, golden color enhances the feel and enjoyment; hoppiness is subdued, making for a drinkable American IPA; aged in wood; look for the rebus on the underside of the bottle cap. Goes well with meat loaf, pickled beets, and rustic, whole-grain breads.

BANDERSNATCH BIG HORN
PREMIUM ALE (draft)   **BP**   **3.4**
(Tempe, Arizona)
Sweet and a bit heavy, with a thickish hop taste pretty much hidden from view; flowery aroma and yeast presence make for an attractive combination; continued hoppiness; a bit thin, with a finish that is too sweet. Try it with summery seafood salads.

BANDERSNATCH EDINBREW
SEASONAL ALE (draft)   **BP**   **2.9**
(Tempe, Arizona)
Slight wisp of musty aroma; chewier with more fruitiness than its pale ale cousin, as if they used less water; vaguely cloudy; smooth with well-hidden, but present, hops; unobtrusive by itself, it stays compatibly in the background with food; mildly entertaining, like a vacation-read bestseller—easy to hold and linger over, but not all that memorable; finishes full and fruity, but lacks grittiness. Accompanies chicken or tuna salad sandwiches.

BANDERSNATCH MILK STOUT (draft)   **BP**   **4.0**
(Tempe, Arizona)
Burnt, subdued taste is an immediate hit; smoothly creamy and mellow; less thick than traditional stouts; moderate alcohol presence creeps up quickly and pleasantly, leaving you with a final, mellowing buzz; perfect deep-brown color; a virtual meal in a glass; I always look forward to sampling this delightful concoction. Accompanies cooked fish and shellfish.

BANDERSNATCH PALE ALE (draft)   **BP**   **1.8**
(Tempe, Arizona)
Citrusy and light with a mild, sour aftertaste; relatively flat and not very balanced or integrated, with or without food.

BANDERSNATCH RED ALE (draft)   **BP**   **3.7**
(Tempe, Arizona)
Fruity, warm, and eminently appropriate; lively hops with minimum texture; increasing alcoholic and ambient warmth only add to the enjoyment with a bowl of chips; nice, yeasty aroma; well-made and drinkable.

BANDERSNATCH SCOTTISH ALE
(draft)   BP   3.3
(Tempe, Arizona)

Attenuated bitterness goes down smoothly and without com-
plaint; subdued fizziness attests to the beer's integrity; almost a
50-50 balance between hops and malts; no yeastiness to speak
of; remains smooth and quietly attractive; glowing red color is
not in keeping with expected deeper hue, but is attractive nonetheless; some bitterness with food; gentle upsurge of alcohol; though
too weak and thin texturally for ale, it is worth trying anyway.
Enjoyable with spicy pasta salads and lightly-seasoned vegetables.

BANGKOK BEER Pilsener   CB   1.6
(Bangkok, Thailand)

Highly carbonated; a thick, knotty taste at the back of the throat;
somewhat cold and aloof with no ingratiating components; keeps
you at arm's length; cloudy paleness adds to the depressed, un-
warm feeling; hint of rawness also comes through; for export
only—which perhaps tells us something.

BANKS BEER Lager   CB   2.1
(Cincinnati, Ohio)

Light, a bit yeasty, and soft; pleasant, mild, and unassuming; remains weak with food; very pale color with robust, nicely shaped
Brussels lace; low-grade in taste, temperament, and overall satisfaction; more fulfilling with salted peanuts; alone, its tenacious
blandness becomes too boring to finish; touted as a Guyana-
Caribbean product on the label.

BARLEY'S FAIR DINKUM AMBER ALE
(draft)   BP   2.4
(Phoenix, Arizona)

Full, sticky, and sweet, as expected; filigreed, dainty Brussels lace;
a little too flat and passive; sweetness quickly builds to too high
a level, overshadowing the other taste components; eventually
eases off and finishes dry.

B E E R   F A C T

*F*air Dinkum takes its name from the Australian
expression meaning "genuine, honest, on the
level"—clearly the attitude the brewer wishes
the drinker to take away after a pint or two of this
brew.

BARLEY'S IPA (draft)   **BP**   **2.3**
(Phoenix, Arizona)

Not as hoppy as expected for an IPA; malt sweetness plays too large a role; soft rather than sharp and bitter; minimally appealing taste, but not energetic or typical—needs drastic hop infusion; good Brussels lace.

BARLEY'S STRANGLER STOUT (draft)   **BP**   **2.9**
(Phoenix, Arizona)

Smooth, with a hint of bitterness; full-bodied and mildly roasted; not complex enough, but good approximation of a milk stout; sticks affectionately to the roof of the mouth; best alone.

BARLEY'S TOBY STOUT (draft)   **BP**   **3.1**
(Phoenix, Arizona)

Tart, creamy, coffee mouthfeel with chocolate accompaniment; semi-robust, like a good demitasse; coffee taste and lactose are very well balanced with emerging sweetness that lays a bit too long on the tongue; smooth with an appealing roughness on the edges; dark, but still a lighter version of a typical milk stout; minimally chewy. Good with chocolate cake.

BARLEY'S TRICK PALE ALE (draft)   **BP**   **3.2**
(Phoenix, Arizona)

Fruity and citrusy with a lingering tang that coasts into a fizzy mini-cauldron of zestiness; the sides of the glass stay covered with silken Brussels lace; color is appropriate for style—relatively pale, compared to black and brown ales; remains sharp and focused, almost like a pilsener; a big thickish on the tongue; style-appropriate bittersweet finish, but too much emphasis on sweetness; delicate and appealing from beginning to end. Goes hand-in-hand with a garden salad with lots of tomatoes.

BARRIL CLARA Pilsener (draft)   **CB**   **3.8**
(Mexico City, Mexico)

Light blond; maltier and a touch more carbonated than the Barril Oscura; slight musty aroma; thin head and reasonable Brussels lace; refreshing and thirst-quenching even without the requisite lime; acceptable and appropriate with any kind of meal. Knows how to please the food before it.

BARRIL OSCURA Pilsener (draft)   **CB**   **4.0**
(Mexico City, Mexico)

Soft, creamy, smooth, and delicious, even (especially?) when served on the warm side; somewhat light mouthfeel which, with minimum carbonation, makes for good sipping; fluctuating balance of malts and hops; gains appealing thickness with spicy, garlicky foods; subdued, but clearly present, ingredients; eventually weakens, not surprisingly, from the onslaught of spiciness, but that in no way diminishes the overall enjoyment; an unassuming, quite entertaining red-copper beer. Also excellent with shellfish.

BASS PALE ALE   **CB**   **3.8**
(Burton-on-Trent, England)
Calm, quick, sweet initial taste; sweet, unobtrusive, zesty aroma has a hint of caramel; while it has difficulty holding its own with spicy dishes, it is subtle and understated with plainer foods; not flashy, but very predictable in a comforting way.

B E E R   F A C T

*T*he red triangle on the Bass label is England's first registered trademark (1876). Bass is the largest brewery in England.

BATEMAN'S DARK VICTORY ALE   **CB**   **3.8**
(Wainfleet, England)
Nice, erect copper head sits atop sparkling, roasted maltiness with just the right touch of burnt flavor; certainly stands up to food; mild fruitiness leads to a stately finish and caps a winsomeness that encourages you to ask for more; cool, appealing fullness adds to the spiciness and texture of food. Accompanies meatballs and spaghetti and other pastas with tomato-based sauce.

BATEMAN'S XXXB ALE   **CB**   **3.7**
(Wainfleet, England)
Bitter flavor with abundant hops from start to last sip, with clearly defined maltiness to complete the balance; fizziness drops away as air comes in contact with beer; fine nutty warmth eventually takes over; maintains soft, foamy head throughout; high alcohol content is obvious; typical English bitter, with abundant hop strength; substance and character add to the pleasure of the meal. Goes well with Chinese food. (The B after the XXX in the name indicates bitter.)

B E E R   F A C T

*O*n a label, "X" traditionally denotes the relative amount of alcohol: "XXX" means there is more alcohol in this bottle than in an "X" or "XX" bottle.

BAVARIA LAGER   **CB**   **3.0**
(Lieshout, Holland)
Nice initial balance between hops and malt with moderated sharpness; slight, but pleasant, hint of yeast-hoppiness emerges and blends effortlessly with spicy foods, as a weaker partner; tasty and flavorful by itself at the end, with a warmth that is beguiling; a beer with substance, it takes its time announcing itself; more or less worth the wait. Goes well with fajitas and other Mexican favorites.

BEAMISH IRISH CREAM STOUT   **CB**   **3.2**
(Cork, Ireland)
Crisper, sharper stout with some underlying softness; satisfying fizzy head; bit thinner and sharper than other stouts; classically put together with its own special twist. Perhaps better alone than with food, but compatible with pastas and salads.

BECK'S Pilsener   **CB**   **3.1**
(Bremen, Germany)
Sharp, light, and likeable; predictable and unchanging from start to finish, with dominating hop presence that makes you take notice; good, but not distinguished or unique; certainly an amiable companion, though not one to create excitement or produce new thoughts; nice with a tuna salad sandwich.

BECK'S DARK Pilsener   **CB**   **2.6**
(Bremen, Germany)
Mildly roasted, familiarly carbonated, and filled with reassuring hints of standard hops and malts, especially malts; straightforward, sharp sweetness that is not cute or cloying; too demanding for spicy foods; though the beer itself is well-made, it is clearly a commercial product; essentially no head, no Brussels lace, and a somewhat muddied, deep-auburn color; finish is sweet and malty; good choice for someone who wants a different beer, but without an abrupt taste departure from the usual fare.

BECK'S OKTOBERFEST (annual)
Lager   **CB**   **3.7**
(Bremen, Germany)
Nice effervescence with apple taste, all preceded by a hint of caramel; well-balanced malt and hops; charming ruby-red amber sets off accelerating sharpness of hops; very grainy, with matching alcohol content; maintains robust composure throughout; strong and wholesome, with staying power; finishes with soothing caramel aroma; similar to typical European amber; far better warm than cold; worth looking for as the leaves start turning gold.

BEER Lager   **CB**   **1.0**
(Calgary, Alberta, Canada)
Harsh, crisp, neighborhood-bar beer; a hint of greenness is pre-

sent; not meant for fancy meals or fancy restaurants—or, even, other locations where you wish a decent beer accompaniment.

BELGRADE GOLD Pilsener   CB   2.9
(Belgrade, the former Yugoslavia)
Sweet, honeyed thickness with visual, but not tangible, effervescence; turns sour and citrusy with sauces and dressings; bitter hoppiness emerges and remains to the end of the bottle, along with honey taste; cloudy, pale-golden color with no head; variable, but not unappealing; sweet finish. Goes best with Middle Eastern dishes such as falafel, couscous, and tabouleh.

BELHAVEN SCOTTISH ALE   CB   4.0
(Dunbar, Scotland)
Tiny bubbles, tingly carbonation; constrained high-quality alcohol and gentle, sweetish hops; creamy, gentle fruitiness; effervescence doesn't push itself on you—mellow, thick, light-tan, foamy head encourages enjoyment; I can't say enough for the marvelous support and delectability this ale adds to food; light and easy to handle, it keeps its composure through thick (a favorite barbecue sauce) and thin (corn on the cob); mild, playful presence of caramel aroma and taste at the end, with a hint of what seems to be licorice flavor; stylish and composed. An excellent match for chicken main dishes.

B E E R   F A C T

*D*unbar, the birthplace of the famed conservationist John Muir, is also the site of a Benedictine monastery brewery that dates to the Middle Ages.

BELMONT LONG BEACH CRUDE Porter MB/BP   2.1
(Long Beach, California)
Immediately weak, though smooth and mildly chocolatey; roastiness is well-hidden, but mild roasty bitterness becomes apparent at mid-glass, providing motivation for finishing the drink; the promise is more satisfying than the reality; in the end, too weak, thin, and one-dimensional to rave about. Try it with a hamburger and tossed salad.

BELMONT LONG BEACH CRUDE NUT BROWN ALE MB/BP   2.8
(Long Beach, California)
Fruity with vague suggestion of molasses; chocolate and coffee are also in there somewhere; fades quickly, but retains some character; nice, warm alcohol aftertaste keeps it within acceptable bounds; finish is slightly bitter; ostensible oatmeal presence is nowhere to be found. I like this with fish and chips.

BELMONT MARATHON ALE   **MB/BP**   **1.8**
(Long Beach, California)
Clear, textureless, and essentially aromaless, with a hint of soap
mixed in; no guts and no body; dull and placid; too fluffy for its
own good; definitely a beer made for American taste and consumption.

BELMONT PETTIFOGGER Ale   **MB/BP**   **3.4**
(Long Beach, California)
This beer is made from part Belmont Crude and part Top Sail.
Simple fourth-grade math mandates a 2.7 when working out the
average of Crude's 2.8 and Top Sail's 2.6, but happily those numbers don't add up when combining Crude and Top Sail, a mixture that produces the best of Belmont's brews: flavorful, zesty,
and nicely balanced, this black-and-tan combination is highly
recommended; deep, dark amber color adds to the attraction, as
does the resulting fullness. Try it with fresh tuna or other mildly
flavored fresh fish.

BELMONT STRAWBERRY BLONDE Ale   **MB/BP**   **2.2**
(Long Beach, California)
Smells like Barbie doll perfume—very soda pop-like, but thankfully not overwhelmingly so; flat texture makes for a watery, light-
hearted concoction; more plain than bitter; a summertime drink
that is easy to handle, if you like a beer that is really not a beer.

BELMONT TOP SAIL ALE   **MB/BP**   **2.8**
(Long Beach, California)
Sweet maltiness presents something tangible with which to deal;
reasonably balanced between hops and malt; mild bitterness creates interest if not idolatry; light-amber color. Try it with salty
chips, nuts, or pretzels.

BERGHOFF Lager   **CB**   **2.9**
(Monroe, Wisconsin)
Thickish with a flat taste; a bit sweeter and softer than most
lagers; predictable taste from start to finish; maintains calm underpinning with Mexican food, but neither adds to nor detracts
from the food—it's sort of just there; some complexity and zest
emerge at the end of the bottle; food to be eaten with it should
be chosen carefully. Best with salted nuts and pretzels.

BERGHOFF BOCK   **CB**   **2.4**
(Monroe, Wisconsin)
Variable honey-sweet initial aroma collides head-on with a tangy
dollop of taste that ends flat and unexciting; texture remains surprisingly bland; expected alcohol zestiness never materializes;
muddy brown, with little redeeming red to it; mild maltiness remains and becomes essentially the sole distinguishing feature in
its uphill battle with food; heartiness and fullness finally become

evident, but remain far removed from the malty alcohol features expected from a good bock; slightly acidic at the finish; this isn't a bad beer, just not a good beer. Okay with Italian food.

BERGHOFF DARK Lager   **CB**   **3.3**
(Monroe, Wisconsin)
Vague but persistent caramel flavor is complemented by relative thickness that is charming and encouraging; a little watery with food; deep red-amber color matches "feel" of the beer perfectly; head hardly exists; good American dark beer; Silver Medal winner at the 1993 Great American Beer Festival. Accompanies steak and salad.

BERGHOFF DORTMUNDER Lager   **CB**   **2.6**
(Monroe, Wisconsin)
Fresh, slightly yeasty aroma, but stale, uninvigorating first taste; cranky sharpness accompanies this full-bodied representative of the style; remains malty sharp and texturally kind with food; Brussels lace is nicely wispy and has staying power; finishes warm and almost sweet. Good with standard American fare such as meat loaf.

BEER FACT

*D*ortmund was one of the four dominant lager styles in nineteenth-century Europe. Each was named after the city in which it was first brewed; the other three are Munich, Vienna, and Pilsen. The city of Dortmund, in western Germany, brews more beer than any other city in a country that boasts well over one-third of the world's breweries.

BERLINER PILS   **CB**   **2.5**
(Berlin, Germany)
Dry, crisp, and light—meant for the ballpark—but has a bit more character; depressed texture and flavor don't integrate well with food; mild honey taste rises to the top, along with wispy warmth and decreased sharpness; okay for a quick thirst-quencher on the run.

BERLINER RATSKELLER LAGER   **CB**   **2.2**
(Berlin, Germany)
Typical, crisp lager with hoppy undertone; sudsy Brussels lace on sides of the glass and thin, sudsy head on top of the beer; individual ingredients suggest that the totality should be more

inviting than the overall taste—but that is not to be; in the end, it is boring and uneventful, though balanced; a run-of-the-mill brew. Probably best with salted nuts or pretzels.

BEVERLY HILLS HARVEST ALE   CT   0.4
(New Ulm, Minnesota)
An overpowering clove impact immediately on the tongue, in the nose, around the mouth—wow!; fleeting chemical presence passes by as clove flavor battles accompanying food; except for a hint of hop bitterness, clove is the only discernible ingredient; as beer further warms, the intensity of the clove taste weakens, permitting a pungent sweetness to emerge that borders on the medicinal; winds up tasting like bubble gum; visually uninteresting; flat texture; no head; no point to this ale.

BIECKERT ESPECIAL Pilsener   CB   4.2
(Antartida, Argentina)
Strikingly fresh, crisp, attentive, and immediately very satisfying; malt and hops are in pleasant, interactive balance, depending on the food requirements of the moment; just the right amount of fizz, but a flat-to-nonexistent head; maintains its own delectable dignity with food; excellent. Goes well with Mexican fare.

BIG APPLE PREMIUM Pilsener   CT   2.4
(brewed in Milwaukee, Wisconsin, by Pabst)
Sour-sweet with restrained cloying sensation; soft sweetness trails off to a mild backdrop to food; residual fruitiness lingers on the tongue; essentially flat with no complexity; brewed for that "exquisite New York taste," according to the label, whatever that might be.

BIG BARREL Lager   CB   3.0
(Leabrook, South Australia, Australia)
Smooth and easy going down; vague corn flavor subtly hidden behind first swallow, awaiting contact with deeper taste buds at the back of the mouth, where slight bitterness emerges; calm, tepid brew; taste is maintained throughout a meal, not necessarily a favor to the beer. Accompanies barbecued burgers served with plenty of condiments.

BIG ROCK BITTER PALE ALE   MB   3.1
(Calgary, Alberta, Canada)
Chocolate aroma and encouraging fruity taste make first sips very pleasant; rising, full-bodied bitterness evens out to fine combination of malt sweetness and hop sharpness; pleasant light-golden color; some fizziness at the roof of the mouth is distracting; nice mellowing at the end, with a touch of honey finishing it off. Accompanies egg salad and other traditional sandwich fillings.

BIG ROCK BUZZARD BREATH ALE   MB   1.7
(Calgary, Alberta, Canada)
Smells of overripe apples on the ground in an orchard; flavor itself is flat and uninspiring; no head; amber color is too faded to be appealing; some emerging fruitiness and depth as it warms, but not enough to change the thumbs down on this bland, uncomplex, and unmotivated beer.

BIG ROCK COCK O' THE ROCK
PORTER   MB   2.4
(Calgary, Alberta, Canada)
Too sweet on first sip; a bit too thin; uncomplex and rather uninspiring; hint of roastedness tentatively appears, then fades away, leaving no taste trace in the mouth. Becomes more integrated and flavorful with broiled meat dishes.

BIG ROCK COLD COCK
WINTER PORTER   MB   3.1
(Calgary, Alberta, Canada)
Mellow, subdued, appealing burnt taste, with passing whiff of same as this relatively high-alcohol concoction settles into the glass; medium-bodied; remains constant and consistent with spicy Cajun dishes, but turns a bit sharp with milder fare—sautéed Dover sole or linguine with clam sauce, for example—which is okay, given that the food is soft and relatively bland; cooling sweetness at the end reveals molasses provenance; a little too watery, but still has substance.

BIG ROCK GRASSHOPPER WHEAT ALE CB   2.5
(Calgary, Alberta, Canada)
Faintly sweet, faintly honey, and definitely smooth and silky; becomes tart and fizzy, with a downplaying of the major ingredients; tantalizing malt flavor is coaxed out by seafood accompaniment; a calm, gentle yeastiness settles on the tongue alongside the food; malt and hops become more noticeable at the end of the bottle, with a malt imbalance; amiable, though unexciting. Nicely suited to shrimp salad and other seafood salad sandwiches.

BIG ROCK ROYAL COACHMAN
DRY ALE   CB   3.9
(Calgary, Alberta, Canada)
Surprisingly attractive, fruity aroma and taste on first sip; fizzy bubbles quickly dissipate; far more flavorful and rounded than most Canadian beers; attenuated sweetness; faint molasses taste enhances overall ambience; if it were a bit thicker, it would easily rank over 4.0. Best with beef.

BIG ROCK SPRINGBOK ALE   MB   2.1
(Calgary, Alberta, Canada)
Plain, unassuming, but not unpleasant; hard to sort out any def-

inite qualities; does leave slight whisper of aftertaste at the back of the tongue; fizzy apple fruitiness with a dry finish and an increased physical presence. Accompanies pork dishes.

BIG ROCK WARTHOG ALE   **MB**   **2.5**
(Calgary, Alberta, Canada)
Misleading fruit presence on first sip; distinctive plum-apple taste fades as beer is consumed; thin head presages and reflects thin mouthfeel, but taste nonetheless is teased out by food; hops and malts and yeast all remain unintegrated; yeast aroma and slight fruity zippiness finish the bottle; not a beer to drink without food; a step or two short of being memorable, but I would drink it again. Good with egg dishes—plain or spicy.

BIG ROCK XO LAGER   **MB**   **3.4**
(Calgary, Alberta, Canada)
Clean, fruity, flavorful taste with only a hint of hops; subtly complex; flattens and sours perceptibly as food is eaten; remains crisp, however, even as the taste deteriorates; a good light lager that continues to do well even after several bottles. Goes well with a fresh green salad dressed with plenty of black pepper and lemon juice.

BIG TIME BHAGWANS BEST INDIA
PALE ALE   **MB/BP**   **2.0**
(Seattle, Washington)
Insufficiently hoppy; too obviously citrusy (grapefruit) without enough zest, though some oomph is present; too little carbonation; won't hold up over the long haul (say, a second bottle); too much red in the color spoils overall effect; too many departures from style to even begin to make this attractive—not to mention that, regardless of style, it doesn't have a good taste.

BIG TIME OLD WOOLY BARLEY WINE   **MB/BP**   **2.8**
(Seattle, Washington)
Moderated alcohol presence; typical, bittersweet barley wine taste; thick and full but, pleasantly, not too potent; light, somewhat murky copper color; grainy undertow; too weak, it needs more work to define itself as a clear example of the style; Bronze Medal winner at the 1993 Great American Beer Festival. Fine with a fresh fruit salad served early in the meal.

BINTANG PILSENER   **CB**   **3.9**
(Surabaya, Indonesia)
Appealing creaminess, overlaid with smartly crackling carbonation underneath; zesty freshness; light-golden color; subdued, flavorful, restrained hoppy bitterness; grains move to the foreground with red meats; stays sharp and clear throughout; fine Brussels lace remaining at the end; typical dry finish with a light, feathery touch. Match with steak and potatoes.

BIOS COPPER ALE   CB   1.4
(Ertvelde, Belgium)
Weak, but distinct, lemon-tart taste; layered, rather than full, mouthfeel evolves into cherry and/or pear taste which diminishes when accompanying food; thick, bubbly head tops off the strangeness of the body; very fruity; yeast residue at the bottom. Better as a *digestif*/after-dinner drink.

BITBURGER PILSENER   CB   3.3
(Bitburg, Germany)
Quickly sparkly and quite hoppy with an ingratiating ambience; mellow and cooling with spicy food; lends a tempered balance to hot foods; not bitter but quite dry; relatively low alcohol content; almost delicate in taste and quite pale in color; a very light, able-bodied pilsener to while away the day, rather than concentrate on the drinking experience; a nice little beer. Try it with Indian food, especially curries.

BLACK CLOUD PORTER   MB   2.6
(Santa Fe, New Mexico)
A promising start—complete with tangy bitterness—that becomes too sweet and slightly cloying too soon; strong burnt toastiness has too much wateriness at the edges for a complete, rounded taste; imbalanced but not unpleasantly so; attractive, dark, chocolate-brown color; yeast resides at the bottom from bottle-conditioning; aroma and taste are consistent and parallel; decent but not outstanding; sweet, toasty finish with satisfying fullness in the mouth. Rich and appropriately bitter with New Mexican food.

BLACK HILLS GOLD LABEL LAGER   CT   2.7
(Monroe, Wisconsin)
Immediately sharp and to the point, but the texture quickly rounds out and weakens; vague lemon presence; settles into a relatively balanced brew; more texture than flavor; maintains steady and tangible backbone; thick, lasting head with big bubbles suggests artificial carbonation; consistent from start to finish, with a touch of textural integrity. Accompanies plain, home-style foods.

BLACK LABEL Lager   CB   2.1
(Seattle, Washington; La Crosse, Wisconsin; et. al.)
Although clear and crisp, this beer is also watery and weak with more mini-fizz than taste; does remain evenhanded and predictable, however, a testament to this big commercial brewery's quality control; mixed with tomato juice it attains body and palate that are more satisfying and appropriately layered; this combination of juice and beer is particularly satisfying with pepper steak, rice, and tomatoes.

BLANCHE DE BRUGES Wheat   CB   3.9
(Bruges, Belgium)
Very yeasty, pale, and delicate, like Champagne; taste and effect
are enhanced in bowl-shaped wine or snifter glass; blond in color;
bottle-conditioned, it makes good use of the grain; almost wine-
like in character and in relation to food; wispy Brussels lace stays
under the liquid. Gentleness and citrus ambience are comforting
alongside meat and potatoes.

BLUE HEN Lager   CT   2.9
(Newark, Delaware)
Flowery, sharp, very slight citrus-honey taste; relatively complex
with favorable hop presence; slight upper palate aftertaste; an all-
malt beer (no adjuncts), it serves up a reasonable balance with
malty sweetness; balance and sweetness diminish, but don't disappear, with food; carefully made. Try it with cold cuts and other
deli favorites.

B E E R   F A C T

A Delaware product, the name Blue Hen honors
the Fighting Blue Hens, a Revolutionary War
state militia known, according to the brewer, "for
bravery and tenacity in battle."

BOAGS PREMIUM LAGER   CB   2.2
(Hobart, Tasmania, Australia)
Skunky aroma and fizzily sharp; remains thick and unappetizing
with food; prickliness remains in mouth for awhile after the beer
is gone; lasting impression, both literally and figuratively, is not
a good one.

B E E R   F A C T

B oags, named for one of its founders, is the longest
continuously operating manufacturing company
in Australia.

BOHANNON MARKET STREET
GOLDEN ALE   MB/BP   2.1
(Nashville, Tennessee)
Chemical sweetness fades quickly; Brussels lace is also chemically
induced, with random, rather than even, pattern; slight, warm
citrus/fruity mouthfeel; clearly weak, but a bit more palatable at
the finish, with a touch of hops missing earlier.

BOHANNON MARKET STREET
OKTOBERFEST Lager   MB/BP   0.3
(Nashville, Tennessee)

Too sweet, no strength, no body, no carbonation, and sticks too much to the roof of the mouth; big bubbles suggest artificial carbonation; not in the Oktoberfest style.

> ### B E E R   F A C T
>
> *T*he mid South's first microbrewery, Bohannon, is located on the river overlook site of Nashville's now defunct pioneer commercial brewery, Crossman & Drucker, which started pouring beer in the pre-Civil War year of 1859.

BOHEMIA PILSENER   CB   1.7
(Monterrey, Mexico)

Slight, bitter hoppiness, with smooth, fizzy accompaniment; warmth, unexpectedly, brings out sweetish, bitter, malty complexity of flavors; hint of perfume comes and goes; settles into slightly sour, flattish, far less complex offering with salty foods; finishes more integrated than the beginning, but still several notches below average.

BOON GUEUZE Lambic   CB   2.2
(Lembeek, Belgium)

Very yeasty and acidic; skunky (an intentional flavor element); very light, dainty head stays at about a quarter-inch throughout—a very good sign (generally, heads should be half the thickness of the original after one minute); soft mouthfeel encourages liquid to go down gently; settles into an even keel with alcohol finally offering up its warmth; finish remains very yeasty, almost to the exclusion of all else; Brussels lace stays in sheets on sides of glass; tartly sweet, like a just-ripening grape; bottle-conditioned, and it shows. Best savored as an *apéritif* or with dessert.

BORSOD PREMIUM Pilsener   CB   2.5
(Bocsarlapujto, Hungary)

Hint of pleasant bitterness greets the tongue, followed by a whisper of maltiness at the back of the mouth; light, airy, and dry; crisp and relatively sharp—far more texture than taste, though taste itself is at best benign, at worst nonexistent; irregular, thick Brussels lace suggests more substance than is actually present in the pale-golden body; an inoffensive summer drink that doesn't interfere with food; unexpected fullness at the end, along with a mild sweetness and mild bitterness, as if all the substance of this beer sank to the bottom of the bottle. Serve it with bagels, cream

BOULDER EXTRA PALE ALE   MB/BP   3.6
(Boulder, Colorado)

Pleasantly light, smoothly refreshing; muted amber color is eye-catching, and crisp, hop aroma is nose-catching—both are a beer-lover's joy; remains unencumbering; a bit of an off-taste rapidly disappears; solid tasting and sweet; don't gulp this one down. Stands up to spicy finger foods, such as barbecued chicken wings.

B E E R   F A C T

*B*oulder Brewing, started in 1979 and now called Rockies Brewing, is the oldest existing microbrewery in the United States.

BOULDER PORTER   MB/BP   2.7
(Boulder, Colorado)

Bitter hops and bland texture—not a good combination; burnt taste is acceptable, but not intense enough; more effective chilled than warm; lacks alcoholic strength and depth, but is mildly interesting and satisfying enough to want more. Serve with munchies such as potato chips, nuts, and crackers.

BOULDER STOUT   MB/BP   2.2
(Boulder, Colorado)

Very smooth and creamy; initially sweet, then mixed sweet-sour taste that eventually turns stale in the mouth; essentially more texture than taste; chocolatey burnt feel at the end of the bottle with no food accompaniment; hairy mouthfeel also at the finish; aftertaste reduces the rating precipitously. Silver Medal winner at the 1994 Great American Beer Festival.

BOULEVARD "BULLY" PORTER   MB   3.8
(Kansas City, Missouri)

Tasty, with a sizzle of zest embedded in the balance of sweet and tart; deep red-brown stops short of deeper black associated with most porters; entertaining, but doesn't live up to its promise; foamy and relatively long-lasting head, leaving an even, substantial ring of Brussels lace; predictable. Quite appealing with a rich bread pudding or similar dessert; beer and food leave a comfortable, nostalgic taste in mouth.

BRAHMA Pilsener   CB   3.8
(Rio de Janeiro, Brazil)

Very nice, malty sweetness reminiscent of better Mexican beers; fresh in bouquet and palate; although light, it does retain a stable heartiness without food; tends to weaken against only mildly hot guacamole and chips; pleasant and attractive; crisp throughout; the label calls it "The best selling beer in all Latin America." Goes with pasta or fish.

BRAHMA CHOPP Pilsener CB 3.7
(Rio de Janeiro, Brazil)

Light, fluffy, and slightly carbonated; mild graininess; very feathery on the tongue and palate; nicely integrated with a sweet blend of malt and hops that stays politely in the background; pretty wisps of Brussels lace dance on top of straw-colored body; all in perfect symmetry and balance; finish is weak with a hint of earlier strength that includes a thickish sweetness that is not part of the rest of the can; appropriate for a beginner interested in building a foreign beer portfolio. Try it with your next Mexican meal.

BEER FACT

*B*razil, the largest country in South America, is the sixth-ranked brewing nation in the world, just ahead of China and a step behind Japan. Rio de Janeiro-based Brahma is the world's tenth-largest brewer. Oddly, Brazil doesn't even show up on the top 20 list of beer-consuming countries.

BRAND Pilsener CB 2.5
(Limburg, Holland)

Acidic with light undertaste; very hoppy and some skunkiness; all taste differential—good, bad, indifferent—is flattened out and rendered irrelevant with food; keeps minimal but recognizable head; flavors and aroma are not that attractive; dry from start to finish. Should accompany bland dishes such as spaghetti with unspicy meat sauce.

BRASSEURS BIERE DE PARIS Lager CB 1.3
(Bonneuil, France)

Wimpy, unpleasant aroma and palate; cloudy, reddish color, just short of caramel; smooth, bland, and very unassuming; ingredients aside (please), it tastes more like good, fresh springwater than anything else; pleasant head but appearance doesn't make up for lack of substance.

BRASSEURS GRAND CRU Lager CB 3.5
(Bonneuil, France)

Sweet, honey taste with moderate body; mild caramel flavor takes over from taste of honey as the beer warms; cloudy, amber color suggests a softness versus flattened sparkle of carbonation on the tongue; a bit too sweet for, say, a spicy meal, but evolves into a gentle pastime by itself or with pre-drink snack food.

BRAUMEISTER PILSENER   CT   2.5
(Monroe, Wisconsin)
Brittle top layer with softer fullness underneath; not particularly
fizzy; filmy aftertaste lingers at the top and sides of the mouth;
quick, initial freshness fades into the throat, leaving behind moderate thirst-quenching qualities; typical, predictable pilsener—
friendly, but not overly solicitous; good for a couple of quick
ones while waiting for the game to start.

TAP TIP

Air and Space

*T*he air space between bottle cap and liquid, called
ullage, should not be more than 1 to 1½ inches.
Extra air causes oxidation, which spoils the taste
and aroma of the beer in rather short order. Too much
space also means you're paying more per ounce of liquid in the bottle and getting less. While you're at it,
check the inside of the bottle neck; grit is highly suggestive of bacterial contamination. In this case, you're
paying for *more* than you want; you don't want that,
either.

BRECKENRIDGE AVALANCHE
AMBER Ale   MB/BP   0.4
(Breckenridge, Colorado)
Too smooth and too much off-taste; no real roasted flavor; sticks
to the roof of the mouth; feels somewhat raw and stomach-turn-
ing; stay away from this one.

BRECKENRIDGE INDIA PALE ALE   MB   2.4
(Denver, Colorado)
Cardboardy, papery taste, mildly bitter, and relatively uncarbonated; yeasty; moderately sour; soft, smooth texture—not bold, as
label proclaims; decent, circumscribed Brussels lace stays layered
in thin sheets; hint of sweetness; essentially, quality ingredients
make their presence known, but still not bitter, full, or bold
enough to be a fullblown IPA; hoppy finish; has the makings to
become a decent beer.

BREUG LAGER   CB   2.7
(Roubaix, France)
Hoppy and a bit skunky; tart and sharp; strong maltiness quickly
comes up; achieves good balance with sandwiches, hors d'oeuvres,
dip, and marinated olives; also integrates aroma, taste, and visual

appeal—light, golden color; tangy and lighter than most lagers, but surprisingly tasty for a French beer; it helps that it's from Flanders.

BREWSKI'S AZTEC AMBER Lager
(draft) BP 2.9
(San Diego, California)
Mild bitterness with caramel maltiness; minimally carbonated; nicely balanced; golden light, pale color; wispy, quickly disappearing Brussels lace; pleasant companion without food.

BREWSKI'S DOWNTOWN CHESTNUT
BROWN ALE (draft) BP 0.5
(San Diego, California)
Bland, tasteless, and medium-bodied; fizzy smoothness; watery and unpleasant; there's hardly any beer there.

BREWSKI'S DRY HONEY ALE (draft) BP 3.0
(San Diego, California)
Fresh and yeasty with not much carbonation; hint of honey is not intrusive; very light taste, texture, color; dry and flavorful; fruity finish encourages you to ask for more. Serve with soft cheese before dinner.

BREWSKI'S OATMEAL STOUT (draft) BP 2.2
(San Diego, California)
Strong; more bitter than roasted; coffee-like taste without any sweetish balance; irrelevant with food; much too acidic; no deep, satisfying flavor is discerned.

BREWSKI'S RED SAILS ALE (draft) BP 2.8
(San Diego, California)
Strong, coppery visual presence with textural balance; likewise, good balance between moderately rich maltiness and light-to-the-touch hops; a satisfying, if not very exciting, beer. Try it with grilled burgers.

BREWSKI'S TWO-BERRY ALE (draft) BP 1.7
(San Diego, California)
Moderated sweetness with distinct, but not overly sweet, berry taste; no carbonation to speak of; uncomplex; weak; makes a better *apéritif.*

BRICK LAGER CB 3.1
(Waterloo, Ontario, Canada)
Quick rush of flavor along with sharp bubbles that dissipate at the back of the mouth; texture is flat but taste is flavorful and apparent; not filled with adjuncts typically found in American lagers; somewhat smooth and silky. Accompanies oversized sandwiches on crusty bread.

BRIDGEPORT BLUE HERON PALE ALE   MB/BP   2.4
(Portland, Oregon)
Fruity, viscous; leaves thin layer of aftertaste on the roof of the
mouth; remains staunchly fruity and warm with herbal tang alongside Southwestern and Mexican foods; flattens at the end, losing
much of its effervescence; finishes slightly heavy and gamey. Try
with green chile stew, grilled seafood, and vegetables.

BRIDGEPORT OLD KNUCKLEHEAD
BARLEY WINE STYLE ALE   MB/BP   4.0
(Portland, Oregon)
Rounded, honey taste with barley sharpness; lastingly sweet, but
fades and turns mildly cloying on the tongue; firmly entrenched
grain taste; very high in alcohol; rich and strong; label identifies
it as a sipping ale—it would be hard to down it any quicker; recommended for those wishing a powerful, tasty, well-made mouthful. A delightful *digestif* to sip slowly after a hearty meal.

BRIGAND BELGIAN ALE   CB   3.8
(Ingelmunster, Belgium)
Old-straw aroma and pungent sweetness greet first sip; soft, spongy
mouthfeel; highly yeasty and hoppy; cloudy, pale, creamy orange
bordering on peach-blush color; almost opaque; tingly robustness forthrightly integrates and balances the various ingredients
into a coherent alcoholic whole; well-made, but doesn't appeal
to me personally; finishes smooth and sharply sweet, with some
roughness at the edges. Serve with smoked salmon, soft cheeses,
or fresh fruit.

BRISA Lager   CB   2.8
(Guadalajara, Mexico)
Light, sharp, good-tasting; simultaneously malty and sparkly;
good brew to sip during a ballgame. Fine with hot dogs.

BROAD RIPPLE EXTRA
SPECIAL BITTER Ale   MB/BP   2.6
(Indianapolis, Indiana)
Harsh, aromatic, and refreshing with bright, deep-golden color;
keeps foamy head (with large bubbles); citrus/hoppiness helps retain freshness throughout; despite nonassertiveness, it is good-
tasting, but weak for a bitter—extra special or otherwise.

BROKEN HILL LAGER   CB   2.0
(Thebarton/Adelaide, South Australia, Australia)
Too bitter for lager; sharp and hoppy; stays crisp with golden,
slight honey impression underneath; smooth and full, but one
step up from bland; even when food is not particularly spicy, it
overshadows this beer that goes nowhere; finishes watery with
hint of hop graininess.

TAP TIP

Measuring Alcohol Strength

*T*he amount of alcohol in a beer is measured in two ways: by weight (percentage of weight of alcohol compared to weight of total amount of beer in the container) and volume (percentage of alcohol in a given volume of liquid, e.g., pint, quart, liter). Brewers in the United States use the alcohol/weight standard; elsewhere (and in the U.S. wine industry), the standard is alcohol/volume. Thus, comparing alcohol percentages between American, and say, European beers is difficult; further complicating the matter is the law, in the process of being changed, prohibiting American brewers from listing alcohol content on the label—by weight, volume, or any other measurement. A rough rule of thumb: 4% alcohol/weight (fairly standard for an American lager)=approximately 5% alcohol/volume (fairly standard for a British lager).

BROOKLYN BROWN DARK ALE   **CT**   **3.1**
(Utica, New York)
Fresh flowery aroma; dainty on the back of the tongue; reddish-caramel color is not overly pleasing to the eye; a complement and adjunct to food; possesses warmth with cool, alcoholic core, especially as the beer itself warms up; not complex or particularly integrated. Serve alongside steak and other grilled beef dishes.

BROOKLYN LAGER   **CT**   **2.3**
(Utica, New York)
Sharp and like a typical American lager: smooth, essentially flat texture with minimum of complexity; a bit above pedestrian; easy to ignore, though malty sweetness gently emerges in the finish; neck label is misleading—a beer from Brooklyn should have more pizzazz (and, indeed, this beer is not from Brooklyn).

BROOKLYN LAGER DRAFT   **CT**   **3.6**
(Utica, New York)
Nicely winey and smooth, with well-presented Brussels lace; back-of-the-throat sharpness; very pleasant fruitiness stays stable throughout; finishes gently hoppy; nicely attractive—makes you want to have more. Serve with roast chicken and mashed potatoes.

BROWN DERBY Pilsener   **CT**   **0.3**
(brewed for Safeway in Tumwater, Washington)
Musty graininess presages green taste with no vivacity; has tang, but remains somewhat watery; light essence throughout; not filling and rather unobtrusive; this made-for-TV beer is not worth the effort it takes to swallow.

BROYHAN PREMIUM Lager   **CB**   **1.8**
(Hannover, Germany)
Tartly hoppy with a mushy mouthfeel; texture flattens rather rapidly, becoming mild and reserved; food may coax a bit of hoppiness back out—this beer obviously needs to be urged to give up anything positive; light-bodied and light-colored, with thin, faint Brussels lace; musty, mild malty finish; an uninteresting brew.

BRUIN PALE ALE   **CB**   **1.0**
(Cincinnati, Ohio)
Slight light-struck mouthfeel, followed by a flat aftertaste after an initial sip or two; mild perfumey, mild hoppy taste with a chemical underflow; not bitter, sharp, or particularly alcoholic like this ale should be—rather like a watered-down pilsener without the carbonated punch; tepid alone or with food; weak-tea color with no visual texture; minor softness and sweetness surfaces at end of bottle (but at this point, so what?); lowest common denominator beer.

B E E R   F A C T

*"P*ale ale" is the term often used to indicate a brewery's premium bitter. Traditionally offered in a bottle, it is increasingly served from the tap.

BUCKERFIELD'S APPLETON
BROWN ALE   **BP**   **3.3**
(Victoria, British Columbia, Canada)
Nice, tender, smooth flow from the tip of the tongue to the back of the throat; remains friendly throughout; good and quasi-creamy. Goes nicely with fried finger foods, such as chicken wings and mushrooms.

BUCKERFIELD'S CYGNET ALE   **BP**   **2.0**
(Victoria, British Columbia, Canada)
A little watery; retains very mild, fruity taste; becomes more palpable with bland cooked foods but fades into mild sourness; not really worth the effort.

BUCKERFIELD'S PANDORA PALE ALE BP 2.9
(Victoria, British Columbia, Canada)
Immediate citrus (orange-grapefruit) taste; fresh, buttery ambience; soft, rounded fragrance; ends up being something of a lightweight, but creates some fun getting there. Goes well with shellfish.

**BUCKERFIELD'S SWANS
OATMEAL STOUT** BP 3.8
(Victoria, British Columbia, Canada)
Subdued, rounded, burnt taste; much less threatening than the deep-brown color would suggest; retains nicely moderated richness; roasted malts stay unobtrusive; very well-balanced; surprisingly refreshing and not filling; well deserving of several pints and a return engagement. Serve with pork.

BUCKHORN Pilsener CB 0.1
(Milwaukee, Wisconsin)
Light, uncarbonated, toxic-tasting, and downright repellant; several sips are all you need, and several sips was all I needed; perhaps the worst American beer I have ever tasted.

BUDWEISER Lager CB 1.1
(St. Louis, Missouri)
Crackly, thin, and watery; sweetish rice flavor floats up immediately; visually bland, thin, and faded; head disappears quickly; no aroma or even a suggestion that hops are present; some bitterness is coaxed out by food; absolutely no nuance or subtlety, or for that matter, taste; thickens a bit at finish; very predictable at a low, superficial (or is it artificial?) level; blandness is so predominant that a negative taste or aroma sensation would raise the rating. It has to be the savvy advertising campaigns and not the beer that makes Budweiser so popular. Bronze Medal winner at the 1994 Great American Beer Festival.

BUFFALO BLIZZARD BOCK Draft MB 0.9
(Buffalo, New York)
Rather shallow and uncomplicated, hardly resembling bock; not very alcoholic or substantive; very fuzzy gray-brown color is too light for an American bock, which is usually dark or deep brown; lightly malted; more carbonation than beer taste, as if to hide its overall lackluster presentation; finishes with characterless warmth.

BUFFALO GOLD PREMIUM ALE MB 3.7
(Boulder, Colorado)
Sharp and crisp, unlike ale style; tasty and mildly alcoholic with understated sweetness; mild texture, but rough enough to raise your interest; gentle, integrated blend; flavor is too flat and tends to fade; slight cloudiness detracts from pale gold color; finishes with a welcoming, mild bitterness. Accompanies pasta salads and traditional Italian favorites.

BULL ICE MALT LIQUOR   **CB**   **1.0**
(Detroit, Michigan)
Peach perfume in a malt liquor!—not the best beginning; chemical taste at top of the palate, followed by unpleasant exhalation; quickly fading crispness and rapidly diminishing head don't distract you enough from slight-sour alcohol taste; full-bodied with a sneaky, perfumey sweetness; settles into a no-frills, bulldozing attempt to get you polluted (6.13% alcohol/weight), even with a texture that is squishy-soft.

BULLDOG Pale Ale   **CB**   **3.3**
(Reading, England)
Pointed, sharp yeastiness with a clean-tasting fruitiness; body is light to medium; finishes nicely complex, hoppy and dry, but leaves a slight bitter aftertaste. Fine with roast beef and a baked potato.

BUNKERHILL LAGER   **CT**   **1.8**
(Wilkes-Barre, Pennsylvania)
Quite hoppy and sharp; more effervescent than flavorful, with dullish aftertaste on the roof of the mouth; no complexity, thin head; adds nothing in taste or as a general accompaniment to food; lackluster in color and mouthfeel; somewhat malty finish with a touch of sweetness doesn't fully redeem this beer by any means.

BUSCH Lager   **CB**   **1.0**
(St. Louis, Missouri)
Lightweight with a lot of fizz; adjuncts predominate, making taste bland, light, but acceptable to many; in the end, uneventful and tasteless.

BUUR BEER DELUXE Lager   **CB**   **3.4**
(Randers, Denmark)
Rounded and sugary, with no head to speak of; sharply alcoholic, but not otherwise texturally complex; evenhanded malt-hop balance; a bit winey at the top of the mouth; gets warmer as the bottle bottoms out; clearly a well-made beer, crafted attentively and with quality in mind. Good with a barbecued burger.

CABRO EXTRA Pilsener   **CB**   **1.7**
(Guatemala City, Guatemala)
Flat, unrevealing taste—you wait for something to happen and it doesn't; slight, quickly fading fizziness; weak undercurrent of sweetness is evident midway, along with some graininess, with hops predominating; in the end, a low-end, palatable beer with minimal interest—doesn't come close to meeting expectations; flat, semi-bland, and steady-as-it-goes—which isn't very far.

CALGARY AMBER LAGER   **CB**   **2.4**
(Toronto, Ontario, Canada)
Sharp at the front of the tongue and mellower than usual Canadian beer; not complex; almost woody taste, good draft-style bar beer; no head to speak of; obviously not interested in going beyond the beginnings of a run-of-the-mill brew. Okay with tortilla chips and dip.

CALLAO PILSEN   **CB**   **2.3**
(Callao, Peru)
Acidic; some yeasty bitterness; very mild aroma; not bland, but undistinguished—like ginger ale in texture; smooth and unobtrusive; unexciting and rather routine. Compatible with deli-style foods.

CANADA COUNTRY LAGER   **CB**   **3.0**
(Vancouver, British Columbia, Canada)
Sharp and lusty mouthful; surprising but pleasant sweetness as it is swallowed; retains crispness and freshness even as frosted mug loses its iciness; decent, but not noteworthy. Try it with bland pastas.

CANADIAN LAGER   **CB**   **2.0**
**(brewed by Molson in Vancouver,
British Columbia, Canada)**
Smooth, light, and easy-to-drink with light food, musty and day-old tasting without; somewhat thin and watery; label proclaims, "An honest brew makes its own friends"—a good brew, of course, makes even more friends.

CAPITAL GARTENBRAU DARK Lager   **MB**   **3.2**
(Middleton, Wisconsin)
Mellow, slightly coffee-sweet, and full in the mouth; rounded with sharpness at the edges; piles on tinginess on the tongue; deep, ruby-red body makes the long-lasting, quarter-inch-thick head seem to float gently on the liquid; makes for soft and gentle sipping throughout a warm spring afternoon; unsophisticated taste—just aims to please. Nice accompaniment to chips and dips.

CAPITAL GARTENBRAU LAGER   **MB**   **3.3**
(Middleton, Wisconsin)
Deep, golden hue accompanied by average texture; nice, rounded, malty fullness not generally found in American beers; stern with abundant touches of grain taste; as meal progresses, it becomes an integrated and pleasantly unobtrusive part of the meal; lingering unpleasant aftertaste mars overall effect, however. Try it with cold soups such as gazpacho or vichyssoise.

CAPITAL GARTENBRAU OKTOBERFEST
Lager   MB   2.5
(Middleton, Wisconsin)
Mild, burnt maltiness and soft palate give immediate attractive
impression; its hallmarks are warmth and softness; remains a one-
note beer, with some slight but noticeable increase in sweetness
as bottle empties; cloying at the roof of the mouth with thickish
honey-like feel is not a good impression to leave. Accompanies
green olives, pickled tomatoes, garlic-cheese bread, and other
cocktail hour nibbles.

CAPITAL GARTENBRAU
WILD RICE Lager   MB   2.4
(Middleton, Wisconsin)
Underpinning of honey; somewhat flat with no head; eventually
displays warmth that envelops tongue and insulates entire mouth
from the flavor of accompanying food; disappointing in its sim-
plicity; more honey aroma at finish, with associated sweetness.

CARDINAL LAGER   CB   4.0
(Fribourg, Switzerland)
Very light and fluffy, with a mild, quite attractive astringency;
wonderful use of hops which appear to be timid at first, but blos-
som into a complex, moderated fullness as you swallow; head is
thick and captivating, leaving substantial, well-configured Brussels lace to linger on the sides of the frosty mug; aromaless, but
more than made up for in taste and texture; very similar to a
wheat beer, including its thirst-quenching abilities; easy to drink,
it finishes smooth and satisfying. Light enough for tuna salad
and interesting enough to be enjoyed alone.

CARIBE Lager   CB   3.3
(Trinidad, West Indies)
Mild but insinuating in a pleasant way; light-honey taste emerges;
maintains its identity even with a variety of food flavors con-
tending for attention; distinctive and noticeable; ranges from
fruity balance to mild spiciness; minimal sour aftertaste smoothly
attenuates the honey taste; pale-yellow color inadvertently signifies more lightness than actually is present. Accompanies thick
deli sandwiches.

CARIB LAGER   CB   2.5
(Trinidad, West Indies)
Immediately fuller body than appearance would suggest, but just
as immediately the body dissipates into flat thinness; slightly
acrid, throaty maltiness is another surprise; a rather wholesome,
common beer, just a step away from something I would buy
again. Try it with hot dogs.

CARLSBERG Lager   CB   3.3
(Copenhagen, Denmark)

Pilsener-like, typical pale lager; thick sweetness deteriorates in the mouth; continuing interplay of barley and hops maintains interest and pleasant unpredictability; settles down into a slightly rough but stylish rhythm; attractive, thickly bubbled head is a soft preface to the sharpness of the body and its mild maltiness. Goes well with the usual pilsener-appropriate foods, from fresh pineapple to freshwater fish.

B E E R   F A C T

*T*he Carlsberg headquarters in Copenhagen boasts what many call the prettiest brewhouse in the world. While the company still is brewing beer (lots of it), it has also set itself up as a foundation in support of the sciences and arts.

CARTA BLANCA Lager   CB   3.6
(Monterrey, Mexico)

Light but with significant body; flavorful without being obtrusive; good workman-like beer that still has style and creativity; can be sipped alone without embarrassment or loss of enjoyment; I get teased a lot about this, but Carta Blanca is one of my favorite everyday, drink-with-anything-or-nothing-at-all brews; taste for yourself.

CARVER AMBER ALE   BP   2.5
(Durango, Colorado)

Soft and weak; hops in evidence, but passive and subservient; doesn't go anywhere after first swallow or two; Brussels lace is spotty and head is less than minimal; no alcohol presence to speak of, but stays within style; dry, with less malt than advertised.

CARVER ANASAZI WHEAT   BP   0.9
(Durango, Colorado)

No fruitiness, no cloves, no citrus, no sharpness; rather mushy and almost gooey; green, yeasty, vague citrus mouthfeel emerges as you sip it; cloying at the finish.

CARVER DURANGO DARK Stout   BP   2.9
(Durango, Colorado)

Strong, roasted, Spanish-peanut taste; flat and unassuming; increasing malt presence parallels the roastedness; some mustiness on the tongue remains and is distracting; stays light and fluffy, with late-blooming floral feel.

CARVER HONEY PILSENER   **BP**   **1.6**
(Durango, Colorado)
Very yeasty aroma; fruity and smooth with a mild citrus sourness, but flat, with no pizzazz at all; lies there hoping the flavor will pull it through; fine Brussels lace sticks to the sides until the glass is drained; far more like an ale than a pilsener.

CARVER IPA   **BP**   **2.1**
(Durango, Colorado)
Minimal hop bitterness, but no alcohol kick or carbonation to speak of; floating Brussels lace makes the almost too-dark, coppery color look more faded than it actually is; too flat (a commonality of Carver beers); balance is okay, but flatness is pervasive; low alcohol and overall blandness are what you notice; ingredients are appropriate and brewing process is professional; better at the end than the beginning.

CARVER IRON HORSE STOUT   **BP**   **2.6**
(Durango, Colorado)
Appealing, light-chocolate aroma; soft milk stout with quick flash of malty roastiness; thick Brussels lace; opaque, deep-brown color; medium-bodied; close to coffee-tasting with lingering dryness on the roof of the mouth; not zesty or pungent enough; improves with each additional sip; overall, too fragile—needs more hop backbone. Good with this brewpub's pastry desserts.

CARVER RASPBERRY WHEAT   **BP**   **0.5**
(Durango, Colorado)
Wispy raspberry aroma and taste, but not sweet; essentially raspberry juice—watery, flat, with no characteristics of wheat beer; orange-copper color; no head to speak of.

CASSEL SCHLOSS Amber Lager   **CB**   **2.5**
(Noerten-Hardenberg, Germany)
Sweet and yeasty; slightly spicy odor is more attractive than the taste, which is like modeling clay; pale Champagne color; zero head; flat-looking texture; taste sharpness dulls halfway through; turns a bit sour; remains absolutely listless from start to finish in the company of food; malt-hop balance seems to fluctuate from sip to sip.

CASTELLO Pilsener   **CB**   **2.2**
(San Giorgio di Nogaro, Italy)
Sweet, dry taste—typical of pilsener; fresh with a subdued, musty crispness; in the end weak and somewhat watery. Not bad with Mexican food.

CASTLEMAINE XXXX LAGER   **CB**   **3.3**
(Brisbane, Queensland, Australia)
Crisp and a bit flowery with a swift thirst-quenching rush when nicely chilled; some hoppiness becomes apparent with grilled red

meats; cloudiness, atypical of lager, misleads you into expecting some yeastiness and grain taste; interest fades as meal progresses; more entertaining at the beginning than the end.

CATAMOUNT AMBER ALE   **MB**   **0.2**
(White River Junction, Vermont)
Flat, watery, and some skunkiness; faint, wispy, fruity aroma that clears out quickly; deep-down sulfur taste sticks like a lump in the throat and is reminiscent of a polluted river; turns into simple blandness as it warms; this beer is obviously weak and poorly thought out.

CATAMOUNT CHRISTMAS ALE
(annual)   **MB**   **2.4**
(White River Junction, Vermont)
Sprightly and spicy, with a mixed blend of taste, texture, and aroma; thickish, with some tongue-coated aftertaste; sweet and tart, with a bit of syrupiness; mild alcohol presence; light, without many of its own advertised taste features; important to wait for this ale to warm in order to get a good sampling of its myriad ingredients; unfortunately, not all of them are worth waiting for; finish is sour and bland with a faint outdoorsy smell. Appropriate accompaniment to nuts, crackers, and pretzels.

CATAMOUNT PORTER   **MB**   **3.8**
(White River Junction, Vermont)
Sharper than expected with attenuated bitterness that is slightly off-flavor; head is immediately thin but it doesn't matter, given the luscious, deep, purple-brown color uniform throughout; warms into mellower, more exactingly balanced brew as it embraces mild foods; reaches nice, bittersweet, hop-malt balanced stride at the bottom of the bottle, but also gets a bit watery; mildly bitter aftertaste; sharp, clean finish—a handsome brew. Try it with roast chicken or turkey.

CAVE CREEK CHILI BEER Lager   **MB/BP**   **0.6**
(Cave Creek, Arizona)
Rapidly rising, very sharp, jalapeño taste and texture immediately lodge in the throat—sort of like inhaling a mouthful of crushed red peppers; set in light pale liquid with no mouthfeel of its own, the beer just says hot-hot-hot; harsh and much too distracting for plain foods; slim, small jalapeño pepper in bottle is difficult to remove, unfortunately; defiantly a one-note (very sharp) beer with no accompanying melody or rhythm; gimmicky with few redeeming qualities.

CELIS GOLDEN Ale   **MB**   **2.4**
(Austin, Texas)
Plain and somewhat timid; very little floral aroma to this light blond ale; rather uncomplex with rising mild sweetness toward

the end. Serve with soft, nonaggressive food such as pasta or chicken.

CELIS GRAND CRU Ale   MB   2.4
(Austin, Texas)

Vague, fruity aroma followed by somewhat spoiled-fruit taste, coming close, but not quite to, rotten-egg taste; highly yeasty with very little carbonation; tart sweetness is reined in along with off-flavored fruitiness with curries and other traditional Indian dishes; engaging crispness emerges; tightly packed Brussels lace adheres to the sides of the glass; finishes with a sharp hoppiness that redeems (somewhat) the earlier spoiled presentation; yeast aroma, however, remains throughout; clearly quality ingredients, but only a knowledgeable palate can begin to appreciate the totality of their taste, if even that is possible.

CELIS PALE BOCK   MB   3.4
(Austin, Texas)

Pleasant warming rush on first sip, with dry aftertaste at the roof of the mouth; accommodatingly bristly with an alcoholic undercurrent; light and tingly; alcohol presence less than it should be; reasonable balance between sweet maltiness and moderately bitter hops; well-made, but essentially a weakened American bock; sweet, dainty finish. Accompanies broiled meats.

CELIS WHITE Hefe-Weizen   MB   4.0
(Austin, Texas)

Sharp and highly yeasty; quick lemon aftertaste matches cloudy, weak lemonade color; wispy Brussels lace slides gracefully down sides of mug; remains steady and forthcoming, maintaining its integrity and predictability despite the potential roadblocks and derailing possibilities of spicy food; throws off the spiciness and cuts forward with pronounced dryness; steady threat of cloves and pungent yeastiness make the brew exciting; clearly brewed by someone who knows what to do; a good representative of this style—and made in the U.S., no less. Silver Medal winner at the 1994 Great American Beer Festival.

CERES ROYAL EXPORT Lager   CB   3.3
(Arthus, Denmark)

Full and hoppy; quickly sweetens and warms up with food; yeast and grains emerge at mid-bottle, lending a nice balance to the sharp hoppiness and adding a mellow, understated mouthfeel; faint bitter/sourness clings to the roof of the mouth, even after swallowing; needs to be highly chilled for full enjoyment—an iced mug would be appropriate; flavor continues throughout; neatly patterned Brussels lace remains until the last drop is gone— a sign of brewing quality; finishes warm, with a hint of hop bitterness. Goes well with fish dishes.

CERVEZA AGUILA Pilsener   CB   2.3
(Barranquilla, Colombia)

Malty effervescence and lighthearted ambience; light straw color with some integrity; remains quite grainy; minimal solidity fades in the stretch at the same time it turns somewhat bland texturally; light, weak, but tasty; finishes gently sweet and freshly grainy, but remains so-so overall. Accompanies vegetable salads.

CHANGLEE LAGER   CB   2.6
(Sanshui, China)

Zesty and ricey with clean, fresh water taste (brewed with mineral water—you can tell); barest hint of honey on the throat arrives slowly and leaves quickly when food is introduced; somewhat wimpy overall, including faded, honey color; entertaining without food, it slides down without any complexity, but certainly not unpalatable.

CHERRYLAND CHERRY RAIL LAGER   BP/CT   2.9
(Sturgeon Bay, Wisconsin)

A shot of cherries is quickly and forcefully present, and stays around; never gets nasty or presumptuously sweet or tacky, though it has the ingredients to head off in that direction; with light coming through the glass, golden, ruby-brown color echoes a thick, newly ripe Bing cherry; acceptable fruit beer with little attention to malt, even though it is all-malt. Looking for something slightly different? You could do worse. Best imbibed without food.

CHERRYLAND GOLDEN RAIL LAGER   **BP/CT**   **2.8**
(Sturgeon Bay, Wisconsin)
Sour and thin, with only a hint of texture; settles down and the
balance becomes apparent; mid-bottle warmth comes through as
sharpness remains at the edges; gets sweeter with malty features;
finishes more palatable than it began; worth trying.

CHERRYLAND SILVER RAIL LAGER   **BP/CT**   **2.2**
(Sturgeon Bay, Wisconsin)
Sweet and sour, leaning toward the former; light and fluffy with
little complexity; warm with a bit of snap, but mushy and mild
with food; no head; generally flat texture; decent starter beer for
those worried about sharpness and surprises—neither of which
is present here.

CHESTER GOLDEN ALE   **CB**   **2.9**
(Cheshire, England)
Very appropriate hint of bitters with fresh, almost sweet wheat/grain
ambience; modulated crispness that flatters the palate unaccompanied by food; not as creamy as other similarly styled English
ales; honest aroma; leaves you somewhat thirsty after the last sip
(too much sugar?); good and sweet, but flags at the end.

CHICAGO'S BIG SHOULDERS PORTER   **MB**   **4.0**
(Chicago, Illinois)
Deep-roasted aroma and flavor along with whiff of plum essence
cheerily greet you on first sip; evolves into a chocolate taste, with
hops holding a mild maltiness at bay; remains alert and sharp
throughout; deep-brown color with glowing auburn core and
tawny, thin head enhance the enjoyment; soft texture and robust
taste—a nice combo; rich and flavorful, it finishes malty—hops
now are secondary—gently urging you to request another bottle; too much musty aftertaste and a little too watery to make
this a 100% winner, but it's well on its way. Try with a first course,
such as artichoke hearts vinaigrette and asparagus.

CHICAGO'S LEGACY LAGER   **MB**   **2.1**
(Chicago, Illinois)
Light-struck with hazy opaqueness that is atypical of lager; somewhat acrid and unenticing; taste disappears into my standby accompaniment of grilled hamburger with green chilies; texturally
lacking luster; heavy-handed hops; not complex; brown specks
on the bottom of the glass, along with the tepid blond color, enhance the impression that this is really tea in a malt beverage dis-
guise.

CHICAGO'S LEGACY RED ALE   **MB**   **1.8**
(Chicago, Illinois)
Lively fresh taste and aroma with mild, accommodating piquancy
and distant, but nice, fruitiness; the bad news: turns a bit rancid

after several sips; prevailing yeastiness is somewhat unsettling with foods other than salty snacks; finishes between bland and vaguely skunky; dry, unpleasant hoppiness at the end.

CHIHUAHUA Lager   CB   2.7
(Monterrey, Mexico)

Middle-of-the-road taste; good for homey foods; familiar, everyday beer; light, mildly hopped, sharp, and fresh-tasting; the choice at the neighborhood bar. Goes well with salsa and chips.

CHIMAY PERES TRAPPISTES ALE—
GRANDE RESERVE (gold label)   AB   2.5
(Chimay Abbey, Belgium)

Fizzier and more wine-like than its red-labeled Première cousin; alcohol predominates from tip of the tongue to back of the throat, tending to overwhelm the anticipated fruitiness; amber cloudiness from fresh yeast added just prior to bottling; in the end, too sharp and harsh with an unfortunate hint of greenness. Try with red meats.

B E E R   F A C T

*T*rappist fathers of Chimay produce a trio of very strong ales (of which I've tasted and rated two), each identified by a different-colored cork; gold-corked Grande Réserve is the highest in alcohol content of the three (8.9% volume). Each of these ales is vintage-dated. While true of all sedimented ales, it is especially important that Chimay be poured slowly, to make certain the sediment stays at the bottom of the bottle.

CHIMAY PERES TRAPPISTES ALE—
PREMIERE (red label)   AB   4.7
(Chimay Abbey, Belgium)

Soft, sweet taste is mellow going in, integrated going down; lots and lots of yeast—in the nose, on the palate, at the bottom of the glass, in the color, which is milky brown; sly fruitiness edges around the tongue while you're dealing with the yeast; soft with gentle but pervasive alcohol presence; apple-juice appearance and implication; delicious, like a good sipping port; best alone, as a gentle and appealing *digestif* without culinary distraction; one of the best I've tasted.

CHINA CLIPPER Lager   CB   2.5
(Guangzhou, China)

Fresh, with vague medicinal undercurrent; strikingly unnuanced, with malts and hops clearly defined and unintegrated; light, unobtrusive texture; dry finish and humdrum memory; best to sample this without food.

CHINA GOLD Pilsener   CB   1.8
(Guangzhou, China)

No effervescence and slightly watery; strong physical mouthfeel; essentially bland with a slight ping; not a memorable brew. Okay with a hamburger.

CHINA LUXURY LAGER   CB   2.9
(Taipei, Taiwan)

Immediate rice-wine taste with soft crispness; clean, fresh, faintly vanilla mouthfeel; smooth and easy going down; not very complex, suggesting that boredom would set in after several bottles; trace of burnt molasses serves as a good finish with sharpness and sourness not noticed before. Subdued companion to linguine with clam sauce and other Italian food.

CHRISTIAN MOERLEIN BOCK   CB   2.6
(Cincinnati, Ohio)

Watery on first sip, but a jolt of textural graininess catches you at the back of the throat; almost satisfying in its attempt at bock richness; less creamy and rich than advertised; clearly better without spicy or sharp food; tantalizes with the promise, but not the fulfillment, of satisfaction.

CHRISTIAN MOERLEIN—
CINCINNATI SELECT BEER Pilsener   CB   2.5
(Cincinnati, Ohio)

Relatively full and undistinguished on first sip; smartly rising bubbles end in a big-bubbled, rather airy head; exhibits reasonable balance of malt and hops; neither-here-nor-there textural ambience lightens up a bit and serves as calming, settling, balance/counterpoint to food; not particularly exciting without a meal. Try it with a burger or grilled chicken breast sandwich piled high with green chilies.

BEER FACT

*C*ontrary to a seemingly indestructible myth, bock beer, such as the Christian Moerlein Bock, is not the residue scrubbed out of the kettles during a brewery's annual spring cleaning. It is a distinct style, a strong warming lager meant to be consumed when cool weather is changing. Perhaps the myth stems from confusion about the brewing of Märzenbier (Oktoberfest), which was traditionally brewed in March, placed in cool caves, and consumed each fall in celebratory fashion. The kegs were then ceremonially drained of their fully fermented and enjoyable contents.

CHRISTIAN MOERLEIN
DOPPEL DARK Lager   CB   2.9
(Cincinnati, Ohio)

Spritzy and almost full-bodied with callow, moderated, burnt-caramel taste; fizzy head; retains crispness throughout but vigorous taste fades and turns acrid and almost rancid with food; without food, it is promising; beginning sips taste as if tomato juice were put into the beer; changes temperament with a display of warmth and comfort. Bland seafood beats zesty fowl with this deep, dark Midwestern brew.

CHRISTOFFEL BIER LAGER   MB   2.5
(Roermond, Holland)

Fresh, doughy taste with bitterness at the back of the throat; more fruity than the usual lager; prolonged sharpness matches pinprick by pinprick sharpness of spicy foods; somewhat moderating after food is gone, with potential warmth that never really arrives; noticeable graininess, but too hoppy in the end. Goes well with Southwestern dishes.

CHUNG HUA Pilsener   CB   3.4
(Guangzhou, China)

Fresh, crisp taste with sweet undertow; pleasant, with an easy-going rhythm; a bit on the dry side, it remains appealing and enjoyable from start to finish. A good match with Asian food.

CHURCHILL AMBER Lager   CB   3.3
(Redruth, England)

Slight molasses-malty taste disappears after passing over the tongue; this is not a bowl-you-over beer, but instead a gentle sipping brew at the neighborhood pub; smooth, fading-in-and-out maltiness stays throughout, alternatingly enticing and neutral (or is it a

mild caramel taste that comes and goes?); come-hither attraction
leaves you at the end with a desire for more. Try this with bagels
and lox—a surprise delight.

T A P   T I P

What Time of Day Is It Best to Drink?

While it is not recommended that you make a habit of drinking beer shortly after getting out of bed, that time of the day, especially mid-morning to lunchtime, is in fact the period when your senses are at their most acute. Taste and smell are just getting revved up and are receptive to sensory input, making the two-to-three-hour window of opportunity ideal for pure judging and taste comparison purposes. More appropriate for the ordinary social pleasures of tasting and drinking beer, however, are the several hours prior to suppertime, which as fortune should have it, is the time period also generally considered the next-best sense-sensitivity period. Alas, fortune is not always precisely prescient: The senses lose some of their sharpness during and immediately after a meal, and flavor, olfactory, and other characteristics become less readily identifiable.

CHURCHILL DRY Lager   CB   2.3
(Redruth, England)
Dry, citrusy, and surprisingly smooth; full-bodied with hop emphasis, but well-balanced between malt and hops; maltiness increases when accompanying food; dulled thickness takes over; mixed bag, somewhat unpredictable; faded, pale yellow with no head.

CHURCHILL LAGER   CB   3.6
(Redruth, England)
Full, hoppy taste quickly followed by pinpricks of subdued fruity bitterness; hearty and somewhat assertive; very pale color; spring water plays leading role in the taste; full, balanced, and maturely integrated at the end with a sweet, lingering taste on the tongue; smooth and medium-dry; appropriate for the novice interested in something different. Try with broiled or roasted pork.

CLARA ESTRELLA DORADA Lager   CB   1.0
(Guadalajara, Mexico)
Rather musty and a bit raw; hard to discern any particular ingredients; sly sweetness creeps out when slice of citrus fruit is squeezed into the glass; essentially no distinctive character—texture, taste, or otherwise; light and thin; pass on this one.

CLARK'S GREAT CANADIAN Lager   CB   1.0
(Vancouver, British Columbia, Canada)
Bold and rugged, just as the label proclaims, but without much flavor or aroma to go with those northern Canadian virtues; the goal here is to muscle its way onto your taste buds, minus much evident concern for the niceties of, say, balance, nuance, and/or consistency; label also boasts, in italics, about its "genuine rugged Canadian bottles"; when the packaging is of more interest to the brewer than the ingredients, watch out.

CLAUSEN EXPORT Pilsener   CB   3.0
(Bogota, Colombia)
Faded off-taste, but crisp and tangible; rice presence is covered by freshness of the water and sweet tang of malt; ingredients become more integrated toward end of can; serviceable and thirst-quenching; tasty by itself. Good with chowder or gumbo.

CLUB Lager   CB   2.7
(brewed by Labatt in Toronto, Ontario,
and elsewhere in Canada)
Straightforward classic lager with fading taste as it is swallowed; bland toward the bottom; in the end, too weak for highly flavored food; evolves into moderately sweet, rounded finish. Try it with relatively bland pasta or vegetable dishes.

CLUB PREMIUM Lager   CB   2.1
(Quito, Ecuador)
Weak and not charming; minimal fizz; builds airy head quickly; very foamy and full of air; average but apparent grain/malt ambience; glimmer of interest at end of bottle with a hint of character via a malty finish; pedestrian and run-of-the-mill. Serviceable with puréed soups such as tomato, pea, or potato.

COLD SPRING EXPORT Lager   CB   3.5
(Cold Spring, Minnesota)
Clean and bright without much texture; mild, pleasant effervescence; light and fizzy enough to allow both food and the beer to express themselves; a good domestic brew. Fine with a tuna or egg salad sandwich.

COLD SPRING SELECT STOCK Lager   CB   4.0
(Cold Spring, Minnesota)
Fresh, fruity aroma with a band of cold hops on initial sip; malt quickly catches up, resulting in sharp, balanced, carbonated beer;

touch of honey taste arises in mid-bottle; Brussels lace beautifully decorates sides of glass with aesthetic design remaining parallel throughout; well-made with a thick creamy head atop light-golden body—a visual feast; finishes with slight yeasty-sour taste that is a nice, pleasant ending to a very accommodating and mouth-friendly beer. Goes well with Mandarin chicken and other Chinese food favorites.

COLLIN COUNTY BLACK GOLD
Pilsener   MB   2.6
(Plano, Texas)

Slight burnt taste on the palate stays after liquid is swallowed; sharpness persists; uncomplicated, consistent drink from start to finish unaccompanied by any food; turns thick after a bottle or two; a bit acidic, almost sour coffee-like mouthfeel; distinctive but not unique; dark-amber color.

COLLIN COUNTY PURE GOLD Pilsener   MB   3.0
(Plano, Texas)

Light-amber color matches its distinctive boldness and clarity of taste; steady, modulated, uncertain character makes drinking this somewhat of an adventure; overwhelms with the smell of herbs and flowers; body is firm and straightforward. Good accompaniment to gazpacho or sushi.

COLTS BERG Pilsener   CB   2.1
(Bangalore, India)

Hint of clove, with some sourness; thinnish, light-yellow concoction; vague sharpness; some malty warmth surfaces occasionally; prickly on the tongue; in the end, more benign than unappealing; weak and undemanding.

COOK'S GOLDBLUME Lager   CB   0.5
(Evansville, Indiana)

Sharply carbonated; slight sour odor; apparently loaded with adjuncts, giving it taste uniformity, not to mention taste boredom; light, weak, and inattentive with food; carbonation disappears at the end; leaves a slight musty aftertaste; standard, low-priced, barroom can of beer with nothing really to recommend it.

COOPERSMITH'S ALBERT
DAMM BITTER Ale   BP   3.0
(Fort Collins, Colorado)

High hoppiness is brought down to acceptable size with yeasty maltiness that is encouraging and beguiling; not very bitter, the predominant texture is smooth and tending to flatness; attractive yeast aroma counterbalances the appropriate diminishing fruitiness as ale warms; while alcohol content makes up for some of the lack of carbonation texture, this bitter ale could still use more working-class grittiness; deep hoppiness is missing. Nice with a variety of cheeses and tart fresh fruit.

COOPERSMITH'S CHRISTMAS ALE
(annual)   **BP**   **3.2**
(Fort Collins, Colorado)

Though ingredients and nuances are modified from year to year, you can generally expect to find a holiday treat that is gently and subtly spiced; mellow cider feel on first sip; thin, but bulked up with many tasty Christmas ingredients, including cloves, ginger, nutmeg, cinnamon; maintains integrity and balance with food; though too thin and texturally weak, remains smooth; allows spices a nice showcase. Try it with a bowl of chili or hearty winter soup.

COOPERSMITH'S HAVEL'S VIENNA
LAGER   **BP**   **2.7**
(Fort Collins, Colorado)

Smooth in aroma, taste, and, initially, texture; texture eventually reveals itself as flat and relatively formless; clear, thin apple-cider color with suggestions of green undertones; mild bite; decreasing aroma; filling and rather even-tempered; offers a dainty crispness; in the end, too changeable for continuous or predictable enjoyment with food.

COOPERSMITH'S HORSETOOTH
STOUT   **BP**   **4.0**
(Fort Collins, Colorado)

Luscious, rich, burnt, roasted-malt flavor; relatively flat and texturally smooth and silky; deep, deep brown, almost-black color mirrors the rich flavor; classic example of milk stout; a second gallon was too alcoholic. (At this brewpub, as at many others, you can get a returnable gallon jug to go.) Overall, the richness of the ingredients and diminished alcohol are just right with oysters and other shellfish.

COOPERSMITH'S IMPERIAL STOUT   **BP**   **3.0**
(Fort Collins, Colorado)

Rich, smooth, and thinly creamy with no sparkly zest at all; deeply luminescent dark, dark brown sets off nicely in conjunction with tongue-tantalizing light burnt-molasses taste that almost in passing becomes the core of this stout; milky and silky, but where's the alcohol?; some spicy tones are almost indistinguishable from one another. Best with chowders and deli foods; meatballs and linguine also do well.

COOPERSMITH'S MAC SCOOTER'S
Scottish Ale   **BP**   **0.3**
(Fort Collins, Colorado)

Sweet, smooth, and silky with an unsettling hit of medicinal taste that turns ugly with food, but lessens alone; definite phenolic presence from aroma to, especially, aftertaste; acid, strong, and medicinal; not worth it.

COOPERSMITH'S MOUNTAIN
AVENUE WHEAT   BP   1.8
(Fort Collins, Colorado)
Yeasty aroma; burst of flavor in the mouth with clear citrus feel;
yeast sediment on bottom clouds this thin pale ale; no clove taste
at all; quite hoppy and somewhat rough; far too yeasty for its
own good; tastes unfinished.

COOPERSMITH'S NOT BROWN ALE   BP   2.7
(Fort Collins, Colorado)
Touch of sweet maltiness; smooth, with no ripples; slightly toasted;
deep, rich color; nice interacting Brussels lace; sweetish aroma;
hint of annoying, cloying aftertaste. Okay with Asian food.

COOPERSMITH'S POUDRE ALE   BP   2.4
(Fort Collins, Colorado)
Flowery, almost perfumey, with continuing aftertaste; smooth
with wine-like feel, but alcohol is not noticeable until the end;
stays stable and uninteresting with very little carbonation; finishes with some mild sharpness; disappointing in the weakness
of its ingredients.

COOPERSMITH'S PUNJABI
INDIA PALE ALE   BP   3.8
(Fort Collins, Colorado)
Yeasty and fruity (especially grapefruity); light mouthful settles
fully and more thickly on the tongue; hops are unassuming, but
present in the form of tangy, moderated bitterness; substance rises
to the occasion, but falls a hair short with food; smooth but not
gritty; the genteel alcohol accumulates subtly and engagingly, but
quality fades rapidly. Bronze Medal winner at the 1993 Great
American Beer Festival. Fine with pasta.

COOPERSMITH'S SIGDA'S
GREEN CHILE Ale   BP   2.2
(Fort Collins, Colorado)
Sharply pungent chile taste comes and lingers; overwhelms bland
foods; nicely in balance with spicy dishes; chile taste has depth
and subtlety with spirited spike of texture; strong, powerful, almost overwhelming.

COORS Pilsener   CB   1.4
(Golden, Colorado)
I agree with the ads—it's the water; take away that crisp, clean,
fresh liquid, and it's hard to tell what you have left; the malt,
hops, and adjuncts, such as they are, are very difficult to discern,
although a thin, faint maltiness does make its presence known,
if you pay close enough attention; very light, almost prim texture. Featureless with food (even salty snacks), it doesn't get much
tastier alone.

COORS EISBOCK   **CB**   **2.2**
(Golden, Colorado)
Pale-amber color is at the lighter end of the bock spectrum; tastes like regular Coors with a pinch of body, though when you concentrate, you come up with more sensation than flavor; perhaps, however, it is more bitter, suggesting there really are hops (or, at the least, fewer intervening adjuncts) in this incarnation; a tight, constricted, but clearly present sweetness emerges with food; malty aroma is stirred up as the liquid is agitated when it is poured; label says this is a stout, which suggests this bock may indeed have higher alcohol content than the regulations for lager beer ordinarily allow; finishes uncomplex and flat.

COORS EXTRA GOLD Pilsener   **CB**   **1.8**
(Golden, Colorado)
Sharp, light, and tasteless; at first it seems to be a quality beer, but quickly subsides into a typical pedestrian brew, even on a summer picnic with cold cuts and salads; touted as "A full-bodied beer"—yes, in comparison to Coors regular pilsener.

COORS EXTRA GOLD DRAFT Pilsener   **CB**   **0.5**
(Golden, Colorado)
Flat, bland, and fizzy; there is no question that this beer is wet—clearly water is the main ingredient; "A full-bodied, robust beer," it says on the label—Ha!

COORS WEIZENBIER   **CB**   **2.9**
(Golden, Colorado)
Slightly perfumey and softly foamy; attenuated bitterness; surprisingly hearty; fresh, clean, and relatively substantive; head is quite thick (typical of the style), too foamy and long-lasting, and tends to interfere with the drinking; dry with barely noticeable fruity aftertaste; with about 4.5% alcohol/weight, it packs less punch by at least 0.5% than the more classic wheats, but is a mild, acceptable version of a true wheat beer; Brussels lace, when not hidden by the thick head, is nicely patterned in parallel, mug-circumscribing arrangements; no aroma; caramel-malt smoothness helps turn this into a pleasant drink; this is perhaps the best of the Coors products. Bronze Medal winner at the 1994 Great American Beer Festival.

COORS WINTERFEST Lager (annual)   **CB**   **3.1**
(Golden, Colorado)
I have found a fair amount of variability from year to year with this annual offering; more recent editions have been weaker in alcohol content than other Christmas beers and moderate-bodied rather than full-bodied; at least one earlier version was quite smooth and palpably sweet-tasting (it had a pleasant glow of color and a friendly aroma; more beerlike than the close-to-water stuff of regular Coors); with the unevenness of past experience, there's

probably a 50-50 chance that you will wind up with something at least nearly worthy of the holiday season; try and cajole a sample sip beforehand.

NOTE: The 1993-1994 version, a 1993 Silver Medal winner at the Great American Beer Festival (Specialty division), is labeled "stout"; it tasted like turpentine sap from a pine tree, was mildly/lightly fruity, and in no way resembled stout; be wary of this imposter in the future; I gave it a 1.5. The Coors company informs me that the Bureau of Alcohol, Tobacco, and Firearms allowed the stout identification because Winterfest—along with Eisbock and Weizenbier—has an alcohol content above the specified limits for lager. A malted beverage that exceeds those limits must be labeled ale, stout, porter, or malt liquor. However, none of those three Coors products is even close to a stout in style. So, in the end, not only do consumers not know the alcohol content—laws prohibit its listing on the label—but we are also misled about the style of the beer for which we just paid good money.

CORDOBA-DORADA Pilsener   **CB**   **3.7**
(Cordoba, Argentina)
Simultaneously dull and sharp texture, especially when cold; hint of rice with good everyday journeyman's taste; soothing undertow with spicy foods; essentially a good, tasty, middle-of-the-road brew that accommodates itself to the food at hand; recommended. Good with broiled or roasted chicken, steaks, and most spicy foods.

CORONA EXTRA Pilsener   **CB**   **1.5**
(Mexico City, Mexico)
Slight fizzy acidity; very light, airy, and essentially tasteless, unless lemon slice is added; hard put to keep up with even mildly salty snacks; hint of skunkiness—not surprising from this clear glass bottle; weak and mass-produced; cold, it is refreshing—but, then, so is plain water; we need a little more textural and taste heft in Corona.

CORSENDONK MONK'S BROWN ALE   **AB**   **3.8**
(Sigillum Monastery, Belgium)
Silky smooth and clean smelling, with color of luscious dark chocolate and commensurate appeal; not complicated at all; nice, unobtrusive fruity undertow; bottled with its natural yeast, the yeastiness emerges calmly and accommodatingly as beer warms at the end of the bottle; gentle and slightly aromatic, with qualities for the novice as well as the more experienced drinker; a visual delight. Perfect for relatively bland food.

CORSENDONK MONK'S PALE ALE   **AB**   **4.0**
(Sigillum Monastery, Belgium)
Highly yeasty, but moderated and calm; creamy, finger-thick head

tops off warm, golden body with touch of red; plenty of fast-rising bubbles; a bit murky, as expected; mildly bitter sweetness; tart citrus taste emerges out of nowhere in mid-bottle; Brussels lace hangs in sheets like finely webbed curtain on sides of glass; hearty and to the point; strikingly smooth and warm; well put-together. Good with spicy shrimp cocktail.

B E E R   F A C T

*C*orsendonk monks started their brewery in 1400, closing it in 1784 when the entire abbey was shuttered by Austria's Jozef II. The religious order's brewing tradition was revived in 1906 with the founding of a secular brewery by Antonius Keersmaekers. Responding to consumers' presumed sensibilities, what is known as Monk's Brown Ale in the United States is called Pater Noster (Our Father) in Europe. *Sic transit* marketing.

COYOTE SPRINGS AMBER ALE　　　BP　　　2.0
(Phoenix, Arizona)

You need to concentrate and think hard to notice any roastedness; too fruity; Brussels lace hangs in there and maintains its substance; alcohol kicks in after 2 to 3 sips, but detracts from the toastedness; a hint of complexity suggests promise, which remains unfulfilled; warmish finish with a slight nutty taste.

COYOTE SPRINGS CHRISTMAS ALE
(annual)　　　　　　　　　BP　　　2.5
(Phoenix, Arizona)

Immediate hit of cloves, in the nose and in the mouth—wow!—covers any other spices that might be present; no zest to this beer, just sweet cloves, which isn't enough to celebrate about (or with); too sticky sweet to drink more than one bottle—save one for New Year's Eve and have it with spicy Cajun chicken breast.

COYOTE SPRINGS FOREVER
AMBER ALE Draft　　　　　　BP　　　3.0
(Phoenix, Arizona)

Perfumey and bitter are the ongoing chronic characteristics; quickly apparent this ale requires stalwart food; remains dominating throughout a meal; persistent flavor—no fading or weakness; could have a lot more integrity, but it unabashedly demands attention; strangely, for all its attraction-getting powers, it doesn't project commensurate titillating excitement; thuds to a balanced malt-hop finish, but you will certainly remember the ride. Match with hot Thai or Mexican dishes.

COYOTE SPRINGS OATMEAL STOUT   BP   1.2
(Phoenix, Arizona)

Spicy oatmeal stout that doesn't quite make it; approaches appropriate smoothness and (mild) bitterness with very nice, substantial Brussels lace; decent, but too subdued, especially with spicy foods; poor head on too-brown body; misses out with lots of the defining qualities of the style, including taste; ultimately too bitter and mostly devoid of roasted barley taste.

BEER FACT

*B*ecause of its warming, calming nature, oatmeal stout was at one time offered as a nutritional drink as well as a wholesome beverage for lactating mothers.

COYOTE SPRINGS PACIFIC
NORTHWEST PALE ALE Draft   BP   2.9
(Phoenix, Arizona)

Floral aroma and hop/floral taste with decent, lasting head; well-configured Brussels lace hangs around; short-lasting, pleasing bitterness; full-bodied; assertive hoppiness; dry finish. Try it with ham and Swiss cheese on rye or similar deli sandwiches.

COYOTE SPRINGS VIENNA
PALE LAGER   BP   1.0
(Phoenix, Arizona)

Thickish and yeasty with essentially no fizz; acceptable bitterness remains subdued and attenuated, but this is far too bitter and smooth for lager; color, too, is a bit too brown for pale; flat-tasting with little balance or complexity; sparse, scraggly Brussels lace; musty, too-dry aftertaste.

CRAZY ED'S BLACK MOUNTAIN GOLD
Lager   MB/BP   2.5
(Cave Creek, Arizona)

Surprisingly soft in texture, but harsh, with a touch of greenness, in taste; meshes wonderfully with marinated green olives—in fact, the two go together divinely; cloudy-pale; good barroom drink; fullness and controlled sweetness at the end; has character for a rather commonplace, mediocre beer. Companionable with appetizers like stuffed mushrooms.

CRAZY HORSE MALT LIQUOR   CB   1.9
(La Crosse, Wisconsin)

Hint of skunkiness; taste varies, bordering on a honey-sweetness sometimes, other times on a sour acidity; head is full and foamy, but, alas, artificially induced; fast-rising bubbles provide good visual carbonation effect in the glass; soft mouthfeel, with no real oomph; lacking the punch associated with malt liquor; sweet finish with, finally, a dollop of alcohol; generally unappealing.

B E E R　　F A C T

*A*Minnesota law, effective August 1, 1994, prohibits the use of the Crazy Horse name on malt liquor or any similar product that suggests "a connection with an actual living or dead American Indian leader." Minnesota and Washington are, so far, the only two states where agencies accordingly have banned the sale of Crazy Horse.

CRESTED BUTTE RED LADY ALE　　　MB/BP　　　2.3
(Crested Butte, Colorado)
Sour citrus taste emphasizes the alcohol; hint of hoppiness helps to propel this ale forward; bland and yeasty; thin head; reasonably filigreed Brussels lace; yeasty finish; not flavorful enough; malt is too subdued.

CRISTAL PREMIUM Lager　　　CB　　　3.2
(Chiclayo/Lima, Peru)
Quickly and satisfyingly refreshing with initial brief touch of alcohol; bubbly and even-tempered, but not particularly flavorful or nuanced; not pushy or intrusive with food; has the same thirst-satisfying qualities of water with added quality of being beer; slightly soapy aftertaste. Enhances New Mexican foods.

CRISTAL PILSENER　　　CB　　　1.3
(Limache, Chile)
Very flat with quickly passing thick taste at the back of tongue; benzene taste starts at mid-bottle and lingers; a no-frills beer; sole interest is a minimal sharpness; no character. Matches the mildness of cheese empanadas.

CROWN Lager　　　CB　　　2.2
(Seoul, Korea)
Weak Asian beer without much zest—typical of the area; lacks distinction; watery and lifeless; essentially unassertive; ingredients are hard to discern; okay in a pinch. Picks up somewhat with plain pork chops and baked potato.

CROWN LAGER　　　CB　　　2.3
(Belize City, Belize)
Very soft; mild fizziness; distinctive grain taste; musty, almost dusty aroma goes up nose with a little irritation; nice complexity; some wine-like flavor; foam clings to sides of glass but oth-

erwise does not do justice to the beer; head also stays intact with bubbly, lighthearted airiness. Some fruitiness emerges with beef stew; remains uncomplicated and relatively lifeless with food.

CUZCO Pilsener   CB   **3.2**
(Cuzco, Peru)

Mixture of tastes and textures: fizzy, fruity, and malty, sharp and smooth; pale gold with intense coppery core; moderate carbonation; user-friendly and mellow-minded—it's there to please, not to dominate or intrude; some citrus aftertaste spoils the finish; good beer for the novice drinker. Retains delightful filigree of malt grains even up against spicy foods.

D'AGOSTINO PUB BEER Lager   CT   **2.2**
(Utica, New York)

Rather tasteless and without texture; nice initial head quickly dissipates; muddy and a bit bloating with food; mild warmth and touch of caramel sweetness gently and faintly emerge at end of bottle. Better alone or with nuts, rather than with a meal.

DALLAS COUNTY OLD DEPOT
PALE ALE (draft)   MB/BP   **2.4**
(Adel, Iowa)

Slightly musty aroma accompanies a grainy, sour taste with no grittiness; harsh, but not unappealing, mouthfeel; clings to the roof of the mouth without offering tasteworthy features; no malt counterbalance to the hops, unfortunately; seems to sweeten minimally when mouth is full of beer; finish is thinly bitter, finally making it feel more like a pale ale. Serve this with sliced smoked salmon and raw onion.

DALLAS GOLD Pilsener   MB   **1.0**
(Dallas, Texas)

Malty, far too watery and textureless, with no head; hint of toastedness, in Vienna amber style, but even then falls short; some acidity spoils overall effect; tastes too much like a home brew—unfinished, unintegrated, unbalanced; deep, malty aroma accompanies definite chocolate taste at the finish, but there is no texture or nuance to mitigate the strong sensations; some orange fruity aroma at last sniff; definitely not in the pilsener style at all; soothes the stomach at the end; lifeless; unappealing with food.

DAMM Pilsener   CB   **3.8**
(Barcelona/Valencia, Spain)

Nice, grainy, zesty flavor fills the mouth; similar aroma fills the nose; smooth with a bit of an off-taste, but gets back on track; neither heavy nor light, it appears to be just right for the food at hand, as well as later on, when a meal is finished; thirst-quenching, and satisfying. Good with a thick Cheddar cheese sandwich.

D'AQUINO ITALIAN BEER Pilsener   CB   2.3
(Induno, Italy)

Malty, fruity, and quite zesty with light, pale color; becomes somewhat Spartan, letting texture overwhelm taste; workman-like, soc-
cer-stadium beer that would go well with pasta and other everyday
food; unprepossessing when all is said and done; finish is malty
and without much flash.

DARRYL'S PREMIUM LAGER   CT   2.6
(Dubuque, Iowa)

Surprisingly soft and agreeable on first sip; subdued sharpness turns
flat at sides of the tongue; creamy, relatively lasting head tastes a
little soapy; not particularly complex; pedestrian, with hints of im-
pending surprise and potential interest—all undelivered; unexciting accompaniment to food; good try for a contracted beer.

DEININGER KRISTALL WEIZEN   CB   2.2
(Hof, Germany)

Yeasty with rounded crispness and fullness on first sip; lighter
than usual sweetness, but overall not above average; maintains
mild tartness; a bit less bitter and more palatable when warmed.
Nice counterpoint to spicy, big-flavored foods.

DEMPSEY'S ALE   CT   2.4
(Monroe, Wisconsin)

Flat aroma and somewhat salty, acrid taste on first sip; rather
musty and old-tasting; basically bland and ticklish on the roof
of the mouth; neatly, but uninterestingly, goes hand-in-hand with
food; undistinguished by itself, even as it warms; tastes more like
Scotch than ale. Accompanies roasted pork dishes.

DENTERGEMS WHITE ALE   CB   0.6
(Dentergem, Belgium)

Rose-petal perfumey taste and aroma; blond and bland with essentially very little texture; a disappointing boudoir beer—pale,
light, and very frivolous, like chamomile tea; conditioned in the
bottle, which is painted white to give it a ceramic look; feh!

B E E R   F A C T

*B*eginning operations in 1896—comparatively recent by most European standards—Dentergems
is now the best-selling wheat beer in Holland
and Belgium. Like most wheat beers, its tart character can be enlivened with a thin slice of lemon or a
drop or two of fruit syrup—raspberry is ideal. Given
my low rating of this ale, it is strongly advised that
fruit be added.

DESCHUTES BACHELOR BITTER   MB/BP   3.1
(Bend, Oregon)

Mildy malty and less than mildy bitter, but decently flavored; increases in circumscribed bitterness with food, becoming mellower and creamier; red, coppery color; increasing complexity make it pleasing and easy to drink; weakens slightly at the finish, but retains its quality character.

DESCHUTES BLACK BUTTE PORTER
(draft)   MB   3.7
(Bend, Oregon)

Relatively light for porter, with forthright alcohol presence (appropriate for porter); deep, velvety brown-nearly-black color is a real attraction; emerging fruitiness and toastiness are refreshing, though texture remains flat; almost food-like in its ability to be filling; calming, satisfying with even-tempered complexity; fuller-bodied and mellower at the end of the glass. Goes well with shellfish—oysters, clams, and shrimp, for example.

DEVIL MOUNTAIN
DEVIL'S BREW PORTER   MB   2.3
(Benicia, California)

Soft, mildly carbonated, and gently sweet; appropriately bitter, but, unfortunately, with a hint of medicinal flavor; far too watery; no depth or chewiness; serious lack of effervescence diminishes the delivery and overall effect; weak, roasted aroma doesn't deliver; diminishes further with food; finishes mildly bitter (a relief), but, alas, unexciting; slight musty aftertaste.

DEVIL MOUNTAIN GAYLE'S PALE ALE   MB   2.4
(Benicia, California)

Relatively little energy; subdued floweriness; some chewiness; muddied sweetness emerges at mid-glass; has lots of promise, no delivery: cloudiness and color of fermented apple cider suggest more aroma than it offers; sediment on bottom makes it look hardier than it is; pleasant nonetheless—won't offend nor will it challenge; too many unrealized ambitions. Fullness emerges with pineapple-topped baked ham.

DEVIL MOUNTAIN IRONHORSE ALT   MB   2.8
(Benicia, California)

Underlying fruitiness overridden by thin sourness; rich body, flavor, and overall impact; head is fizzy and thick, though not as airy as other beers; a thinnish head remains atop the misty, copper-colored beer throughout; more interesting to look at than to taste; apricot bouquet at end (see label); much more appealing after being opened and recapped for two to three days—just be patient. Good flavor and textural match for highly spiced main courses.

DEVIL MOUNTAIN IRONHORSE STOUT MB 2.6
(Benicia, California)

Appealing, light chocolate aroma; soft milky taste with a quick flash of malty roastiness that later resembles coffee; thick Brussels lace; vague, deep-brown color; soft, gentle maltiness; medium-bodied; lingering dryness on the roof of the mouth; not zesty or pungent enough; improves with each sip, but needs more hop backbone. Drink as an after-meal *digestif.*

DEVIL MOUNTAIN RAILROAD ALE MB 3.6
(Benicia, California)

Immediate tang comes through heavy foam; alcoholic warmth moderates the tanginess; some cloying, sticky sweetness at the roof and back of the mouth; cloudy amber color; ambiguous yet quite drinkable; aroma makes up for underwhelming bitterness. Good with a burger or a bowl of chicken noodle soup.

DIAMOND HEAD DRY Lager MB 2.9
(Honolulu, Hawaii)

Moderately thick and somewhat strong in character; hoppiness predominates with background of faint fizziness; forces you to pay attention to its power; settles into more compact, less forceful brew at the bottom, but its presence remains felt all through the bottle (or meal); strength suggests European origins. Remains dominant with a meal of breaded pork chops and candied yams.

DIEKIRCH Pilsener CB 2.9
(Diekirch, Luxembourg)

Nice, sweet, grain bouquet with muddied yellow appearance; sharp with quickly rounded end note; crisp and clean from head to toe with fulfilling mid-range body; does yeoman service against hot, spicy dishes; still, it is more appropriate with blander food.

DILLON'S SIX SHOOTER RED ALE CT 3.8
(Chatsworth, California)

Lovely, sweet-caramel malt taste lingers on tongue; appropriate, rich, deep-ruby, apple-cider color with pure white, lasting head; smooth and carefully balanced; malt remains in the nose as an attractive come-on; opaqueness (from yeast) adds to the attraction; ends a bit watery; a visual and gustatory delight. Nicely contains hotness of spicy food while maintaining its own integrity and separateness.

DILLON'S STRAIGHT SHOOTER
PALE ALE CT 2.3
(Chatsworth, California)

Sweetish, caramel taste; smooth tending-to-bland texture; head quickly disappears; tamped-down fruitiness is the major characteristic of this style; malt presence does add to relative sweetness, making this more like Vienna amber than ale; lingering whiff of skunky odor diminishes overall effect; light amber opacity is too dark for pale. Good with a pot pie or shepherd's pie.

DILWORTH ALBEMARLE ALE   MB/BP   2.4
(Charlotte, North Carolina)
Weakly alcoholic with subdued fruitiness; very flavorful; drier than most ales with a sneaky alcohol finish; could be mellower; waits for food, or something, to take the lead; not assertive enough.

DINKELACKER Pilsener   CB   2.9
(Stuttgart, Germany)
Cloudy, milky, unobtrusive; good complementary background taste; dry, minimally fruity and light-bodied; hop taste is soft, but present; a good, sturdy beer that is not particularly complex. Serve it with fresh salmon or other favorite fish.

DINKELACKER DARK Lager   CB   3.4
(Stuttgart, Germany)
Moderate, chewy sweetness that almost immediately turns a bit sharp and yummy; slight burnt-caramel taste lingers and remains tantalizingly around the roof of the mouth; maltier, rather than hoppier, with attendant, almost bland smoothness; not really dark in color, but medium-brown with orange-red overtones and some murkiness; weakens at bottom of the bottle. With this malt liquor, try a barbecued chicken sandwich.

DIXIE Lager   CB   3.5
(New Orleans, Louisiana)
Great uplifting spirit entering and leaving the palate; crisp and refreshing; brewed for an appreciative popular taste; texture out-plays flavor, but end result is a comprehensive beer worthy of re-peat performances. Accompanies (what else?) oysters on the half-shell, crawfish, and spicy shrimp.

DIXIE BLACKENED VOODOO
LAGER   MB   2.4
(New Orleans, Louisiana)
Teasing sweetness with pungency in background, punctuated by snappy pinpricks of fizz; texture is tamped down and smoothed out in mid-bottle; flatness rapidly settles in, underscoring lack of complexity and integration of ingredients; fades toward water; rich, reddish brown with hint of purple when held up to the light; faint fruity, molasses feel at finish, along with the return of a malty aroma; in the end, disappointing. Full and almost fruity with linguine with clam sauce.

B E E R   F A C T

*D*ixie Blackened Voodoo Lager gained a measure
of notoriety when it was introduced to the public in 1992. A number of localities tried to ban
the brew because, it was alleged, images on the label
were too suggestive of sorcery, charms, and other
voodoo practices. The company, of course, couldn't
have bought better publicity, and the fledgling boy-
cotts quickly disappeared into the swamps.

DIXIE JAZZ AMBER LIGHT Pilsener   **CB**   **2.0**
(New Orleans, Louisiana)
Fruity and sparkly on the first sip, with medium-lasting carbonation; no head; slightly sour flavor; hoppy at the back of the
throat, which proves to be somewhat unsettling; fades precipitously to bland, essentially becoming irrelevant with fiery food;
regains some tangible fruitiness, but still stays relatively flat; finishes watery and light; the wrong Dixie to have in Dixie.

B E E R   F A C T

*W*ood barrels made of Louisiana cypress are
used to age Dixie lager. Once in the bottle,
however, Dixie, like most beers, does not improve with age. A good rule: drink your beer within
one week of purchase.

DOCK STREET AMBER Ale   **CT**   **3.1**
(Utica, New York)
Front-of-mouth fruitiness, followed by fizziness at the back of
the throat; thick and robust with grilled London broil—noticeable sweetness mellows out and integrates, nicely enhancing the
red meat; body gets fuller, too; warmth and fruitiness are finishing trademarks.

DORADA PILSENER   **CB**   **3.3**
(Talca, Chile)
Starts off with fresh onrushing hops taste that calms down to an
integrated, more balanced drink with some mellowness; hoppiness remains ascendant and agreeable; a heavy pilsener that continues to weigh heavily. Serve with solid, meat and potatoes-style
meals.

DORTMUNDER AKTIEN ALT   CB   1.2
(Dortmund, Germany)
Complex and balanced aromatic interaction between malts and
hops is featured at the outset; sweet, fresh wood taste quickly disappears, to be replaced by a rather bland, unentertaining, and
cloying mouthfeel that stays for the duration; a curious beer that
holds promise, but ultimately doesn't deliver.

DORTMUNDER UNION DARK Lager   CB   0.1
(Dortmund, Germany)
Creamy head; hint of bitterness at the back of the throat; has a
funny fish-like taste with some foods; mild and smooth with a
medium body; exudes an almost rancid chocolate taste; remains
creamy and slightly chewy throughout.

DORTMUNDER UNION ORIGINAL
Pilsener   CB   3.6
(Dortmund, Germany)
Cold, this mildly hoppy creation squarely hits the spot after an
hour or so of lazing in the sun; aftertaste is dry and hoppy; head
is thinnish but smooth and very much a part of the full body;
achieves faint sweetness with kalamata olives, as the salt of the
olives appears to draw out the flavor of the hops; nicely put together; low carbonation level, with resultant smooth texture.

**DOS EQUIS CLARA—LAGER ESPECIAL CB   3.2
(Guadalajara, Mexico)
Mild, pleasant, and responsive; light rice taste appears to come
from brewing ingredients rather than addition of adjuncts; flat-
tened sharpness is well-balanced; weakens after a bottle or two.
Appropriate with pasta in a garlicky seafood sauce.

B E E R   F A C T

*D*ouble Diamond (below) gets its name from
the twin diamonds chalked a century ago on
the brewery's wooden casks to mark the best of
the brew. Today the bottle label shows an updated version of the original geometric design.

DOUBLE DIAMOND ALE   CB   2.5
(Burton-on-Trent, England)
Starts with a honeyed, fruity palate; cold on the sides of the
tongue; wraparound taste quickly dissipates with food; sharp fin-

ish with unexpected savory sourness to match; overall, more texture than taste, but that's not necessarily a drawback; malty warmth along with roughened smoothness finally emerges at the end. Accompanies roast chicken with plain vegetables.

DOUBLE EAGLE Lager MB 1.4
(Addison, Texas)
Clear, but with no taste and devoid of aroma; water is obviously a major ingredient; not unpleasant, but essentially nothing is there with or without food—but it's good water.

DOUBLE HAPPINESS Lager CB 2.3
(Guangzhou, China)
Pedestrian Asian beer with faint rice taste that is plain rather than enhancing; thin and somewhat pallid; completely overwhelmed by spicy or highly flavorful foods; clearly tries to be a good companion to food, but ingredients are not integrated enough to allow it to perform the task; I would come back to this in a year or two, to see if any changes have been made.

DOUGLAS SCOTCH BRAND ALE CB 3.9
(Antwerp, Belgium)
Creamy, alcoholic fruitiness greets the nose and mouth with just a hint of underlying cloyingness; constant burnt-caramel taste, particularly on the tongue; alcohol emerges with great depth and insistence with food; tightly bubbled Brussels lace surrounds the beer, adding to creamy, smooth context; cream-white head sits like crown on deep-red body; malt accent; drink this nifty concoction in a brandy snifter for best results, or try it with pasta dishes and lightly seasoned pork chops.

DOWN UNDER Lager CB 2.6
(Perth, Western Australia,
Australia)
Creamier than other Australian beers, with a smoky aftertaste; smooth, mellow, and easy going down; in the end, turns thin and a bit sour; ultimately less robust than at first sip. Pleasant with pan-fried fish.

DRAGON STOUT CB 3.3
(Kingston, Jamaica)
Creamy and very sweet, with mild, burnt follow-through; warmth, comfort, and emerging alcohol strength make your heart (and cheeks) glow; deep-brown color is classic in its luminescence; strong, high-alcohol aroma; finishes pleasingly bitter and smooth, smooth, smooth; typical milk stout, but perhaps too sweet. A nice *digestif*, try this with chocolate cake or chocolate pudding after a meal.

Empty Glasses

*B*eer brewing is often a fleeting enterprise. Brews and breweries come and go, and it is not unusual to unexpectedly discover that a familiar companion—or a just-acquired friend—is no longer available. Sometimes they reappear in a different guise (different company, different label, hoppier, smoother). Over the years, several good beers, as well as some that perhaps should never have been made in the first place, have disappeared. Here are a few remembered favorites, offered to you fondly and with the hope that someday they may return—for my renewed, and your new-found, enjoyment.

Three lagers stand out—Snake River (Caldwell, Idaho), Trapper (Red Deer, Ontario, Canada), and Dark Horse Amber (Virginia Beach, Virginia). Dark Horse, which I rated 4.0, was one of the best American beers I've ever had—fresh-tasting, fruity, and well-balanced. Snake River, which I savored in the brewery's small taproom surrounded by fields of growing hops and rated 3.9, had a creamy smoothness, roasted aroma and taste, and chewiness at the back of the mouth. Trapper, 3.7, was crisp and effervescent, with a mild, sweetish tartness. You still can buy a product called Trapper, but, although it's made in Canada, it's not the same beer, company, or brewery location.

Other vanished beers include Boulder Sport, a surprisingly good contract brew from Shiner, Texas (3.5) and Zele, a lager from Prince George, British Columbia, Canada (3.2).

The moral? Enjoy your beer, but don't get too attached to it. Although smaller breweries have a higher overall success rate than, say, restaurants, the mortality level still warrants caution. A conservative figure suggests that one in every 4 to 5 brewpubs goes belly-up shortly after opening. On the other hand, one brewpub a week opens somewhere in the country. A second moral (*caveat emptor* division): the success of a beer is not necessarily related to its taste—as if most of us didn't already know that.

DRAKE'S ALE   **MB**   **2.1**
(San Leandro, California)
Smooth and malty with faint fizz; good when warm; hint of apple comes and goes; relatively uncomplex, with no predictable distinctive taste; too weak for a true ale.

DREHER PILSENER   **CB**   **2.1**
(Milan, Italy)
Creamy, smooth head tops off mild, laid-back hoppiness; soft, gentle fizziness, but virtually tasteless; parallel, uniform Brussels lace circumnavigates the glass; beer plays second fiddle to heavy food; visually more balanced than texturally; pale-golden color; some integration in the palpably dry finish; subdued—not exciting, but neither is it a turnoff. Try it with pasta, fish, or chicken.

DRESSLER Pilsener   **CB**   **2.0**
(Bremen, Germany)
Honey taste and aroma as if from bees using very strong malt-flavor source; almost like a mild Scotch whiskey; no effervescence; flat, sparkleless texture; alcohol seems to be more spread out, not concentrated; not unlike water, but with some backbone; ends with continuing honey taste, but overall rather lifeless and dull.

DRUMMOND DRAFT LAGER   **CB**   **2.4**
(Calgary, Alberta, Canada)
Light and citrusy; pale color underneath airy, rapidly diminishing head; very plain with no pretensions; not filling or obtrusive.

DRUMMOND DRY Lager   **CB**   **0.8**
(Red Deer, Alberta, Canada)
Light and faint-tasting, reminiscent of other Canadian beers; sharp at the top of the mouth, but that's about all it has to offer in the way of impact; some greenness; continuing less-than-bland taste/texture is completely irrelevant to and submerged by even the plainest food; cheap-tasting, almost perfumey.

DUFFY'S ALE (draft)   **BP**   **4.1**
(Vancouver, British Columbia, Canada)
Nice, rounded, contained, balanced sweetness; smooth and energetic, though not very alcoholic and not fruity at all; thin but tangible head over reddish body; retains its flavor and body without food; warm yet quenching; some zest is lost at the end; delicious and well-made. Goes very nicely with fresh fruit such as peaches and nectarines.

DURANGO Pilsener   **CB**   **0.8**
(Del Sur, Guatemala)
Tastes as pale as its color, which is very pale—virtually colorless through green glass of the bottle; sort of like flavored water—the Guatemalan answer to Coors; old, musty taste with faintly

sweet undertow doesn't deviate with food; the colder it is, the more it tastes like water; an obviously mass-produced beer with little to recommed it.

DURANGO COLORFEST Lager
(annual)   MB   3.5
(Durango, Colorado)

Thin head on top of a thin, pale amber body; refreshingly fruity and tangy with aggressive sharpness; nicely balanced with attenuated hop bitterness; compact, nicely detailed, with a bit of residual chewiness unusual in an Oktoberfest; refreshed, warming fullness is manifestly present when imbibed alone or with blander main dishes; rolling-around-the-mouth flavor; well-balanced hops and malt are a real pleasure despite persistent yeasty aroma; don't let peach-blond coloring put you off, this does contain some alcohol. Good with grilled burgers, chicken or fish.

DURANGO DARK Lager   MB   2.7
(Durango, Colorado)

Immediate light-chocolate aroma and taste are essentially its most telling features; gentle roastedness obscures both malt and hops, though malt is a bit more apparent; medium-bodied; connects to antipasto-type hors d'oeuvres; no head to speak of; middle-of-the-road—a beer for all foods and all seasons.

DURANGO WINTER ALE
(annual)   MB   3.2
(Durango, Colorado)

Definitely fresh-tasting, but somewhat aroma-spoiled; high fruitiness and too much froth on first pour; long-lasting but sporadic Brussels lace; enticing alcoholic spiciness with flat texture settles down into tantalizing yeastiness with faint tones of citrus fruitiness; malt and hops become far more balanced and integrated as it warms, engendering a very pleasant light touch on the tongue; evolves into charming glass-filler; this rather mild ale should be imbibed at room temperature. Works surprisingly well with red beans and rice with a splash of hot sauce.

DUVEL Ale   CB   2.9
(Breendonk, Belgium)

Big head with flat, musty taste does not make for a good introduction; fruity wine flavor; soft, thin, and obviously highly alcoholic both by weight and volume; gains in warmth and mellowness; rather light body; all-malt; smells like raw yeast—but that's the tradeoff for its distinctive fruitiness; for those of you who ask a little more from your beer. Perfect with poultry.

EAU CLAIRE ALL-MALT LAGER　　　MB　　　3.7
(Eau Claire, Wisconsin)

Simultaneously sharp and creamy mellow; very similar to London Pride and amber malt liquors, but a bit sharper and thinner; caramel aroma complements soft texture and caramel taste; clearly brewed in the European tradition—distinctively and with care. Goes well with Cajun dishes.

EDELWEISS DUNKEL DARK Wheat　　　CB　　　3.0
(Salzburg, Austria)

Apparent but more subdued clove taste than its cousin Hefetrüb; with clove diminished, the taste is more enchanting; retains freshness without cloyingness, somewhat unexpected for a dark beer; unassuming and clear-tasting; circumscribed warmth. A good companion with baked or roasted chicken.

EDELWEISS HEFETRUB Wheat　　　CB　　　2.4
(Salzburg, Austria)

Very light and fizzy, with distinct hint of clove; becomes rather airy, almost nondescript; golden, translucent cloudiness gives the iced glass a frosty appearance; delicate flavor is a bit too cute, not to say disconcerting, in an Austrian/German beer; lightly hopped; drink with lemon slice, as recommended on the label. Food is unnecessary with this beer.

EDELWEISS KRISTALLKLAR
WEIZENBIER　　　CB　　　4.0
(Salzburg, Austria)

Immediate clove palate and softened sharpness; dry; golden, pale color with long-lasting creamy-puffy head; soothing in the stomach while nourishing in the mouth; fresh and hardy for wheat beer; textural sweetness, clove-like in substance, finishes the bottle; like a well-tempered symphony with engaging opening, sublime middle, and smooth finish; strong, thirst-quenching example of this style. (Labeled malt liquor for U.S. consumption.) Serve with spicy food or fish.

EDELWEISS LUXURY GRADE
MALT LIQUOR   CB   1.4
(Dresden, Germany)
Flat and stolid in texture with faint, hard taste of honey; no complexity; hops are evident with accompanying dryness; malt is downplayed; mild cloudiness subverts light amber-color; even the alcohol in this malt liquor is not apparent; an unattractive, much too predictable brew.

EFES Pilsener   CB   1.1
(Izmir, Turkey)
Fresh and restrained on the first sip; sweet and sour at the same time; mixed aftertaste is more unpleasant than pleasant; reminiscent of cheap perfume or old turpentine; an aroma better suited to cleaning fluid than to beer.

EGGENBERG URBOCK   CB   2.3
(Salzburg/Linz, Austria)
Sweet at the tip of the tongue, bitter at the back of the tongue, smooth all over the tongue; golden color draws attention away from the taste; sort of parallels food rather than complementing it; some fruity taste; a bit sour and cloying; round, alcoholic taste; far from memorable.

EINBECKER UR-BOCK   CB   3.0
(Einbeck, Germany)
Smooth; pleasantly integrated with unexpected lightness; weakly alcoholic, mellow, and somewhat undistinguished, but not without distinctiveness; tastes far better without food to obscure its gentle nature.

EKU DARK HEFE WEISBIER   CB   3.8
(Kulmbach, Germany)
Pinprick sharpness, with underlying smoothness, accompanied by lemon-clove taste; mild and gentle on the palate; creamy tan head remains thick and comforting with tiny, well-shaped bubbles; tart, tangy, and richly yeasty; dry bite; no aftertaste; contrast between head and copper-brown body is aesthetically pleasing and emotionally calming; well-made; nice, stately brew you can serve proudly to guests. A pleasant companion to pasta dishes.

EKU EDELBOCK   CB   3.7
(Kulmbach, Germany)
Sweetly and sharply hopped with restrained alcoholic upflow on just the first sip, sturdy and assertive thereafter; aroma and taste

match each other perfectly, while texture remains supple and smooth; malt can be ascertained in the aroma; relatively higher alcohol content remains under control and presents itself gradually rather than being overwhelming; a step above the usual brews of this style; nice warm maltiness finishes the bottle. Accompanies various types of deli meats and cheeses.

EKU KULMBACHER PILS   **CB**   **3.9**
(Kulmbach, Germany)
Fresh taste; appropriately sweet graininess; smooth, yet agreeably textured; sparkly and well-proportioned; finish is mildly dry. Serve with clams or oysters on the half-shell; taste circulates and seems to improve after every bite of food, not to mention every swallow of beer.

EKU KULMBACHER RUBIN Lager   **CB**   **1.9**
(Kulmbach, Germany)
Rather mild and run-of-the-mill with tantalizing hint of almost fruity sweetness; flat texture; imbalanced in the direction of maltiness; attractive ruby-red amber leads you to believe it's a better brew than performance suggests; uninteresting and fades further in the stretch.

EKU KULMINATOR URTYP HELL
MALT LIQUOR   **CB**   **0.2**
(Kulmbach, Germany)
Overwhelmingly sweet and syrupy with lasting coating all over the mouth; remains strongly unpalatable, with increased alcohol content adding to the unpleasantness; food is ruined by the taste of the beer; even deep-red color doesn't take attention away from its sticky cloyingness; far too strong, potent, and aggressive for food—by itself, it is unfinishable.

ELEPHANT MALT LIQUOR   **CB**   **3.1**
(Copenhagen, Denmark)
Crisp, relatively full taste with muted floweriness; nice malt/yeast aroma is good counterpoint to the sharpness of the texture. Pick your food carefully with this beer: It is enhanced by New York strip steak, at odds with shellfish.

BEER FACT

*M*alt liquors come in the same range as do other beers: dark, pale, hoppy, sweet, dry, and so forth. However, malt liquors, while malty (though not strongly so), are not true liquors; that is, they are not distilled as are vodka or gin.

EMERALD CITY ALE   MB   1.3
(Seattle, Washington)

Surprisingly lifeless with backdrop of vinegar on the tongue; malty, but remains flat and listless; sudsy head; adds no taste or texture to foods; hops sort of wander off by themselves and are not integrated into overall taste; transient, spotted Brussels lace detracts from enjoyment; too weak and unfruity for an ale.

EMPEROR ALE   CT   3.2
(Modesto, California)

Fruity, honeyed citrus taste; full and perfumey; remains sharp with just a hint of butteriness; warm, light amber color; minimum head; appears to be high in alcoholic content; good alone; maintains rich, fruity aroma; loses some flavor at the end. (This is a Vietnamese beer, made by St. Stan's Brewery, under the direction of brewer Chau Tien.)

EMPERORS GOLD Pilsener   CB   3.5
(Guangzhou, China)

Somewhat vivacious with touch of hoppy aroma at first sip; pale-golden color and minimal head suggest lighter feel than is actually the case; almost perfect balance between malt and hops; loses some fizziness as bottle is drained; good and serviceable—unusual from this country; finish is warm, attractive, and satisfying. Serve with broiled meat.

ERDINGER WEISSBIER—DUNKEL   CB   4.0
(Erding, Germany)

Tawny-tan, thick, creamy head sits atop a root-beer-brown body—a great visual beginning; controlled, mild yeastiness is chewy and very attractive, with just the right hint of lemon-clove taste; about midway through the bottle, a charming vanilla flavor emerges as a delighful accompaniment; fresh, with a constrained tartness and appealing, rich maltiness—marks of a good dunkel weissbier; quite spritzy and invigorating; slight roasted taste keeps things interesting; remains tart throughout; yeast sediment collected at the bottom of the bottle turns the color apple-cider hazy; quality product from this reliable Bavarian brewery. Goes well with veal scaloppine and fresh vegetables.

ERDINGER WEISSBIER HEFETRUB   CB   4.4
(Erding, Germany)

Fluffy with a wonderful clove-lemon balance and blend; crisp and nicely carbonated, making it delightful to drink and savor; smells like fresh air off of a mountain lake, so much so, you might want to keep your nose in the glass all evening; head stays thick and creamy; tastes every bit as fresh as the aroma; slightly opaque, though relatively clear, despite presence of yeast in the bottle;

small, moderately fast-rising bubbles continue until the last sip; quality ingredients and quality-brewed; finish is mildly pungent and sweetly tangy—a joy to behold and to drink. Goes perfectly with shrimp and other seafood salads.

ERDINGER WEIZENBOCK   CB   3.8
(Erding, Germany)
Spicy and flowery, with a moderated pungency; finely tuned caramel taste and accompanying smooth mouthfeel; creamy at the front of the mouth and bitter at the back, adding just the right touch of character, muddy nut-brown color is the result of sediment in the bottle; aroma is reminiscent of macaroni and cheese; cloyingness on the tongue at mid-bottle wears off and the beer remains quite dependable from there forward; thick maltiness intrudes toward the end, detracting from the previous good cheer; surging alcoholic finish caps this dark, flavorful beer. Try it with fried fresh fish.

ERLANGER MARZEN BIER AMBER
Lager   CB   2.8
(Dubuque, Iowa)
Light, mellow body with undercurrent of appropriate malt/cooked taste; mild flavor can't cope with food; should be drunk alone; comes close to the identified style; but there's not enough toasted malt flavor and aroma, and it has uncertain hop bitterness.

ESCUDO PILSENER   CB   2.9
(Osorno, Chile)
Very hoppy; bubbly head; not subtle—direct and to the point; strong graininess; for those who want their beer cold, but with some taste so as to know they're not drinking water. Assertive with pickled cold meats and cheese, and spicy empanadas.

BEER FACT

*I*n Chile, "pilsener" signifies more hops; *cerveza* (beer in Spanish) means less.

ESCUDO SCHOP (draft) Pilsener   CB   2.4
(Santiago, Chile)
Somewhat thick-tasting with a hint of sourness; provokes some interest, which is passive rather than active; thickness at back of tongue doesn't linger; flat and unmotivating at the end.

B E E R   F A C T

*I*n South America, where many countries have a large German population, *schop(p)* means "draft." It is based on *schoppen*, which in German means a "glass of beer."

ESKE'S ALT BIER   BP   1.4
(Taos, New Mexico)
Somewhat fruity and acidic; weak, without staying power; flat; tends to lose its taste; in the end, undistinguished and not worth the effort.

ESKE'S BOCK   BP   3.8
(Taos, New Mexico)
Creamy, smooth, and roasted; fine, strong example of this higher-alcohol style; slips down the throat without a hitch, while relatively unassertive flavor clings to the roof of the mouth; a little too supple, with no backbone to speak of; light-headed concoction of charm and piquancy; a bit cloying in the end, but why quibble? Appropriately assertive with strongly-flavored meats such as mutton, lamb, and game.

ESKE'S EL JEFE WEIZEN   BP   3.0
(Taos, New Mexico)
Clearly filled with wheat malt; diminished hoppiness; thickish aftertaste on the back of the tongue turns somewhat acidic as it remains there; dry, with rounded sharpness; full, with light underpinning of citrus presence. Try it with a tuna salad or American cheese sandwich.

ESKE'S SMOKEHOUSE ALE   BP   2.2
(Taos, New Mexico)
Fills the mouth with fishy smokiness, though it dissipates relatively quickly; warm and soft on the palate with no readily discernible texture; smokiness resumes its fishiness at the end; choose this one carefully—*caveat emptor*. A match for smoked cheeses and fresh-water fish.

ESKE'S SPECIAL BITTER   BP   3.5
(Taos, New Mexico)
Fresh and fruity, but not sweet or sappy; nice, restrained taste with some flat, fizzy aftertaste at mid-glass; flavor and texture fade with some foods; drink first half of glass quickly to get the best out of it; finishes warm and comforting. Match with a hamburger and French fries.

ESKE'S TAOS GREEN CHILI   **BP**   **2.7**
(Taos, New Mexico)

Fresh green-chile aroma and taste with lingering, roasted mouth-feel; texture is flat and liquid without much pizzazz; gentle roll on the tongue accompanies nice, mild chile aftertaste; chile presence is handled well—subdued, but clearly a player; agreeable change of pace. Try it with a grilled cheese sandwich.

ESQUIRE EXTRA DRY Lager   **MB**   **0.9**
(Smithton, Pennsylvania)

Dry, light, and tasteless; very pale faded color; uninspiring, uninteresting, unintegrated; possesses a certain fruitiness that saves it from complete condemnation; someone must have liked it, however: Silver Medal winner at the 1993 Great American Beer Festival.

ETTALER KLOSTER DUNKEL Lager   **AB**   **4.5**
(Ettal, Germany)

Rich, flavorful, and immediately—and immensely—satisfying; flat, hoppy taste is tantalizingly bitter, and quite fresh, even after its journey across the ocean; golden, red-brown color suggests it is lighter than it actually is, but who's complaining? A lovely, gentle blend of aroma, taste, and texture with an integrated, layered complexity; out of the tap, this beer must be a knockout; finishes with a hint of caramel and sturdy malt sweetness; an exciting import. Sweetens gently, while malt mellows into a feathery texture with couscous and chicken breast with honey-mustard sauce.

EUGENE ALE   **CT**   **2.0**
(Helena, Montana)

Very effervescent with mildly creamy tartness; looks like root beer; tastes somewhat watery; ends up being passively responsive to food, the food taking precedence over the liquid's taste, texture, and aroma; unassuming and uncomplicated.

EUGENER-WEIZEN Wheat   **CT**   **1.1**
(Helena, Montana)

Flat and musty, without expected citrus fruitiness of wheat beer; rather tasteless with pretzels as well as by itself; essentially unmemorable, except for thirst-quenching attributes.

EUROPA Lager   **CB**   **3.1**
(Lisbon, Portugal)

Mild hoppiness; easy on the nose, palate, and tongue; slightly perfumey; light, somewhat airy taste and pale-blond color; uncomplicated; calm, honey-sweetness emerges with determination, pleasantly balancing and complementing saltiness of some foods; malts take over gently and gradually, turning this brew into a more interesting and desirable drink; finishes smooth and mellow; good to have with food or without. Try it with an Italian hero sandwich.

EXCALIBUR Stout   **MB**   **0.6**
(Chico, California)
Overly burnt taste; much too bitter; roasted barley presence is so strong it nearly overwhelms; muddy and ill-defined; harsh, bordering on raw; watery underneath the rough texture; touted as "the stout with an edge"—unfortunately, the edge is quite ragged.

TAP TIP

Changing Temperatures

*B*itter flavors are intensified by colder temperatures, which also lessen malt sweetness and body fullness. Beers meant to be served at higher temperatures, like many ales, are generally less bitter, more full-bodied, and less dry (sweeter).

F AND A Lager   **CB**   **3.1**
(Toronto, Ontario, Canada)
Subdued freshness fills the palate; more texture than taste; sweet, soft, and variably mellow; unintrusive malt-hop mix stays in the background; worth trying. Serve with warm bread and soft cheeses.

FALSTAFF Lager   **CB**   **2.3**
(San Antonio, Texas)
Quickly refreshing and crisp, but just as quickly develops thickness on the tongue and palate; freshness and some zip; taste is rather attenuated and bland, but like a cold glass of water, it does offer thirst-quenching qualities; too many adjuncts to be anywhere near distinctive; decent lightweight brew. Try it with Indian food.

FELINFOEL DOUBLE DRAGON ALE   **CB**   **4.1**
(Llanelli, Wales)
Sweet-wine taste; touch of bitterness fits nicely into the sweetness; appealing, smooth, rich-amber color; attenuated fresh effervescence; sweet smelling; clean rather then fizzy after swallowing; versatile; hearty, strong, and determined to help out with hearty, strong, rich food—succeeds nicely in that respect. Try with a meal of thick-sliced roast beef, gravy, and mashed potatoes, and a gooey concoction for dessert.

BEER FACT

*F*elinfoel has redesigned its label so that its products are now sold under the name Welsh, with "Felinfoel" displayed less prominently. In 1935, the company was the first in Great Britain to can its beer.

FELINFOEL DRAGON ALE   CB   4.0
(Llanelli, Wales)
Sharp and biting on first sip; gently increasing honey-tainted sweetness and mellowness trickle upwards as the ale warms; fullness reaches appetizing midpoint, stops and stays there; moderately lasting head with small bubbles tops a dusty-brown body with orange undertones; remote fruitiness adds mystery to this tender ale; alcohol remains warming and unobtrusive; yeasty aroma at finish. Goes well with chowders and grilled chicken.

FELINFOEL HERCULES ALE   CB   4.0
(Llanelli, Wales)
Combination wine-beer taste is quite winning; thin and thick at the same time; sweet and bitter; alcohol strength copes well with tangy food; finishes on an upbeat, hoppy note, warming as you swallow the last drop; good cold-weather warmer. Surprisingly appropriate with barbecued dishes.

FELINFOEL WELSH ALE   CB   3.9
(Llanelli, Wales)
Nicely balanced, with controlled sweetness laced with mild, fruity-citrus taste; full-bodied and soft with a tart edge that revives at every sip; yeast cloudiness and fruitiness are full and consistent; sweeter at the bottom of the bottle as the alcohol becomes more noticeable; mature balance of sweet and sharp; nicely put together. A near-perfect accompaniment with grilled tuna or salmon steak.

FELINFOEL WELSH BITTER Ale   CB   2.4
(Llanelli, Wales)
Rich without bitter bite on first sip; flat and uniform rather than complex in texture and taste; no aroma; prickly mouthfeel; somewhat tentative; not intrusive—surprising for a bitter; if possible, sample a few sips before ordering a pint of your own. Accompanies fresh fruit, such as mangoes and apple slices.

FELINFOEL WELSH PORTER   CB   1.8
(Llanelli, Wales)
Flat, thin, and without zip; no aroma; remains uninteresting; some maltiness in the nose as you drink it; hoppy finish is not typical of porter, nor is it thick, or dark, or sweetish; watery and untasty.

FEST BIER Malt Liquor   **CB**   **2.4**
(Bayreuth, Germany)
Soft taste at the top of the glass, with sharp underlay on first sip; rather neutral with food; unassuming and uneventful except for quantity (comes in 16.9-ounce bottle); ordinary.

FIEDLERS BOCK IM STEIN   **CB**   **2.5**
(Koblenz, Germany)
Sweet and somewhat cloying; smooth and easy going down; remains constant and predictable; almost plain with diminished sweetness when imbibed with food; alcohol gets warm and comforting about halfway through the crock; in the end it has an up-and-down attraction, quite different from the beginning sips; doesn't reflect a typical bock in ingredients or quality; bottled in a stoneware crock, traditionally used to "shield its contents from harmful light and heat for thousands of years," according to the label. Accompanies grilled poultry dishes.

FIEDLERS PILS IM STEIN   **CB**   **2.3**
(Koblenz, Germany)
Mild freshness immediately followed by a dullness that lasts as slight tannic aftertaste; changes and becomes unpleasantly filling, eventually subsiding—all this without food; filmy aftertaste remains on the roof of the mouth; mellows and sweetens considerably with food; better at the beginning, but still a little too flat and thick-tasting for pilsener. Try it with broiled meat dishes.

FISCHER D'ALSACE AMBER
Malt Liquor   **CB**   **3.2**
(Schiltigheim, France)
Hearty, thick, and creamy; full-bodied with hint of sharpness; not much alcohol presence; soothing, smooth; some dryness and flatness at the end. Appropriate accompaniment to pork dishes.

FISH EYE IPA (draft)   **BP**   **0.5**
(Olympia, Washington)
Fruity aroma; mellow and faintly sweet with a hint of acrid lemon flavor; peach/almond marzipan taste adds to the impression that the brewing process was incomplete—more reminiscent of a homebrew; yeast is sour and off-tasting; weak and hard to finish; skip this one until further notice.

FITSPATRICK STOUT   **BP**   **3.1**
(Seattle, Washington)
Creamy-smooth and soft; roasted barley taste is obvious, even with food; clearly quality-made; integrated and complex throughout; gives feeling of lightness and airiness, although its substance is tangibly present. Try it with seafood dishes.

FLYING HORSE ROYAL LAGER CB 2.7
(Bangalore, India)
Sour citrusy taste and a bit gauzy; turns pleasantly bitter early on; dainty sheets of Brussels lace enhance the ambience, while a touch of medicinal taste at the back of the throat inhibits it; hoppy rather than malty, but overall rather evenhanded and middle-of-the-road; aromatic hops are pleasant if not exciting; medium-bodied; in the end, the whole turns out to be more interesting than the individual parts. Goes well with seafood salads.

FOECKING PREMIUM Lager CT 0.3
(Monroe, Wisconsin)
Sour, winey taste accompanies hint of honey sweetness—the latter planned, the former not; thick, brutish texture as well; flat and watery with no carbonation; muddy-gold color; insults the taste of food; blotches of stuff (yeast?) float around the glass; its only redeeming feature is the honey aroma and taste, even at the end.

FOSTER'S LAGER CB 3.4
(Melbourne, Victoria, Australia; Toronto, Ontario, Canada)
Expectedly fresh and crisp on contact; full palate and smoothness around the sides of the mouth; generally even-tempered and predictable throughout; head is very white with clearly distinguishable bubbles; nicely patterned Brussels lace adds to the soft feel; a quite pleasing, flavorful lager with backbone; Australian version is essentially identical, except for definitely lighter carbonation. Try it with spicy Mexican fare.

FOSTER'S LIGHT LAGER CB 3.2
(Melbourne, Victoria, Australia)
Light, citrusy flavor; typical lager texture and body; mild hoppiness fades into background after several sips; as beer warms, ingredients seem to flow and blend; head is creamy-looking, but appears to be pumped up by additives, not naturally. Accompanies Chinese food nicely.

FRANKENMUTH DARK Lager MB 3.1
(Frankenmuth, Michigan)
Very pleasant honey-fruit aroma with underlying tartness; consistent flavor that doesn't attack your taste buds; not as texturally firm or full-bodied as it should be; warmth is relatively characterless; minimal integration of ingredients; hint of clove spiciness at the bottom of the bottle; creamy head quickly thins out; good but not great. Drink alongside broiled pork chops and other broiled meat dishes.

FRANKENMUTH GERMAN-STYLE
BOCK   **MB**   **2.4**
(Frankenmuth, Michigan)
Full and darkly hearty; mushy taste with a cloying mouthfeel; heavy maltiness disrupts enjoyment of a variety of ordinary foods—this is not a food-friendly beer; slight bitterness disappears very quickly; deep brown matches color of the bottle; malty sweetness turns a bit bitter at the end, and is not pleasant; malt aroma, however, redeems the overall impression somewhat.

FRANKENMUTH PILSENER   **MB**   **1.2**
(Frankenmuth, Michigan)
Immediately juicy flavor, followed by sharp, tangy, citrus taste; full and satisfying; many bubbles suggest high carbonation, but texture is flat, flat, flat; provides very little energy for food; weakens further as bottle is drained; intricate, thin, relatively short-lived Brussels lace; weak, cloudy, pale-yellow color adds to the overall poor presentation; gets downright blah and watery at the end, with low-level sourness.

FREE STATE OATMEAL STOUT   **MB**   **1.2**
(Lawrence, Kansas)
Rather bland; medium-light; no burnt-roasted favor; tame with faintly underlying complexity; too weak and uninteresting.

B E E R   F A C T

*F*ree State Brewing Company, established in 1989, is the first legal brewery in Kansas since state prohibition, begun in 1880, was repealed. It occupies a renovated inter-urban trolley station in downtown Lawrence. Free State refers to Kansas' role in the Civil War.

FRYDENLUND Pilsener   **CB**   **2.9**
(Oslo, Norway)
Sharp with rounded, restrained edge; remains crisp and concise throughout; taste stays consistently attentuated; texture is far more exciting; aroma is essentially nonexistent. Okay alongside smoked fish and the like.

FULL SAIL BROWN ALE (draft)   **MB/BP**   **2.8**
(Hood River, Oregon)
Immediate malt hit in the mouth; deep, roasted mouthfeel, with lovely sidebar of hops; no aftertaste; full-bodied and almost succulent in its richness; not as complex as it should be; needs more alcoholic pizzazz to lift it above average; some hops finally enter the picture at the end. Good with pub fare.

FULL SAIL GOLDEN ALE   MB/BP   2.3
(Hood River, Oregon)
Mild, quickly dissipating fruitiness; melts into background and lets the flavor of the food have its way; gentle and unassuming with moderate fullness and dryness at the roof of the mouth; fruitiness increases again at the end of a meal; finish is weak-kneed. Okay with grilled steak and a tossed salad.

FULL SAIL WASSAIL WINTER ALE
(annual)   MB/BP   2.7
(Hood River, Oregon)
Strong, almost perfumey, chocolatey burnt-caramel taste and aroma, with prominent lacing of bitterness; full-bodied and smooth, with a core of softness; becomes more pungent and citrus-flowery with hot foods; emerging spiciness at the bottom of the bottle proves this is a seasoned beer; very hoppy beginning, middle, finish, and aroma—wow!—strong stuff; more than two are likely to produce some discomfort. Very good match with Southwestern–Mexican food.

FULLER'S E.S.B. EXPORT ALE   CB   2.5
(London, England)
Full, mushy (slightly gooey) mouthful with sweet taste of mustiness; similar to London Pride but with more bite; maintains a consistent, forward-thrusting, unfading presence from the tip of the tongue to the back of the throat; its advertised bitterness can be clearly dominant (and off-putting); a good beer to share with a friend; voted "Britain's Best" at the Great British Beer Festival in 1985. Nicely complements lightly barbecued pork chops.

FULLER'S LONDON PRIDE Ale   CB   3.8
(London, England)
Tastes like Sugar Daddy lollipops, with nuttiness thrown in; reasonably full; caramel flavor; overall, delicious, soft, slosh-around-mouth taste/texture; sip this gently, take your time, and swallow slowly. Delicious with maple syrup-enhanced baked beans.

FURSTENBERG Pilsener   CB   3.6
(Donaueschingen, Germany)
Fresh and hoppy but without sparkle, despite the many quickly rising bubbles; smooth, almost to the point of becoming bland; conservative and constrained; keeps its distance, but its presence is gentle with subtle strength and backbone. Try it with pastas, salads, and fruit (it turns a bit sour, but remains a worthwhile food companion nonetheless).

GAMBRINUS LAGER   CB   2.9
(Pilsen, Czechoslovakia)
Crisp and edgy with underlying composed flatness; emerging sweetness counterbalances the earlier sharpness; not fizzy; no head to speak of; malt takes precedence over hops toward the end,

then reverts to a hoppy, dry finish. Remains sharp enough to slice right to the core of an open-face deli sandwich.

GARDEN ALLEY AMBER ALE   CT   0.1
(New Ulm, Minnesota)
Skunky and unpleasantly acrid; quick hit of fruitiness immediately sours and fades—thankfully; yeasty harshness and no carbonation to speak of; raw and unfinished: malt tastes as if it still needs some cooking, while the hops are very sparse and indistinct; overall, underpowered in taste and strength of ingredients; liquid seems to sag in the glass, topped off by patches of flotsam; soft mouthfeel is its best characteristic; forget this beer.

GATOR LAGER   CT   2.3
(Auburndale, Florida)
Very neutral in taste, aroma, and ambience; no bite, though it does have a comforting nothingness that has a nice calming or settling effect on hot foods, almost like a friendly analgesic; relative robustness not found in similar, locally brewed American lagers; only the texture has any lasting impact, and that's relative; the label proclaims, "The beer with a bite"—toothless, at best. Try it with hot dogs topped with everything.

GEARY'S PALE ALE   MB   2.4
(Portland, Maine)
Crisp, caramel ale taste with core of sweetness and body; holds its own with food but syrupy sweetness detracts from any kind of well-rounded flavor; devoid of hop presence for about two-thirds of the bottle; not unfriendly, just standoffish.

GENESEE Lager   CB   2.5
(Rochester, New York)
Opens crisp and to the point with the quick disappearance of both characteristics as it is swallowed; light-bodied with some complexity of hops and barley—a taste that can easily get tiring; forget food with this brew, but feel free to call it up in a local bar with friends; nice Brussels lace evolves from head on sides of

glass; highly carbonated; gains in fullness and satisfaction as evening progresses; slight touch of sourness in the finish.

GENESEE CREAM ALE   CB   2.7
(Rochester, New York)
Creamy, smooth, and mellow; maintains this pattern evenly and consistently with food, for which it provides good working background; modulated thickness occasionally intrudes; texture more noteworthy than taste; Silver Medal winner at the 1993 and 1994 Great American Beer Festivals. Goes well with grilled shrimp.

GENESEE 12 HORSE ALE   CB   3.4
(Rochester, New York)
Fittingly light-tasting; full-bodied core makes the first sips very pleasant and fulfilling; evolves into smooth, relatively soft drink; a beer to sit back with on the front porch while shooting the breeze; creamy with a quick-to-detect underlying fruitiness; not difficult to enjoy. Try it with pizza.

GENGHIS KHAN Lager   CB   1.1
(Guangzhou, China)
Muddled sharpness, with no particular evidence of taste; remains unflavorful although somewhat thirst-quenching; not obnoxious, but essentially not worth the effort.

GENTLE BEN'S BIG HORN
OATMEAL STOUT   BP   2.2
(Tucson, Arizona)
Burnt-malt taste with a bitter finish that stays on the sides of the mouth and interferes with food; not thick or creamy enough; as it warms it balances well with red meats, but loses flavor with other foods; too constrained without the complexity necessary for a top stout; aroma is more attractive (and appropriate to style) than taste.

GENTLE BEN'S CATALINA KOLSCH
PALE ALE   BP   2.0
(Tucson, Arizona)
Hint of citrus fruitiness; aftertaste coating on the tongue and mouth; subdued hint of yeast hides malt and barley nicely; too weak and dry in the end.

GENTLE BEN'S COPPERHEAD ALE   BP   0.6
(Tucson, Arizona)
Musty, soapy smell; nondescript, washed-out taste; not exactly unpalatable, but gets close.

GENTLE BEN'S RED CAT AMBER   BP   2.3
(Tucson, Arizona)
Lightly malted with a faint warmth and a gentle dollop of alcohol; color is appropriate with good balance and integration of ingredients; approximates traditional amber but is not hefty or malted enough.

GENTLE BEN'S T.J.'S RASPBERRY
Ale   BP   2.4
(Tucson, Arizona)
Gently fruited with a lot of fizz making it more like raspberry
soda; light and gentle with good Brussels lace; too weak but not
too sweet, it teeters between beer and a frilly summertime drink;
malt and hoppiness are subdued, so any balance is hard to detect; sip this without food to whet your appetite, then order a
real lager—without fruit in it.

GERST AMBER   CB   3.2
(Evansville, Indiana)
Beautiful, newly polished, ruby-copper color prefaces very fizzy,
smooth mouthfeel; light and watery with sweet malt taste; nice
Midwestern beer—rather direct and accommodating; got universal rave reviews from a mixture of indifferent and experienced
beer drinkers during a recent holiday season. Great for mild pre-
meal snacks.

GILA MONSTER Lager   CT   1.8
(St. Paul, Minnesota)
Aromaless and tasteless on first sip; whiff of malty aroma and
roastedness eventually, begrudgingly, rises without much complexity, suggesting a Vienna-style beer; seems to have been thrown
together without a lot of thought as to balance, integration, or
presentation; washed-out amber color implies more character than
there is; smoky flavor on exhalation, sour on inhalation; weak
even with a salad; not unpalatable, just uninteresting; its label is
cute as a button: the charm of a handmade label without the
charm of a handmade beer.

GIRAF MALT LIQUOR   CB   2.3
(Odense, Denmark)
Slight, quick, initial bitter taste, then crisp and undistinguished;
never seems to get started and recedes as full impact of food is
felt; well-meaning, but not assertive enough.

GLACIER BAY LAGER   CB   1.1
(Toronto, Ontario, Canada)
Crisp and oozing adjuncts; a notch or two above ballpark beer,
especially with hot dogs on a bun smeared with yellow mustard;
flat-tasting and off-tasting as meal progesses; a bit more filling
than most lagers, but repellent by the time you get to the bottom of the bottle; much too variable to risk buying again.

GLARNER LAGER   CB   3.1
(Zurich, Switzerland)
Hoppy fullness with strength at the back (bitter) and sides (sour)
of the tongue; depth and charm remain circumscribed and "top
out" just when you expect the beer to continue its interest and

your enjoyment; while the texture is flat, the taste with food is appealingly sharp and almost palpable; a food's beer—well-made, but not particularly distinctive. Try it with caviar or other salty hors d'oeuvres.

GLENWALTER WEE HEAVY
SCOTCH ALE   MB   1.5
(Burlington, Vermont)
Like the gooey stuff that comes from local trees, this Vermont product is mellow and lightly syrupy; nicely touched with alcohol as well; however, there is a spoiled pungency to it that is clearly detracting; deeply malted within the Scottish-ale style; but off-taste lurking throughout is a major flaw.

GOA PILSNER DRY   CB   2.9
(Goa, India)
Full and immediately satisfying; hint of rich maltiness; texturally too smooth for this style; sharply sweet, with improving flavor as you drink it; cloudy, pale yellow with barest suggestion of golden color; no head; wispy Brussels lace; in general, not compatible with food; too filling; finishes with an autumnal smell.

GOEBEL GOLDEN LAGER   CB   2.1
(Detroit, Michigan)
Filled with taste-flattening adjuncts; starts off bland and watery, although there is some amount of fizzy sharpness; not awful, but remains rather tasteless, uninspired, and completely inattentive to food; hint of warmth/sweetness hardly makes its presence felt; light and thin.

GOLDEN CROWN PALE DRY   CT   0.1
(Tumwater, Washington)
Green, full of adjuncts, and rather bland; off-taste is grumpy and clotted at the roof of the mouth; harsh and overbearing, this concoction is a pale imitation of a pale dry.

GOLDEN DRAGON Pilsener   CB   3.1
(Guangzhou, China)
Flattish liquid with bubbly effervescence on the surface; immediately undistinguished; however, it gets more interestingly complex and attractive—developing a honeyish, almost fruity, overtone—as food interacts with the brew; if you don't believe a beer can grow and improve before your very eyes—or on your own lips—try this one, but with mild-mannered food.

GOLDEN EAGLE LAGER   CB   3.5
(Madras, Tamil Nadu, India)
Strong, sweet wine bouquet; smooth, full-bodied texture; blond color; a bit watery with food, but comfortable and palatable; a touch lightweight in the end. Goes well with flavorful hors d'oeuvres, such as sweet-and-sour meatballs and chicken wings.

GOLDEN HARPOON LAGER   CT   3.1
(Utica, New York)
Warm on the first gulp, which soothes the ensuing sour sharpness; moderate body and crispness with an outdoorsy, airy ambience; good, crisp balance of malt and hops, with occasional predominance of hops; appropriate alone or with mild, uncomplicated food; above-average American lager; unevenness lowers ranking in the end. Compatible with beef stew.

GOLDEN PACIFIC CABLE CAR
CLASSIC LAGER   MB   3.0
(Emeryville, California)
Full-bodied and almost rich-tasting; hop aroma abounds and ultimately defines this beer; strong but secondary malt presence plays well against the dryish hoppiness; agreeably carbonated; balance fluctuates too much to be predictable; weakens in the end—a well-made beer that finishes with less flash than promised at the beginning. Goes well with salty food like Caesar salad with plenty of anchovies.

GOLDEN PACIFIC CASCADE WHOLE
MALT Lager   MB   2.5
(Emeryville, California)
Fruity wine smell; overwhelming head with airy nonfizzy bubbles; tasteless on first sip; cloudy-blond color; more flavorful when sampled with a cheeseburger; a little raw-tasting; sediment at the bottom; much too hoppy for me, though those who like hop bitterness might rate it higher.

GOLDEN PACIFIC GOLDEN BEAR
DARK MALT LIQUOR   MB   3.3
(Emeryville, California)
Not your everyday malt liquor—nicely tangy and fresh with moderate burnt-malt middle; smooth and easy going down; good, but not exciting; a bit sour at the end; lasting taste. Balanced tang and sweetness make this compatible with marinated chicken and boiled potatoes.

GOLDEN PACIFIC GOLDEN GATE
MALT LIQUOR   MB   3.1
(Emeryville, California)
Surprising hint of caramel in a malt liquor; sour, yeasty maltiness not unpleasingly integrated into a subtle, but consistent, sweetness; amber color enhances the overall effect; quality is present, but overall not completely satisfying; however, a certain warmth does come through; yeast is an important ingredient; bottle-conditioned (not pasteurized). Try it with poultry.

GOLDEN PACIFIC THOUSAND OAKS
LAGER   MB   3.0
(Emeryville, California)
Immediate fresh fruit, almost grapefruit, taste—a bit of an astringent, unpleasant start; sweetness and a nice streak of bitterness appear with food; cloudiness is reminiscent of ginger ale, and like ginger ale, it maintains an even-tempered freshness and sparkly newness throughout; nicely thirst-quenching. A good match with barbecue.

GOLDEN PROMISE ALE   CB   2.8
(Edinburgh, Scotland)
Subdued, integrated fruitiness and yeastiness; thin texture; weak but balanced; splash of alcohol occurs on second or third sip; generally attends to the differing demands and flavors of food; reddish-copper color (not golden) with thin head; a little too rough around the edges.

GOLDEN VALLEY RED THISTLE ALE
(draft)   BP   1.0
(McMinnville, Oregon)
Burnt aroma, perfumey taste, and black-coffee color greet the senses; less-than-mild bitterness parallels an emerging grassy aroma, which ultimately predominates; caramel maltiness offers some hope (false, it turns out) that things will get better; taste comes and goes quickly, which in this case is a blessing; too weak and watery for the style; where are the alcohol and hops?

GOLDHORN CLUB Pilsener   CB   3.4
(Lasko, the former Yugoslavia)
Fresh, fruity aroma and sharp clove taste greet first sips; soft, quickly diminishing head; honey-like sweetness plays second-fiddle as bottle is emptied; I like the way this beer and food interact—grainy ingredients are well-matched; cloudy yeast haze creates translucent blond color; slightly sour, dry/sweet finish, suggesting a cross between wheat and pilsener styles. Accompanies noodle dishes, including noodle soup.

GOOSE ISLAND DUNKEL
WEIZEN BOCK   BP   2.2
(Chicago, Illinois)
Light and a bit perfumey; slight roof-of-the-mouth cloyingness; deep malty sweetness is distinctive and creates a furry aftertaste; minimal hint of alcohol; strength weakens further with even plain-cooked foods; apparently a bock that prefers no competition—especially from food.

GOSSER PALE Lager   CB   2.6
(Leaben Goss, Austria)
Creamy, smooth, fluffy, and lots of air; dark taste belies its mildly

cloudy, pale color; restrained flavor ends at the back of the tongue; overall, more American in its blandness, although it does have a fuller body generally absent in U.S. brews; foam bunches up thickly as a head, even when most of the beer in the glass is gone; the steel (not aluminum) can says, "Especially brewed for export, ships and aircraft." Appropriate with sandwiches.

GOSSER STIFTSBRAU Lager   CB   3.5
(Graz, Austria)

Mild-mellow burnt taste with very little carbonation; relative thinness; remains consistent and evenhanded by itself and with salty snacks; modest depth and hearty, well-defined, sweet, malty taste; clearly defined textural boundaries—you easily can tell when strength gives way to smoothness, for example; gets stronger at the end of the bottle. Serve with barbecue- or mesquite-flavored potato chips.

GOUDEN CAROLUS ALE   CB   3.9
(Mechelen, Belgium)

Sweet, almost cherry aroma, turning into mild, tentative clove aroma; well made; deep, golden-amber color with a dollop of red; rich, tan, long-lasting head and haphazard Brussels lace; strong, warming alcoholic presence that tenderly envelops food; yeast at bottom clouds the end of the drink; sweet, very malty finish. Nicely accompanies Italian food.

B E E R   F A C T

*G*ouden *Carolus*, which translates from Latin into Golden Charles, is named for the bright metal coinage of the Holy Roman Emperors Charlemagne and at least one Charles V. Brewed since the middle of the fourteenth century, this brown ale is reported in historical documents to have been popular at royal fox hunts because "it fired both rider and steed with such enthusiasm for galloping that the hunt took place in the best possible atmosphere." Later, when he was no longer monarch, Charles V declared "this daughter of the grain [to be] superior to the blood of the grape."

GRANT'S CELTIC ALE   MB   3.1
(Yakima, Washington)

Classic burnt taste is overpowered by a hop sharpness unbecoming to an American ale (Yakima is hop country, after all); good tip-of-the-tongue fruity sweetness; with food there is a more beguiling warmth and evenhanded balance between taste and texture; mild, as noted on the label, and appealingly hopped; winds up being a bit too watery; sweet, burnt finish. Try with sharp cheeses, like Cheddar, or savor as an after-dinner drink.

GRANT'S IMPERIAL STOUT   MB   4.2
(Yakima, Washington)
Incredibly dark, rich, and full of body; sweetness surrounds burnt taste, resulting in an essence of chocolate syrup; gets sweeter, mellower, and more incredibly integrated with grilled New York strip steak and green chilies; character strengthens until the bottom of the glass; a classy, sturdy offering.

B E E R   F A C T

*I*mperial stout was the Russian battlefield and peacetime winter warmer of choice of Czar Alexander's troops. Its significantly higher alcohol content helped preserve freshness as it traveled from England to Moscow, St. Petersburg, and beyond. Several breweries carry on the potent part of the tradition, though far less of it finds its way to the former Soviet Union nowadays.

GRANT'S INDIA PALE ALE   MB   3.6
(Yakima, Washington)
Crisp and sharp with an ebb and flow of mildly fruity wine taste; sweetness with a hint of sourness emerges, then mellows into an obviously well-made brew, retaining sharpness and pungency at the edges, and an anticipated, but not quite obtained, warmth on the tongue; you certainly can taste the hops; cloudy appearance; neck label pronounces this a "faithful reproduction of the 19th century ale. . . ." Delicious with smoked or grilled fresh fish and crusty bread.

GRANT'S SCOTTISH ALE   MB   2.0
(Yakima, Washington)
Sour fruitiness pervades, coats the mouth and stays there; remains too winey to be satisfying or greatly appreciated; a let-down compared to other Grant's styles, although a sturdy cheese sandwich improves the taste.

GRANT'S SPICED ALE   MB   3.9
(Yakima, Washington)
Powerful, spicy, clove aroma with corresponding taste; visually and texturally very watery; liquid looks almost lifeless; no head; no fizz or pizzazz—it's all spiciness and fruitiness, like fermented

apple cider; clove and fruity taste meld and integrate somewhat with food; becomes a warm, enchanting, and far more enticing drink as the meal progresses; flavor and texture balance and substance becomes more pronounced; honey component eventually comes to the fore. Drink warm with pork chops; also particularly good at room temperature or slightly warmer with *pan dulce* or other kinds of sweet pastry.

GRANT'S WEIS BEER   MB   2.8
(Yakima, Washington)

Stale and grainy on first sip; light with a tangible body throughout the rest of the bottle; well-balanced and pleasantly integrated with hearty foods; modulated bitterness creeps into the mouth as the bottle is drained; loses its minimal fizziness, but gains some flat warmth; mild fruitiness lingers in the nose. Try it with beef soups and stews.

GRANVILLE ISLAND BOCK   MB   4.2
(Vancouver, British Columbia, Canada)

Lovely, integrated sweetness and mellowness with a hint of carbonation; remains charming, intact, and approachable with food; taste weakens as alcohol (6.5%/volume) becomes more apparent; warm, professionally created beer that ranks among the best of American and Canadian microbrewed products; mature and ready to drink. Very good with pub fare such as English sausage rolls and pork pies; also a nice match with a steamed artichoke.

GRANVILLE ISLAND LAGER   MB   2.9
(Vancouver, British Columbia, Canada)

Mild, fruity-caramel taste with little carbonation, but sustaining interest; taste is silky and pleasantly grainy; professionally done brew. Nice with main-course pork dishes, baked beans, or winter vegetables.

GRANVILLE ISLAND LORD GRANVILLE
Lager   MB   2.6
(Vancouver, British Columbia, Canada)

Very effervescent; light and airy with ginger-ale ambience; settles into calming, no-waves beer; mild, honey-like taste remains as an undercurrent throughout; basically falls in the range of average Canadian lagers, with perhaps a bit more complexity. Accompanies Asian food.

GREAT WALL Lager   CB   2.9
(Hebei, China)

Immediate, sweet, honey-like taste; sharp with rounded edges; faint, back-of-the-mouth rice presence; needs bland food, like rice or egg noodles, to show off the complexity and malt character that is only hinted at; the first super-premium Chinese beer.

GREEN ROOSTER Lager   **CB**   **0.0**
(Copenhagen, Denmark)
Soapy, sticky, unpleasant, green (I'm not making that up); reminiscent of dishwashing liquid, only not as tasty; color was chosen as an alcoholic bow to spring; perhaps the worst beer I ever have encountered; I couldn't finish it.

GREENALLS BITTER Ale   **CB**   **2.4**
(Warrington, England)
Deft, creamy smoothness and attractive softness circulate around the mouth and then gently slide down the throat; turns acidic then ultimately fades in the presence of the food; thin with a bubbly head; expected bitterness is surprisingly low-key; clearly not a connoisseur's beer, but a pleasant pub diversion with a few chips rather than hot/spicy food; complexity diminishes at the middle and almost disappears at the end.

GREENALL'S CHESHIRE
ENGLISH PUB BEER Ale   **CB**   **3.1**
(Warrington, England)
Thin, fruity, winey foretaste with nicely layered maltiness primarily at the back of the tongue; warm honeyness evolves underneath a fizziness that is a little too sharply intrusive; settles into a droll companion with hints of excitement and unpredictability; too much imbalance between taste (fruity warmth) and texture (sharp, cold, and prickly). Try it with pork or lamb dishes.

GRENZQUELL GERMAN PILSNER   **CB**   **3.1**
(Hamburg, Germany)
Smooth hops feel, enticing, Old-World aroma (complex and dainty); sharp bitterness turns into a film all over the mouth; 100% barley malt. Best with food, such as veal or white meat of turkey.

GRIMBERGEN DOUBLE ALE   **MY**   **4.0**
(Waterloo, Belgium)
Soft, creamy, and richly medium-bodied with a weighty lightness; emerging fruity sweetness with an unwanted hint of cloying mouthfeel; thick, creamy foam lasts down to the bottom of bottle—sits like meringue atop the beer; durable softness and changing flavor with food (from minimal sweetness to appropriately mild bitterness); a laid-back, mellow delight that sort of surrounds and gently absorbs the food in a cushion of deep amber; texture is especially attractive; the alcohol tastes like the alcohol in a delicious fruitcake; very easy to get along with. Good company with London broil and green chile stew.

B E E R   F A C T

*G*rimbergen Abbey, constructed in 1128 by St. Norbert, is typical of the monastery brewing tradition; abbeys doubled as inns for pilgrims, providing room, board, and good drink. Many centuries-old brewing recipes remain appealing today. The monks recommend serving their ale in a chalice glass at 53°F.

GRINGO EXTRA LAGER   **CT**   **0.8**
(Evansville, Indiana)
Light, fluffy, airy, with a faint, seemingly pleasant whiff of fruiti-ness; very, very faint hop taste, as if it were put in just to prove this is actually beer—not unpleasant, but ultimately rather point-less; Brussels lace sticks to the sides of an iced mug in clumps, suggesting either poor carbonation and/or too many artificial in-gredients; finish is a little sweet and a bit chewy, but also some-what metallic; contains cereal grains as adjuncts (unspecified, undoubtedly corn, perhaps rice); from "original 1877 recipe, Santa Fe, New Mexico Territory"; obviously, bad beers were made back then, too, but why advertise that fact?

GRIZZLY Lager   **CB**   **0.6**
(Hamilton, Ontario, Canada)
Heavy, obtrusive odor; off-taste; green-tasting—all of which strongly suggested I forego the possibility of having my meal spoiled by this beer; so, no food with this one—and no expec-tation of trying another bottle, either.

GROLSCH Pilsener   **CB**   **3.1**
(Groenlo, Holland)
Fresh, crisp, and sharp with a quick, dulling aftertaste; mildly distinctive, almost-malt taste; relatively full-bodied; dry; unpas-teurized (pasteurization tends to dull the flavors and subtleties of a beer); levered stopper in the bottle. Works well with Caesar salad with lots of anchovies and crunchy croutons.

GROLSCH AUTUMN AMBER ALE   **CB**   **3.6**
(Groenlo, Holland)
Mellow and pleasant with immediately apparent fresh mouthfeel; slight hint of caramel malt adds to the increasing enjoyment; tasty and mild—makes you want more of whatever they put in this; rich, amber-brown color with creamy, tan head is ad-copy perfect and quite inviting; rising hoppiness; unpasteurized, it holds its flavor; despite being a beer without an intense taste, it nonetheless has lasting flavor; finishes malty, carbonated, and al-coholic—all to its credit. Good with shellfish.

GROLSCH DARK LAGER   CB   3.2
(Groenlo, Holland)

Mild aroma and taste greet the first sip; balanced sharpness and creaminess make this beer pleasantly unpredictable, though its relative lightness (for a dark beer) remains constant; laid-back dark malt/slightly burnt taste emerges and increases in mellowness and flavor when interacting with food—a good sign; not the best-quality ingredients, however, but a decent mass-market beer; Brussels lace forms at the bottom of the glass. Try it with broiled or roasted meats, expecially pork or ham.

GROLSCH DRY DRAFT Pilsener   CB   3.0
(Groenlo, Holland)

Crisp, fresh, substantive texture—a good thirst-quencher on a hot day; a bit of staleness in mid-taste; with food, the beer becomes more mellow and seamless; nicely calibrated; strong, holds its own nicely. Accompanies guacamole, salsa, other favorite dips with chips.

GUINNESS EXTRA STOUT   CB   3.8
(Dublin, Ireland)

Rich, brown, toasted bouquet and palate; exudes a warmth both charming and insulating against the tasty hot breath of a hamburger with green chilies; interestingly, the burnt-toasted taste fades rather quickly and emerges as a firm underpinning to the food; soft, creamy, calming, and smooth at the end; a sturdy, yeasty presence brings this classic brew to a pleasant close. Guinness Extra Stout is traditionally used to create a Black and Tan (see page 132).

GUINNESS GOLD LAGER   CB   3.3
(Dundalk, Ireland)

Freshness and an encouraging attenuated hoppiness greet you at the outset; reaches an integrated balance; prickly sharpness remains throughout; overall, a mild, passive beer; good for beginners and the less adventuresome; after all of the food is eaten, the last few sips produce a mild aftertaste; quality with substance. Especially good with smoked fish, cream herring, cream cheese, sliced onions, tomatoes, and bagels—Sunday brunch.

GUINNESS PUB DRAUGHT Stout   CB   3.9
(Dublin, Ireland)

Mushy, mellow, soft, mildly bitter with an almost roasted-chocolatey elegance; stays smoothly balanced in texture and taste with food; constrained, expertly calibrated maltiness; classy and very satisfying; they've come winningly close to having this packaged beer taste like it just came out of the tap; it is now my canned beer of choice, although a bit too foamy and airy—a mechanical problem with the clever nitrogen gas capsule in the specially designed can needs reengineering; nonetheless, a clear winner. Especially good with baked fish or roasted chicken.

B E E R   F A C T

*B*lack and Tan is a popular mixture of draft lager and stout (usually Harp and Guinness), or ale and stout, and apparently is a political reference to the color of the uniforms of the English military busy in certain parts of Ireland in the 1920s. The practiced barkeep first pours a half-pint of the golden lager. Then, placing a spoon under the tap containing the stout, the bartender carefully rolls the darker liquid from the spigot onto the spoon and onto the top of the lager. When done properly, the two styles don't mix in the glass—brown-black on top, pristine gold on the bottom—producing perhaps the most esthetically appealing glass of beer in all the world. In response to its popularity among the current generation of drinkers, several companies now bottle a blend of the two styles; alas, so far they haven't figured out how to keep the black and the tan separate. The precursor to Black and Tan was a mixture of bitter ale and stout called "Arf 'n' Arf."

GURU LAGER   **CT**   **2.2**
(London, England)

Tangy, citrusy, and sharp; settles down after a few sips into a malt-oriented lager that is a bit too soft and uncertain about where it's going; citrus theme and mini-fizziness continue throughout; no head or other distractions to speak of; a bit watery under the quickly disappearing fizz; in the end, uninspired. Okay with roasted meats.

HACKER-PSCHORR DARK LAGER   **CB**   **2.5**
(Munich, Germany)

Reasonable, dark taste, but too watery for any depth to take hold; initial sweetness dissipates and appropriately disappears into food; somewhat dry; decent, middling beer. Weakly soothing with hot/spicy foods.

HACKERBRAU EDELHELL MUNICH
LAGER MALT LIQUOR   **CB**   **3.3**
(Munich, Germany)

Obviously a lager with too much alcohol for the U.S. authorities (hence the malt liquor appellation) and typically high enough for German consumption (hence the Munich-style prefix); starts off very grainy, slightly fizzy, and mildly bitter; rich, pale-golden color with a touch of red; bitterness sweetens and increases with food; emerging strong alcohol presence; ongoing, clean aroma; medium-bodied; consistent texture and mouthfeel; tasty and attractive, though not my cup of tea; malty, mellow finish; well-made, it progresses and changes, all in a positive direction; a strong lager, regardless of what it's called in this country. Try it with Mexican as well as German dishes.

HALE'S IPA (draft)   MB   4.4
(Colville, Washington)

Hoppy, hoppy, hoppy—but well-controlled and smoothed over by healthy dollops of malt; fruity, fermented initial aroma; bitterness takes over your entire mouth, but it is so well-done, you can't complain; lovely patterned curtains of Brussels lace stick around in wide parallel configurations; retains perfect balance, with all ingredients in convivial harmony; lusty, musty grain aroma finishes the glass along with a full-bodied fruitiness; slight hop weakness at the end, but so what—the ride getting there was fun; a well-crafted, tasty beer; I couldn't stop drinking this, with food or without, although I enjoyed it more with seared chicken breast and almonds.

HALE'S PALE ALE   MB   2.2
(Colville, Washington)

Deep fruitiness with subdued bitterness; soft throughout the mouth; flowery aura is evident; a little too precious and thin to make this worthwhile, even with food.

HAMM'S Pilsener   CB   2.5
(brewed by Pabst in Milwaukee, Wisconsin)

Fruity aroma which turns musty; sharp swallow at the back of the throat; offers some warmth and some substance and complexity, though not enough; fuller than other megabrews, with longer-lasting flavor; hops and malt are virtually impossible to discern; carries a certain grittiness, providing texture to let you know it went through a brewing, rather than a blanching, process; if you need a six-pack of mass-produced beer, this is it.

HAMPSHIRE SPECIAL ALE (annual)   MB   2.4
(Portland, Maine)

An annual event, this Christmas beer has proven to be alcoholic, spicy, and clove-like with a smooth, small-bubble mouthfeel; echoes of strength and quality with depth; mellows, but remains distinctly alcoholic with food; tamps down into calm, organized, somewhat complicated brew; still, compared with other Christmas beers, it leaves much to be desired, though, as a seasonal offering, changes do occur yearly; among other things, it's not spicy enough; higher alcohol content is not integrated with the other ingredients and complexity fluctuates; musty, reddish color with tannish, foamy head; finishes with a fresh yeasty aroma—but let's see what happens next year.

HANSA DARK Pilsener   CB   4.1
(Bergen, Norway)
Hint of burnt caramel doesn't alienate; constrained sweetness; distinctive; mellow yet sharp and crackling at the back of the tongue; defined, subtle, roasted taste combines with an undertone of malt, resulting in a pleasant, pungent package; taste comes around subtly, smoothly, and uniformly. Complements oysters or boiled shrimp with sharp horseradish or cocktail sauce.

HANSA LIGHT Pilsener   CB   2.6
(Bergen, Norway)
Significantly thinner, paler texture than the dark, but same overall taste and aroma. Too tame for oysters, shrimp, and similar seafoods; much better alone.

HARLEY-DAVIDSON HEAVY BEER
Pilsener (annual)   CT   2.4
(brewed by Joseph Huber Brewing in
Monroe, Wisconsin, for
the Harley-Davidson Co.)
Surprising softness and engaging thinness given the name, which immediately raises expectations; however, finish is bland and a bit flat; slight greenness; even with its gimmicky packaging (a 1989 edition was designed to look like an oil can), it is more appealing than anticipated; two to three at a time would probably help improve its taste; sweetness surfaces throughout; about average for an American beer; brewed annually for motorcycle events in Daytona, Florida, and Sturges, South Dakota, so check the date on this. Try it with a turkey sausage sandwich.

HARP Lager   CB   3.5
(Dublin, Ireland)
Immediate, rich taste without being overwhelming; balanced blend of flavors lingers on the tongue; sharp and very pleasantly fizzy; for people who have not fully developed their beer taste buds, this may come close to top-of-the-line; nice and solid, with integrity; a good food beer. It stands up to pizza with lots of cheese and has the guts to stand up to stronger dishes. Harp is also my lager of choice in a Black and Tan (see page 132).

HARPOON ALE   CT   2.7
(Utica, New York)
Vaguely sour, almost bitter, with a citrus fruitiness; thin body; gentle fizziness with flowery dryness at the back of the throat; soothing; engages several senses at once; classy presentation, but still not up to the great ones; dry and austere; meant for the connoisseur rather than the casual beer-lover, but misses the mark with both. It doesn't miss the mark, however, with mildly spicy Thai food.

TAP TIP

Listen When Your Beer Speaks

As with our other senses, hearing plays a role in the appreciation of drinking beer, though we aren't always aware of it. Listen to the "psssst" of the air escaping as you open the can or bottle. Is it strong and steady, or weak and very brief? The more noticeable the hiss, the more certain it is that the liquid has been packaged correctly and is ready to drink. Return the bottle or can if no sound is heard as you pop the top. Similarly, once beer has been poured, cock your ear to the top of the glass. Are the bubbles crackling and sharp-sounding, especially in a lager or pilsener? If so, carbonation levels are probably okay, and that pleasing, appropriate sound to the ear is likely to translate to a pleasing, enjoyable taste on the palate. As they say at Munich's Weihenstephan School of Brewing, a good beer "... must snap in the ear. . . ." So, listen up.

HART SPHINX STOUT   MB   2.7
(Kalama, Washington)
Stark, burnt taste; sharp, with mellow surround; surprisingly light and even-tempered; deep-brown color with practically no head; goes down easy without food; nicely patterned Brussels lace. Match with strong-flavored game.

HAZEL DELL RED ZONE PALE ALE
(draft)   BP   0.2
(Vancouver, Washington)
Sharply fruity taste and aroma; somewhat hoppy with a tart aftertaste on the roof of the mouth; apple-cider color; begins to taste like burnt rubber and coats the mouth; unpleasant ensuing citrus taste curls in on itself; simply not well-made.

HECKLER BRAU PALE LAGER   CT   2.2
(New Ulm, Minnesota)
Fresh, fruity, faint hit of lemon comes and goes too quickly, followed by mild tartness that turns bitter; dollop of sweet maltiness also quickly appears and disappears; some roastedness, suggesting a Vienna-style match with the amber color; faint, distracting medicinal overtones; overall, taste is interesting when it

is present; not very complex, with increasing flatness; hard to ratebecause it's hard to get a grip on it; finishes bland; needs more punch and staying power.

HEINEKEN LAGER   CB   3.4
(Amsterdam, Holland)
An old, familiar standby with crunchy sharpness in both taste and texture; substantive quality and predictable rhythm; consistent palate; although its taste is not the most inspiring, it is a solid all-around beer. As good with a burger as it is with shrimp and other seafood.

B E E R   F A C T

*H*eineken Lager is the number-one beer imported into the United States. It is reputed to be the first beer legally brought into the United States after Prohibition. Its presence and initial popularity in this country are attributed to Leo van Munching, a baggage manager with a trans-Atlantic shipping line who carted a few cases westward on the *S.S. Statendam* at the behest of a friend of his who was well placed with Heineken. The New York response to the beer was so positive that sales quickly zoomed and in short order van Munching was made Heineken's distributor in the U.S. His name still appears on all cans and bottles of the brand sold here.

HEINEKEN SPECIAL DARK Lager   CB   2.4
(Amsterdam, Holland)
Light, sharp, and fizzy, unlike the usual middle-European darks; taste is mild, clammy, and accompanies an uninteresting seltzer-like texture; best alone rather than with food; not worth the hype and label.

HENNESSEY'S LAGER   CT   1.8
(brewed in Seattle, Washington; bottled in Dubuque, Iowa; tasted in Seal Beach, California)
All-malt, "private stock," with vinegar overtones; ingratiating warmth marred by flat aftertaste; unexpected complexity; expected thinness and muddied mouthfeel; fades and becomes unmemorable; a generic beer that has a restaurant's own label on it—I tried it at Hennessey's Tavern, hence the name.

HENNINGER DARK Lager   CB   2.5
(Frankfurt, Germany)
Mild, slightly burnt taste; pretty much zestless and punchless;

the taste at the back of the throat turns a bit acrid as it settles in; hint of caramel; stays unperturbed, neither bolstering nor subtracting from a variety of foods; some musty mouthfeel at the end, along with sweetish accompaniment; neither exciting nor unexciting.

HENNINGER KAISER PILSNER   **CB**   **3.0**
(Frankfurt, Germany)
Sharp, crisp, and "guzzleable" on first sips; smooth and prickly in moderation, with a hint of non-fruity sweetness; modest and unobtrusive with vague hint of hoppy floweriness in the finish; moderately dry; malty flourish at the bottom of the bottle. Needs food to add interest, so serve with a deli sandwich and fries.

HENNINGER LIGHT Pilsener   **CB**   **1.9**
(Frankfurt, Germany)
Quick mustiness develops rapidly into flat, superficial taste; effervescence and staying power save this from being labeled nondescript; somewhat wispy and light, with similar color; for a weak-appearing beer it remains determined to help out in whatever way it can. Try it with lamb, or at brunch with spicy scrambled eggs.

HENNINGER MEISTER PILS   **CB**   **3.2**
(Hamilton, Ontario, Canada)
Simultaneously lightly crinkly and smooth; taste and freshness remain constant with food; quality ingredients enhance the enjoyment; overall, keeps your interest, though not exciting. Goes well with a crab salad.

HENRY WEINHARD'S DARK Lager   **CB**   **2.3**
(Portland, Oregon)
Sharp to bland, with no head to speak of; thin, with a slight malty, roasted flavor that just manages to differentiate it from the usual American beer; no depth or character; an attempt at giving the impression of a quality brew, but in the end rather ordinary; slight warmth comes through at bottom of glass; Bronze Medal winner at the 1993 Great American Beer Festival. Try it with salami on rye.

HERMAN JOSEPH'S DRAFT Lager   **CB**   **2.6**
(Golden, Colorado)
Quickly fading sharpness with a fruity undertaste; settles into a routine of thickness and sweetness; finishes as a relatively bland American brew with some textural distinction; there is a robustness that lasts throughout. All right with red-sauced pastas.

HERRENBRAU PILSNER
MALT LIQUOR   **CB**   **2.4**
(Bayreuth, Germany)
Strong, very appetizing, honey/grainy taste and aroma; slides a

little roughly down the gullet; maintains honey flavor with blander dishes although the texture is too watery to fully complement most foods; fades in interest as meal continues; encroaching sourness further pushes it downhill.

HERRENHAUSER PILSENER
MALT LIQUOR   CB   1.2
(Hannover, Germany)
Odorless, tasteless, and textureless; hints of clove and honey appear midway with food; smooth and dry, but so what? More complexity at the end of bottle—slight acidity and thickness on the tongue.

HINANO Lager   CB   2.1
(Papeete, Tahiti)
Slightly sour and flat-tasting on the tongue; mild fizziness quickly dissipates; French brewing influence is evident in the cutting texture and winey sharpness; has a fullness not always found in better-tasting beers; better with food than by itself. Try it with seafood.

HOBOKEN SPECIAL ALE   MB   2.8
(New Haven, Connecticut)
Cloves and other spices tantalize you on first sip; orange-rind smell percolates up; not as hearty as anticipated for an ale advertised as typical on board old-time clipper ships sailing the world; nice balance of malt sweetness and hops bitterness; thick head, no Brussels lace, and murky blond color; languid and smooth with beguiling, warming maltiness; best at the end. Try it with a meat loaf sandwich.

HOEGAARDEN GRAND CRU ALE   CB   0.9
(Hoegaarden, Belgium)
Perfumey aroma and taste discourage finishing this ale; made exclusively with barley malt; fruity, almost rancid, sourness and pale-golden haze leave a great deal to be desired; unpasteurized and bottle-conditioned; according to the label, Grand Cru was the secret of medieval noblemen, but the reputed allure of its taste still remains a secret.

HOEGAARDEN WHITE Wheat   CB   2.6
(Hoegaarden Belgium)
Immediate, winey, almost vinegary, aroma; fruity, perfumey sour taste at the sides of the tongue; quickly dissipating fresh, flat texture; sweetens to honey with food; much more palatable at the end than at the beginning; shimmering cloudiness; hints of coriander and curaçao, both common flavoring ingredients used before hops. Good with Italian food as well as brunch dishes.

HOFBRAU BAVARIA DARK RESERVE
Lager CB 2.5
(Kulmbach, Germany)

No aroma; ripe-apple flavor; texture wavers between thin and thicker; remains balanced (sweet/bland) with foods; a friendly, unassuming beer for the novice who wants to start trying dark beers; decent drink for any food regardless of spiciness; eventually fades into the woodwork.

HOFBRAU BAVARIAN LIGHT RESERVE
Lager CB 2.7
(Kulmbach, Germany)

Light, flavorful, and crisp with a smooth blend of hops and malt; flat aftertaste leaves slight burnt feel, even several minutes after last sip; sturdy and predictable. Fine with deli sandwiches.

HOFBRAU MUNCHENER OKTOBERFEST
Lager (annual) CB 3.3
(Munich, Germany)

Full in the mouth and slightly bitter, with a minimum of fizziness; nice balance between taste and texture; mild burnt-caramel taste appears throughout; this beer doesn't overwhelm you—it remains steady from start to finish with manageable complexity, balance, and overall flavor; good choice for those wanting an introduction to Märzenbier. Accompanies lemon chicken and rice nicely.

BEER FACT

*H*ofbräu, "court brew" in German, is made by Hofbraühaus, the famous beer garden in Munich that was originally the Bavarian Royal Court Brewery, founded in 1589.

HOFBRAU ROYAL BAVARIAN LAGER CB 3.1
(Munich, Germany)

Zippy, hoppy, crisp, and grainy; classic lager taste, but with more fullness and complexity; a good beer for those wanting something basic, yet somewhat challenging; aroma and taste match perfectly; well-made, but not overly exciting. Goes well with thick meat loaf or meatball sandwiches.

HOLSTEN Pilsener CB 3.0
(Hamburg, Germany)

Neutral taste and texture, leaning toward soft; hop aroma increases as food is consumed; still, you have to pay close attention to appreciate this beer; tapers off to a more pronounced dryness at the end. Enhances sushi and gazpacho.

HOLSTEN DRY Pilsener   CB   2.9
(Hamburg, Germany)
Sharp graininess at outset; sourness and sharpness increase with
spicy foods; medium body with mellow, golden hue; well-presented balance of sweetness and dryness, essentially substituting
taste for texture; good example of a dry beer. Try it with bagels,
lox, and cream cheese.

HOMBRE Lager   CB   2.9
(Ciudad Juarez, Mexico)
Sweet-tasting; very smooth and easy going down; gritty character is more malt- than hop-based; a little watery, but I would
drink it again. Enjoy with corn on the cob—a great beer/food
combination.

HOPFENPERLE Pilsener   CB   2.6
(Rheinfelden, Switzerland)
Affecting fruit aroma on first sniff, followed by pleasantly flat
maltiness that lingers on the tongue; surprisingly mild for a Swiss
beer; no acidity or alcohol bitterness; good basis for a malt beverage, but taste, texture, color, and body all need to be built up.
Goes well with Sloppy Joes and the like.

HOPFENPERLE SPECIAL Lager   CB   2.9
(Rheinfelden, Switzerland)
Dry, light, and flat on the tongue with an accompanying thickness; turns warming and honeyed with the right food—nicely
mellows out the fire of grilled chicken with green chilies; kinder
at the end then the beginning.

HOPS AMBER ALE   BP   2.4
(Scottsdale, Arizona)
Long-lasting head; perfumey, light, and dainty; minimally cloying, but enough to negatively affect pairing it with food; an unpredictable ebb and flow of sweetness, which is submerged by
the end of the bottle, may surface without warning.

HOPS BOCK   BP   3.1
(Scottsdale, Arizona)
Sheets of Brussels lace set off the deep brown of this seasonal
beer, making for a charming visual context; gently alcoholic and
somewhat sticky; appropriately hopped; remains weak to mild
for a bock, which in this case makes for an acceptable mellowness; I enjoyed this, but would not return for another.

HOPS PILSENER   BP   3.2
(Scottsdale, Arizona)
I first sampled this at the 1991 Great American Beer Festival in
Denver. Served in tiny plastic glasses, it was not fizzy, too sweet,
and too malty; the color was too yellow. I didn't consider it a
true pilsener, and rated it close to 0. A year or so later, I tried it

again, fresh from the tap at the brewery in Scottsdale, and *voilà*! without the knocking around, it tasted sweet, sharp, and crisp, with more appropriate carbonation; though still a bit flat on the tongue, it was an attractive, malty brew; firm and fulfilling; pale color was still too faded; and now, with a well-filled glass, Brussels lace tantalizingly coated the sides. Try it with a toasted bagel and smoked trout—a delightful combination.

HOPS WHEAT BP 2.3
(Scottsdale, Arizona)
Restrained citrus taste; fresh and alluring; sweetness is weak, but lasting; not as thirst-quenching as a wheat should be; an ordinary beer; dryish finish.

HOSTER WHITE TOP WHEAT MB/BP 2.5
(Columbus, Ohio)
Much-too-faint clove aroma; not sharp or thirst-quenching enough for wheat beer; much more like a plain, run-of-the-mill lager; flat, but not unattractive; undistinguished; a beer without a style. Improves with plain foods such as liverwurst or ham sandwiches.

HUA NAN Lager CB 3.8
(Guangzhou, China)
Very sweet, light, and delicately refreshing; easy on the hops, it is a little too weak for spicy or barbecued food; enjoyable alone or with plain beans and rice or steamed vegetables.

HUBCAP RAZZLE DAZZLE BERRY
Wheat Ale BP 1.0
(Vail, Colorado)
Weak, watery cranberry juice; consistency of cheap wine; weak red-brown color doesn't help; not unpleasantly sweet with hint of counterbalancing bitterness; more gimmick than beer.

HUE BEER Lager CB 0.6
(Hue, Vietnam)
Salty, sour, and bitter with sharp carbonation—all obscuring any real taste sensations; sweet, perfumey presence is felt at the back of the throat as the fizziness subsides; dry, flat aftertaste lingers on the roof of the mouth; no head, no lace, and no complexity; cloudy, faded yellow-golden color; while some malt appears at the end, this concoction is oddly unbeer-like; finishes cold and unforgiving.

HUMBOLDT GOLD RUSH EXTRA
PALE ALE MB 2.3
(Arcata, California)
Fresh, fruity aroma along with flat, rancid taste greet first sip; yeasty cloudiness and bitterness become driving forces at mid-bottle; cloudy, pale-blond color blends naturally with thin but lasting head; weak and static, with potential; needs more inte-

gration and assertiveness; finishes with semi-appealing sweetness; aftertaste lingers too long and too unpleasantly but improves somewhat with old-fashioned salty beer nuts.

HUMBOLDT RED NECTAR ALE   MB/BP   2.8
(Arcata, California)

Fresh-baked aroma with emerging citrus taste, particularly at the back of the throat; maintains its keen bite; gets into the crevices of the mouth with a comforting, watery feel; each pour creates a new, somewhat fluffy/spongy head that lasts until the next pour; raw at the end; serviceable, but not outstanding.

HURLIMANN SWISS DARK LAGER   CB   2.4
(Zurich, Switzerland)

Malty and pinprick sharp at the beginning of the bottle, followed by a light backbone with concentrated yet short-lived boldness; unenticing dryness flattens on the tongue and, thankfully, goes away; sharpness fades into fizziness; overall integration of ingredients as beer warms—surprising for a lager, which usually does its best when chilled. Fine with bread and cheese.

B E E R   F A C T

*H*urlimann, which is called Hexenbrau, or "witches' brew," in Switzerland, is a dark, brooding mixture allegedly brewed only when the moon is full.

HUSSONG'S CERVEZA CLARA
Pilsener   CB   3.4
(Guadalajara, Mexico)

Smooth body that dissipates quickly; sharpness on palate fades pleasantly and gently; slight aftertaste integrates well with each subsequent sip; constrained sweetness; tingly and good tasting, but served with food, the same sweetness lowers the score. Goes well with paella or other seafood and rice dishes.

ICEHOUSE ICE BEER MALT LIQUOR   CB   3.3
(Milwaukee, Wisconsin)

Stiff-backed and bold; surprising hop bitterness that slowly erodes; harsh, full sweetness follows first swallow with food; remains fresh and invigorating; very dry; plain and clean-tasting; not bothered by complexity or nuances in texture or flavor; malts and hops are carefully calibrated; a tangible physical "feel" distinguishes this beer; the taste is almost an afterthought, but there is a purity that is central to its appeal, not to mention the 5.5% alcohol/volume; Bronze Medal winner at the 1994 Great American Beer Festival. An uncomplicated companion for hearty sandwiches and snacks.

IDAHO CENTENNIAL PILSENER   CT   1.1
(Helena, Montana)
Large bubbles of foam signal artificial enhancers; a musty aroma further alarms you; while bubbles continue to rise rapidly, there is no genuine pizzazz or fizziness; dry, bland, rather lifeless beer; hops are flat; malt seems nonexistent; first brewed to celebrate this state's centennial (1890 to 1990).

IMPERIAL Lager   CB   1.3
(San Jose, Costa Rica)
Brief front-end flavor that quickly goes flat and bland; mild hops and almost nonexistent malt make this beer weak at the end.

IMPERIAL PILSENER   CB   2.9
(Punta Arenas, Chile)
Crisp with warmth and minimal sweetness alongside food; malt and hops play off each other with finesse; thick, high head with flat, uncomplex taste and a faraway sharpness that forces you to rely on the food at hand for flavor; some thick, bitter aftertaste around the tongue and sides of the mouth doesn't make you look forward to drinking this alone; color is impure, off-yellow. A thirst-quenching companion to salty salamis and pickled condiments.

INDIA Lager   CB   1.1
(Mayaguez, Puerto Rico)
Thick, essentially indiscernible taste and texture; ginger-ale color; barely satisfying; remains stale-tasting with food; "La Cerveza de Puerto Rico" is rather harsh and discordant; fortunately, it comes in a nonstandard 10-ounce can.

INDIANAPOLIS DUESSELDORFER
DRAFT ALE   MB   2.5
(Indianapolis, Indiana)
Yeast aroma quickly rises to the nose as very bruised-apple-like sharp taste hits the throat; hazy, pale golden, yeast-laden color with thick, big-bubbled head; yeast turns musty toward the end, along with an increase in the fermented apple mouthfeel; not highly distinctive; essentially for those with the patience to allow for an acquired taste. Sharpness is tempered and made sweeter with Italian hero sandwiches topped with peppers, onions, and tomato sauce.

INDIANAPOLIS MAIN STREET
PREMIUM LAGER   MB   3.1
(Indianapolis, Indiana)
Could be sharper and fizzier; possesses a certain edge and Midwestern graininess that suggest it is a wholesome, unexciting food companion; hops dominate malt in an unaffected, modest manner; beguiling and subtle. Goes with "Main Street" American foods such as hot dogs, corn on the cob, and fast food.

INDIO OSCURA Lager   **CB**   **1.6**
(Monterrey, Mexico)

Minimally thick, sweet, and somewhat bland; no zest or carbonation; almost smoky, musty aftertaste toward the end, at which
point it begins to lose its flavor and rapidly goes downhill; rich,
amber color rescues it from visual obscurity.

IRISH BRIGADE Ale   **CB**   **3.0**
(Warrington, England)

Toasty; slightly winey taste; mellow; dark red; smooth; soothingly
works its way around the mouth and tongue, encouraging food
to display its full flavor and texture; finishes warm and mellow,
like a good friend. Just right with hearty meat dishes such as
stews, barbecue, grilled steaks with onion rings.

IRONS HELLBENDER ALE   **MB**   **2.3**
(Lakewood, Colorado)

Flowery and light in taste and aroma; soft, subdued mouthfeel;
slight hop bitterness tends toward sour; even-handed with or
without food; a bit coarse-textured throughout; hazy, thinnish,
amber color; no head or Brussels lace; turns sweet, malty, and
flat; restrained, almost incomplete finish; essentially starts nowhere
and goes nowhere; the name is more exciting than the ale.

ISENBECK Lager   **CB**   **3.4**
(Hamm, Germany)

Smooth, pleasant, fruity taste; lacks zest; hoppiness at the end
helps; goes down easily, with grainy finish that is not harsh or
bothersome. A good match for sharp cheeses and mustards, specialty meats such as smoked ham, spicy salamis, and German
wursts.

IVANHOE ALE   **CT**   **0.1**
(Chico, California)

Handmade English-style ale; very smoky, cloudy, and carbonated; hovers between a somewhat repellent taste and no taste at
all; lots of fizzing and textural huffing and puffing; chemical taste
throughout; continuing effervescence is (almost) its only redeeming
feature; bad; I couldn't finish it.

JAMAICA BRAND RED ALE   **MB**   **3.3**
(Blue Lake, California)

Rich-looking and rich-tasting, with a quickly disappearing bitterness; turns thin as you swallow; gentle, light fruitiness has a
suggestion of nutty undertones; flowery hop taste becomes quite
powerful after several sips, presaging a big flavor that emerges
with food; yeasty, apple-cider aroma provides an invigorating up-
lift halfway through the bottle at the same time the beer regains
its full-bodied stature; not as crisp as label suggests, but still well
done; milk-chocolate color and yeast cloudiness and sediment at

the bottom of the glass; considering the complexity and balance requirements of this style, the brewer is to be commended for displaying a certain degree of daring to produce this commercially—and with panache. Goes well with grain dishes.

JAMES BOWIE KENTUCKY HILLS
LTD. PILSNER   CB   2.0
(La Crosse, Wisconsin)
Raw, tart, and flat, with a sharpness at the back of the mouth that keeps your attention; tea color is beguiling and unpilsener-like; plain and less invigorating than most American pilseners, but with slightly more taste; aftertaste lacks complexity or strength; gets blander as the bottle drains; boredom is a distinct possibility, but patience reveals that stage to be a precursor: the 40-ounce container, packaged to resemble a large whiskey bottle, offers a (very) slow mellowing out—giving you the chance to decide whether the wait is worth it. Best suited to light luncheon fare and plain sandwiches.

JAX Pilsener   CB   3.0
(San Antonio, Texas)
Light, but with enough grit to go along with hot or spicy foods; visually and nosewise similar to its even lighter cousin, Pearl; sweet, malt presence and carbonated vivacity distinguish it from other summertime throwaways; unpretentious; a tried-and-true thirst-quencher. I had my first one in Gulfport, Mississippi, back when the county was legally dry. A bottle went for 25 cents, and you and your friends could have five longnecks brought to the table for a grand total of one dollar. It helped pass the dog days of August, and will likely do the same for you. Well-suited to spicy Cajun and hot Southwestern dishes; also fried fish.

JENLAIN FRENCH COUNTRY ALE   CB   2.3
(Jenlain, France)
Sweet, plum-like taste with silky, wine smoothness; similar to a pale rosé wine; remains warm and somewhat removed from itself. Best after a meal, as a mellow *digestif.*

B E E R   F A C T

*T*echnically, Jenlain is in the specialty French *bière de garde* style—traditionally strong, full-flavored, fruity, bottle-conditioned, and all malt. The style originated in northern France near the Belgian border. Up until the early 1900s, more than 2,000 farmhouse breweries operated in France; Jenlain is one of about 30 that remain active today.

JET CITY ALE   CT   2.4
(Seattle, Washington)
Aroma is slightly oxidized, but taste is smooth and creamy with
apple-cider tang; medium-bodied and not complex at all—indeed, hops and malt and yeast kind of just sit there, neither as-
serting themselves nor interacting with each other; malt finally
takes over as the ale warms; eventually turns watery and uninteresting; starts much better than it finishes. (Although a major
brewery actually produces this beer, Jet City owner-brewer Jeff
Leggett uses his own recipe and ingredients and oversees the brewing process.)

JINDAO Lager   CB   4.0
(Qingdao, China)
Fresh, creamy, and refreshing—something of a surprise given its
cloudy paleness; lends a not-overwhelming sweetness to a meal;
could be a bit heavier texturally; holds its own overall; a very
drinkable beer. Excellent accompaniment to Chinese food, especially seafood-based dishes with shrimp or lobster.

JOHN BULL Ale   CB   2.9
(Burton-on-Trent, England)
Rather flat and tasteless with a cold crispness that makes for the
only excitement; decent, but essentially uninteresting; there is
substance to the texture, but that's not enough to put it over the
top. Good with heroes and other overstuffed sandwiches.

BEER FACT

*B*urton-on-Trent, known especially for its ales, is
probably the most famous brewing center in
Britain. It originally gained renown because of
the quality of its drinking water, which may be the
hardest in the world used in commercial brewing.

JOHN COURAGE EXPORT Lager   CB   2.8
(Bristol, England)
Cross between pale and dark beer, leaning toward dark; so-so in
the bottle without the positive attributes of either pale (prominent bitterness) or dark (crisp and clean); the draft version is
much more mellow, smooth, and satisfying. An all-purpose accompaniment to most cuisines.

JOHN PEEL Ale   CB   2.8
(Blackburn, England)
Sweet, caramel taste, soft and smooth; rising, pleasant, modulated sharpness as beer integrates with food; subtle fruit flavor,
almost cider-like in its wateriness; in the end, however, flatness

pervades and comes to be what is remembered. Try it with raw vegetables and dips.

JOSEPH MEENS' HOLLAND PREMIUM
Lager   **CB**   **1.0**
(Schinnen, Holland)
Nondescript sweetness rises to flatness on the roof of the mouth; remains unchallenging and rather devoid of balance and tangible ingredients; pale-golden color and very white head are the only things that attract your attention; slight off-tasting maltiness is last memory—not a good beer.

JUDGE BALDWIN'S BROWN ALE   **MB/BP**   **1.8**
(Colorado Springs, Colorado)
Cloves (distinctly not to style), some sweetness (true to style), low in alcohol (true to style), lots of flatness, and no fruitiness; hint of molasses?; faint citrus sharpness in finish. Sends too many mixed messages to be worthwhile.

JULIUS ECHTER HEFE-WEISSBIER   **CB**   **3.0**
(Wurzburg, Germany)
Combination buttered popcorn and distinct clove taste, with tart citrus accompaniment; passing sweetness; becomes a warmer, gentler blend as ingredients settle down; ultimately dry, with no aftertaste; somewhat watery; cloudy, faded-blond color, as expected from bottle-conditioning; drink when warm. Best with moderately seasoned pastas, turkey or chicken pot pies, and other dishes with crusts to absorb and mellow the harshness of the yeast and alcohol.

JUMPING COW AMBER ALE   **CT**   **2.3**
(New Ulm, Minnesota)
Fruity aroma, malty taste, smooth texture; goes from sweet to bitter to sour in one mouthful; fruitiness disappears and is replaced by sweet maltiness; sour finish; mildly filling; slight chocolate taste creates some excitement, but in the end this is a run-of-the-mill brew; doesn't grow on you, though it does tell you what it is right up front and goes downhill from there; it is finishable, however.

KAISER Pilsener   **CB**   **0.8**
(Queimados, Brazil)
Light, light, light; faint hint of old-fashioned ballpark beer, which really is nothing more (quite literally) than a canful of adjuncts— or cereals, as the label points out in Portuguese; something of a head, perhaps due more to the travails of travel and the wonders of brewing chemistry than to anything intrinsic to the beer; slightly sour at the back of the tongue; wispy mustiness lazily reaches the nose; quite weak texturally; cheaply made and cheap-tasting.

KAISER PILSENER   **CB**   **0.5**
(Frankfurt, Germany)
Very malty and flat; quite unpilsener-like; more reminiscent of a

chocolate malted; mild burnt flavor; no pizzazz at all; watery, flat, and entirely uninspiring; no hops of any consequence.

KAISERDOM EXTRA DRY Lager   CB   3.9
(Bamberg, Germany)

Very nicely balanced between malt and hops; homey, attractive malt aroma; remains crisp and evenly balanced with knife-like dryness and keen texture; durable yet fancy at the same time; mild, enhancing honey taste and aroma add to the strong finish; comes in a tasteful, all-black bottle with strong gold-lettered label; a nice package, inside and out. Try it with baked ham, pork chops, or a bacon, lettuce, and tomato sandwich.

KAISERDOM RAUCHBIER—
SMOKED BAVARIAN DARK   CB   3.9
(Bamberg, Germany)

Immediately smoky-tasting, but subordinated to a clear coldness on the palate; distinctive, restrained, and not overwhelming; a truly interesting and enlightening brew; purportedly the only smoked beer imported into the U.S. Goes with smoked trout, smoked oysters, or lox and cream cheese on a bagel.

B E E R   F A C T

*R*auch is the German word for "smoke." The area around Bamberg is famous for the smoked malts which characterize this unusual specialty beer.

KALYANI BLACK LABEL
PREMIUM LAGER   CB   3.5
(Bangalore, India)

Tart, sharp, and hoppy with dry, satisfying swallow; balanced and complex with strong backbone; surprisingly smooth; tasty and serviceable for beginners and experienced drinkers alike; finish is full and fresh. Works well with Mexican fare.

KAPUZINER WEIZEN KRISTALLKLAR   CB   3.1
(Kulmbach, Germany)

Subdued, smooth, clove taste and creamy texture; full, white head nicely tops red-golden body; clear and filtered, rather than the more typical *weizen* cloudiness from the bottle-conditioned yeast; emerging yeast taste at the finish; remains smooth and creamy to the end; could be a bit spritzier; lasting quality. Remains evenly balanced and tempered with Chinese food.

KAREL IV LAGER CB 3.6
(Czech Republic)

Lots of fresh graininess on first sip; mild hoppiness is appropriately gritty at the back of the throat; dry and a bit musty on the roof of the mouth; damp soil/wet straw aroma attests to its earthy origins, with a similar, but less enchanting, aftertaste; typical pale-golden color with small-bubbled head presents a classic lager picture; substantial sheets of Brussels lace add to the enjoyment; firm, forthright body from beginning to end; malty aromatic finish tops off a solid representation of the style. Fine with rice dishes such as risottos and pilafs, and with veal.

KARLSBEER Pilsener CB 3.2
(Karlovac, Yugoslavia)

Rounded, honeyed taste that quickly flattens and becomes a bit musty; somewhat thick on the tongue, but with a hoppy sharpness; malty aroma emerges as does an attenuated hop bitterness that is contained, not widespread, over the palate; may lose some of its complexity in its travels from the brewery; settles into a predictable, smooth companion. Try with vegetarian Japanese dishes such as vegetable teriyaki or tempura.

KB AUSTRALIAN Lager CB 2.9
(Sydney, New South Wales, Australia)

Tastier, with more gumption than its compatriot, Foster's; unpleasant sour aftertaste makes this beer difficult to drink without food or some other distraction; sharp, grainy taste returns and stays; okay in moderate amounts. Good with picnic fare or hearty roasted meat sandwiches.

KEO Lager CB 3.1
(Limassol, Cyprus)

Malty aroma, hoppy taste, with a dash of fishiness just to make things interesting; grainy presence comes forward, especially with spicy or salty foods; improves—tastier, more complex, better balanced—the more you drink it; reasonably steady Brussels lace diverts the eye from washed-out yellow color; finishes pleasantly grainy, but with little-to-no carbonation and definitely no head; generally friendly beer. Try with cheese/jalapeño nachos, kalamata olives, and salty snack foods.

**KESSLER LORELEI EXTRA PALE
LAGER** MB 3.2
(Helena, Montana)

Soft crispness and mild, placid flavor make this beer easy to handle; fruitiness emerges in mid-bottle; appropriate balance and complexity finish this surprisingly approachable beer. Try with meat or chicken pot pies, rice and beans, and sourdough bread with cheese.

KEY DARK Lager   CB   1.2
(Victoria, British Columbia, Canada)
Too smooth and watery; no immediate—or eventual—discernible
taste; mildly bitter, but that's about it; slight alcoholic warmth
eventually pushes its way through, but not enough to really notice; try something else.

KEYSTONE Pilsener   CB   0.9
(Golden, Colorado)
Mildly acrid, citrus taste, with paper-thin body and somewhat
old mouthfeel; chemically-induced head stays throughout; remains green-tasting and unfulfilling despite can's special inner
lining designed to reduce metallic taste; what we have here is not
the "Quality bottled beer taste" it bills itself as providing.

KILLIAN'S RED ALE   CB   2.3
**(Brewed by Coors in Golden,
Colorado)**
Vague, cherry lollipop taste with sharp, pinprick texture; cloying
sweetness at the back of the tongue needs starchy, absorbent food
to temper it; distinctive, non-American taste; thin in texture; bad
tendency for the round, sweet caramel-like taste to rapidly give
way to modulated sharpness.

KING COBRA MALT LIQUOR   CB   2.2
(St. Louis, Missouri)
Rounded, mild taste, with raw, green overlay; remains even-tast-
ing throughout a meal; some fizziness, though it is essentially
flat-tasting; not much body; Bronze Medal winner at the 1993
Great American Beer Festival.

KINGFISHER LAGER   CT   2.8
**(brewed and bottled in England for United Breweries,
Bangalore, India)**
Robust and tasty grain presence; integrated flavor is underpinned
by cold-water blandness; early on, the taste unpredictably peaks
and flattens out from sip to sip; persistent tangy sweetness offers
a cooling balance to spicy foods; oddly enough, with food, the
up-and-down vagaries of the beer settle into an interesting routine. A calming complement to curried rice, Tandoori chicken,
and other Indian dishes.

KINGPIN Lager   CB   1.0
(Mansfield, England)
Pallid, flat, thin, and essentially unexpressive; slight body appears
tentatively and fleetingly; label advises, "Best consumed within
3 days of opening"—that's being presumptuous—and optimistic;
A "college" beer meant for large-scale consumption, without much
attention to quality. Drink with dorm or pub food.

KIRIN DRAFT Lager   CB   2.3
(Brewed and bought in Tokyo, Japan)

Brewed for the Japanese market, not exported; sharp and attention-getting, with brief, flowery follow-through; close to full-bodied; flavor comes and quickly goes, replaced by flat, almost metallic
taste; doesn't integrate well with food; leaves a thickish aftertaste
on the tongue; hard to discern the ingredients in this beer; too
sharp and unforgiving.

KIRIN DRAFT Pilsener   CB   3.9
(Vancouver, British Columbia, Canada)

Sharp, straightforward taste and texture; mellow crispness accompanies an airy top with a heavy underpinning; emotionally
and spiritually satisfying, but not physically filling, making it easy
to enjoy more than one; retains aesthetic vigor to the last drop;
smooth and charming throughout. Nice with crisp raw vegetables, salads with sprouts, or mild, soft cheeses with unsalted
crackers.

KIRIN DRY DRAFT Pilsener   CB   4.0
(Tokyo, Japan)

Crisp and immediately satisfying, with inviting freshness; bit of
flat, off-taste on palate; stable, predictable, and full of flavor;
nicely balanced with pinpoints of appealing sparkle and body.
Goes well with grilled Japanese specialties such as yakitori (grilled
bits of skewered, marinated chicken) or negamaki (beef).

KIRIN ICHIBAN MALT LIQUOR   CB   4.0
(Tokyo, Japan)

Hoppy, sweet tang greets nose immediately, with follow-up cold,
rounded sharp taste that prepares the tongue for more; grain presence is full and complex; dry; tends to cling to the roof of the
mouth; strength and character mesh well with food; higher alcohol content is well hidden within the nuances of malt and
hops; strong and full of character; clearly a quality, well-thought-
out product. Goes well with barbecued and grilled foods.

KIRIN LAGER   CB   3.9
(Tokyo, Japan)

Crisp, but not sharp on the first and subsequent sips; malt is tangible and accommodating to food; clearly high quality, and clearly
made for mass consumption, with none of the nuances or little
touches that often personalize a beer as well-put-together as this
one. Excellent with fruited meat dishes and Japanese cuisine.

KIWI LAGER   CB   4.0
(Timaru, New Zealand)

Nicely crisp and fresh throughout; satisfyingly fills the mouth
with tantalizing faint, hop/barley taste that perfectly fits ongoing crackliness of texture; grain taste is even more deliciously ap-

parent; fresh and invigorating—have more than one to gain full pleasure. A good complement to all but hot/spicy foods.

KLOSTER SCHWARZBIER—MONKSHOF
Lager   **CB**   2.9
(Kulmbach, Germany)
Texturally complex, with a thread of sweetness from start to finish; pleasant, lingering taste; dark and brooding; too syrupy to be rated higher. But a good complement to a barbecued chicken sandwich.

KLOSTERBOCK MONKSHOF
Malt Liquor   **CB**   2.3
(Kulmbach, Germany)
Faint, quickly disappearing, burnt taste that is more acute at the back of the mouth; sweet but not cloying; transient, somewhat watery taste; drink this without food.

KODIAK PREMIUM LAGER   **CB**   2.5
(Saskatoon, Saskatchewan, Canada)
Mild; a bit sour, but pleasantly hoppy; well-balanced and roughly smooth; becomes more subdued with food; sweetness stretches toward the end; mild and somewhat matter-of-fact; recommended for those just beginning to sample the wonderful world of beer and others who just want a non-threatening, easy sipping drink; finishes with a hint of yeasty aroma; disappoints in the end— clearly its potential has not been approached.

KOFF Lager   **CB**   3.6
(Helsinki, Finland)
Flat on first taste; restrained aftertaste with small bubbles providing nice fizziness at the back of the throat; in general, invigorating, playing very well to taste expectations; soft, modulated finish is somewhat surprising, but certainly acceptable. Quite compatible with chicken and pasta.

KOKANEE GLACIER PILSENER (draft) **CB**   3.4
(Creston, British Columbia, Canada)
Creamy, soft, and chewy; calm and laid-back; flavorful and substantive with integrated graininess that remains intact and consistent with food; crisp, with staying power; appropriate for a warm, not hot, day, with time to idle away. Try it with summer seafood dishes.

KO'OLAU LAGER   **CB**   3.1
(Honolulu, Hawaii)
Appropriately mild, caramel taste; full-bodied, with subdued bitterness; strong, malty mouthfeel; pliable, textured drink that can be savored at leisure; caramel aroma enhances the enjoyment; creamy body at the end; a beer to enjoy on its own.

KOSMOS RESERVE LAGER (draft) **CB** **3.0**
(Shiner, Texas)
Full-bodied and quite chewy with distinct hop bitterness that follows a rounded bittersweetness on the roof of the mouth; gentle, lasting, figurative Brussels lace—its presence makes you pay attention to the undulating, alive taste and texture; vague citrus feel lurks in background; enjoyable fullness three-quarters of the way through; good—but be careful of the follow-through, it may pucker the sides of your mouth without warning. Pair with a good old mustard-slathered American hot dog.

KRAKUS LIGHT Pilsener **CB** **2.1**
(Zywiec, Poland)
Very pleasant wheat aroma that quickly falters; thin and watery with virtually no zest or fizz; no head or smoothness; sweet and pleasant, though clearly not fully developed; charming, but unable to offer a whole lot with food.

KRONEN CLASSIC ALL DARK Lager **CB** **2.1**
(Dortmund, Germany)
Rather undistinguished—you wait for an increase in appeal and nothing happens; flat-to-no head with faded, deep-red color; hint of warmth and caramel sweetness toward the end; flat, bland, and, unfortunately, very predictable.

KRONENBOURG PALE Lager **CB** **3.1**
(Strasbourg, France)
Rich, golden color; sparkling, malty, and strong; combined wine/beer taste, as befits its geographic location; medium-bodied and nicely balanced; some sharpness; has potential to wear thin too soon. Goes very well with duck and chicken.

KROPF DARK DRAFT Lager **CB** **2.6**
(Kassel, Germany)
Molasses aroma precedes light, but sharp, fizziness with a rounded, appealing swallow; satisfying without being challenging or pushy; finishes with a hint of sweetness and subtle malt; pleasant, but not exciting. A friendly backdrop to casual lunch foods such as a grilled cheese sandwich.

KROPF DRAFT Lager **CB** **2.3**
(Kassel, Germany)
Fruity, musty taste with sharp texture on first sip; fullness grows but fades into the background; some solidity and mild warmth are maintained; complexity tentatively emerges along with an appealing roundedness at the end of the bottle. Good with steaks and hamburgers.

TAP TIP

Your Nose, Your Glass, and You

P roper attention to glasses can make a great difference when tasting beers. Lack of a good head of foam might indicate the presence of grease or detergent film on the glass. Next time you're at a bar, smell an empty glass. A musty odor indicates the probable presence of dishwashing detergent. At home, rinse the glass with hot water and let stand to dry.

Also, the thinner the sides of the glass, the quicker your beer will warm up, particularly if you wrap your hand around the glass. That's one reason beers meant to be consumed warm—e.g., most ales—are generally served in goblets or tumblers that can be held by wrapping your hand around the glass; on the other hand, cold beers, like lagers, are often offered in mugs with handles to keep body warmth away from the thick glass surrounding the liquid.

KROPF EDEL PILS   **CB**   **2.9**
(Kassel, Germany)
Kind of hoppy at the outset; bland foretaste succeeded by subtle, complex, on-going taste involving the malts and yeast and hops; after the first bottle, the beer becomes lifeless and loses distinction; lack of depth hinders its staying power. Good with hot dogs with sauerkraut or grilled sausage sandwiches.

KUNSTMANN LAGER   **MB**   **2.7**
(Valdivia, Chile)
Uplifting effervescence brings along a sweetish clove taste that is a little flat on the tongue; sharp; slowly evolving licorice taste; texture tends toward flatness; pleasurable malt-hop balance.

KWAK Ale   **CB**   **2.1**
(Buggenhout, Belgium)
Wine bouquet with dull, sweet, fruity, wine taste that settles generously on the tongue; sweet acidity lingers on the palate, detracting from the taste of food; deep-amber color misleads you into expecting a more full-bodied, caramel taste, though there is some of that; sweetness increases as the glass is emptied, turning it into a rather unwanted experience: you do need a particular interest in this assertively tart, dry style (known as *zuur* in Flanders) to enjoy it; food is important to help absorb some of the alcohol and acidity. Try it with strong cheese before a meal.

LABATT CLASSIC Lager   CB   3.8
(Toronto, Ontario, Canada)

Smooth and mellow with some fizziness at the back of the throat; subtle complexity; smooth maltiness is the centerpiece of this calming, unaffected, quality brew; conservative, but with presence; gets a little too flat and a touch thick at the bottom of the glass; companionable and easy—very easy—going down. Try it with grilled salmon steaks.

LABATT'S Pilsener   CB   3.1
(Vancouver, British Columbia, Canada)

Uncomplicated, but good taste, in the back of the mouth; some crispness offset by rounded, sweetish malt body; taste tends to flatten relatively quickly; label proudly announces, "Union Made." Okay with hamburgers and other sandwiches.

LABATT'S BLUE PILSENER   CB   3.1
(Vancouver, British Columbia, Canada)

Tasty and fresh; consistent taste and texture, though lacking in subtlety; crispness increases with food, but ingredients remain relatively subdued; falls short of its promise. Compatible with fresh seafood.

LABATT'S 50 Ale   CB   3.7
(Vancouver, British Columbia, Canada)

Understatedly crisp and fresh, with not-quite-fruity aroma; taste grows on you, steadily and consistently; finishes with a hint of sourness that may or may not be attributable to food; warm and friendly enough to request another bottle. Subtly compatible with Italian foods.

LABATT'S VELVET CREAM STOUT   CB   3.1
(Edmonton, Alberta, Canada)

Fullness at the back of the throat, thin at the sides of the tongue; sweet fullness with a rim of bitterness at the back of the tongue; deep brown-black color is a bit muddy with a hint of red; no head to speak of; mushy at the end. Good with mildly flavored chicken dishes and relatively bland grain and rice dishes.

LA BELLE STRASBOURGEOISE Lager   CB   2.9
(Schiltigheim, France)

Heartier and sharper than some German and/or Austrian beers, but not as heavy or hoppy; pleasing sharpness distracts you, but not enough to keep you from wondering why you didn't order a stronger beer. Overwhelmed by full-flavored foods.

LA CANADA PALE ALE   MB   0.9
(Santa Fe, New Mexico)

Flat, fruity aroma matched by flat, fruity taste; hint of mustiness; uncomplicated and bland; yeast haze hides pale-gold color; medicinal, hospital taste emerges halfway through the bottle; insipid and uninteresting; hint of fruitiness lingers helpfully to let you know this is an ale; no head; weak in hops and malt; decent mild, semi-citrus sweetness remains throughout.

LA JOLLA PUMPHOUSE PORTER   MB/BP   0.0
(La Jolla, California)
Faintly sulfurous, more so as you drink it; flat, bland, utterly uninteresting, and distinctly unpleasant.

LANDLORD STRONG PALE ALE   CB   2.9
(Keighley, England)
Clover-honey sweetness goes directly to the upper palate; restrained hoppiness settles into the main flow of the liquid; emerging bitterness is acceptable after sweetness passes; definitely mellows as it warms; finish is dry with subtle character; a beer that definitely improves during the course of a meal, the rating is primarily based on its finish. Up-and-coming graininess matches nicely with well-spiced dishes like beef fajitas.

LANDSKRON PILS   CB   3.8
(Radeberg, Germany)
Immediate yeast/grain aroma and taste; texture is duller than expected; appealing honey sweetness remains central; color is light and golden; less carbonation and not as zippy and zesty as many other pilseners, but pleasing and almost sensuous. A good match with barbecue, spicy sausages, choucroute garni.

LAPIN KULTA Lager   CB   2.2
(Helsinki, Finland)
Fresh, clean, and semi-sharp; relatively tasteless and short on nuance; remains low-key and unassertive, but not unpleasant; hard to detect alcohol content, though it is supposedly present; ditto for hops and malt; texture is more attractive than taste, leaving you less than half satisfied, which is not enough to try this again.

BEER FACT

*F*inland, like its neighboring countries, restricts beer advertising, usually allowing it only for the lowest alcohol content brews. Unadvertised Lapin Kulta is in Class IVA, giving it an alcohol strength a little above the typical American pilsener (2.9 to 3.9%/weight) and about the same as an American premium pilsener (3.6 to 4.4%/weight).

LA TRAPPE ALE   AB   3.9
(Tilburg, Holland)
Not overwhelmingly fruity; mildly acidic; moderated sweetness

with sharp after-bite; hazy, reddish-brown color adds to the European ambience; remains crisp and fresh with cidery overtones; fizzy, loosely bubbled head diminishes quickly, but adds to the sharpness while it lasts; holds character and balance from start to finish; predominance of tangy hops makes itself apparent; good example of style; nicely settled sediment on the bottom; definitely well-made, but not to my taste; ends on a sweet note. Works well with sweetened pork dishes.

LEAVENWORTH HODGSON'S IPA
(draft)   BP   2.5
(Leavenworth, Washington)
Filling and fruity, but lacking in strength; zesty and fresh-tasting, though not particularly complex; malty fruitiness makes for a nice balance with the less-than-full hops flavor; light-amber color; minimal carbonation; keeps your interest; on the way to being a good IPA, but not yet there. Try it with pizza.

LEEUW PILSENER   CB   3.2
(Limburg, Holland)
Clean and flavorful overall; moderate effervescence; soft, inviting taste; invigorating, distinctive mouthfeel slides into mildly sour aftertaste; well-made, good example of a Dutch pilsener without any pretensions. Goes with cheese or ham sandwiches.

LEFFE BLOND ALE   MY   3.1
(Leffe, Belgium)
Tart and sharp with slight mustiness; full, yeast taste increases as beer warms; nice balance between hops and malt, with gentle bitterness predominating; slight haze fuzzes up pale-blond color; minimal winey aroma; sweet alcohol finish; in general, good representative of the style. A nice match for Southern-style foods, such as fried chicken and honey-glazed baked ham.

LEFT HAND MOTHERLODE
GOLDEN ALE   MB   2.4
(Longmont, Colorado)
Light and perfumey on first sip, followed by superficial floral aroma and taste; rather flighty and lacking substance; slight malt/hops presence; caramel aroma and taste emerge as it warms; humdrum and ordinary, generally flat and uninvigorating; golden color; finishes with pleasant, faint malty sweetness, with no aftertaste or cloyingness; this may be headed in the right direction, but it's hard to say. Partner it with bagels and lox.

LE GARDE Ale   CT   3.5
(White River Junction, Vermont)
French country beer, with amber-style roasted maltiness; not too alcoholic; moderated honey sweetness and flat texture; balance of hops and malt pleasingly integrated with the yeast and water

so no single ingredient steals or spoils the show; a good beer, delicious on its own, made with ingredients that are best savored without food.

LEINENKUGEL'S ORIGINAL PREMIUM
Lager   CB   3.1
(Chippewa Falls, Wisconsin)

Thin, light, and sweet; thick, airy head remains for at least half of the bottle; even-tasting; almost flat, but not distracting; distinctive in its mildly sweet blandness; may just grow on you after two to three bottles; typically Midwestern: mild, beguiling, and undemanding; Gold Medal winner at the 1993 Great American Beer Festival. Try it with grilled or barbecued red meats, baked beans, or a hearty black bean soup.

LEINENKUGEL RED LAGER   CB   2.1
(Chippewa Falls, Wisconsin)

Brutish and fizzy, with no complexity; a nasty undertow; unstylish and straightforward; hint of sweetness; fast-disappearing Brussels lace and dirty amber-chocolate color reflect neither a good lager nor a good example of the namesake color; some substance struggles through at the end, but essentially a disappointment; flat and uninvigorating.

LEON DE ORO CERVEZA ESPECIAL
Lager   CB   3.8
(Antartida, Argentina)

Warm, enveloping, honey aroma accompanies warm, filling, honey taste underpinned by lightning strike of carbonation/fizziness and hint of lemon; flattens and weakens but hangs on to its core flavor by the end of the bottle; essentially tasty and attractive; based on one note, it still holds promise. Satisfying with burritos, empanadas, and other South-of-the-border foods.

LEOPARD DELUXE Pilsener   CB   3.0
(Hastings, New Zealand)

Bland but tasty; bitter initial taste; smooth and unobtrusive; appealing, mild hop presence and faint fruitiness enhance this light- to medium-bodied brew; increasing strength halfway through the bottle. A reliable seafood companion.

LIEFMANS KRIEKBIER CB 3.9
(Oudenaarde, Belgium)

Queen Anne cherry red; mild and smooth with a sweet and sour balance; cross between beer and wine; minor sparkle on the tongue; if this were a delicate wine, it would be overwhelmed by any food; subdued, cherry flavor nicely balanced by fermentation and the yeastiness itself; charming and delightful; some stick-to-your-tongue texture; full and musty at the end. Perfect for sipping after dinner with chocolate desserts.

BEER FACT

*B*rewed once a year at the time of the July harvest of Schaerbeeck cherries, Liefmans Kriekbier is made with the addition of one pound of this relatively scarce shiny red fruit to each gallon of six-month-aged Goudenband Brown Ale. The resulting product is then matured for eight months, after which it is filtered and bottled in Champagne-like bottles and stored in the brewery's caves. It is at least two years old by the time it reaches retailers' shelves.

LIMACHE CERVEZA TIPO CRUDA
Lager CB 3.2
(Limache, Chile)

Fills the mouth on the first sip; fresh and peppy in the throat, with a hint of acidity that is acceptable and refreshing; flavors are uninhibited, allowed to circulate and percolate though the texture is a bit flat; it maintains its integrity and character nonetheless; a little thin and almost salty at the end; when this beer is drunk fresh it is integrated and has interest. Try with a *completo* (Chilean sausages with garnishes).

LIND RASPBERRY WHEAT MB 1.2
(San Leandro, California)

Raspberry flavor is full and genuine, but tastes and smells like soda pop, without the fizz; overall, flat and boring; uncomplicated, with no interesting features.

LINDEMANS KRIEK—LAMBIC CB 2.0
(Vlezenbeek, Belgium)

This red, Belgian, cherry-flavored brew tastes and smells like the cherry sodas I knew as a kid—with more bite, of course, but the same amount of sparkle; resembles a spritzy wine cooler; indeed, is more of a wine than a beer; clearly a pre-dinner drink or one to accompany a fruit dessert; label touts it as one of the five best beers in the world, but it's too thin, light, and sweetly fruity to be on my best beers list; comes in a thick, green, corked bottle; drink in a Champagne or thistle-shaped glass. A pre-dinner drink or after-meal companion for fresh fruit with cheese.

LINDEMANS PECHE LAMBIC   CB   1.3
(Vlezenbeek, Belgium)

Immediate peach aroma—like a peach liqueur with Sprite: sweet and overachieving; similar to peach-flavored Champagne—hard to know it's a beer; ingredients from different worlds are brought together in a cheap, wine-cooler taste; too fruity to go with food; finish is like old, canned juice or semi-alcoholic cider; sticks to the roof of the mouth. An after-dinner drink.

LITTLE KING'S CREAM ALE   CB   2.0
(Cincinnati, Ohio)

Soft and creamy; hint of bitterness; mellow, quick refreshment with little substance or flavor profile—basically, it does its appointed job, which is to cool you down, quench your thirst, and encourage enjoyment of the food—so why complain? Good with grilled meat or poultry.

LONDON LIGHT Pilsener   CB   2.2
(London, England)

Watery and very lightly carbonated; empty-tasting, as if there are no innards; not unpleasant going down; a bit sour at the end—but at least that suggests it's alive. Nice with tomato soup and a ham sandwich.

LONE STAR Lager   CB   3.1
(San Antonio, Texas)

Traditional, crisp, common-beer mouthfeel; a workingman's brew with minimal body; fresh-tasting and to the point; a beer you could drink a lot of, but wouldn't necessarily write home about. "The National Beer of Texas"; Silver Medal winner at the 1993 Great American Beer Festival and Bronze Medal winner in 1994. Pour with down-home dishes such as chicken-fried steak with mashed potatoes and black-eyed peas.

LONE STAR NATURAL BOCK   CB   2.0
(San Antonio, Texas)

Creamy taste and texture, with only a quick, slight hint of sourness; mild, rather weak taste plays around on the upper palate and back of the mouth; smooth and easy going down; light amber-copper color holds a minimal but tangible head; nicely fashioned thick rings of Brussels lace stay just above the liquid as the beer level goes down; not full-tasting; relatively characterless; with more taste, it very well could have been a contender, but in the end it couldn't assert its presence—a genuine bock would easily knock it out of the ring. Pleasant with unfussy chicken dishes or garden salads with a good vinaigrette.

LONGXIANG Pilsener   CB   2.1
(Beijing, China)

Mildly fruity with thickness on the tongue; lightly carbonated; remains flat, but with promise that unfortunately goes nowhere; sweet, benign malt taste; not quite bland but certainly not full of flavor; actually more watery taste as bottle is emptied; needs good, zesty fistful of roasted nuts to pep it up. Match with Szechuan and Hunan food.

LORD CHESTERFIELD ALE   CB   2.5
(Pottsville, Pennsylvania)

Light and fizzy with ongoing aftertaste; ordinary golden color; moderate hop aroma; rather unassuming without hint of briskness; sweetness emerges after awhile so it is much better at midbottle than at outset; quietly competent and unexceptional. Serve with pork chops or simple chicken entrées.

LORIMER'S SCOTTISH BEER Ale   CB   2.6
(Edinburgh, Scotland)

Sharp, honey aroma and taste, with expected jolt from fizz not apparent; burnt, smoky, paper taste comes on quickly and dominates; dark, apple-cider color with gilt-brown undertones, shades, and shadows; malty and mildly pungent at the finish, with a thinnish texture as if running out of oomph; almost, but not quite, an ale. Doesn't quite keep up with accompanying foods.

LOS GATOS OKTOBERFEST Ale
(draft)   BP   0.1
(Los Gatos, California)

A little bit of citrus with a taste of sulphur which even the hops can't hide; remains uninviting, with an unpleasantly sour emphasis; green and raw; hard to finish (starting wasn't easy, either).

LOST COAST DOWNTOWN
BROWN ALE   MB   3.2
(Eureka, California)

Full, tasty, and entertainingly balanced; smooth with pleasant yeast aroma; nice, creamy smoothness, with thin but consistent head; lends mildly fruity, faint, and tart counterbalance to roasted main dishes; well-made; taste and texture flatten at the end; Bronze Medal winner at the 1993 Great American Beer Festival. Fine with roasted poultry and meats or a green salad.

LOST COAST STOUT   MB   3.3
(Eureka, California)

Appropriately bitter burnt-malt taste; smooth with rough edges; coppery, somewhat thin head; quickly becomes flat, especially up against spicy dishes; not as mouth-filling as stout should be, but otherwise has most style characteristics; step or two away from being a top-quality confection; sweet, gentle, finish; very good beginning, but maker must learn to master the ending as well. Serve with game meats, grilled mushrooms.

LOWENBRAU Pilsener   **CB**   **2.9**
(brewed by Miller in Albany, Georgia;
Fulton, New York;
and Milwaukee, Wisconsin)
Malty, grainy aroma that encourages the taste to spread out, covering the tongue and sides of the mouth; hint of sweetness with spicy foods improves the beer, but lessens the food's desirability; well-calibrated balance between malt and hops eases the passage from mid-bottle forward while making evident a firmness otherwise hidden; finishes relatively hoppy, with emphasis on relative; at one time this was considered an exotic import, but in the increasingly competitive and more sophisticated world of beer, it is now simply average. Goes with a pastrami sandwich.

LOWENBRAU ZURICH Pilsener   **CB**   **3.0**
(Zurich, Switzerland)
Soft, full grain taste with flavor that quickly drops off; tangy and smooth; a lot of promise, but not enough follow-through with highly flavored foods; sweet mellowness takes over after the food is gone, accompanied by fullness that was missing earlier. Appropriate for relatively bland main-course chicken dishes.

LUCIFER Ale/Lager   **CB**   **1.1**
(Dentergem, Belgium)
Sour bitterness with thin texture; faint odor of fresh varnish (turpey); needs to be forced down to finish it; unlike its stronger, more assertive cousin, Duvel, this beer is less sharp and lacking in character; not the best example of the usually well-regarded Belgian beers.

LUCKY LAGER   **CB**   **0.8**
(brewed by Labatt in Vancouver, British Columbia, Canada)
Tasteless, light, watery, and bland, with almost undetectable harshness that thankfully breaks up the monotony; despite relatively average alcohol content (5%/volume), this weak beer remains boring.

MacANDREW'S SCOTCH ALE   **CB**   **3.2**
(Edinburgh, Scotland)
Amazingly creamy with satisfying mix of bitter and sweet, with emphasis on the former; lovely, clouded-amber color, topped nicely with a waxy, milky foam; distinct wine taste emerges as the food settles; appears to be more sour with food, sweeter and more mellow alone; contains some surprises, not all of them pleasant. Goes with sausages, sharp cheeses.

MACCABEE Lager   **CB**   **2.2**
(Netanya, Israel)

Sharp and bitter with flat aftertaste; evolves into sourness with some rounding off at the edges; bile-like at the back of the throat; hint of grain; end is clearly better than the beginning; establishes some warmth and calmness, but still no complexity.

MACKESON TRIPLE XXX STOUT   **CB**   **4.1**
(London, England)

Good, dark, sweet, burnt taste; silky and enjoyable; tasty with a wide range of foods as its subdued zest quickly integrates with the food; remarkably balanced, with taste and texture very close to perfectly complementing each other; a good example of a traditional milk stout. I've never had a better match of food and beer. Fantastic with any highly-spiced or barbecued foods; equally good with rich stews, duck, and game.

MACK-ØL ARCTIC BEER PILSNER   **CB**   **2.9**
(Tromsø, Norway)

Wheat taste at the back of the mouth on first sip, but fades quickly; even-tempered and sharp; nicely subtle texture and taste go well with sweet grain mouthfeel with bit of edge on it. Goes with a broad range of foods.

B E E R   F A C T

*S*ituated north of the Arctic Circle, Mack claims to be the most northerly brewery in the world. *Øl* means "beer" in Norwegian.

MAES PILS   **CB**   **3.0**
(Waterloo, Belgium)

Sharp and mildly sour with a cleansing palate; no head and very light color make it look puny; mellows into tart sweetness at the end of a meal; prickly edge, not unappetizing, remains attributable to the hops; delicate bouquet is reflected in the light texture of the beer; passively dry; tantalizing, but not entirely satisfying. Bland thickness holds steady alongside grilled meats and mild cheeses.

MAGNUM MALT LIQUOR   **CB**   **1.4**
(brewed by Miller in Milwaukee,
Wisconsin; Fort Wayne, Indiana; et. al.)

Silky smooth to the point of wishy-washy; tasteless; no texture or complexity—indeed, no hint of any ingredients; no gustatory intrusions, except for a bit of perfume; a beer no one can complain about since it doesn't engage you when you drink it; the makers of this beer clearly had the goal of not scaring off any potential American drinkers—except, of course, those who enjoy beer; Silver Medal winner at the 1993 Great American Beer Festival.

MAISEL'S HEFE WEISSE   **CB**   **4.0**
(Bayreuth, Germany)
Pinch of clove kicks in on the second sip and lingers long after you get your mouth out of the creamy foam that tops off the hazy, amber color pockmarked with gently rising golden bubbles; cloves remain dominant, gently turning sweet; a touch of astringency going down the throat; texture, taste, and aroma balance and integrate about halfway through the bottle, resulting in a pleasant, good example of what *weissbier* is supposed to be; matches the nuances of food very well; tinge of sharpness permeates the inner recesses of the mouth; quite yeasty and rather softly full-bodied; finishes with a clove/yeast flourish. A good pairing with barbecued baby spareribs.

MAISEL'S WEIZEN   **CB**   **2.0**
(Bayreuth, Germany)
Light for a *weizen*; almost tasteless with well-seasoned or spicy foods; very foamy; unimpressive and without redeeming characteristics; no real negative qualities, just no positive ones.

MAISEL'S WEIZEN KRISTALL-KLAR   **CB**   **2.5**
(Bayreuth, Germany)
Very fine bubbles and a direct hit of cloves as the first swallow finds the back of the mouth; finely tuned with a soft, lacy backbone; remains soft and pliable with soft-textured foods; head stays creamy and smooth throughout; hint of rising bitterness toward the bottom of the bottle; warming and sweetish at the end. Enveloping pungent sweetness develops with barbecued foods and Sloppy Joe sandwiches.

MAMBA Malt Liquor   **CB**   **3.1**
(Abidjan, Ivory Coast)
Surprising chewiness along with a prickly sharpness that evolves into a flatness on the sides of the tongue; this is a golden beer with a substantial but rapidly disappearing head; creamy texture in the entire mouth, along with a fruity wine mouthfeel; becomes more mellow and even-tempered well into a meal; almost syrupy in its wine-like mouthfeel; not complex; silky; tending toward bland; aftertaste is too sweet. Good with duck, steaks, and cold cuts.

MANHATTAN BRITISH BITTER (draft)   **MB/BP**   **2.1**
(New York, New York)
Fruity, fresh lime taste roams around the palate and finds its way

into all of the crevices of the mouth; very yeasty; citrus presence comes to the fore without food; tends toward wateriness—too much so.

MANHATTAN EXTRA STOUT (draft)   MB/BP   4.0
(New York, New York)
Long-lasting beige head on top of almost perfect deep-brown/black body; highly alcoholic; mild and very attractive burnt-malt taste, the bitterness of which doesn't linger, while the chocolatey taste does; develops a hard creaminess with an attention-getting edge; full and almost rich; delicious on its own.

MANHATTAN GOLD Lager   CT   2.1
(Wilkes-Barre, Pennsylvania)
Tangy-tart with no real texture, but nice color; warmer and more integrated with "comfort" foods; has an iron, river-water taste; too much hoppiness for its own good. Serve with meat loaf or Salisbury steak with mashed potatoes.

MANHATTAN ROYAL AMBER (draft)   MB/BP   3.2
(New York, New York)
Airy, light head on top of deep-red, serious body that is forthright in taste and overall presence; some citrus tone; restrained freshness is invigorating; gentle maltiness is felt throughout; increasingly fruity as it warms; a bit prepubescent, but headed in the right direction. Good with grilled fish.

MANHATTAN SPECIAL STOUT (draft)   MB/BP   3.3
(New York, New York)
Very soft, restrained, burnt taste; not heavy at all; flatness on the tongue; without food, it remains smooth and goes down gently and unobtrusively; feels as if you could drink it forever and it would remain smooth and easy. Try it with chocolate candy or a sweet dessert.

MANHATTAN TAILSPIN BROWN ALE
(draft)   MB/BP   3.1
(New York, New York)
Soft and somewhat chewy; vaguely integrated with mild spiciness and fruitiness; seeks and finds the crevices of your mouth; calming and plain in an attractive way; perfectly enjoyable without food, especially on a cold day. Try with slices of baked Virginia ham or medium-sharp cheeses.

NOTE: The Manhattan Brewing Company has changed ownership. Check to see which beers have come and gone and which are new.

T A P   T I P

Flat, Fizzy Fixes

*I*s your draft beer flat? A leak in the keg or lines or improper keg pressure can cause a freshly tapped brew to lose its zest. Bottom-of-the-barrel remnants could also be the culprit.

Is your beer too fizzy? Partially clogged or dented lines, or lines not kept sufficiently cold, may result in too much carbonation.

Ask the bartender or server for bottled beer if you are served a draft with either of these defects.

MANHATTAN WINTER WARMER
Ale (draft; annual)   **MB/BP**   **3.8**
(New York, New York)

Very soft with a hearty dollop of alcohol-wrapped sweetness, making it almost cider-like; similar to a decent barley wine; like any good winter brew, this one packs quite a wallop, leaving a nice lingering glow in its 10%-alcohol wake; drink in front of a roaring fire. Interesting alone or with desserts such as sponge cake or fruit cobbler.

MANILA GOLD PALE PILSEN   **CB**   **3.1**
(Cabuyao, Philippines)

Moderated freshness, quickly flattening into prolonged dryness; remains appropriately malty and thick on the roof of the mouth with food; a little heavier than a standard pilsener; generally flat and not complex; sharpness on the edges of the tongue; unassuming, dry finish with a tantalizing hint of rice; tasty and flavorful, as is true of Filipino beers in general. Good with deli food.

MAREDSOUS ABBEY ALE   **AB**   **4.1**
(Denee, Belgium)

Fresh, clean aroma greets first sip, with a nice, fruity backdrop; cloudy, yeasty look gives off a glowing, frosty appearance topped by a thin layer of long-lasting head; sharp, readily apparent alcohol presence; full-bodied, very obvious yeast presence; appropriately balanced fruitiness has banana overtones; heavy on the hops and malt with reduced fruitiness and increased alcohol as the bottle is finished; good example of solid, traditional abbey ale with backbone and palpable presence; not for the fainthearted; finish is warm and satisfying. Sip this slowy, like a brandy, after a hearty meal.

MARIN OLD DIPSEA BARLEY WINE   **MB**   **3.0**
(Larkspur, California)

Strong; rich, fruity taste fills the mouth nicely; quite hoppy, with subtle maltiness; almost whiskey-like; a bit thin; has staying power; be careful not to drink too much—its potency is potentially overwhelming. Sip and savor after dinner accompanied by chocolates.

MARITIME FLAGSHIP RED ALE
(draft)   **MB**   **3.0**
(Seattle, Washington)

Flowery and bitter caramel tastes balance each other on initial sip, while a toasted aroma wafts pleasantly in the background; malty smoothness with a touch of coffee taste; copper-brown color; a bit cloying, but not enough to be troublesome. A friendly accompaniment to a bagel with cream cheese.

MARITIME ISLANDER PALE ALE
(draft)   **MB**   **2.8**
(Seattle, Washington)

Fresh, clean aroma with the pleasant bitterness of a pale ale plus a sharp fruitiness; color is classically pale-gold; highly hopped and a little chewy; stimulates the appetite, thereby increasing the enjoyment of food; one-dimensional, uncomplex hop character; sheets of Brussels lace testify to its freshness; finishes like it started: clean and bitter/dry; unfortunately, it leaves you thirstier than when you started. Goes with a tomato-and-cheese sandwich.

MARITIME NIGHTWATCH ALE
(draft)   **MB**   **3.0**
(Seattle, Washington)

Warm and smooth with tantalizing pinch of hops at the back of the mouth; auburn-brown color and curtains of Brussels lace make for an attractive visual package; fresh-bread aroma stays throughout; calm maltiness; no apparent fruitiness or yeast presence; tepid but flavorful—a beer to calm your stomach and massage your senses. Complements bean and grain dishes, especially black bean soup.

MARKSMAN LAGER   **CB**   **3.3**
(Mansfield, England)

Sharply crisp with mild mustiness; light-hearted and direct with restrained sweetness that underpins sparkling heartiness; maintains a certain fruitiness that is not interfering; pleasant and entertaining; smooth and robust in the English manner. A subtle complement to seafood pasta dishes.

MARTIN'S PALE ALE   **CB**   **3.5**
(Antwerp, Belgium)

Honeyed smoothness and soft backbone greet the palate; steady, retained head tops off the acid underlying the rest of the body;

subtle balance with a warmth and mild maltiness; fluffy pieces of foam cling to the side of the glass; some complexity and strength are lost at the end—a shame. Delicious with broiled steak or a snack of aged Cheddar cheese with crunchy apple wedges.

MATEEN TRIPLE ALE   AB   3.4
(Melle/Ghent, Belgium)

Light and dainty with a beguiling combination of alcohol and mild hops; brewed in the monastery style, its soft, foamy head remains thick and bubbly; soothing, accommodating, unobtrusive light color is a bit (appropriately) cloudy; finish is a touch fruity; yeasty in taste and visually quite pleasant but stumbles briefly at the end of the bottle, then recovers nicely, thanks to the presence of yeast. A tasty companion for a bagel with smoked salmon and cream cheese.

MAUI LAGER   CB   3.9
(Wailuku, Maui, Hawaii)

Immediate inviting odor transforms easily into sweet taste at the front of the palate and sharp, sour taste at the back; well-founded, continuing integration of smooth and sharp, but sharp eventually predominates and detracts from overall body, aroma, and subtlety; grain taste remains as a nice underlay; an attractive partner at mealtime. Accompanies fish from the deep sea, such as mahi mahi or tuna.

MAXIMATOR DARK DOPPELBOCK   CB   3.5
(Munich, Germany)

Coca-Cola–colored; smoky-tasting with very little carbonation; very flavorful, with body and character; malt dominates; increasing complexity, strength, and backbone with food; smoothes out at the end of the bottle with a touch of fruity aroma; strong and chewy; gives you a run for your money. Try it with Danish pastry or similar desserts.

McEWAN'S EXPORT INDIA PALE ALE   CB   4.0
(Edinburgh, Scotland)

Attractive, hoppy fruitiness and sharp fizziness greet you; full in flavor and satisfying; remains fresh and zesty throughout; dainty Brussels lace in layered patterns lasts until the glass is empty, and beyond; thick head; overall, flavor stays strong, constant, and predictable; clearly a quality, well-thought-out product. Accompanies rare roast beef, baked ham, beef Wellington.

McEWAN'S SCOTCH ALE   CB   3.8
(Edinburgh, Scotland)

Full, thick, and perhaps too sweet; virtually chewable; deep-bodied; flavorful burnt-caramel taste; food should be chosen carefully for this handsome, silky, molasses-like brew. Best as an after-dinner drink, but pleasant with Virginia ham or smoked turkey.

McFARLAND GOLDEN FIRE Ale CB 3.9
(Milan, Italy)

Restrained crispness with perimeter of sharp hoppiness that sticks to the roof of the mouth; malt kicks in after two to three sips; remains fresh and motivates you to drink more, even though balance is sequential rather than simultaneous; passive, golden color; mere hint of head appropriately tops off this understated and not entirely satisfying brew; assertively tasty, but quietly so; grain and malt bouquet emerge in the finish; malt is nicely hidden, though with presence. I drank this in a tulip-shaped wine glass, quite suitable to the gentleness of the ingredients. Good with cheese and fresh fruit.

**McMENAMINS BLACK RABBIT
PORTER** BP 2.7
(Portland, Oregon)

Gentle, roasted malts and smooth mouthfeel make this a well-calibrated beer with pleasant taste and textural balance; unfortunately, the texture part of the equation is relatively thin, ultimately resulting in the mellow roastedness becoming the main player; rich, amber-brown color; some spiciness pops up at the end—a nice touch; an attractive, though not outstanding, porter. Good with shellfish.

McMENAMINS FREUDIAN SIP ALE BP 3.3
(Portland, Oregon)

Fresh and lightly fruity, incorporating a grapefruit tang with apple aroma; subdued hoppiness; pleasingly patterned, fragile Brussels lace lasts all the way through; ingredients are carefully calibrated to maximize the general public's acceptance and the knowledgeable drinker's interest (McMenamins excels like no one else in striking this hard-to-identify balance with all of its dozen or so brews); hint of cloves on exhalation; even-tempered and very easy to drink; a good beer for the novice ale customer. Very nice with cold seafood dishes.

**McMENAMINS HAMMERHEAD
AMBER ALE** BP 2.0
(Portland, Oregon)

Somewhat flat and deficient in hops; vague, fruity aroma kind of drifts around; medium-bodied; spotty, unpatterned Brussels lace; exudes some warmth with food, but stops short of any real interest; intimations of being good, but doesn't deliver; finishes with a surprisingly gentle hoppiness.

McMENAMINS NEBRASKA BITTER Ale BP 2.9
(Portland, Oregon)

Light, fruity, and gently bitter; fantastic patterns of Brussels lace decorate the circumference of the glass; rich, yellow color adds to the visuals (and orals); fizzy hoppiness increases alongside food;

citrus aroma emerges and becomes full-blown at the end; unfortunately, the flavor flattens at the same time—too bad: This beer is definitely headed in the right direction. Try it with chicken dishes.

McMENAMINS RUBY RASPBERRY ALE   BP   3.0
(Portland, Oregon)

Looks like pink grapefruit juice, tastes mildly of raspberries; sipping sweet, not cloying or overwhelming like many other fruit beers; light and texturally unobtrusive; quite appealing as a novelty drink, and a good match with a pastry dessert, especially a chocolate one.

McMENAMINS TERMINATOR STOUT   BP   2.1
(Portland, Oregon)

More bitter than roasted; remains too flat and simplistic, lacking nuance and alcohol; bitterness increases further, along with an insignificant sweet taste; mild, roasted aroma; the brewer has calibrated it to be an obvious stout that is also palatable to the general public; good commercial instincts, but shy of the real thing. Ask for oysters with this, and hope for the best.

McNALLY'S EXTRA ALE   CB   1.9
(Calgary, Alberta, Canada)

No head; full, apple-juice flavor with no fizz or pizzazz—almost as if it came right out of the cider press; aromatic flavor; not a good match with food; more filling at the end, but not enough to change my opinion.

McSORLEY'S ALE   CT   2.0
(La Crosse, Wisconsin)

Pungent, citrus-honey aroma mellows after two to three sniffs; warm, gentle taste with faint hops and quality water; rather simple and uncomplicated; light-bodied and unfruity; some yeasty fruitiness begins to emerge as it warms, but remains faint; pleasant and undemanding; overall, weak and lacking character; go to McSorley's for the ambience, not for this ale.

B E E R   F A C T

*M*cSorley's Old Ale House, a Manhattan landmark since 1864, is known for its conviviality as well as the grandeur of its massive wooden bar. The draft ale served there is brewed in Philadelphia. The bottled ale is made in La Crosse, Wisconsin, and its label proclaims: "The older the fiddle, the sweeter the tune."

McTARNAHAN'S SCOTTISH ALE MB 3.8
(Portland, Oregon)
Nice, malty, food-like aroma with a hint of floweriness; almost like drinking bread; rich, creamy mouthfeel with light caramel color and taste; finishes with a pleasant caramel aroma, taste, warmth, and color; well-made and professionally balanced; perfect with roast chicken.

MEDALLA DE ORO LAGER CB 2.3
(Guatemala City, Guatemala)
Dull and fruity on first sip; relatively rapid flatness occurring on surface of the tongue; some flavor and relative warmth oozes up at end of the bottle; fruity aroma, but stale smelliness remains throughout; cereal/grain taste is also evident from start to finish.

MEDALLA LIGHT Pilsener CB 0.8
(San Juan, Puerto Rico)
Very fizzy; mildly light with a back-of-the-tongue aftertaste; doesn't contribute to or detract from food; clearly is attempting to appeal to the lowest common denominator; hint of warmth is its only redeeming feature; thickness occurs at the end; it's not bad-tasting, just no-tasting.

MENDOCINO BLACK HAWK STOUT MB 3.4
(Hopland, California)
Somewhat flat with no head and a fizzy bitter undertow; burnt flavor dissipates quickly; deep-brown color and malty nose enhance the stout definition; a good, sweet balance with smoked fish—the food enhances and sets off the stout and vice versa—a sweet combination; settles into a predictable, languid flow with less texture, peak-performing hops, and modulated sweetness; appears to have enviable ability to reflect the best in the food though it retains some immaturity throughout. Delicious with smoked salmon; an equally interesting match with barbecued ribs.

MENDOCINO RED TAIL ALE MB/BP 2.5
(Hopland, California)
Sharply fruity with fast-disappearing fizziness; too much tang at the outset; with warmth, the unwanted zip diminishes; better without food; some energizing fruitiness, but not outstanding.

MESSINA PILSENER CB 4.1
(Milan, Italy)
Typical pilsener reminiscent of Rheingold and Schaefer at the ballparks; hoppy and purely satisfying in a direct, uninhibited way; nicely balanced with constantly refreshing palate; light and uplifting with substance and piquancy; fun to drink. Tasty accompaniment to antipasto, pastas, and Italian specialty meats that aren't very spicy.

MICHAEL SHEA'S IRISH AMBER
Lager (draft)   **CT**   **3.0**
(Utica, New York)

Light and fluffy with sedated hoppiness that fades into a soda-like texture; similar to flavored water, but in a positive, tasty sense; foggy, deep amber is reminiscent of Irish bogs; remains clean and unfilling, yet satisfying; you could probably drink gallons of this stuff without feeling it too much; pleasant, even without food. Try with salty snacks such as nuts and pretzels.

MICHELOB DARK Lager   CB   1.8
(brewed by Anheuser-Busch in St. Louis, Missouri)

Tastier and maltier than its dry cousin, but still weak and relatively boring; toasted flavor redeems it somewhat; diminishing hop presence makes it seem sweeter than it actually is; a minimally serviceable brew.

MICHELOB DRY Lager   CB   2.1
**(brewed by Anheuser-Busch in
St. Louis, Missouri)**

Softly pallid, clean, and bold, but with taste that doesn't match the promise; relies on texture rather than aroma, taste, or complexity; distinctive but not significantly so; not a good complement to food.

B E E R   F A C T

*T*he Michelob name was adapted from a town in Czechoslovakia named Michalovce. It's not the first time Anheuser-Busch found inspiration in European geography to name a beer, however. In 1876, Adolphus Busch wished to invest his newly created brew with Old World character, so named it Budweiser, after the royal Bohemian town of Budweis (formerly Ceske Budejovice). The local brew in Budweis, known as the "beer of kings," also inspired Busch to call his the "king of beers."

MICKEY'S MALT LIQUOR   CB   3.1
(La Crosse, Wisconsin)

Smooth, light, and easy-flowing; even-tempered and predictable throughout; surprisingly pleasant. Gold Medal winner at the 1993 Great American Beer Festival. Accompanies virtually anything.

MIDNIGHT DRAGON GOLD
RESERVE ALE   **CT**   **1.5**
(La Crosse, Wisconsin)

Malty, hoppy, sweet-and-sour on first sips; ingredients quickly settle down into uniform, slightly sweetish, thickish mixture; not enough bulk and backbone; eventually becomes mildly interesting; gives too little, too late; no fruitiness, no alcohol presence, and hardly any yeast—not exactly the signs of a good ale.

MIDNIGHT DRAGON MALT LIQUOR   CT   1.1
(La Crosse, Wisconsin)

Alternatingly strong and weak, and very soft on the palate—hard to tell it's malt liquor; slight chunky sweetness emerges; essentially benign and sympathetic with plain foods; pale, almost pallid color, with thin "look" overall; bland and tasteless—close to tea, except tea usually has more pizzazz; finishes weaker than it began.

MIDNIGHT DRAGON ROYAL
RESERVE LAGER   CT   0.5
(La Crosse, Wisconsin)

High, prickly carbonation with orange-juice-concentrate aroma that rapidly rises through the nostrils; not especially disgusting, but certainly not wonderful; rounded sourness; carbonation almost completely disappears; very tea-like; begins to turn skunky; this is a sequential beer—it goes from bad to worse; rough texture at the end; hard to finish.

MILLER HIGH LIFE Pilsener   CB   2.4
(Milwaukee, Wisconsin)

Attractive, clean smell, with no grit that might make it interesting; on the other hand, it's clear, inoffensive, and devoid of chemical taste; no intimations of adventure, but no signs of danger, either; compared to other mass-produced beers, this at least has the beginnings of complexity; stays restrainedly refreshing and mildly interesting with food; tissue-thin dusting of foam stays on top of the liquid, while some adheres tentatively to sides of glass; very faint, grainy odor at end; one of the better of the megabrewed products. Try with a bacon-wrapped filet mignon and tossed green salad.

MILLER HIGHLIFE Pilsener   CB   2.2
(Toronto, Ontario, Canada)

Smoother and softer than the American version, with a flavor built from quality adjuncts and the usual malt and barley; cooling and refreshing at first; in the end, watery and washed out as far as taste, texture, and visual "feel" are concerned; no aroma or complexity—just your basic okay bland beer with some hint of interest.

MILLER RESERVE BARLEY DRAFT
Lager   CB   2.6
(Milwaukee, Wisconsin)

Gritty and distinctly malted; dry and persistent in its relatively thick textural presence; barley maltiness is pumped up with basically no aroma; some heft, settling down into sturdy routine; more substance, presence, and taste than most American mass-produced beers; takes some getting used to for the American palate; slightly bitter finish; thin film on the roof of the mouth five to ten minutes after the end of the bottle. Good with barbecued chicken and grilled vegetables.

MILLER RESERVE VELVET STOUT   CB   1.9
(Milwaukee, Wisconsin)
Smartly crackly, with barest hint of malted hops—and, if you concentrate closely, the malt seems to be roasted; bitter and a bit harsh—certainly not velvety; sheets, rather than complex designs, of Brussels lace, quickly fade into a thin film of moisture; plain, coffee color makes it look more like a dark lager than any kind of stout (so does the taste); quickly mellows and becomes soft, almost smooth, with food; after a while, the beer simply disappears as a player in the meal, its taste weakening further at the end of the bottle; vaguely malty aroma remains throughout; the folks who made this need to retake the beginner's level course in "Beer Styles: How to Differentiate Among Them."

MILLSTREAM LAGER   MB   3.8
(Amana, Iowa)
Fresh and malty at the beginning, which leads you to expect a fuller, mellower taste; sharp and effervescent; good malt-hop balance; straightforward; zestier than other Midwestern beers; finish is medium-dry with a flavor that makes you want to try another; crosscurrents of texture make it interesting with or without food; a touch flat and metallic, leaving you disappointed and perplexed on final sip. Sweetness comes through with dishes such as chicken with Cajun spices or gumbo.

MILLSTREAM SCHILD BRAU AMBER
Lager   MB   2.7
(Amana, Iowa)
Nice, rounded maltiness with complementary minimal carbonation; faint, but in-depth sweetness adds upbeat note; remains relatively consistent throughout; appropriate sourness emerges with food; bland yet a bit interesting, with subtle, tangible complexity; food is necessary to add substance to this beer—not a brew that creates excitement by itself. Good with mustard-slathered hot dogs or wurst.

MILLSTREAM WHEAT   MB   0.3
(Amana, Iowa)
Not in wheat style at all—no cloves, no fruitiness, no zip, not even refreshing; hard to tell this is even beer; rather staid and unassertive, especially with spicy foods; dry and characterless.

MILWAUKEE 1851 Pilsener   **CB**   **0.4**
(La Crosse, Wisconsin)
Chemical-tasting and somewhat sharp; water is the predominant feature, though some hop suggestion is also present in the far background; light-to-medium-bodied; starts going flat one-quarter of the way through the can; taste turns unpleasantly bitter, metallic, coarse, intrusive; gives a new meaning to the cliché, "It leaves a bad taste in your mouth"; forget about this one.

MINOTT'S BLACK STAR LAGER   **CB**   **2.7**
(St. Paul, Minnesota)
Floral aroma with clean but not crisp taste; flat and headless; increasingly flowery taste doesn't linger; some malt/hop balance emerges, but is faint and superficial; unobtrusive with food; sweetens and gets its act together a bit at the end, but never really establishes itself as the double-hopped beer the label claims; needs more than one bottle for its character to flourish.

MIRROR POND PALE ALE (draft)   **MB**   **1.2**
(Bend, Oregon)
Wispy and fruity with similar aftertaste; I find it to be not much of a drink with or without food, but between my first tasting and 1994 it improved. Try it for yourself and decide; Gold Medal winner at the 1994 Great American Beer Festival.

MODELO ESPECIAL Vienna Lager   **CB**   **2.9**
(Mexico City, Mexico)
Sharp with a tantalizing sweetness that comes to the upper palate, and then diffuses; slight afterbite; golden hue suggests it's more lightweight than it is; there's chocolate in there somewhere; flavorful and motivating. Maintains malty sweetness and character with Mexican food and pasta.

MOLSON BRADOR MALT LIQUOR   **CB**   **2.7**
**(Montreal, Québec; Toronto, Ontario; Vancouver,
British Columbia, Canada)**
Fading crispness on first sip; predictable, somewhat malty, without much kick from the supposedly higher alcohol content; a lager-like beer; neither offensive nor attractive. A fitting partner for a burger topped with green chilies.

MOLSON EXPORT ALE   **CB**   **3.2**
**(Montreal, Québec; Toronto, Ontario; Vancouver,
British Columbia, Canada)**
A little stronger and fuller than the lager, with a hoppier taste; crispness is a bit rounded at the edges; remains satisfying, filling, and fresh; straightforward; satisfies different tastes; thirst-quenching when very cold; not much complexity. Good with grilled chicken or fish.

MOLSON GOLDEN Ale   CB   2.4
(Montreal, Québec; Toronto, Ontario;
Vancouver, British Columbia, Canada)
Immediate first impression of substance begins to fade into relatively bland taste and non-existent aroma after a swallow or two; a certain crispness remains as long as the beer stays cold; light, thin hoppiness; creamy head and unpredictable, intricate Brussels lace last until final drop; attractive, mild bitterness finishes the bottle, with accompanying hop aroma; a one sip, one whiff beer—beyond that, not much to experience; "An Honest Beer," says the label, "Makes Its Own Friends"—true enough. Fine with a ham and cheese or salami sandwich.

MOLSON ICE Lager   CB   3.5
(Vancouver, British Columbia, Canada)
Fresh, crisp, and cold (it's from Canada, after all), with a predominance of hops; medium-bodied; uncomplicated; remains firm; strong brew for hot-weather thirst (5.6% alcohol by volume—higher than most American lagers). Serve with hearty beef stew, well-seasoned meat loaf, or braised oxtail.

MOLSON SPECIAL DRY Lager   CB   2.5
(Toronto, Ontario, Canada)
Smooth and soothing; a seriously dry beer, with no hint of sweetness or cloyingness; remains cool, calm and collected; hangs together tenuously, as if the wrong food would destroy its attractiveness; not flavorful or complex enough to be ranked very high. Compatible with relatively bland foods such as a turkey burger or a club sandwich.

MON-LEI Lager   CB   2.6
(Beijing, China)
Immediate wheat/wine taste, fading into some sourness; settles into a balance between grain and acidity; sharpness at the back of the throat remains even several minutes after swallowing; alcoholic presence throughout; some spritziness; thin and watery; complexity increases from start to finish; Try it with pasta dishes.

MONROVIA CLUB BEER Lager   CB   3.0
(Monrovia, Liberia)
European-style lager; dry without much carbonation; settles into tasty, nicely balanced beer that sets off food well; dry, flattish finish lingers. Companionable accompaniment to Caesar salad with grilled chicken breast or a chef salad.

MONTE CARLO LAGER   CB   2.8
(Guatemala City, Guatemala)
Crisp, sharp, and neutral-tasting on first sip; medium body with nice spritziness; flavor develops when matched with food, but

texture flattens out; greenness toward the end; slight attractive fruitiness. Goes with spicy Mexican foods.

MONTEREY KILLER WHALE
AMBER ALE   MB/BP   0.2
(Monterey, California)
Highly yeasty and acidic; spoiled aroma and taste; raw and unfinished, and as it turns out, unfinishable; does get points, however, for rich, apple-cider appearance; stay away from this killer.

MONTEREY SEA LION STOUT   MB/BP   0.0
(Monterey, California)
Stings the mouth and irritates the stomach—great beginning; it's a struggle to get through the burnt taste of the malt; deep, coffee color; no head; no fullness or thickness; strong, astringent, and watery; bitter, bitter, bad.

MONTEZUMA DE BARRIL Lager
(draft)   CB   3.3
(Mexico City, Mexico)
Dark and tasty; I sampled it with street food in Mexico City's Zona Rosa, where the beer served mainly as a grease-cutter, but its deep maltiness and faintly sharp hops hinted that it could be enjoyed without food. It is a delectable choice on its own or as a perfect foil for snacks such as Buffalo-style chicken wings and jalapeño-topped nachos.

MOONLIGHT TWIST OF FATE
BITTER ALE   MB   3.3
(Windsor, California)
Harsh with citrus overtones, but appealing—a true bitter, with hop aroma to match; delicate Brussels lace belies the strength of the contents; musty aftertaste at the roof of the mouth; dry finish, sturdy and forthright. Serve as an intriguing *apéritif* accompanied by unsalted walnuts, cashews, and smoked almonds.

MOOSEHEAD CANADIAN LAGER   CB   1.4
(St. John, New Brunswick, Canada)
Foamy, creamy head covers a very pale, less-than-carbonated, weak body; dainty, light-lemon mouthfeel suggests a barely flavored bottled spring water; faint, beery aroma fades rapidly as does the transient bitterness; a hardly-there beer; the best word for this brew is flimsy—no taste buds need apply.

MORETTI BIRRA FRIULANA Pilsener   CB   1.3
(Udine, Italy)
Immediate cardboard/paper aroma, the dreaded hallmark of oxidation; very perfumey; mild, light-bodied, flat, uncomplex; airy, sweet, corn-like taste; finish is soda-like, with fizz and raspberry flavor; a second bottle doesn't contain the oxidized off-flavor; drink-

able, but not enough stamina to stand up to bland foods; too variable to recommend.

MORETTI LA ROSSA ALL MALT
Lager   **CB**   **3.1**
(Udine, Italy)
Caramel flavor, thick foam, and full body—all unexpected from an Italian beer; very much like an ale, except for the alcohol—there doesn't seem to be any; silky and smooth throughout; malty with a hint of acidity and sweetness; malt-rich aroma and taste from start to finish; deep-red color. Try with Cornish hens or veal chops.

MORETTI LA ROSSA DOPPIOMALTO
Amber Lager   **CB**   **2.7**
(Udine, Italy)
Malty and mildly roasted, as expected; smooth; light- to medium-bodied; increasingly cloying; hoppiness arises at mid-bottle, nicely counterbalancing the slight fruity sweetness; rather unobtrusive; unappetizing without food. Good with chicken and seafood pasta dishes.

MOSCOVA Lager   **CB**   **1.9**
(Moscow, Russia)
Malty and hoppy at the same time, with a hint of spoilage; flat and relatively textureless; rather indifferent, both by itself and with food; slight honey aroma and taste appear at the end of the bottle; medium-dry; flat viscosity; typical of Russian beer; uninteresting and slightly spoiled.

MOSS BAY AMBER ALE (draft)   **MB**   **1.0**
(Kirkland, Washington)
Fruity at the beginning; full-bodiedness and complexity disappear almost completely after the beer sits for five minutes or so—and I got this fresh out of the tap; retains a slight floral taste, but everything else dramatically flattens out; some roasted aroma pops up momentarily, but is really of no consequence; starts out with promise, but ends up as forgettable.

MOUNTAIN CREST Pilsener   **CB**   **0.9**
(Toronto, Ontario, Canada)
Tries to imitate American beers, and unfortunately, has succeeded; undistinguished; drink water instead.

MOZA BOCK   **CB**   **2.9**
(Guatemala City, Guatemala)
Spritzy and flavorful; texture a bit watery; maintains appealing slightly sour mustiness; flattens out to a pleasant blandness; mildly agreeable burnt taste at the back of the throat; not complex; weakens at the end of the bottle. Good with rice or grain dishes.

MULTNOMAH FIGUREHEAD
EXTRA SPECIAL BITTER/PALE ALE   **MB**   **2.0**
(draft)
(Portland, Oregon)
Cocoa taste wrapped in a full body offers an attractive initial impression; displays a smooth texture with rough edges and a pleasant, but unexciting malty aroma; evolving malt-chocolate flavor becomes lifeless as does the brown-amber color; too much hop off-taste spoils the benign calm; aftertaste coating on the tongue lowers the rating even further; not ready for prime time.

MURPHY'S IRISH STOUT   **CB**   **2.5**
(Cork, Ireland)
Surprisingly flat and tasteless, though soft and creamy, almost velvety; hint of wine meanders in and out; predictable creamy smoothness gently, seamlessly insinuates itself into food, mainly because it has no real core of its own; deep, dark brown; thick tan head; virtually non-existent aroma; neither complex nor balanced; more integrated, textured presence at finish, with some emerging warmth; a disappointment despite its new pressurized-can packaging, especially compared to the real draft version. Okay with a grilled chicken or sharp Cheddar cheese sandwich.

MURPHY'S STOUT (draft)   **CB**   **3.5**
(Cork, Ireland)
Soft on the mouth, lips, and palate; sharp hoppiness evolves into mellow, smooth, burnt flavor; brown-black body and milky-brown level head create perfect visual balance for this spicy-tart stout; stays smooth throughout, with evergreen spiciness; classic, clinging Brussels lace; solid and above average. Good with raw oysters, chips and salsa, or potato chips with clam dip.

NARRAGANSETT Lager   **CB**   **3.0**
(Cranston, Rhode Island)
Smooth and prickly at the same time; mellows and becomes pleasurably tame with food; average beer for average food on an average day at a baseball game. Goes well with salami and cheese sandwiches.

NAVIDAD CERVEZA COMMEMORATIVA
Lager (annual)   **CB**   **0.1–3.4**
(Monterrey, Mexico)
A popular Christmas beer that has, in my experience, varied wildly in acceptability; my first bottle in 1986 was flat and lifeless—no zip, no zest; some fruitiness was present but it was pallid, thin, and weak; more recently, I have found the body to be pleasing—not too heavy, with a flavorful, unobtrusive roasty taste; sharpness on the front of the tongue turns sweet with spicy foods; not fully thirst-quenching, but worth searching for during the end-of-year holiday season.

NEGRA MODELO DARK ALE   CB   3.5
(Mexico City, Mexico)

Delicious, creamy, and remarkably smooth; subdued crispness; loses mellowness with highly seasoned meat dishes; much sweeter and more palatable with blander flavors; thirst-quenching and extremely pleasant. Very good with food, especially pork and lamb.

NEKTAR LIGHT Pilsener   CB   1.4
(Banja Luka, the former Yugoslavia)

Watery, flat and distinctly unfizzy; however, its warming, mellow honey flavor is likeable with crunchy, salty snacks; lightweight by itself, this beer is really textureless; hazy, yellow-brown color looks dirty; tasty but empty. A suitable match for Bavarian-style pretzels dipped in honey mustard.

NEUWEILER BLACK AND TAN
Porter/Lager   CT   2.5
(Wilkes-Barre, Pennsylvania)

No aroma; bland tasting; deep, copper-red color; a hint of malty sweetness pops up now and then; remains frustratingly predictable—given its quality ingredients and thoughtful brewing; this beer, unfortunately, goes nowhere. (For more on Black and Tan, see page 132.)

NEW AMSTERDAM AMBER Lager   CT   3.6
(Utica, New York)

Watery, apple flavor with sharpness early and flatness later; smooth, malty mouthfeel; enhances the sharpness of very spicy foods; roasted freshness throughout; amber color is too light, but gustatory sensations more than make up for the visual deficit. A nice match with Thai food.

NEW AMSTERDAM NEW YORK ALE   CT   3.3
(Utica, New York)

Fruity aroma and strong citrus taste on first sip; appropriately thin and texturally evenhanded; some complexity and balance emerge as it warms; bitter aftertaste and spiciness trail the main part of the drink; zesty; all ingredients come together pleasantly at the end, making for a good adolescent beer that would gain from maturity. Try it with Mexican food.

NEW BELGIUM FAT TIRE AMBER ALE BP   3.9
(Fort Collins, Colorado)

Tightly compacted, fizzily foaming bubbles in head; attenuated fruitiness; is immediately and appropriately cut down to manageable size with the first bite of food; bounces back with a modulated sweetness that plays off a hoppy aroma and slightly nutty malt flavor; some yeast in the bottle helps to give it body and a cloudy amber color; even-tempered, respectful ale, though lack-

ing complexity; too sweet without food. Accommodating with
foods such as lamb chops with mint sauce.

NEW ENGLAND ATLANTIC AMBER Alt   MB   3.1
(Norwalk, Connecticut)

Far too fruity and alcoholic for this style, but inviting and satisfying nonetheless; a nice, foamy head; soft and mellow; hint of
tangy sourness passes quickly; carbonation is quickly minimized;
lively fruitiness combines with rich, hoppy bitterness; finishes
with an attractive mustiness and warmth, although too thin; Gold
Medal winner at the 1993 Great American Beer Festival. Try this
with boiled, spicy jumbo shrimp.

NEW ENGLAND HOLIDAY ALE
(annual)   MB   4.0
(Norwalk, Connecticut)

A little sweet, even a little gummy; a mini-concoction of delectable scents and spices, mainly evergreen and cloves, in varying
intensities; full and tasty with rich, velvety, red-brown color, giving it an enticing glow; an undertone of chocolate unites all of
the diverse but complementary ingredients; the ale's spiciness
heats up the tongue and ultimately takes over most foods; perfect, discernible alliance of aroma and taste—you get what you
smell; remains consistent from beginning to end; an enchanting
holiday drink; highly recommended. A festive match for a traditional roasted turkey dinner with all the trimmings.

NEW HAVEN ELM CITY
CONNECTICUT ALE   MB   2.9
(New Haven, Connecticut)

Rather uncomplex with a faint blush of fruitiness; smooth and
medium-bodied; cools and calms spicy foods, which may turn
the beer a little sour; slight caramel aroma; weak yellow-amber
color; minimal yeast sediment; richer and more complex as it
warms, although generally too thin.

NEW YORK HARBOR ALE   CT   1.9
(Steven's Point, Wisconsin)

Suggestion of fruitiness quickly turns mildly bitter; clear, golden-
amber with no head; some malt sweetness; good intentions, but
of disappointing quality; aroma is heartier than the taste; hop
finish; texturally smooth.

NEW ZEALAND LAGER   CB   2.4
(Auckland, New Zealand)

Thin and grainy with minimal spritziness; takes on an attractive
molasses-like sweetness served with pork; pale-golden color with
a ruby undertone; head thins down very quickly; hint of hoppiness and dryness finishes off this good-hearted but uninteresting
beer.

NEWCASTLE BROWN ALE   **CB**   **2.0**
(Newcastle-upon-Tyne, England)
Sharp, almost metallic taste; not very flavorful; very little body.
Serve with fish and chips.

TAP TIP

What About the Bubbles?

*C*arbonation offers a clue to the quality of the beer you drink—or don't drink. Small bubbles are found in a naturally carbonated product, generally resulting in a smoother, creamier brew. Larger, fast-rising bubbles are usually an indication that carbonation has been artificially introduced. This commercial carbonic injection process results in shorter brewing and aging periods and generally less care than naturally carbonated beverages, potentially rushing the beer to market before its time. It also allows for fewer carbonation-related serving problems at the tap, and hence, the potential for fewer irritated customers. Large bubbles and a rapidly collapsing head may also be the result of insufficient malt.

NEWCASTLE BROWN ALE (draft)   **CB**   **3.3**
(Newcastle-upon-Tyne, England)
Full-bodied and very satisfying—gets immediately to the core of
your taste buds on first sip; fresh malty aroma; hearty and stalwart with minimal carbonation; quality medium-brown color
and sweet chewy maltiness create a smooth, soft mellowness; hops
slowly creep up onto the roof of the mouth about half-way through
the glass; bit of thickish aftertaste lowers the rating; finishes
smooth, smooth, smooth. I had this with chewy strips of licorice
candy—an unusual combination I recommend highly, but it
would also be good with a tuna salad sandwich.

NGOK' MALT LIQUOR   **CB**   **1.8**
(Pointe Noire, Zaire)
Skunky and strong tasting—a surprise, given its light-golden
color; turns tasteless and lifeless; hoppy presence and relatively
dry finish; disappointing; lacks interest, even with the hoppy
punch.

NGOMA MALT LIQUOR   **CB**   **2.1**
(Lome, Togo)
Musty aroma with a mild caramel flavor; increasing taste of old alcohol; sharply hoppy with a cloying hint of malt sweetness; alcohol predominates and detracts from the texture and flavor of most foods; finish is milder, sweeter, and less alcoholic, but still somewhat raw.

NGOMA TOGO PILS   **CB**   **2.7**
(Lome, Togo)
Immediate grain taste with subdued, but evenhanded texture; no head or Brussels lace to speak of; goes flat halfway through the bottle; a rather bland drink for foods; taste is better than texture; mildly warming; rating is based primarily on strength of its taste.

NIKSICKO PIVO Pilsener   **CB**   **3.1**
(Niksic, the former Yugoslavia)
Slight musky odor followed by mellow, warm taste with little pizzazz; rather flat texture; much more flavorful alone than with food; gentle sweetness, almost juiciness, remains throughout; won awards in (among other places) London, 1976; Paris, 1932, 1973, 1979; Brussels, 1971, 1974, 1987; Lisbon, 1985; Plovidiv, 1985; Luxembourg, 1977—decide for yourself.

NINE STAR Lager   **CB**   **2.9**
(Beijing, China)
Sharp and rice-tasting, but overwhelmed by spicy or highly seasoned foods; comes out refreshed and balanced, and not as weak as at the outset; a grain-hoppiness begins to take over at the finish; label calls this the "Beer For State Banquets." Try it with rice and beans.

NOCHE BUENA Lager (annual)   **CB**   **2.4–3.3**
(brewed by Moctezuma in Orizaba, Mexico)
A much sought-after Christmas beer that, in my experience, is above average, though it has been known to fail to reach that level occasionally; negative qualities include a mild, cloying sweetness with bland texture; can switch gears quickly and without warning; sometimes too watery; however, at its best, it is strong, full, and flavorful with richness that complements salty foods; its sweetness and sharpness make a nicely balanced beer; a taste of clove; thick, rich, and bountiful; start looking for this annual release in late October, as it is often difficult to find in the U.S.

NORTH COAST OKTOBERFEST ALE
(annual)   **MB/BP**   **0.8**
(Fort Bragg, California)
Sweet-sour accent with mild aroma and taste; fruitiness has been sapped out of this ale, leaving it wimpy and without substance; even alcohol content is diminished; clouded, brown color with

purple overtones; these folks need to scrap everything and start this one all over again.

NORTH COAST OLD NO. 38 STOUT   MB/BP   3.1
(Fort Bragg, California)

Malty aroma; astringent, without flat taste on first sip; crusty, chocolatey underlying flavor moves into caramel; on second pouring, it displays a thick, tan head; smooth; vanilla hidden in the deep, brown-red body; sweet milkiness emerges when served with poultry; remains "green" tasting; overall, integrates nicely as the bottle empties; representative of the style; Silver Medal winner at the 1993 Great American Beer Festival. A very good match with duck.

NORTH COAST RED SEAL ALE   MB/BP   2.4
(Fort Bragg, California)

Fruity and flat, but encourages you to have more; nice, reddish-amber color complements taste; remains watery and textureless—you can tell this is made by unskilled, but presumably well-intentioned, hands; premise is promising, but not fulfilled; a mild, essentially textureless ale subtle enough to interact with food flavors; mild, in the English tradition; alas, the label is more enchanting than the beer. Try it with barley or cream of mushroom soup served with rustic whole-grain bread.

NORTH COAST SCRIMSHAW
PILSENER   MB/BP   3.1
(Fort Bragg, California)

Begins soft, gentle, and warm with no ingredient complexity; daintiness takes over and lightly entices; faint—perhaps imagined—honey flavor; ingredients eventually become more complex when accompanying food; cloudy, light-brown color; not exciting, but definitely companionable; good choice for a novice to try. Nicely accompanies fresh tuna, swordfish, and other seafood steaks.

NORTH COAST TRADITIONAL BOCK
MALT LIQUOR   MB/BP   2.8
(Fort Bragg, California)

Fruity and alcoholic, with a deep coolness apparent on first sip; fruitiness flattens while texture disappears; a wine taste begins to seep in at mid-bottle; somewhat watery; mild caramel, almost nutty, flavor emerges with food; finishes better than it starts. Okay with burgers, hot dogs, and French fries.

NORTHAMPTON OLD BROWN
DOG ALE (draft)   BP   3.3
(Northampton, Massachusetts)

Strongly alcoholic and malty in taste and aroma; this is clearly a strong beer, even after having traveled cross-country; fresh and sharp, with staying power; good, flavorful mixture of malt, hops, and yeast; some chewiness adds to the enjoyment; well-coordinated and pleasantly balanced; a calm, attractive brew that finishes with a mild caramel taste. Goes well with mild cheeses and strong-tasting crackers.

NUDE BEER Lager   **CT**   **1.5**
(Wilkes-Barre, Pennsylvania)
Tasteless and cold (and the cold isn't from too much refrigeration); a generic beer with no special qualities; not pleasant or unpleasant—just there.

OB LAGER   **CB**   **2.5**
(Seoul, Korea)
Light, not very tasty; some wine overtones; neither complicated nor simple; nonassertive and predictable, it follows the lead of food. Good with mild-flavored pasta and noodle dishes.

OBERDORFER DARK HEFEWEIZEN   **CB**   **3.1**
(Marktoberdorf, Germany)
Apple aroma; slightly musty; maintains soft fizziness throughout, adding tang to its already smooth character; head stays foamy but thin; nice interplay of taste, texture, and aroma; interesting by itself, but not outstanding, even with a twist of lemon. A thirst-quencher to drink with salty snacks such as potato chips and olives.

ODELL'S DUNKEL WEIZEN
BARLEY WINE   **MP**   **3.5**
(Fort Collins, Colorado)
Immediate clove aroma with even stronger clove taste; delightful, emerging citrus-orange backdrop; appropriate textural roughness, rounded at the edges; full, uniform, long-lasting Brussels lace; nicely balanced and calibrated; pleasant, interesting and even-tempered; a bit too thin and green. Serve as an after-dinner drink, or try with pork.

ODELL'S 90 SHILLING ALE   **MB**   **3.7**
(Fort Collins, Colorado)
Like grapefruit juice with malt and alcohol; citrus fruitiness settles into predictable, smooth palate; nicely integrated; light, and not too fluffy; consistent foam from start to finish.

OKANAGAN SPRING PREMIUM LAGER   **MB**   **1.1**
(Vernon, British Columbia, Canada)
Flat texture, woody taste, some water; poor integration of ingredients; but it does leave a nice layer of Brussels lace.

OKANAGAN SPRING ST. PATRICK
STOUT   **MB**   **1.3**
(Vernon, British Columbia, Canada)
Shallow caramel flavor is too flat for maximum savoring; thin,

with nice tartness and a fruity tang; watery and lacks punch with food; no flavor develops as this stout warms up, dashing initial expectations; no maltiness or any real feel for this brew's ingredients—other than water; at bottom of glass, a burnt flavor emerges as it should have earlier; not full-bodied; so smooth it puts you to sleep—but not soon enough.

O'KEEFE ALE   **CB**   **3.1**
(Toronto, Ontario, Canada)
Soft head contrasts with the sharpness of the hazy, pale-golden color of the body; moderate complexity in the rounded, almost fruity taste; a hint of alcohol; unassuming, nonintrusive Canadian overtones; grows warm and comforting; pleasant, but not scintillating company. A good match with Chinese or Japanese noodle dishes.

O'KEEFE'S EXTRA OLD STOCK
MALT LIQUOR   **CB**   **2.9**
(Vancouver, British Columbia, Canada)
Stark, crisp, and light, with unexpected substance; reasonable head; relatively high alcohol content (5.65% by volume); nice balance of taste and texture—at least by itself without food; not exceptional, but a decent everyday companion; proudly says "Union Made" on the can. A good companion with virtually any food.

OKOCIM O.K. FULL LIGHT Pilsener   **CB**   **2.2**
(Warsaw, Poland)
Sweet and airy; flattened texture; smooth mouthfeel; back-of-the-throat sourness comes through with food; mild fruitiness ebbs and flows; pleasantly bland; neither surprising nor memorable.

OKOCIM O.K. PILS   **CB**   **0.3**
(Warsaw, Poland)
Lacks flavor and has minimal zest; odd lamb chop taste; pallid, honey-yellow color with no head; does not resemble a pilsener; Brussels lace is spotty and ragged—dribbles sit on top of the liquid in the glass; spoiled-fruit aroma with vague malt; far from delightful.

OLD AUSTRALIA STOUT   **CB**   **3.8**
(Thebarton, South Australia, Australia)
Inviting head, substantive body, almost black color, and pleasant caramel taste on first sip; a hint of sweetness/syrupyness; tangy and sharp; with a bit more body, this would be a good example of traditional stout; winey aftertaste turns sour in the throat; still, worth asking for. Enjoy with shepherd's pie and other pub grub.

OLD CHICAGO LAGER   **CB**   1.2
(Chicago, Illinois)
Somewhat stale and quite hoppy; pale, straw color; poorly integrated ingredients; slightly sour, with citrus overtones; for the fainthearted.

OLD COLUMBIA AMBER LAGER   **BP**   2.9
(San Diego, California)
Smooth texture and hop spiciness sit together nicely on first sip; sweetness slips through almost unnoticed, providing soothing, cooling backdrop to spicy food; increasing complexity stops short of full-blown, integrated charm; has more presence with milder flavored foods; its ready responsiveness to food makes it hard to evaluate—not necessarily a bad sign, just a gentle warning; Old Columbia considers this its signature beer—only problem is, it's a little too hard to read.

OLD COLUMBIA BLACK'S BEACH
EXTRA DARK PORTER (draft)   **BP**   4.0
(San Diego, California)
Nutty, toasty, and surprisingly easy to drink, this distinctive porter has an unusually light body; nicely calibrated, not overwhelming or intrusive; respects food while retaining its own dignity; very satisfying and smooth. Fine with charbroiled burgers.

OLD COLUMBIA DOWNTOWN AFTER
DARK BROWN ALE (draft)   **BP**   3.3
(San Diego, California)
Firm, very malty, and toasty; more complex than its namesake cousins; appropriate sweetness is modulated and does not linger; fresh, rich, and not cloying. Try it with minestrone or tomato soup with a grilled cheese sandwich.

OLD COLUMBIA GAS LAMP
GOLD ALE (draft)   **BP**   2.7
(San Diego, California)
Nicely moderated sweetness, thin creaminess, and pale-amber color with a sweet, lingering aftertaste; not as bold or creamy as advertised. Goes with light pasta main courses.

OLD COLUMBIA PORT LOMA
LIGHTHOUSE LIGHT LAGER (draft)   **BP**   1.1
(San Diego, California)
Tasty for a light beer, but too musty and, ultimately, uninspiring; leaves thick aftertaste on the roof of the mouth, which is as thick—or substantial—as this lager gets.

OLD COLUMBIA RED TROLLEY ALE
(draft)   BP   3.1
(San Diego, California)
Super fruitiness wells up as you're drinking; aftertaste is less compelling and dissipates relatively quickly; without food, it's too
fruity; bright red color; well-made, but not a favorite of mine.
Good with salty snacks such as nuts or potato chips; believe it
or not, an interesting match with apple pie à la mode.

OLD DETROIT AMBER ALE   CT   3.8
(Frankenmuth, Michigan)
Fruitiness stays in background while a sweet nuttiness takes over;
nicely restrained overall ambience, as if waiting for food; full and
sharp; not as rich as it should or could be; distinct fruitiness
emerges, as it warms, as does a touch of caramel flavor; a surprise find. Good with a steak and baked potato dinner.

OLD MILWAUKEE Lager   CB   0.8
(Detroit, Michigan)
Sour mustiness greets you and stays throughout; no complexity
to speak of; hint of greenness; loaded with adjuncts (corn, for
example) which make for a weak overall impression.

OLD PECULIER ALE   CB   3.8
(Masham, England)
Rounded, burnt-caramel flavor thickens into fuzzy aftertaste; rich
and creamy without food; mildly sticky aftertaste adheres to the
roof of the mouth; faint nut aroma; lightly carbonated; increasing sweetness suggests this would not go well with food, though
this turns out not to be the case; immediately frothy and creamy;
smooth and texturally appealing; flavorful, well-balanced; complements the taste of red meats; whiff of alcohol lingers; warm
finish and caramel aroma; the label calls this "traditionally brewed
Yorkshire Ale"; an excellent choice for the newcomer who wishes
to try a moderately dark/moderately alcoholic, distinctive style
of ale. Good with prime beef dishes.

OLD STYLE PILSNER   CB   2.4
(Vancouver, British Columbia, Canada)
Both light and thick; fuzzy aftertaste; bubbly head thins down
and stays down; hops are evident; a rather ordinary beer with
some character and strength. Fine with plain, everyday fare.

OLD VIENNA Lager   CB   3.0
(Toronto, Ontario, Canada)
Fresh, with a beguiling hint of mustiness; has more complexity
than American lagers; fullness and sweetness emerge with sweet
and sour foods; typically crisp, though lighter than most Canadian beers; retains its freshness; better than average. A good choice
with barbecued spare ribs.

OLD WEST AMBER Lager   CT   2.2
(New Ulm, Minnesota)
Slight, fast-fading honey-citrus taste; prickly fizziness; generally balanced, but with too much emerging hoppiness; weakens considerably with food; faint roasted taste is typical of the style, but other style elements are missing or diminished; flat, bitter aftertaste; within style or not, this is not an attractive brew; Gold Medal winner at the 1993 Great American Beer Festival.

OLDE ENGLISH 800 Malt Liquor   CB   2.9
(brewed by Pabst in Milwaukee, Wisconsin)
Very smooth; appropriately sweet; flavorful but unobtrusive with food; adequately balanced between hops and malts; surprisingly pleasant, warming finish; Gold Medal winner at the 1994 Great American Beer Festival. Good with roast beef or ham.

OLDE HEURICH MAERZEN   CT   2.6
(Pittsburgh, Pennsylvania)
Mildly fruity and pleasantly sweet; relatively flat in texture; somewhat watery as the bottle progresses; tea-like color and taste; on the mild side; similar in caramel maltiness to Vienna amber, with little intrusion by the hops; not as smooth as advertised on the label; sweet malt finish and aroma. Good with pizza.

OLDENBERG PREMIUM VERUM Lager   MB/BP   2.6
(Fort Mitchell, Kentucky)
Malty, Vienna-amber sweetness is struck immediately in the middle of the tongue by a (purposefully) sour jolt; full-bodied with no head to speak of; strong and uncompromising with too little complexity to make it genuinely interesting; deep burnt-caramel aroma and hazy, yellow-amber color; a mixed bag. Fine with most pasta or rice dishes.

OLDENBERG WEISSE   MB/BP   3.9
(Fort Mitchell, Kentucky)
Feisty and pungent with a reassuring dryness that immediately tackles your thirst; remains fresh and interesting throughout, with an attractive, almost sensual presence; well-balanced; clean, foamy head; light but appealing with a modicum of intrusive yeastiness. Mild citrus presence goes surprisingly well with moderately spicy guacamole; also interesting at breakfast or brunch with scrambled eggs and rye toast.

OLYMPIA Pilsener   CB   2.1
(San Antonio, Texas)
Clean and light in taste, texture, and appearance; mild, malt aroma tantalizes your interest, but never really satisfies—you keep waiting for the taste to kick in or hint that this beer is alive and breathing; perhaps it's the advertising exerting its influence, but the water is ultimately what moves this pale, limp brew along;

drink alone or with cheese and crackers; it's not bad, but there's just not much to it.

ORANJEBOOM PREMIUM LAGER   CB   3.4
(Breda/Rotterdam, Holland)
Strong hops; sharp texture; reasonable head; reddish-golden color; blunt yet restrained; fuller flavor, including rice graininess, as texture diminishes; becomes full-bodied and bold; increasing smooth maltiness; virtues are magnified when imbibed by itself; well-made, firm and moderately lively; label boasts, "Crown Prince of Lagers." Goes well alongside a hamburger with green chilies.

ORVAL TRAPPIST ALE   AB   2.1
(Florenville, Belgium)
Expensive, distinctive, wine/musty/perfume taste; high alcohol content contributes to bitter mouthfeel; cloudy color; many knowledgeable beer drinkers claim this is one of the best made; complex and rich, it can be stored for several years; but sample first before deciding if it's worth the shelf space. Best as an *apéritif* or *digestif*.

OTTAKRINGER GOLD FASSL PILS   CB   2.9
(Vienna, Austria)
Nice rice taste, but also wine sourness; light, even for a pilsener; underlying tastiness isn't readily detected, especially a shame since the pleasant malt sweetness is too deeply hidden to be easily savored. Try it with a cheese pizza.

OTTAKRINGER GOLD FASSL VIENNA
Lager   CB   2.5
(Vienna, Austria)
Full, with an edge; undercurrent of honey; bit of flat aftertaste; not bad, but not memorable, either; a run-of-the-mill beer for run-of-the-mill food.

PABST BLUE RIBBON DRAFT Lager   CB   2.1
(San Antonio, Texas)
Tastes a little like draft, if you concentrate hard and there aren't too many distractions; too many filling adjuncts; relatively soft and creamy for an American beer. Good with salted chips and a creamy dip.

PACENA CENTENARIO Pilsener   CB   2.6
(La Paz, Bolivia)
Light, sweet, and smooth; some emerging citrus with counterpoint of gentleness; head is medium-to-wispy; modulated grain character lowers assertiveness of the 5% alcohol content; easygoing; fizzy; bland except for a pungent yeastiness; thin and sharp; very pale. Primarily a thirst-quencher, but could be matched with mildly seasoned pork dishes.

PACIFIC BEACH BLONDE Wheat   **BP**   **1.6**
(San Diego, California)
Fruity and yeasty with mild citrus flavor—a good fruit juice; flat
and unexpressive; no head; cloudy, light-yellow color; in the end,
weak and too watery; no effervescence.

PACIFIC BEACH MUNICH DARK
LAGER   **BP**   **1.5**
(San Diego, California)
Strong clove taste—not bad if you like that kind of spice, but a
surprise coming from a lager; where are the hops and/or roasted
malts?; those hops that are present are mildly disappointing; erratic Brussels lace hangs in there; no carbonation; quickly disappearing taste; end of swallow turns watery; misnamed.

PACIFIC BEACH OVER-THE-LINE
STOUT   **BP**   **2.7**
(San Diego, California)
Mild, smooth, and soft; weak roasted flavor and some creami-
ness; not alcoholic enough; character tends to wilt in hot sun-
shine; better after a meal than with one.

PACIFIC BEACH STONEHENGE
BROWN ALE   **BP**   **2.7**
(San Diego, California)
Stronger, tastier, and more carbonated than the lighter ales, though
the flavor rapidly fades; erratic, long-lasting Brussels lace; very
thin, almost nonexistent head; acceptable mouthfeel stays put—
no aftertaste and no changes; lightly hopped with moderate body;
cloudy, golden-brown color with slight yeast haze. Good match
for thick-cut French fries accompanied by lots of ketchup.

PACIFIC BEACH SUNSET RED ALE   **BP**   **2.5**
(San Diego, California)
Peachy, red-blush color and apple taste to start; smooth as it glides
down the throat; rich, fruity aroma; no head; gains edge in mid-
glass, turning a bit harsh after several swallows; alcohol begins to
overtake malt/hop taste, unfortunately; too much could be tiresome; falls short of quality ale; best alone, without food.

PACIFIC COAST LAGER   **CT**   **2.4**
(Helena, Montana)
Full, rounded sweetness envelops soft fizziness; yeasty taste and
some sourness interfere with plain foods such as eggs, vegetables,
and grains; muddy rather than luminous appearance; taste and
texture become more balanced as the liquid warms; yeasty grittiness detracts in the end; remains soft to the mouth.

PACIFIC CREST ALE   **MB**   **1.1**
(Kalama, Washington)
Flat, fruity, over-ripe (like fallen apples); headless; watery taste

and weak auburn appearance; hint of caramel doesn't last long enough to improve the overall mood of the beer; harsh edge at the back of the throat; more flavor emerges as it warms, but texture remains essentially blah at the core and jagged at the edge.

PACIFIC DRAFT Pilsener   **CT**   **1.7**
(Vancouver, British Columbia, Canada)
Genuine draft taste (this came in a can); slightly sour; rough texture without food; not high-quality or high-interest; pedestrian at best—why walk with this when you can run with something better? Passable with hot dogs or hamburgers.

PACIFIC HOP EXCHANGE GASLIGHT
PALE ALE   **MB**   **2.5**
(Novato, California)
Fruity, apple-cidery, with busy fizziness; yeast cloudiness; bottle-conditioned; surprisingly bland; malt richness emerges as bottle warms. Warming and gentle with dishes like broiled chicken and spaghetti with herb-garlic sauce; strong apple taste toward the end—but that's appropriate for cider, not for pale ale; doesn't live up to its potential.

PACIFIC HOP EXCHANGE '06 STOUT   **MB**   **2.3**
(Novato, California)
Smooth and roasted; lighter than expected; though appropriately deep, dark-brown color and texture are somewhat lackluster; not very complex; there are clues that this is a stout, but not one of quality, balance, or ingredient integration; in short, too mild and too plain.

PACIFICO CLARO Pilsener   **CB**   **3.1**
(Mazatlan, Mexico)
Sharp, clean taste with curve toward off-taste as it is swallowed; remains smooth and easy; not fancy or complex; spicy food easily blunts and dulls its effects; workmanlike, with no pretensions. Fine for non-spicy Mexican seafood dishes served with rice and beans.

PALERMO ESTRASBURGO Lager   **CB**   **2.2**
(Quilmes, Argentina)
Slight, skunky odor; flat taste and a touch of grain on first sip; faded flavor may be the result of long travels and time in the bottle; too bland for serious beer, especially when the flavor withers next to an egg burrito; tastes like zesty water; moderate body suggests somebody gave some thought to quality, but was apparently overruled in other areas.

PALI HAWAIIAN Lager   **MB**   **1.0**
(Honolulu, Hawaii)
Very pale, almost ginger-ale color, though not as zesty; light and

thin with no texture to speak of; adjuncts (rice, corn) seem to be only substance in this poor imitation of lager.

PALM ALE   **CB**   **3.2**
(Brussels, Belgium)
Thickish, with a nice balance of fruitiness and modulated strength; cloudy, red-golden color adds to the enjoyment; maintains a richness, though there's a hint of interfering sweetness; smoky and toasted malt aroma; taste reminiscent of apples and oranges; easygoing character is not up to hot or spicy food; quickly dissolving head makes you long for more body; retains its interest and appeal throughout, like a longtime friend. Overall, a substantial beer that goes with food you can sink your teeth into.

PANAMA CERVEZA ALLEMANA STYLE
Lager   **CB**   **3.6**
(Panama City, Panama)
More texture than taste; evenhanded, compact malt/hop balance stays throughout; sparkly to start; becomes more integrated as meal progresses; grows on you. Good with shrimp jambalaya or shrimp with hot sauce.

PANDA Pilsener   **CB**   **3.5**
(Shanghai, China)
Nice, immediate rice taste; light but holds its ground with food; even-tempered and predictable; pleasing aftertaste; a good friendly beer. A thirst-quenching choice with barbecued spare ribs; good, light match for meat-and-potatoes suppers.

PASADENA LAGER NATURAL DRAFT   **CT**   **1.0**
(Vancouver, British Columbia, Canada)
Sharp, with quickly diminishing textural breadth and depth; faded background taste with a hint of rancidity; bad aftertaste.

PAULANER ALT MUNCHER DUNKEL   **CB**   **3.9**
(Munich, Germany)
Sharp and sparkly; dark; lightly burnt taste, making for an interesting balance and combination; almost a layered taste effect; dry and quite malty at the end; think of this mellow brew as a deeply satisfying, good example of the German style. Just right with hamburgers or shish kabob.

B E E R   F A C T

*D*unkel means "dark" in German and identifies the classic Munich (Münchner) dark-brown, malty style.

PAULANER HEFE-WEIZEN   **CB**   **2.9**
(Munich, Germany)
As expected, very yeasty and spritzy; head remains foamy and cohesive atop cloudy opaqueness; too yeasty and rancid-fruit tasting to be acceptable overall (rancid=oxidized=rotten, harsh, sour);
mellows and warms as meal progresses; dry, firm finish grudg-
ingly comes and quickly goes; not an all-star, but a beer for individual tastes. Compatible with most red meats.

PAULANER MUNCHEN NR. 1 LAGER   **CB**   **2.2**
(Munich, Germany)
Slightly sour; attractive maltiness greets you and remains; well
integrated and balanced with food, but dull and plodding by itself. Good matched with grilled red meats, green salads with
creamy or blue cheese dressings, baked potatoes with sour cream.

PAULANER OKTOBERFEST Lager   **CB**   **3.8**
(Munich, Germany)
As close to dark beer as you can get without actually being dark-
colored, though, fortunately, many dark-beer attributes are present; full-bodied; some effervescence, but not obtrusive. Good
with simple broiled or grilled chicken dishes.

PAULANER PREMIUM LAGER   **CB**   **3.0**
(Santiago, Chile)
Malty and clove-like with fluffy but decreasing head; grains emerge
and provide roughness against the smoothness of the texture; gentle fizz ends the bottle, and the evening. Nice with lemon-baked
chicken.

PAULANER SALVATOR DOPPELBOCK   **CB**   **4.0**
(Munich, Germany)
Molasses flavor and apple fruitiness with bite and backbone make
you take notice immediately; obvious alcohol content is nicely
wrapped in a creamy, mellow texture with, surprisingly, no head
to speak of; rich, roasted, and filling; drier at the end; roasted
malt feel remains throughout; strong, resilient, and memorable;
a top-notch *doppelbock* with complexity and balance. An excellent choice with spaghetti and meatballs or other red-sauced
pastas.

PAVICHEVICH BADERBRAU PILSENER   MB   2.3
(Elmhurst, Illinois)
Hoppy, somewhat acrid sweetness greets nose and palate; settles down into mildly flowery softness that unfortunately lingers on the sides of the mouth; remains fruity and dry with food; the beer acts as if it were simply another ingredient, another part of the meal—separate but equal; medium-auburn color; dainty, very bubbly head lasts throughout; becomes more integrated as meal progresses; full and assertive; not as spritzy as it should be.

PEARL LAGER   CB   2.3
(San Antonio, Texas)
Solid down the middle, but raggedy at far reaches of the mouth and throat; the water is fresh and sharp, overshadowing weakish hops and washed-out malt; minimal grain taste appears at the bottom of the can; a reasonable choice if you need a quick, straightforward thirst-quencher, but not worth going out of your way to find. Try it with all-American classics such as hot dogs, meat loaf, or fried chicken.

PECAN STREET Lager   CT   2.5
(Shiner, Texas)
Immediate perfumey taste; heavier than a genuine lager; soft texture with virtually no head; perfume taste fades and becomes more interesting, more acceptable, and sharper with grilled meats; respectable, but far from exciting.

PERONI Lager   CB   3.1
(Rome, Italy)
Fresh up front and full at the throat; creamy head; steady flavor remains with food; sharpness on the upper palate persists; retains its fizz throughout; gentle malt taste, reminiscent of bread; mild, but ever-present thickness detracts somewhat; some muddiness at the end; quality with mass appeal. Serve with shrimp and a piquant cocktail sauce or herb-broiled chicken.

PERRY'S MAJESTIC LAGER   CT   2.8
(Frankenmuth, Michigan)

Light and fluffy with a hint of varnish; maltiness evolves into hoppiness, but overall is too weak for strongly flavored foods; light and hardly carbonated; retains a freshness; a thirst-quenching, pleasant, friendly beer that doesn't tax you or your taste buds; nicely integrated at the end; made from organically grown barley and hops. Pair with bland foods such as turkey burgers or plain grilled fish.

PERTOTALE FARO LAMBIC   CB   2.9
(Lembeek, Belgium)

Strong yeast aroma, thick head, slightly sour, fruity taste, and a rush of warmth all greet the senses as soon as you pop the cork from this elongated green bottle; classic off-white head sits atop a medium-amber liquid; surprising hints of orange pekoe and a heavy dose of cloves appear in the alcohol; yeast taste remains subdued, allowing for mellow orange taste; a sweetened, less assertive version of the lambic style (Faro is a type of lambic, with additional sugar or caramel); finish is warm, spicy, and hoppy; orange taste becomes more sweetly pungent as beer warms; dry, lightly fruity finish; toasty and satisfying. Customarily poured with dessert or as an after-dinner drink.

PETE'S GOLD COAST LAGER   CT   3.2
(New Ulm, Minnesota)

Golden (as advertised), quintessential lager (as advertised); hops practically bounce around in your mouth; dry, creamy aftertaste coats the palate; distinctive, mellow taste; flowery aroma appears as long-neck bottle is finished; heady balance of taste, texture, and aroma; hops have the last word; not top-of-the-line, but better American lager than most. A mellow match for hot pastrami on rye or olive-topped pizza.

PETE'S PACIFIC DRY Lager   CT   3.3
(New Ulm, Minnesota)

Appealing honeyed sweetness offset by mild, fruity sourness and fast-rushing, tiny bubbles; not full-bodied enough to be texturally satisfying; warmth expands as meal progresses; rather sweet for a dry beer, but its mild manner is appealing. Good with spicy black bean soup or cold cuts.

PETE'S WICKED ALE   CT   3.8
(New Ulm, Minnesota)

Lovely burnt-caramel taste with fizziness; emerging sweetness as ale warms; silky texture on the tongue fades to dull undertaste at the back of the throat when drunk with smoked foods; grows sweeter with bread and rolls; not as thick and full-bodied as it could be, but still welcoming with its blend of warmth, fruitiness, and smoothness; texture weakens, however; this may be best one bottle at a time rather than multiple bottles at one sitting—too many sips would quickly diminish its attractive textural and taste qualities, which are not insubstantial. Compatible with Chinese noodle dishes, pasta primavera, or pasta with pesto sauce.

> ### B E E R F A C T
>
> *P*ete's Wicked Ale and Pete's Wicked Lager no longer sport the distinctive and attractive picture of Millie, the brewery co-founder's English bull terrier, on their labels. The packaging was changed because the desired image was getting uncomfortably muddied by the logo's resemblance to another canine, the ubiquitous Budweiser dog. Millie has been replaced by a photo of Pete's grandfather.

PETE'S WICKED LAGER   CT   2.9
(St. Paul, Minnesota)
Sharp and highly hopped; lacks complexity and flavor; reasonably stable, long-lasting head and filigreed Brussels lace; perfumey finish is mild, but definitely present. Excellent with spicy guacamole and tortilla chips or a bowl of New England clam chowder.

PETE'S WICKED WINTER BREW—
AMBER ALE (annual)   CT   3.1
(St. Paul, Minnesota)
Mellow spiciness; deep root-beer color; fresh-tasting; subdued flavor; tasty; light, dainty, yet substantive; more complexity and appeal than many other winter brews; oddly, the ½-inch tan-white head foams and stays after most of the bottle has been poured; hint of nutmeg fittingly supports the raspberry taste; despite the fruity sweetness, this is an unusually adaptable drink; finish is thin and creamy smooth, almost textureless; my local supplier ran out of this quickly once the locals discovered it. Tasty accompaniment to spicy Chinese food or peppery-hot main dishes.

PETER'S BRAND PILSENER   CB   2.3
(Amersfoort, Holland)
Rounded sharpness; large bubbles in head suggest artificial carbonation; flattens as bottle empties; consistency of flavor doesn't remain in place from start to finish; ends with dull, mild citrus taste which lessens its attraction. Good with sweet barbecue sauces, herbed pasta salads, and dishes with a lot of cilantro.

PIELS DRAFT Pilsener   **CB**   **1.0**
(Detroit, Michigan)
Thin and mildly crisp; flat, no complexity; very pale, almost lemon in color, which reflects the lack of real substance in the taste; passing hint of skunkiness; no distinctiveness or even a glimmer of identifiable ingredients—other than corn as a filler and lightener; food makes the beer taste better than it really is; a nonbeer.

PIG'S EYE PILSNER   **MB**   **2.5**
(St. Paul, Minnesota)
Undistinguished; not as carbonated as it should be; nice Brussels lace, which fades too quickly to really enjoy; some malt presence at mid-bottle; too sharp and too hard to serve with a meal; remains fresh, but uninteresting; oddly, for a pilsener, it improves as it warms—more flavor and complexity emerge; malty aroma also makes a (tentative) appearance. Serve with salted nuts or chips.

B E E R   F A C T

*A*ccording to legend, Pig's Eye was the original name and site of what is today St. Paul, Minnesota. The town allegedly was named after a famous one-eyed local bootlegger whose snouty features and tiny eye were reminiscent of a certain portly animal.

PIKE PLACE PALE ALE   **MB**   **3.6**
(Seattle, Washington)
Perfumey, grapefruit taste and aroma with emerging clove background; ingredients become well-balanced, but weaken with food; interesting and different; thinner than I'd like, but lovely copper-brown color compensates; mellows, with grapefruit flavor tantalizingly at the forefront, even at the last sip; Bronze Medal winner at the 1993 Great American Beer Festival. Very tasty with lamb.

PILSENER   **CB**   **4.0**
(Quito, Ecuador)
Soft and velvety; smooth going down; wispy; Brussels lace lasts the length of the drink; subdued grain; fresh and enlivening—a very good pilsener. An assertive partner for a hero or submarine sandwich.

PILSENER CLUB PREMIUM   **CB**   **1.0**
(San Antonio/Galveston, Texas)
Green, unfinished taste; cheap, perfumey flavor and aroma; chem-

ical mouthfeel; some yeast makes a fleeting appearance, but, over-all, a narrow band of taste prevails; no aftertaste; it has some thirst-quenching qualities; good in comparison to Old Milwaukee and Schaefer.

PILSENER OF EL SALVADOR   CB   2.5
(San Salvador, El Salvador)

Immediately sweet and appealing, but changes quickly to sharp bitterness; fades into a run-of-the-mill beer with food; alone, it has more body and a modicum of taste integrity; light and dry with corn adjunct—a workingman's beer; the clerk at the store referred to it not by its proper name, but as *Corazón de rojo* (red heart)—exactly what is found on the stark white and red label. A versatile companion for a wide range of foods.

PILSNER URQUELL   CB   3.5
(Pilsen, Czechoslovakia)

Crisp, fresh, and mustily hoppy; pleasant, understated aroma; intensely carbonated; floral mouthfeel contains some bitterness, but it is subtle and well-calibrated; admirable textural strength; slides into tempered sweetness with spicy foods; a first-class beer to be enjoyed in multiples; considered noteworthy from a historical point of view (see below).

B E E R   F A C T

*P*ilsner Urquell is the original pilsener, introduced in 1842. It still sets the standard for pilseners.

PINKUS HOME BREW MUNSTER ALT   CB   1.5
(Münster, Germany)

Sour and tangy; astringent, which fades after a swallow or two; texture is smooth and punchless; maintains a "hard" taste; flat and uninspiring; malt aroma helps mellow overall harshness; aroma is the only element of interest; some honeyed sweetness appears at the end of the bottle.

PINKUS HOME BREW UR PILS   CB   1.9
(Münster, Germany)

Sour, flattening off-taste that evolves into overly hoppy floweriness; light, firm, and typically dry; a bit too astringent; retains rich, creamy head—a nice contrast to the body's pungency; improves and becomes more pilsener-like with food, but never reaches a truly acceptable level; unexpectedly weak; leaves a trellis of Brussels lace the length of the tall pilsener glass. Okay with tuna or salmon steaks.

PINKUS HOME BREW WEIZEN   CB   1.3
(Münster, Germany)
Sparkly, sharp, and somewhat sour; thin and unassuming; no hint
texturally or flavorwise of wheat, clove, or tartness; disappointing with food; smells like the beer left in a glass after a party.

POINT SPECIAL PREMIUM LAGER   CB   2.9
(Stevens Point, Wisconsin)
Smooth; "cool" in texture; laid-back; somewhat dry; interesting,
not-quite-spicy taste; pretensions of being full-bodied (contains
corn grits); smooths out toward the end; an unexciting but well-
made beer; Bronze Medal winner at the 1993 Great American
Beer Festival. Serve with snack foods such as nachos, olives, and
flavored crackers.

POLAR Lager   CB   1.0
(Caracas, Venezuela)
Weak nose (no aroma) and bad legs (low alcohol presence); not
complex; raw and harsh; like a home-brew; doesn't aspire to great-
ness; take it for what it is.

T A P   T I P

Nice Legs

"*L*egs" refers to the mini-streams of liquid that
drip down the insides of the glass. They are usually found in higher alcoholic brews and denote
strength and quality.

POPE'S "1880" Ale   MB/BP   3.6
(Dorchester, England)
Wine-like, fire-brewed taste; very close to a light-style dark beer;
similar to Watney's but a bit more bitter; evident freshness; heightened aroma—due to the type of hops as well as special process-
ing methods—make this strong ale an aromatic delight and
enjoyable experience. Good with mild cheeses or shellfish.

PORT ROYAL EXPORT Pilsener   CB   1.3
(San Pedro Sula, Honduras)
Off-taste crisp mouthfeel in the body, accompanied by softness
attributable to immediately foaming head; deeper taste at the
back of the tongue does little for food; uninteresting, inconsistent and uncertain (can you enjoy it or not? the next sip may
change your mind); continuing fullness is a positive that keeps
it from being a complete dud.

PORTLAND ALE   **MB/BP**   **2.8**
(Portland, Oregon)
Paradoxically astringent and rather bland on first sip; no fruitiness to speak of; overall, far too light-bodied for food with any zip; would be good alone, as a pleasant sipping companion; some apple-cider taste appears at the back of the throat and at the end of the bottle; unobtrusive.

PORTLAND LAGER   **CT**   **2.5**
(Utica, New York)
Stiff, reflecting its New England heritage; a hint of wine taste and virtually no aroma; a bit too taut and tense for my enjoyment; sweetness (finally, some relaxation of its demeanor) develops at the bottom of the bottle. Try it with clam chowder.

PORTLAND MT. HOOD BEER Ale   **MB/BP**   **2.6**
(Portland, Oregon)
Soft, honey aroma and tingly, sharp texture greet the nose and mouth; fresh, grainy taste is also present; character begins to fade after three or four sips, resulting in a less complex, sweeter beer; hops sharpness rebounds nicely; yeasty sweetness predominates; keeps you and your taste buds on the alert; cloudy and not particularly appealing visually; hint of creeping sourness at the end; the bottle I had was apparently several months old, and I was warned by the brewer to "treat it like a collector's item," rather than drink it; I'm glad I drank it. Tasty with herb breads and focaccia.

PORTLAND OREGON DRY HONEY
Ale (draft)   **MB**   **1.5**
(Portland, Oregon)
Obviously honey-based at first, then sweetness fades; flat and zipless soda-like fizziness toward the bottom of the glass doesn't help nor does weak, off-blond color; in the end, quite forgettable.

PORTLAND PORTER Draft   **MB/BP**   **4.0**
(Portland, Oregon)
Thick, burnt-caramel, chocolate ambience with creamy head and deep brown/black color; assertive, but not overwhelming by any means; nicely subdued with food; a little wateriness detracts at the end, but freshness prevails nonetheless. Try it with full-flavored vegetables roasted with garlic, chicken with shallots, or pasta with pesto sauce.

PORTLAND TIMBERLINE ALE (draft)   **MB/BP**   **2.6**
(Portland, Oregon)
Light fruitiness; heightened alcohol/caramel combination; bitter; sweetens with a tang (citrus zestiness) at the end—all without food; a bit too thick on the tongue; amber-colored, medium-bodied. A good choice with Asian food, especially appetizers such as egg rolls, spring rolls, and fried dumplings.

PORTSMOUTH BLACK CAT STOUT   **MB/BP**   **2.4**
(Portsmouth, New Hampshire)
Dainty, fruity aroma with fanciful lightly roasted flavor; smooth with weak but appealing finish; too light and watery for a stout; very little complexity.

POST ROAD REAL ALE   **CT**   **3.6**
(White River Junction, Vermont)
Nicely balanced with mild fruitiness; settles into a subtle consistency; some greenness; slight flavor loss as you drink it; nicely nuanced; not pretentious or overly strong; a good introduction to ale. Complements lamb and pork.

PRESIDENTE PILSENER   **CB**   **3.5**
(Santo Domingo, Dominican Republic)
Foamy first sip with hoppy taste and fine texture; huskiness is appealing, particularly on the sides of the mouth; solid, with tangible body; pleasant, sharp hoppiness; leaves some nicely patterned Brussels lace; there is German influence here. A good choice with spicy Thai food.

PRESTIGE STOUT   **CB**   **4.0**
(Port-au-Prince, Haiti)
Fresh, sweet start subsides quickly and abruptly, but your interest is recaptivated by the hearty texture; musty, controlled sweetness emerges; dark, robust color; sudden wine taste quickly, and thankfully, dissipates; turns silky, smooth, and mellow; provides sweet/bitter balance with poultry; heavily malted with sediment that looks like tea leaves; reaches fullness of character at last sip; chocolatey, caramely, and rich-bodied. A good match with duck or chicken.

PRIMO Lager   CB   2.2
(Van Nuys, California)
Sharp and watery with an appealing hoppy undertone; some body
with food; turns even more watery by itself without food; just a
notch above run-of-the-mill; stale and thin at the end; everyman's
beer.

PRIOR DOUBLE DARK Bock   CT   3.7
(Norristown, Pennsylvania)
Not as strong-tasting as expected; good burnt taste; could be
creamier; rather unobtrusive, but complements hearty food—in
short, a meat-and-potatoes kind of beer; finishes full and smooth,
but leaves room for more; worth a second bottle. Pair with pot
roast or braised veal shanks.

PRIPPS LAGER   CB   2.9
(Gothenburg, Sweden)
Rounded, bitter taste with strong, hoppy bouquet; creamy, smooth,
thick, long-lasting artificial-looking head on top of a pale-gold
body; crisp and straightforward hops; a typical lager; subdued
freshness; dry finish; nearly better than average. Good with simply prepared fish such as cod, snapper, sole, and flounder.

PRIVATE STOCK MALT LIQUOR   CB   1.1
(Cranston, Rhode Island)
Very watery, somewhat fruity, and generally textureless; slight
sourness underpins the fruitiness; tongue-coating aftertaste
remains tangible throughout; virtually no redeeming flavor;
vinegary taste tracks throughout and increases—or seems to—
toward the end of a meal (and bottle); label suggests serving
it on the rocks!—a sure sign this beer is headed for oblivion, and
deservedly so.

PROSPECTOR JOE'S SPECIAL DARK
GOLDEN Lager   CT   2.9
(San Antonio, Texas)
Soft, with a hint of malt and cherry flavor; stunning clear ruby-
red color; effervescent and light-bodied; built like a typical American beer, but without the obvious chemicals; as it warms, a
smooth roasted maltiness gently emerges, reminiscent of Vienna
amber style; maintains some integrity but overall taste flattens,
heading toward bland at the finish. Match with a ham and cheese
sandwich.

PSCHORR-BRAU WEISSE   CB   3.5
(Munich, Germany)
Tangy, apple-citrus taste; yeasty, with soft, gentle mouthfeel; fat
bubbles support ½-inch-thick head; carbonation holds up as does
dusty-yellow color; taste, aroma, texture, color are all nicely

arranged and balanced, but tame for this particular style; flavorful chewiness ends this dry beer on an attractive note. Try it with Indian curries or Middle Eastern rice and grain dishes.

PUNTIGAMER DARK MALT DRAFT
Lager   CB   2.5
(Graz, Austria)

It does have, as advertised, a draft-beer "feel"; bland in a pleasant way with no carbonation to speak of; some faint burnt taste, a result of dark malt; warming and fuller at the bottom of the bottle; best drunk by itself.

PUNTIGAMER PANTHER DRAFT Lager   CB   3.1
(Graz, Austria)

Mixture of citrus and honey with a creamy head and solid, hearty body; forthright hops and malt presence keep this beer moving along; fruit taste lessens somewhat at mid-bottle, but not to its overall detriment; finishes with character and balance. Good with shrimp, chicken, or pasta salads.

PYRAMID ESPRESSO STOUT (draft)   MB   2.9
(Kalama, Washington)

Smooth, bitter roastedness reflects the deep-brown color; smoky aroma and taste similarly match up well; sweetens considerably alongside food; rich and creamy, but unexciting; chocolate undertones add flavor and character; ingredients are interesting, but need to be better integrated for this beer to realize its full potential. Try it with smoked salmon or trout.

PYRAMID PALE ALE   MB   2.5
(Kalama, Washington)

Perfumey and flat with a thin layer of warmth; an even thinner layer of complexity, while it warms; fullness emerges along with a frisson of acidity with a combination of spicy and sweet foods; not complex; fruity finish. Fine with barbecued beef and a slice of cornbread.

PYRAMID SNOW CAP ALE (annual)   MB   2.5
(Kalama, Washington)

Red-black color; roasted bitterness on the sides of the tongue; watery; flowery hoppiness in an otherwise textureless liquid; slightly cloying as the glass is finished; taste is more appropriate to style than are texture and complexity; some balance creeps in at the end; this is an annual winter offering, so expect some variability. Perfect for traditional holiday meats such as roast turkey and baked ham.

PYRAMID WHEATEN ALE (draft)   MB   3.3
(Kalama, Washington)

Chewy with a bit of wateriness; light, smooth, and sweet; nice citrus bitterness is boosted with a slice of lemon; fresh and light;

recommended as a summer beer. No food was eaten with this, but it would probably go well with salad of mixed summer greens.

QUILMES CRISTAL Pilsener CB 1.6
(Buenos Aires, Argentina)
Too light and dainty for its own good; low-key and thin, but not too watery; loses tartness as it goes from the front of the mouth to the back; uninteresting and dull; pale ginger-ale color matches washed-out taste.

RADEGAST ORIGINAL LAGER CB 3.1
(Nosovice, Czechoslovakia)
Texturally pallid; quite hoppy with minimum fizz; consistent, though relatively bland, taste; typical of Czech pilsener, with its requisite hint of bitterness and hop backbone; soft, long-lasting, spongy head; in the end, weak core undermines the strength of the hops; still too hoppy for my taste, but a solid beer that will make an adventurous beer connoisseur happy. Accompanies pretzels.

RAFFO Pilsener CB 3.9
(Rome, Italy)
Light, somewhat fizzy; pleasant, balanced taste; mellow, "warm" texture; not as full as I generally like, but certainly a good "local" beer; lacks the typical flowery pilsener aroma which, in this case, would enhance its attractiveness. Try it with knockwurst or Italian sausages.

RAINIER ALE CB 3.6
(Seattle, Washington)
Mellow, sweet, creamy, and just fruity enough to titillate the salivary glands; pale red-amber color adds to the enjoyment; maintains warmth and some complexity—certainly more so than most other mass-produced U.S. ales; thinner than comparable European brews—a good American beer. Try with a cheese or chicken salad sandwich.

RATTLESNAKE PREMIUM Lager CT 2.4
(Shiner, Texas)
Light; flavorful with unexpected fullness at the back of the throat; tantalizing warmth doesn't come close to fruition; serviceable in a pinch.

RAZOR EDGE LAGER CB 2.5
(Hobart, Tasmania, Australia)
Sharp; mild citrus flavor; freshness increases with food; two levels of taste: one relatively bland, the other shows more pizzazz and complexity; ingredients are less than top quality, with some roughness and rawness; too thin and not crisp enough; on the verge of becoming a good beer.

RED BACK MALTED WHEAT BEER   CB   2.2
(Fremantle, Western Australia, Australia)
Baked-bread aroma on first sniff—enough yeast to make it almost taste warm and just out of the oven—but the enjoyment stops there; tangy citrus accent; highly malty, so there's little hop bitterness to deal with the yeast; flavor and ambience are too unfocused; soft texture, almost mushy.

RED BARON Lager   MB   2.3
(Waterloo, Ontario, Canada)
Fresh and purposely sour; quickly fading presence; even-tempered; a bit bland; flat, with a somewhat pasty taste in the Canadian tradition; warms to turpentine essence at the end; light and very easy going down.

RED BREW-STER Pilsener   CB   2.2
(Ljubljana, the former Yugoslavia)
Skunky smell yields to fresh malt taste—all packaged in pale, faded liquid with rapidly rising bubbles, which don't quite impact on the palate—or anywhere else; slightly honeyed, creating a warming balance to spicy foods; remains unfizzy and uncomplicated as honey sweetness increases; light yet with a dollop of body for the European customer; pleasant and entertaining, but not top-notch; in the end, too thin and lackluster.

RED BULL MALT LIQUOR   CB   1.4
(Detroit, Michigan)
Pretty much what you'd expect from a mass-market, higher alcohol product—drinkable but lacking distinction; a beer to swill; untamed and mildly raw; weak with food.

RED FEATHER PALE ALE   MB   3.5
(Chambersburg, Pennsylvania)
Light, ruby-red color forms backdrop for this light, more malty than hoppy ale; somewhat bland with a hint of complexity; tantalizingly sweet with a sweet/sour ambience that enhances—and is received well by—red meats; improves with warmth; lasting mellow sweetness throughout the meal; nicely balanced with fruity spritziness; decidedly food-friendly. Goes well with a wide variety of cuisines.

RED HOOK BALLARD
BITTER PALE ALE   CB   3.0
(Seattle, Washington)
Caramel-sweet, watery, and beguiling at first taste; musty aftertaste wends its way down the tongue as you swallow; the taste is okay, but the texture is too light; hop tang is present, carbonation is not; label cheerfully proclaims, "Ya sure, Ya betcha," a local high school sports cheer. Pleasant with Chinese hot-and-sour soup, and Asian pork and shrimp dishes.

RED HOOK BLACKHOOK PORTER   CB   4.0
(Seattle, Washington)
Nice, prickly smoothness with very appealing black barley taste; mildly rich; nicely balanced fullness; achieves well-earned, attractive grittiness at the end as it warms; satisfying with or without food; clearly well-made and very carefully prepared; an American-made porter on a par with English versions. A smooth match for barbecued foods.

RED HOOK ESB ALE   CB   3.1
(Seattle, Washington)
Watery bittersweetness coats the tongue and sides of the mouth on first sip; becomes more integrated and smoother with the food; increasingly satisfying as it warms; smoother, rounded, and more body with emerging citrus sweetness; ends as a very nicely balanced beer; probably not more than a two-bottle brew because it's prone to over-sweetness; check the label for detailed information on how to drink this representation of the classic style. Good with hearty pub food.

RED HOOK WHEAT HOOK ALE   CB   2.9
(Seattle, Washington)
Thirst-quenching, subdued freshness; clear, crisp, and sparkling in taste and feel; simpatico with spicy, salty foods; briny, sharp, and musky; well-made, but it gets less than rave reviews due to its weak fruitiness. Match with strongly flavored foods served with hot sauce.

**RED HOOK WINTERHOOK
CHRISTMAS ALE (annual)   CB   3.6**
(Seattle, Washington)
Apple aroma with moderated back-of-the-mouth spritzy sharpness on first sip; nicely balanced between smoothness and some prickliness; unobtrusive, but maintains its identity with food; perhaps a little too watery and thin; segues into bland at the end; may vary from year-to-year. Just right with holiday cookies and cakes.

RED HORSE MALT LIQUOR   **CB**   **3.2**
(Manila, Philippines)
Neutral to pleasantly sweet, with soft, lightweight taste and color;
evolves into a mild, calm drink; unobtrusive and not particularly
engaging on its own; best with bland foods; a good choice for
those who prefer a non-assertive brew. Try it with chicken noodle soup or fried rice.

B E E R   F A C T

*M*alt liquor is a misnomer. Often an American
brewery's strongest non-ale offering, malt
liquors are in fact lagers that are too high in
alcohol to be labeled beer—usually 4–4.5% and up.
That limit, for example, is reached in Texas at 4% by
weight, 7% by weight in Montana, and 3.2% by weight
in Missouri, where an exception at 5% is made specifically for malt liquor. Several states—e.g., New Mexico, Connecticut, Nevada—have no legal limits. But
because of national distribution constraints, the lowest limit becomes the common denominator.

RED STAR SELECT Lager   **CB**   **2.2**
(Berlin, Germany)
Flat with minimal fizzy citrus bubbles; grainy hoppiness ranges
from subtle to hard, depending on the food it accompanies; clear,
golden color suggests it will taste cleaner and fresher than it does;
dull, workmanlike ambience; relatively light body; a thick slice
of lemon enhances the beer tremendously, adding zest and encouraging the hops to do their thing. Okay with a pastrami-on-
rye sandwich.

RED STRIPE LAGER   **CB**   **2.2**
(Kingston, Jamaica)
Weak hops, malt, and color, with immediate overall ballpark-beer
ambience; weakens still further after a sip or two; some lively flavor holds your interest, but not for long; soft fizziness saves it
from blandness; faintly stale odor; plain and not especially memorable; appropriate for novices building their imported beer library; still, remains in the low-average range. Serve with a salami
and cheese sandwich or sourdough pretzels.

BEER FACT

*J*amaica is one of at least ten islands in the Caribbean that have one or more breweries—a legacy from the early European colonists. The others include: Barbados, Cuba, the Dominican Republic, Haiti, Montserrat, Puerto Rico, Trinidad, and the Virgin Islands.

RED, WHITE AND BLUE
SPECIAL LAGER   CB   3.2
(La Crosse, Wisconsin)
Inexpensive, good baseball beer; tastes like Pabst; I'd probably tire of it quickly; light and thin like an American beer, but still maintains a slightly effervescent feel and some distinction in taste with spicy foods; for a mass-produced brew, this is a surprisingly enjoyable find. Good with a mustard-slathered hot dog.

REICHELBRAU BAVARIAN DARK Lager   CB   3.1
(Kulmbach, Germany)
Soft honey aroma is not reflected in the taste, which is initially, at least, sharp and cold; mild, burnt mouthfeel emerges around the edges and increases in vigor as the bottle empties; a bit too sweet in the end; reasonable balance and complement to sweetish meat that, by itself, would otherwise be bland or neutral. Try with braised pork chops, stir-fried pork with vegetables, or roast turkey.

RESCHS PILSNER   CB   2.9
(Sydney, New South Wales, Australia)
Full-bodied for a non-dark beer; background taste is so subtle that too often it appears as if there is no substantive taste; drink alone or with pizza.

RHEINGOLD PREMIUM Pilsener   CB   1.1
(Philadelphia, Pennsylvania)
Some body along with immediate taste of adjuncts (corn, definitely; rice, perhaps); sharpness quickly fades to blandness; a hint of rawness; some complexity saves it from complete failure; still, it's generally unappealing.

RHINELANDER Lager   CB   2.4
(Monroe, Wisconsin)
Light, with thick backbone and weak citrus fruitiness at the back of the mouth; maintains slight sour taste throughout; far more complex and nuanced than most American lagers; smoother, sweeter, and less flavorful at the end. Try it with black beans and rice or other Central American dishes.

RHINO CHASERS AMBER ALE   CT   3.7
(Chatsworth, California)

Well-balanced; delicate intertwining of sweet and dry makes for interest and mature taste; citrus fruitiness accompanies all sips; somewhat mushy texture, but unobtrusive; milky/hazy amber color doesn't match the interest and appeal of the taste; soft; more of a beer than an ale; tepid but competent. Good with sturdy, uncomplicated dishes such as meat loaf, roast beef, or chicken.

B E E R   F A C T

*P*roceeds from Rhino Chasers products are shared with the African Wildlife Foundation for the protection of the rhinoceros and other endangered species.

RHINO CHASERS AMERICAN ALE   CT   2.2
(Chatsworth, California)

Soft on the tongue and palate; hint of acridness in the nose and at the back of the throat; a little too bland; settles down into a mildly sweet ale with no real distinguishing characteristics; hops presence asserts itself midway through; weak tea color echoes the pallid texture and taste; malt touches the tongue at the end; drink this ale shortly after purchase as it tends to quickly lose its freshness.

RHINO CHASERS LAGER   CT   3.7
(Chatsworth, California)

Highly grainy and sharp with an earthy, country aroma that reminds you of health and goodness; crisp and pointed; texture continues to outweigh flavor; hops are evident; gritty sweetness emerges toward the bottom of the bottle; pale-yellow color belies the strength of the drink; smooths out, but maintains attractive boozy interplay. Good with grilled salmon, spicy boiled crawfish, or Chinese seafood combinations.

RHINO CHASERS WINTERFUL Ale
(annual)   CT   2.5
(St. Paul, Minnesota)

Brewed during the winter holiday season; light touch of orange mixed with soft spiciness; pale amber-copper color; cloves rise up as it warms; too sweet and timidly spicy; suggests alcohol strength heartier than is actually present; fruity aroma toward the end; thickish sweetish finish is not counterbalanced enough with alcohol—a disappointment when all is said and done; comes in a bottle with what appears to be a cloudy, milky film coating the glass, obscuring the contents; a holiday ale that, ironically, does not go well with holiday foods; warm the glass in your hand and sip without food.

RICKARD'S RED DRAUGHT ALE   **CB**   2.5
(Calgary, Alberta; Vancouver, British Columbia, Canada)
Malty-sweet beginning becomes aftertaste at the back of the mouth; mildly sharp, but mainly smooth, almost milky texture; generally, a middle-of-the-road brew; hard to define one way or the other. Best alone or with simple pasta dishes.

RIEGELER SPEZIAL EXPORT Lager   **CB**   2.9
(Kaiserstuhl, Germany)
Strong, musky, malty aroma with nearly equivalent initial taste; distinct alcohol presence remains throughout; grainy undertone significantly enhances enjoyment; surprising molasses taste at mid-glass gives the beer a lift; fuller and more complex at the end than at the beginning—warming seems to help; light-golden color contrasts with the full-bodied taste and texture; somewhat hoppy finish. Good with broiled or grilled steaks.

RINCON DRY Pilsener   **CT**   2.3
(Dubuque, Iowa)
Thin, yeasty, and sour, with pale, faded color to match; settles into bittersweetness with relatively little complexity; surprisingly lasting head—foamy but thin; easy-going; lightweight, but decent. Try it with smoked oysters or clams.

RINGNES EXPORT PALE Pilsener   **CB**   4.0
(Oslo, Norway)
Very warm, mellow, wheat-rice taste lasts with food; taste is consistent, not too sharp, and pleasingly integrated; a touch of sweetness gives this light brew a certain roundness; crisp and clean overall, it has more taste than texture; a beer made with the enjoyment of food in mind. Very good with Buffalo-style chicken wings or chicken nuggets with dipping sauce.

RINGNES SPECIAL JUBILEE ALE   **CB**   2.7
(Oslo, Norway)
Malty roastiness disappears and goes flat almost immediately; slowly rising integrated warmth with food; mellow, moderate sweetness also emerges; lovely maltiness appears further on; ultimately lacks the silky firmness and pungency of a first-class ale; basically no head; in the end, a restrained but changeable drink. Serve with grilled chicken.

RIO BRAVO BIG BOB'S
BARLEYWINE (draft)   **BP**   2.6
(Albuquerque, New Mexico)
Nice sweet flavor at start, with full, wine-like taste; lovely sensa-

tion at the front of the mouth unfortunately fades at the back after a few quick sips; fresh and fruity with a hint of grapefruit sourness; aroma more integrated than the taste; sweeter than other barley wines; smooth and filling, a suggestion of diminished alcohol presence; deep, ruby-red color signals this is a close cousin of this brewer's highly regarded pale ale; sticks slightly to the roof of the mouth; needs sharp food accompaniment to cut some of the juicy thickness; much more agreeable to the novice palate than expected. Try it with a sharp cheese, fruit, and cracker platter; tortilla chips with salsa; or grilled artichokes.

RIO BRAVO ESTEBAN DARK PORTER (draft)   BP   4.1
(Albuquerque, New Mexico)

Cooling and soothing on the first sip; sweetens and weakens with food; moderate roasted taste swirls around the mouth; somewhat chewy, with chocolate notes threading in and out; deep, ruby-brown coloration makes up for fleeting appearance of Brussels lace (longevity seems to have improved greatly in subsequent samples); finishes fresh, with attractive, sweet malt taste and aroma; both the brewmaster and my tasting partner noted licorice tones, which I did not; I drink a lot of this without food—virtually a meal in itself, it possesses many nuances and subtleties; for an exhilarating change of pace, have the barkeep pour half a pint of pale ale and top it off with a half a pint of this finely honed, luscious porter. Good with chicken mole.

RIO BRAVO FRUIT ALE (draft)   BP   0.3
(Albuquerque, New Mexico)

Raspberry aroma permeates the glass and fizzless raspberry pop taste spoils the fun; weak and unobtrusive, with seemingly no alcohol at all; poor representation, unless it was meant to come out of a soda bottle; pass up this one.

RIO BRAVO HIGH DESERT PALE ALE (draft)   BP   4.2
(Albuquerque, New Mexico)

Full-bodied, full-flavored; deliciously hoppy and quite dry, with consistent, clearly defined flowery presence; powerful hops take center stage, but remain respectfully in balance with intoxicating aroma and overall ambience; beautifully configured, dainty Brussels lace is long-lasting; ditto for the head; hops mature and remain floral-tasting and dry; gentle yeastiness; I was unable to detect an underlying caramel maltiness that the brewmaster aims for; quite dry at the end; finishes as it starts: fresh, bountiful, and enormously satisfying—a credit to the style; delicious on its own but also unusually tasty alongside thick slices of crusty French bread.

RIO BRAVO KURLY'S KOLSCH
(draft)   BP   2.1
(Albuquerque, New Mexico)

Lightly bitter; somewhat watery; increases in blandness as you drink more—almost hopless, as it should be; texture is nonexistent; decent Brussels lace; minimal aroma with faint, hoppy aftertaste; light and dry; meets the characteristics of the style, but remains unsatisfying and unexciting. Okay with nachos and guacamole.

RIO BRAVO LARRY'S LAGER (draft)   BP   0.6
(Albuquerque, New Mexico)

Smells faintly of old cigarettes—not a good sign; hop imbalance and, alas, a hint of skunkiness; hops turn into sour wateriness early on and remain that way; crisp and fizzy, but too weak overall to be rated higher.

RIO BRAVO O'KEEFE
DRY IRISH STOUT   BP   4.0
(Albuquerque, New Mexico)

Brewer says he meant to make this in the traditional manner, with traditional ingredients: he certainly succeeded, arranging them almost perfectly—smooth, reasonably bitter, mildly roasted, judiciously sweet, and full of mouth-filling malted barley taste; Brussels lace is so appropriately aligned and spaced in thick parallel layers, it looks almost computerized; a bit of thickish aftertaste on the tongue lasts a little too long, but that's the price one pays to continue experiencing its soft mellowness even after the pint glass has been drained dry; try more than one of these, and relax. An unusual, but very good, match with a steamed artichoke; also good with risotto.

RIO GRANDE OUTLAW LAGER   MB   2.8
(Albuquerque, New Mexico)

Thickly fruity, with a hefty hop sharpness; malt sweetness creeps in on second sip, lending beguiling balance to the flavorful bitterness; rather flat and too smooth texturally; ingredients, especially the water, come together in a neat package; yeasty sourness floats forward as the fruity taste diminishes; weakens considerably at the finish; a decent start for a beer that has not been on the market for long. For an interesting taste sensation, try with chocolate cookies or a piece of rich, chocolatey devil's food cake.

RITTERBRAU PALE Lager   CB   4.0
(Dortmund, Germany)

Dark and attractive on first sip—and last; malt and hops appear to be of high quality and professionally brewed, making for delectable, spritzy mouthfeel; worth savoring alone, as well as with food; remains fresh and inviting, with slight mustiness as the bottle empties; finely tuned and unresponsive. A good choice with snapper, mahi mahi, or pompano.

RIVA BLANCHE ALE   **CB**   **2.2**
(Dentergem, Belgium)

Perfumey, yeasty aroma; mini-fizziness; yeast continues to dominate; pale-straw color, with no head; sour and moderately bitter; very cloudy; uninspired vision; meets the style of white ale—a bit orangey (citrus increases) at the end; yeast sediment on the bottom of the glass; you really need to like this style to finish this bottle-conditioned brew.

TAP TIP

Clouds, Agitation, and Beer Storage

*M*ore and more breweries—especially the consumer-conscious microbreweries—are marking their bottles with dates to indicate optimal shelf life. While some clearly identify the pull dates on the label, usually with clearly delineated punch marks, others place essentially indecipherable codes, generally meant for the retailer, on the bottle, can bottom, or neck. One quick and easy way to make some determination about the age of the bottle you have in your hand is to gently turn it upside down. Hold it up to the light; you can be fairly certain it is past its prime if you observe any cloudiness or sediment (this, of course, doesn't work for a wheat or bottle-conditioned product, since its defining characteristics are, in fact, cloudiness and/or sediment). Checking dates is not a futile exercise. I once purchased an expensive French bitter, only to discover that, according to the date markings on the label, it was almost three years old. I returned it to the retailer, who not only gave me credit for future purchases, but immediately had one of his clerks call up the wholesaler and tell him to come by and pick up the whole rotting batch.

Beer should be stored standing up, in order to minimize oxidation and to reduce the possibility of contact between beer and metal (in the cap). Further, don't agitate the liquid, which means keep your bottles and cans in the back of the fridge, not on the door shelf.

ROCKIES DRAFT Ale   **MB**   **3.6**
(Boulder, Colorado)
Freshly brewed and mild; hint of apple; slight textural buzz; full, tightly woven Brussels lace with minimal head; remains pleasantly sweet with a nice hit of hops to keep it gently balanced; refreshing and immensely enjoyable all by itself. A good match with hot dogs or baked beans.

RODENBACH BELGIAN RED ALE   **CB**   **2.9**
(Roeselare, Belgium)
Immediate light-struck (skunky) odor along with highly tart but normal sourness and orange spiciness; chocolate taste comes up with shellfish; rich, deep-copper color leads you to expect more fullness; spice and yeastiness don't really sort themselves out; individual flavors are somewhat muddied; at the end, spicy, hot sauces pleasantly cut through the yeast's tartness; finishes harsh, dry, and fruity; naturally aged for two years in oak casks, it lays claim to being the "most refreshing beer in the world." Try it with hard cheese and sliced cold meats.

ROGUE ALE   **MB/BP**   **3.1**
(Newport, Oregon)
Deep, rich aroma followed by thin taste; smooth and sweet with underlying liveliness; nice balance of hops and malt with appropriate alcohol—not too harsh and not too much—connecting the two; a dollop of honey nestles at the back of the mouth; finishes with yeasty, hoppy palate that enhances hot foods; a little flat overall; final sip exudes warmth and chewiness. Try it with spaghetti with a spicy red meat sauce.

ROGUE GOLDEN ALE   **MB/BP**   **2.4**
(Newport, Oregon)
Fruitiness with an edge of sharpness in the throat; airy, as befits a golden ale; thin layer of aftertaste; murky, faded golden color suggests that further maturing is needed; tastes like an unfinished (green) product; everything softens as it warms, but premature bottling remains evident; to best enjoy this ale, drink a bit and let the remainder stay capped in the cooler for a day or two. A match for pasta with Italian sausages.

ROGUE MAIERBOCK ALE   **MB/BP**   **3.9**
(Newport, Oregon)
Delightfully malty aroma offers not-so-sneak preview of pleasure and enjoyment; light, syrupy, berry taste lingers, but doesn't spoil the aftertaste; light-golden color daintily supports fuzzy, mossy head which pours to a delicious thickness; quick, sharp taste gets nicely lost in sweet smoothness; random sheets of Brussels lace enhance the ambience; rich and moderately hearty; well-balanced in taste, aroma, and color; finishes a touch weak, but with a full, grainy, candied-malt aroma. A good choice with pizza or calzones.

ROGUE MEXICALI ALE   MB/BP   2.5
(Newport, Oregon)

Very pleasant aroma of restrained citrus and spice on first sip, along with cloudy (yeast-laden), light-amber color; almost tea-like in texture, taste, and coloring; weak but satisfying with fizzy carbonation and faint hop taste; lingering tartness perks up the end of the bottle; too watery—not the best representative of this gem of a microbrewery. Nice with roast chicken and a garden salad.

ROGUE MOGUL ALE   MB/BP   3.6
(Newport, Oregon)

Immediate honey-pine aroma that makes you go "yummm . . ." and eagerly look forward to tasting it; soft around the edges with a bite of hops underneath and throughout; good, lasting Brussels lace is nice counterpoint to the medium-deep, red-brown body; clear and balanced; light orange fruitiness becomes more evident with barbecued foods; appears to be less alcoholic than other Rogue ales; smooth, hoppy finish, preceded by subdued liveliness. Pairs well with barbecue or smoked meats.

ROGUE NEW PORTER   MB/BP   3.7
(Newport, Oregon)

Even with the hyperbolic advertising this label doesn't mislead: "a bittersweet balance of malt and hops yet a surprisingly light and refreshing finish"; thickish head and hearty Brussels lace; in general, too texturally weak; substantial, fulfilling mouthfeel; finishes mellow, gentle, and soft. Wonderful with medium-rare roast beef and a baked potato, or with venison.

ROGUE OLD CRUSTACEAN
BARLEY WINE   MB/BP   3.6
(Newport, Oregon)

Tentative apple-cider aroma gently wafts up as soon as the cap comes off the tiny (6.4 ounce) bottle; full mouthfeel as alcohol revs up and takes over, though fruitiness lingers; quite bitter and texturally weak; hazy, brandy color is result of yeast in the bottle; slight mustiness comes along toward the end; a warming, compassionate brew; a bit too thin and unassertive; aroma is simply wonderful and stays steady and available throughout; smooth, not biting; well-made and carefully crafted—a Rogue trademark. A companionable *digestif.*

ROGUE RED ALE   MB/BP   4.4
(Newport, Oregon)

Fresh, yeasty aroma immediately creates interest; smooth, foamy texture perfectly balances the hoppy fizziness; just the right kick of alcohol; remains fresh, if just a bit raw, throughout the bottle; mellow, foamy head sits jauntily atop deep, copper-red colored body; frothy, fresh, and appropriately complex; toastiness everywhere; stunning achievement; belongs in anyone's book of the best beers; cheers for this American brewery; may be the freshest-tasting bottled beer I've ever had. Savor with thick Bavarian-style pretzels and honey mustard.

B E E R   F A C T

*H*op content is measured in a brewer's convention called International Bitterness Units (IBUs). For most drinkers, hop bitterness first becomes noticeable at around 10 IBUs (e.g., Budweiser, Miller). A hearty stout like Guinness checks in at about 50 IBUs. Rogue's Old Crustacean, by strong contrast, is rated at 80 IBUs. *Caveat emptor.*

ROGUE ROGUE-N-BERRY ALE　　　**MB/BP**　　　**3.1**
(Newport, Oregon)
Butterscotch aroma and taste, with rich mouthfeel on first sips; cloudy, light-coffee color; vague berry flavor underlies the heavy yeastiness throughout; stays rich and fruity, almost chewy; finishes light and relatively oomph-less; best without food.

ROGUE SHAKESPEARE STOUT　　　**MB/BP**　　　**4.8**
(Newport, Oregon)
This may well be my favorite bottled beer of all time (well, there *is* Rogue Red Ale); deeply roasted and creamy, with tantalizing bitterness; thick, smooth, and attractive; deeply satisfying; I have sampled this many times with a variety of foods—red meat, pasta, vegetables, and sweet desserts—and my enthusiasm remains at every sip and swallow; a conversation stopper; do try it.

ROGUE SMOKE ALE　　　**MB/BP**　　　**2.0**
(Newport, Oregon)
Smells and tastes like smoked salami but without the spicy edge; hint of garlic; velvety smooth; mild, smoky ambience; deep-amber color; nicely configured Brussels lace quickly slides down sides of glass and disappears; too thin and watery; weakens at the end; mild, lesser version of German *Rauchbier;* a rare, below-average offering from this otherwise fine microbrewery. Drink with beer nuts.

ROGUE ST. ROGUE RED ALE   MB/BP   3.0
(Newport, Oregon)

Fresh, fruity, yeasty aroma; deep-copper color is perfect for this strong, solid ale; mellow sweetness with just an edge of sharpness emerges with food; roasted flavor underpins a slight spruciness that fills the nose and mouth; a bit pedestrian compared to other Rogue styles, but still one of my favorite American breweries; good sipping ale for a relaxed, cold evening.

ROLLING ROCK Lager   CB   3.6
(Latrobe, Pennsylvania)

Very American, but with more flavor than the average domestic beer; taste is evenly distributed on the tongue, palate, and throat; blunted crispness sits well at the back of the tongue; paints its own texture and color; tasty, but not complex or dynamic; one of the better mass-market American beers. Goes with virtually any food.

ROLLING ROCK BOCK   CB   3.5
(Latrobe, Pennsylvania)

Sweet, with a substantial dose of alcohol that refreshes and then fades; sharp and thirst-quenching; controlled sweetness does its job, and then moves on; a bit thickish aftertaste; nicely balanced with noticeable, carefully delineated hops and malt. For an unusual pairing, try this at brunch with Belgian waffles and real maple syrup.

ROYAL BRAND Pilsener   CB   3.4
(Wylre, Holland)

Sharp texture entering the mouth, dull at the back of the tongue; slight off-taste, but in general not much flavor at all: initial distinctive taste becomes integrated at the back of the tongue; retains an interesting and invigorating complexity with food; a second bottle would not be unwarranted. Serve along with olives, morsels of cheese, crackers, and other savory pre-dinner nibbles.

ROYAL EXTRA STOUT   CB   3.7
(Trinidad, West Indies)

Sweet, chocolatey, and full; doesn't present an immediately attractive ambience; sweetness calms down and becomes relatively complementary; deep, dark-brown color with thin, reddish-tan head; still, this is a good example of a mild stout; delectable toasted malt aroma at the end; hint of alcohol also helps dampen the sweetness. Compatible with Caribbean cuisines.

ROYAL GUARD CERVEZA—TIPO
DORTMUND Lager   CB   2.5
(Santiago, Chile)

Thickish on tongue; clearly less hoppy and bitter than its pilsener ~usin (see below); also more run-of-the-mill; medium body;

rather uninteresting without food, but still a cut above most other Chilean beers; malty sweetness eventually appears; in the end, too thick, too much aftertaste; food helps moderate the aftertaste. Goes with savory tidbits such as nachos, Spanish *tapas,* or Greek *meze.*

ROYAL GUARD PILSENER   **CB**   **3.8**
(Santiago, Chile)
Some fizziness; attractive complexity with emphasis on hops; maintains character throughout; golden wheat color; almost wine-like in character (body, balance, and integration); rich and satisfying with or without food. Good with a wide range of foods from mild cheese with crackers to steaks and chicken.

ROYAL OAK PALE ALE   **CB**   **4.4**
(Dorchester, England)
Appealingly soft and fruity, complemented by subtle bitterness; like a soothing, smooth brandy, but fuller with more body; copper color at outset diminishes but remains at the edges; creamy head; finishes with a moderated sweet fruitiness that makes you ask for more; round and mobile at the back of the tongue—a classy act; mouth-filling flavor increases with warmth, though a bit watery; very good alone. Delicious with pork.

RUBENS GOLD Ale   **CT**   **3.0**
(Kontich, Belgium)
Crisp and slightly metallic with a bitter, hoppy presence on the tongue; thick, harsh-tasting head; exquisitely patterned small bubbles mutate into irregular big ones toward the top of the foam; grating, rough texture grabs your attention while the taste remains secondary; head stays foamy, if somewhat light and airy; finish is mild and unassuming; best without food; style is indeterminate; label says top-fermenting, serve chilled—the importer says it has the character of a pilsener; sort of a eunuch beer, but I'd try it again.

B E E R   F A C T

*R*ubens Gold is named for the 17th-century Flemish painter, Peter Paul Rubens, whose vibrant, exuberant, animated style is claimed by the importer to be represented in this lively ale.

RUDDLES BITTER   **CB**   **1.4**
(Rutland, England)
Sweet-to-tasteless with hint of cloyingness; possesses a lightness that is not expected due to its (thin) amber color; certainly not bitter, in fact weak; taste of hops is feeble; an undistinguished beer.

RUDDLES COUNTRY ALE   CB   2.5
(Rutland, England)
Golden-amber color complements thickish, burnt quality of the
initial taste; constant, flat-tasting overtone; slightly unpleasant aftertaste; with food, taste begins to wither in strength and palata-
bility; sweet and robust; best alone, but can be paired with seafood
pilaf or chicken with yellow rice.

RUSKI Lager   CB   3.3
(Kiev, Ukraine)
Immediate sourdough-rye bread aroma with a similar follow-up
taste; solid body; dry and thirst-quenching; reduces to cold water mouthfeel, albeit from a relatively fresh spring; decent head
appears to be artificially carbonated; very wispy Brussels lace; ef-
fortless to swallow, easy to take—a good beginner's beer; finishes
with a hint of clove; refreshing. (Note that there is sometimes a
residue in the rubber liner of the bottlecap—mold?) Serve with
cold meats or fish.

RUSSKOYE LAGER   CB   0.2
(Kiev, Ukraine)
Full grain aroma followed by cold, sharp mouthfeel; relatively
flavorless and almost green tasting; chemical ambience (to stabi-
lize it) doesn't help; really has no quality features—no complexity, no enduring taste, no aroma, no lasting head; faded, translucent
yellow-orange color; basically unappetizing.

SAGRES PREMIUM Lager   CB   2.1
(Lisbon, Portugal)
Gentle and flat with faded texture as it hits the sides of the tongue;
negligible head with nondescript yellow color; some acidity creeps
in with food, paradoxically adding character otherwise missing;
hop imbalance; overall, rather unimpressive.

SAILER PILS   CB   2.8
(Marktoberdorf, Germany)
Not-unpleasant sour taste on first sip; wine-like aftertaste; reminiscent of heavier beer; highly flavored and fills the mouth with
bland but determined hoppiness; faint metallic presence makes
your appreciation more cautious and tentative—it disappears
quickly, and the beer regains its earlier attraction; clearly making
an effort to please, and, except for a momentary lapse, it does.
Compatible with Asian cuisines.

SAINT NICK'S DARK ALE (annual)   CT   3.1
(Helena, Montana)
Creamy, moist, and sweet, unlike many other Christmas brews;
typical burnt-malt taste nicely tempered by smooth texture and
restrained sweetness; enchanting specialty beer whose attitude appears to make it welcome with any food—spicy, plain, or in-be-

tween; some fading of already weak strength at the end; uncomplicated and straightforward; above average.

SAMICHLAUS DARK Lager (annual)   CB   0.1
(Zürich, Switzerland)
Strongly alcoholic, but moderated a bit by fizzy caramel taste; extraordinarily syrupy and acridly tart; clearly more wine-like than beer-like; alcohol is too overwhelming even for highly flavored food; increasing sweetness; malty, faint brown-sugar aroma and brandy-like finish; strong and assertive; clearly has quality ingredients, but their arrangement bothers me; considered a very good brew by some beer lovers; connoisseurs drink this with a dollop of raspberry or strawberry syrup for a more rounded mouthfeel; sip as an *apéritif* or *digestif*. (Due to varying laws regarding alcohol content, "Brown" may be substituted for the word "Dark" on the label in some states, but it is the same beer.)

> **B E E R   F A C T**
>
> *E*ach batch of Samichlaus, which means "Santa Claus" to the Swiss, is brewed on December 6th, naturally aged before bottling, and distributed one year later. Until the introduction of Samuel Adams Triple Bock (17% alcohol by volume), it is reputed to be the world's strongest beer (14% alcohol by volume), and, as a result, has been listed in *The Guinness Book of Records*. Unlike other lagers, Samichlaus should be stored at cellar temperatures in order to enhance its definite ale-like qualities.

SAMUEL ADAMS BOSTON STOCK ALE   CB   2.6
(Boston, Massachusetts)
Tastes more like lager than ale, with a hint of citrus sharpness; a flexible setting for food, both adding support as well as remaining neutral; hint of caramelized malt; not as hearty as advertised, although more multidimensional and complex than most Americans are used to, with crisscrossing textures, flavors, and aromas. Enjoy alongside a grilled hamburger.

SAMUEL ADAMS BREWHOUSE
ORANGE CORIANDER WHEAT BEER   CT/BP   3.1
(Philadelphia, Pennsylvania)
Very flowery, like a poignant marmalade with deflected sweetness; not too overwhelming, but enough to make you want more; nice balance between hops and spice flavors; more than one bottle of this concoction would probably be too much, but drink-

ing it with liquid-absorbing, starchy foods like potatoes or bread increases the likelihood of prolonged enjoyment.

SAMUEL ADAMS CRANBERRY
LAMBIC   CT   3.4
(Pittsburgh, Pennsylvania)

Knife-sharp texture with just a hint of berries—a nice surprise when you expect overly fruity sweetness, but instead get a hit of the true tartness of the cranberry; displays more amber color than cranberry red; people who don't like cranberry sauce (yours truly among them) should not be put off by this incarnation—displays berry's virtues, not negatives; remains tart and snappy and, surprisingly, is a nice accompaniment to certain foods; good thirst-quencher; not much haze; stays tart and dry to the, uh, bitter end; finishes a bit too thin, but remains far less intrusively sweet, unlike European lambics. An interesting match with meat loaf, roast pork, or (no surprise) turkey.

SAMUEL ADAMS CREAM STOUT   CT   2.3
(Utica, New York; Pittsburgh, Pennsylvania)

Burnt, bitter, and roasted—the way a stout should be—although not hearty or integrated enough to be up there with the best stouts, nor is it as rich or smooth; malt needs to be more fully roasted and perhaps also increased in quality—or at least the ratio altered; weak alcohol presence; maybe brewing this at the company's Boston site rather than contracting it out would improve the mix and match.

SAMUEL ADAMS DARK WHEAT   CT   2.7
(Pittsburgh, Pennsylvania)

Subdued wheat taste with musty-dusty aroma; evenhanded and predictable with fine sheets of Brussels lace; integrated balance of hops and malt fits nicely and comfortably with relatively bland foods; emerging hop bitterness with slight carbonation toward the end of the bottle; not very complex or intimidating; good starter for the wheat-drinking newcomer. Accompanies chicken dishes.

SAMUEL ADAMS DOUBLE BOCK
DARK LAGER   CT   3.7
(Pittsburgh, Pennsylvania)

Creamy, tangy, and full; highly malted; deep red-amber color is clear and makes for a nice initial impression; sweet alcohol presence emerges at midstride, quickly subsiding before it gets too cloying or too sweet; thick on the tongue; more than one glass or bottle at a time might prove to be too rich and full-bodied for the average drinker; starchy foods help temper the richness; smooth and entertaining with a high percentage of malt; Bronze Medal winner at the 1993 Great American Beer Festival. Try it with a broiled steak and a baked potato.

SAMUEL ADAMS HONEY PORTER / **CT** 3.3
(Lehigh Valley, Pennsylvania)
Tangy, coffee taste follows a pour of deep ruby-red color; medium-bodied with, as the label rightly proclaims, a full, round flavor; honey tones emerge one by one: a very charming balance between constrained sweetness and bitter roastedness—makes you pay attention to what you are drinking; mild, malty aroma caps things off as the glass is finished; effortlessly done and well worth looking for; delicious by itself or with nuts and dried fruit.

SAMUEL ADAMS OCTOBERFEST
Lager **CB/CT** 3.7
(Boston, Massachusetts;
Pittsburgh, Pennsylvania)
Immediate tangy hops, sparkling but subdued carbonation, and fruity/hoppy nose; malts taste roasted; overall, a strong, deeply textured brew; sprightly, rounded, balanced character, but doesn't integrate well with food; alcohol is felt by the time the bottle is finished; good American version of a traditional German beer.

SAMUEL ADAMS TRIPLE BOCK **CB/CT** 4.7
(brewed at Bronco Winery in
Ceres, California, for the Boston
Brewing Co.)
First whiff (even at a distance) is alcohol, second is maple syrup; deep, tawny color is reminiscent of a beautiful port; wonderfully fruity and woody, filling the mouth with delectable subtleties and nuances; a sweet, ripe, prune-like taste emerges—all delicate and exquisitely balanced; silky smooth and gentle, with none of the burning roughness of a cognac or whiskey; remains layered, rich, and absolutely compelling—the subtle delicacy is memorable; warm, maple-syrup aroma with hints of sweet vanilla lasts throughout; mellow, with a coaxing, tantalizing buzz; one negative: a fuzzy, distinct aftertaste stays on the roof of the mouth for several hours after the last sip—but the good news is it continues to evoke the sultry bock's maple and fruit essence; savor slowly at room temperature in a brandy snifter after dinner.

*I*ntroduced to the public in 1994 in a sleek, "designer" 8.45-ounce cobalt blue bottle with gilt lettering, Samuel Adams Triple Bock claims a record-breaking alcohol content of 17%/volume. Commercially brewed for Samuel Adams at the Bronco Winery in Ceres, California, it is aged for 45 to 60 days in oak barrels that once contained Jack Daniel's Rare Tennessee Whiskey. The company anticipates the triple bock will improve with age and invites interested parties to contact it for periodic updates. I have two bottles resting comfortably in the back of my refrigerator, alongside Thomas Hardy's Ale and Rogue Old Crustacean Barley Wine.

SAMUEL ADAMS WHEAT   **CT**   **2.5**
(Pittsburgh, Pennsylvania)
Immediate, sweet, yeast/citrus taste with unfortunate quick and short-lasting skunkiness; tempered, but warm sweetness gradually climbs out of the morass, making it soft and mellow, rather than zesty and tart; taste fullness is reached at the end: Why did it take so long? Accompanies a lettuce and tomato salad or light pasta dishes.

SAMUEL ADAMS WINTER LAGER
(annual)   **CT**   **2.2–3.9**
(Portland, Oregon)
A seasonal beer with warm, spicy, caramel aroma and similar taste; a bit too thickishly sweet; strong hoppiness; not particularly complex though clearly well-made; rich, red-amber color; generally unexciting; mellows out toward the end, but still remains essentially bland and unobtrusive; indistinct and lumbering; as an annual brew, the quality and enjoyment are necessarily variable—as a general rule, one way to maximize the likelihood of getting a fresh, quality product is to buy a bottle produced at the brewery site closest to where you live (read the label carefully).

SAMUEL SMITH OATMEAL STOUT   **CB**   **4.0**
(Tadcaster, England)
Full-bodied without being filling; good burnt taste; strong, smooth—almost silky; generously sweet, but not to the point of interfering with food; well-made and well worth the expense. Delicious with roast beef, steaks, and game.

SAMUEL SMITH TADCASTER
TADDY PORTER   CB   3.7
(Tadcaster, England)
Subdued wine aroma on first sniff resolves into mini-sharpness,
with mild caramel on the palate; deep-brown color looks like a
full-throated burgundy wine in a tulip-shaped glass; settles
down into a rounded, full-bodied drink with slight sourness; interesting juice taste/texture (sugary, thin, just-off-the-vine) is present
at the end of the bottle; quality wine finish; sequential rather
than integrated taste; since I don't like wine, my ranking is probably less than a wine drinker might give it. Try it with breaded
pork chops or veal cutlets.

SAMUEL SMITH'S IMPERIAL STOUT   CB   4.0
(Tadcaster, England)
Wine/berry aroma; dark, roasted, creamy taste with a dollop of
appropriate sourness; incredibly full-bodied, integrated, and robust, particularly at the end; extraordinarily rich throughout;
cheery and refreshing, with more than a hint of alcohol; caramel
color and burnt-currant taste fill the entire mouth, with the taste
memory lasting long afterward; one of my favorite high-alcohol
brews. Stay away from food with this distinctive beer; savor as
either an *apéritif* or *digestif.*

SAMUEL SMITH'S LAGER   CB   4.0
(Tadcaster, England)
Full-bodied, appealingly hoppy, and clean-tasting, with pale-
golden, healthy-looking hue; a quality beer with undiminished
backbone; maintains its zest and balance of hops and malt from
fresh start to exuberant finish; rounded and made to fit comfortably in the mouth. A versatile, quality lager that can be enjoyed with nearly any food.

SAMUEL SMITH'S NUT BROWN ALE   CB   3.4
(Tadcaster, England)
Mild and pleasantly sweet; slight winey taste; palate-pleasing and
smooth; very similar to Fuller's London Pride; a more full-bodied taste at the back of the tongue; very complementary to plain
foods.

SAMUEL SMITH'S OLD BREWERY
PALE ALE   CB   3.0
(Tadcaster, England)
Sharpness obscures slight caramel-burnt taste; copper-tan color;
minimal sourness; not as satisfying as the heavier, darker, richer
Smith's beers. Good with a chicken salad sandwich on toasted
rye bread.

BEER FACT

*T*adcaster, home of the Samuel Smith brewery, was originally a Roman encampment. Its lake water which lies atop a bed of limestone, is ideal for producing pale ale—the predominant style of beer in Great Britain.

SAMUEL SMITH'S WINTER WELCOME ALE (annual)   **CB**   **2.3–3.8**
(Tadcaster, England)

As an annual offering, there is variability from year to year; overall, I find this to indeed be a warm winter welcome: opening aroma can be musty and dry, with a hint of perfume in the air; first sip is fizzy and crisp, smooth and elegant; straightforward, strong, and hearty with high alcohol content adding to the seasonal cheer; refreshing and almost perfectly balanced, though it can be too textureless for the punch of the taste and aroma; imparts a warm, friendly glow, but, in the end, sometimes not as flavorful as it could be; check out the label: it's a joyous, multicolored testament to attractive packaging, offering a visual suggestion as to what you may find inside; alcoholic strength seems to have increased over the years. Sip as a *digestif*, or serve with rice and other grain dishes.

SAN ANDRES EARTHQUAKE PALE ALE   MB   **3.0**
(Hollister, California)

Very fruity aroma and mouthfeel with flowery smoothness; tastes like its color: cloudy, pale amber; aftertaste bite is pleasantly fleeting; ends with integrated though conflicting appeal of taste, smell, and texture; remains fresh throughout; invites you back again, although its name might suggest otherwise. Try it with crispy chips and dip.

SAN ANDRES KIT FOX AMBER Ale   MB   **1.1**
(Hollister, California)

Flat, flat, flat; tasteless, too, as if the flavor has been drained from it; only taste characteristic is hint of fruity sourness that is coaxed out by food; seems to have the promise of a balanced, flavorful brew, but never quite makes it; perhaps it's not fresh enough; *caveat emptor*.

SAN ANDRES SEISMIC ALE   MB/BP   **1.8**
(Hollister, California)

Sour with barely perceptible fizziness; settles into bland taste and texture; very slight hint of fruity aroma; improves 24 hours after bottle is opened; better without food.

SAN CARLOS ESPECIAL Pilsener   CB   2.3
(San Carlos, Argentina)
Very pale, light-bodied pilsener with a sharp but very restrained opening tang; fluffy, moderately disappearing head is a good counterpoint to slight acridness of the body; relatively satisfying without food (the operative word here is "relatively"); some complexity raises it a notch or so above other ordinary brews.

SAN FRANCISCO CACTUS LAGER   BP   0.8
(Tucson, Arizona)
Fruity and sweet; not particularly sharp; texturally uninteresting and bland; sour, musty aftertaste leaves you not wanting more; unbalanced and relatively tasteless; the only agreeable quality is the Brussels lace that clings tenaciously to the sides of the glass—unfortunately, the taste sticks around, too.

SAN FRANCISCO WILDCAT ALE   BP   1.0
(Tucson, Arizona)
Cloying and sweet; textureless and flat; attempts to offer a big taste and falls far short; sticky and unappealing.

SAN MIGUEL DARK Pilsener   CB   4.4
(Manila, Philippines)
Buoyant and uplifting, fulfilling both its promise and your expectations; creamy richness with very mild, burnt maltiness that's integrated into the fullness and warmth of the texture; finishes a little too watery for my taste, thereby lessening its overall effect; this is a very good beer, one of the best imported beers of those most readily available at local retailers. One of the things I like is its compatibility with both plain and fancy dishes—from a salami sandwich to a butterflied leg of lamb.

SAN MIGUEL PALE PILSEN   CB   2.9
(Manila, Philippines)
Light and fizzy with no stimulating aroma; hint of wheat/grain flavor gently enlivens a mouthfeel that initially fails to gain your attention; sweetens and becomes pleasantly even-tempered with food; moves along; a far cry from San Miguel Dark. Fine with a hamburger or linguine with clam sauce.

BEER FACT

Although San Miguel is often associated with the Philippines, it is actually a Spanish company, with headquarters in Manila.

SAN RAFAEL AMBER ALE　　　　MB　　　　2.4
(Novato, California)
Thick and citrusy (lemon), perhaps a touch sour; not a head in sight; a general fruitiness gradually replaces the singular citrus presence; less interesting alone than with spicy foods; flavor is more complex as it warms, while sourness is subdued; some yeastiness in bottle deepens amber color and increases attractiveness; definitely drink this ale at room temperature. Complements baked ham.

SAN RAFAEL GOLDEN ALE　　　　MB　　　　3.2
(Novato, California)
Light, fruity aroma with textural kick as soon as the bottle is opened and you take your first swallow; fluffy, satisfying mouthfeel; minimal, clouded, golden color; complexity and flavor reach a high point with simple foods; stays true to typical golden ale style, especially light and dry; maintains mild floweriness with appropriate hint of alcohol; could be zestier; overall, a pleasing, albeit not overwhelming, package. Try it with deli sandwiches.

SAN RAFAEL TRADITIONAL ALE　　　　MB　　　　0.4
(Novato, California)
Sour, apparently light-struck, and thinly citrusy; far too fruity even for ale; without any discernible malt or other balancing qualities, a truly one-note brew; yeast runs rampant with no controlling factors; unusually opaque; unintegrated and unfinished; lots of yeast sediment detracts.

SANTA CRUZ LIGHTHOUSE
AMBER Lager　　　　MB　　　　1.1
(Santa Cruz, California)
While aroma is rose-sweet on first contact, it is too sour on the throat; oxidized, which in this case may not be the brewer's fault—but the taste effect is the same, regardless of the culprit.

SANTA CRUZ LIGHTHOUSE LAGER　　　　MB　　　　0.6
(Santa Cruz, California)
Sour and tart, almost like spoiled wheat beer; essentially textureless; fruity and acrid—clearly not lager—this beer is either spoiled or mislabeled; no head, no fizz, no nothing.

SANTA FE CHICKEN KILLER
BARLEY WINE　　　　MB　　　　1.3
(Galisteo, New Mexico)
Light, soft, and balanced; alcohol is gentle rather than harsh; medium amber color; yeasty and young—not fully developed; with short-term storage in the bottle, hops and sweetness diminish and balance changes: bitterness increases, while hop flavors stay put; clingy coating on the tongue; chalky; should age longer—a beer that's not done yet.

SANTA FE FIESTA ALE　　　　　**MB**　　　　　**1.9**
(Galisteo, New Mexico)
Very fruity nose with accompanying flowery taste; not yet ready
for drinking; weak with foods; flat texture and non-command-
ing taste; sweet curlicue at the end doesn't really improve taste
sufficiently.

SANTA FE OLD POJOAQUE PORTER　　**MB**　　　　　**3.5**
(Galisteo, New Mexico)
Creamy, moderated, and full; subtle roasted taste and aroma; perhaps a bit too smooth and watery in the end; slightly, but not
unpleasantly bitter; understated and satisfying even with a hint
of premature bottling; nice creamy head. Accompanies chips and
spicy dips as well as smoked meats and poultry.

SANTA FE PALE ALE　　　　　**MB**　　　　　**2.3**
(Galisteo, New Mexico)
Variety of tastes: mild, sweet palate followed by slightly sour taste
that deadends back to mild and sweet; fresh, piquant, and fruity,
but somewhat watery; settles into an average, evenhanded beer
with a thick, foamy head; an acrid taste emerges with bland foods,
interfering with their enjoyment; faint, flatly sour aftertaste; lingering hint of mustiness clouds the freshness; could use more
depth and character.

SANTA FE RUBIA ESPECIAL Lager　　**CB**　　　　　**3.9**
(Santa Fe, Argentina)
Very apparent, appealing graininess; conveys a fleeting impression of freshness that probably isn't really there; remains steady;
evenly distributed head stays around; good body and mouthfeel;
creamy smoothness emerges with continuing attractive malt and
grain taste; unusually flavorful; hint of auburn in the color. Accompanies Chinese food.

SAPPORO BLACK MALT LIQUOR　　**CB**　　　　　**4.0**
(Tokyo, Japan)
Lovely, modulated caramel-roasted flavor with a touch of wine
taste reflective of higher alcohol content; as the liquid warms,
balanced complexity and integrity meanders pleasantly from the
tip of the tongue to the back of the mouth—all this without food
accompaniment; with food, it remains calm, cushioning spiciness nicely and unobtrusively; sweetness lingers at the end; not
as chewy as it should be. A good choice with sturdy main courses
such as spaghetti and meatballs.

SAPPORO BLACK MALT LIQUOR　　**CB**　　　　　**4.1**
(Tokyo, Japan—brewed for the
Japanese market; not for export)
Smooth, malty, and mildly pungent; muddy brown color with
short-lasting head; relatively sharp backdrop to food; leaves musty

afterglow on the roof of the mouth; strikingly similar to Sapporo Black Malt Liquor (see page 229), purchased in the U.S. Try it with spaghetti and meatballs or pork dishes.

B E E R   F A C T

*S*apporo, brewing since 1876, is Japan's oldest brand of beer. Named after its city of origin, the brewery was founded by the Japanese government. Now privately owned, the firm has breweries in Tokyo as well as Sapporo.

SAPPORO DRAFT Pilsener　　　　**CB**　　　　**2.4**
(Tokyo, Japan)
Slightly sour and acidic with thick texture on the tongue; very little carbonation or balance; unsweet and grainy, especially for a Japanese beer; thin, pale-gold color with absolutely no head; needs a redesign of taste, texture, and visual appeal.

SAPPORO DRAFT DRY MALT LIQUOR　　**CB**　　　**3.2**
(Tokyo, Japan)
Dry, restrained, and a touch sour; water is fresh and spring-like, making the overall effect light and substantively airy; not too filling; well-defined; clearly a quality product. Try it with broiled or grilled chicken, pork, or veal dishes.

SARANAC ADIRONDACK WINTER
SEASON'S BEST HOLIDAY AMBER
(annual)　　　　　　　　**CB**　　　　**3.4**
(Utica, New York)
Piney aroma and sharp, crisp taste with lots of malt overtones are hallmarks of this holiday brew; quite alcoholic; not complex, too much of a one-note taste; smooths out its rough edges when paired with food; stays a bit bitter while showcasing its alcohol; could have more body; finish is nice and relaxed for beer meant to offer good cheer. A festive accompaniment to baked chicken or roasted turkey served with wild rice.

SARANAC BLACK AND TAN
Stout/Lager　　　　　　**CB**　　　　**3.8**
(Utica, New York)
Immediate freshness, depth, and balanced malt-hops; merely a whiff of sweet, malty aroma at the start; hearty and flavorful; minimal, but tangible fizziness nicely counters the beer's smoothness and mellow strength; loses strength, and flavors turn a mite thin at the end of the bottle; dark-amber color adds to the enjoyment; late in the bottle, a pine-spice aroma whispers in the nose, which adds to an underlying, subtle bitterness. Tasty with typical pub fare.

```
B E E R   F A C T
```

*S*aranac Black and Tan is a blend of Irish stout and all-malt German-style lager, a bottled version of the draft of the same name. The visuals in the bottle are quite different from those observed out of the tap. (See page 132.)

SARANAC 1888 LAGER CB 2.2
(Utica, New York)
Simultaneously acrid and fruity, with a hard edge; both qualities remain with food, but display a much lower profile; taste flattens out; in the end, any pizzazz and spiffiness are leached out, leaving a chalky aftertaste.

SARATOGA LAGER DORTMUNDER
STYLE CT 2.4
(White River Junction, Vermont)
Starts with a big body and some dryness that appropriately approximate the style; quickly becomes a run-of-the-mill beer, though pale-golden color maintains the style connection; not carbonated enough; a bit sweet, with hints of citrus sourness; no Brussels lace—in general, no quality details to attract your interest; tantalizing hints of pleasure are simply never realized—sometimes that happens with a contract brew.

SAXER AMBER LAGER MB 2.7
(Lake Oswego, Oregon)
Moderated bitterness on first sip; fast-rising bubbles fizz through reddish, golden-amber body upwards to thin, but firm head; distinct sharpness attacks the tongue while the undertexture stays smooth and bland; sugary, honey ambience rests gently on the tip of the tongue and on down the throat; smooth, malty roundness eventually predominates; in the end, the loss of effervescence dramatically lowers my interest; slight cloudiness also spoils the overall effect; a decent beer that needs to raise its sights; definitely drink this cold in order to squeeze out every bit of thirst-quenching character. Try it with hot dogs, burgers, and fries.

SCALDIS NOEL ALE (annual) CB 2.1
(Pipaix, Belgium)
Caramel taste with thickish, not-quite-cloying mouthfeel; smooth and strong-bodied; thick, big-bubbled, light-tan head stays awhile and complements light-copper color of the body; slight bitterness tends to hide any fruitiness; triple-hopped, it is more of a routine high-alcohol brown ale than a special seasonal drink; harsh and biting; far too strong and thick for most foods. Goes with crackers and slightly sweet, creamy spreads or dips.

SCHAEFER Pilsener CB 2.3
(Detroit, Michigan)
Sour bouquet, with similar but quickly fading taste; overall, taste-less and unmotivating, even with aggressively flavored foods; strangely, it gets mellower and sweeter at the bottom of the glass; good for the ballpark. (It tasted better when I was younger watch-ing the Brooklyn Dodgers at Ebbets Field on TV.)

SCHINCARIOL PILSEN CB 0.2
(Schincariol, Brazil)
Increasing cabbage odor that almost reaches full flower toward the end of the glass; bland texture; spoiled-food ambience con-tinues along with unexciting, not-going-anywhere mouthfeel; dull, heavy, and generally unpleasant; raw—forget it.

SCHLAFLY HEFEWEIZEN (draft) BP 1.1
(St. Louis, Missouri)
Citrusy, weak, and much too flat; sourness at the end of a swal-low; too light, too sweet, and not complex enough; too much yeast without proper malt balance; thin and shallow; Busch, an-other local product, is more satisfying.

SCHLAFLY OATMEAL STOUT (draft) BP 4.0
(St. Louis, Missouri)
Mellow and soft; nice, laid-back, burnt taste with a hint of tang that's virtually perfect; a great example of the style—and tastes great, too; finishes with complexity balanced with a surge of thick-ness; suave and malty with charbroiled chicken; try one, and ask for another…and another. Good with game and rich stews.

SCHLAFLY PALE ALE (draft) BP 2.5
(St. Louis, Missouri)
Fruity aroma and taste, but neither is overwhelming; light touch and feel; tempered sweetness with circumference of citrus that is mellow and appropriately close to, but not quite making, the bit-terness that helps define this style of ale; too weak to entice a second helping—or to fully enjoy the first one.

SCHLAFLY PILS (draft) BP 1.0
(St. Louis, Missouri)
Close to completely lacking in complexity; flat and strikingly without fizziness; tentative aroma and color; just as well this was sampled alone, since food would obviously overwhelm it.

SCHLAFLY WHEAT (draft) BP 1.6
(St. Louis, Missouri)
A bit green; medium-bodied, but sluggish; weak, hardly notice-able cloves and fruitiness, as if they were drained out after hav-ing been present; good, prominent Brussels lace; slightly furry aftertaste; nothing to write home about—not even a postcard.

SCHLITZ Lager   CB   1.8
(Detroit, Michigan)
Quite thin, with feeble attempt at crispness; surprisingly unfizzy; musty "old" aroma; no complexity or intricacy; adjuncts safely hidden from view and taste, except for a slight, weak corn/grain-iness in the background; somewhat turpey (turpentine-like) at the finish, but sweetly so, not acrid or sour; more body at the end, as if everything sank to the bottom in order to prove this really is a beer—it is, but just barely.

SCHLITZ MALT LIQUOR   CB   1.3
(Milwaukee, Wisconsin)
More suggestive of high alcohol content than is actually the case; harshly grainy, with no discernible flavor nuances; ingredients become relatively more integrated toward the end, raising this mass-produced beer to approximately the mediocre level.

SCHMALTZ'S ALT ALE   CB   3.3
(New Ulm, Minnesota)
Sweet, chocolate, burnt-malt taste, with smooth texture and a hit of alcohol; rich and full-bodied, with heft and hoppy character; deep, dark-copper, almost-black color is appropriate match for taste and overall ambience; warming sweetness of the alcohol is too overpowering for most foods; more like porter than ale, but tasty nonetheless; intimations of nuttiness float forward at the finish— a charming surprise. Fine with a hero sandwichs.

B E E R   F A C T

*S*chmaltz came on the market in 1993 and was named after a founder of the August Schell brewery.

SCHMIDT Lager   CB   2.2
(La Crosse, Wisconsin)
Sour, carbonated, and somewhat green mouthfeel; cheap taste; softer, warmer, and more flavorful at the end of the bottle. Good with pasta and grain dishes.

SCHMIDT'S Lager   CB   2.4
(Baltimore, Maryland)
Smooth, neighborhood-bar beer; slight tingle in tandem with smooth, wave-like texture; mellowness swerves off to a bit of sour-ness with food; in the end, cereal grains predominate and enhance the off-taste sourness that becomes increasingly apparent; starts good, but doesn't end well. Okay with a hamburger.

SCHNEIDER CERVEZA RUBIA
ESPECIAL Lager   **CB**   **2.5**
(Santa Fe, Argentina)
Tamped-down texture and taste; prickly and fizzy on the palate; some fruitiness continues throughout; hazy, reddish color with little head; nice ring of Brussels lace; uninspired, almost wispy; leaves a fermented presence on the roof of the mouth, which is not unpleasant; sharp hoppiness. Nice accompaniment to barbecued pork dishes.

TAP TIP

Pass the Woodruff, Please

*M*ost beers suffer if you add anything to them once the beer is poured and waiting to be savored. After all, the brewer has done his or her job, and now you are expected to do yours: Drink it. True, you can add tomato juice. And in the case of some beers served in the traditional manner in a warm clime like Mexico, a slice of lime in a cold glass aids the battle against the tropical heat. However, there are beer styles that are peculiarly accommodating to an intrusion on the finished product. The southern German *weizenbier* is made more refreshing with a lemon slice submerged in a glass of it or with fresh lemon juice squirted directly into the full-flavored liquid. Some examples are August Schell Weizen, Witkap-Pater Singel Abbey Ale, Edelweiss Kristallklar Weizenbier, and Paulaner Hefe-Weizen.

An even more tantalizing tradition is the addition of a dollop of raspberry or cherry syrup, or a pinch of essence of woodruff to help take the wheat-generated astringent edge off a cold Berliner Weisse. If neither of those sweeteners is available, a splash of fruit-flavored liqueur can be a more-than-adequate substitute. It is also not unheard of to use mashed, fresh raspberries in place of the syrup. Good candidates are Pschorr-Brau Weisse, Schultheiss Berliner Weisse, Celis White, and Erdinger Weissbier Hefetrub.

SCHOONER LAGER   **CB**   **1.8**
(Montréal, Québec, Canada)
Very fizzy; nice bite initially, but fades and gets thin and watery;

doesn't develop on the palate, or anywhere else; in the end, weak and uninteresting drunk by itself. Accompany it with a slice of pizza.

SCHOP OSCURO Pilsener   CB   3.4
(Osorno, Chile)

Mildly roasted, mildly sweet, and generously appealing; light on the outside, fuller in the middle; almost soda-like in texture, but with minimal fizz; smooth going down; nicely malted; a bit thin and almost watery; easy to enjoy. (Made by Compania Cervecerias Unidas, S.A., a monopoly that makes all of the beers in southern Chile and most of them elsewhere in the country.) Compatible with mild cheeses, olives, or a sliced tomato and avocado salad.

SCHULTHEISS BERLINER WEISSE   CB   3.0
(Berlin, Germany)

Astringent and highly citrusy; adding a dollop of raspberry syrup—a common practice with this beer style—quickly moderates any sourness or astringency (though it remains palatable without it); typical of the style; sharp, highly carbonated, and acidic; satisfying thirst-quencher; pale, opaque color; almost like drinking grapefruit juice with alcohol; for highly individualized tastes—you may like it, but watch out for its tart bite.

SCHULTHEISS GERMAN PILSENER   CB   0.3
(Berlin, Germany)

Slightly light-struck; pale-golden color is clear and bright; tangy with tangible carbonation; retains semi-fresh yeasty taste, yet becomes increasingly sour and spoiled-tasting; in the end harsh, green, and unsatisfying; too many off-tastes for its own good.

SCHUTZ BIERE D'ALSACE PILS   CB   2.4
(Schiltigheim, France)

Yeasty and quite malty, soft and gentle on the tongue; hop presence increasingly makes itself felt; airy, empty head lingers, but adds nothing of substance except some interest in comparison to the light, faded, pale body; very filling—don't drink too many of these; a slackness at the finish adds to the unappealing, but typically Alsatian character; a curl of honey offers a semi-fond farewell. Try it with spicy pasta dishes.

SCHUTZENBERGER JUBILATOR Bock   CB   3.8
(Schiltigheim, France)

Fruity sweetness with thickness that settles at the back of the tongue; delicately balanced, though a bit biased toward the hops; slightly golden cloudiness; nicely formed Brussels lace, indicating quality ingredients and manufacture; pleasant thread of alcohol remains present throughout; a good French beer, but thins out at the end. Try it with baked Virginia ham accompanied by sweet potatoes.

SCHWEIZERHOF-BRAU LAGER   CB   2.9
(Marktoberdorf, Germany)
Soft and gently carbonated; hop bitterness at the back of the
throat; low-level flavor is rather flat and certainly not complex;
amazingly untasty for a German beer—light, a bit fluffy, and
airy; mild hoppiness finally emerges at the end of the bottle; also
becomes more full-bodied, tastier, and maltier; gives the impression that it needs time to gather its strength in order to perform
at an acceptable level—which it eventually does. Try it with pasta
salads.

SCORPION MALT LIQUOR   CB   2.4
(Evansville, Indiana)
Hint of skunkiness, but sweet and sharply smooth; remains mild
and somewhat malty; balanced overall, though there's really not
much malt or hops to balance; stays prickly in the mouth without interfering with food; aroma remains lightly skunky (due, no
doubt, to its clear-glass bottle); weak for a malt liquor, though
reasonably flavorful—not a bad trade-off. Try it with ham and
Swiss cheese on rye.

SEABRIGHT BANTY ROOSTER IPA   BP   2.4
(Santa Cruz, California)
Fruity, sharp, and within the IPA style, but needs more bitterness; dry and appealing; hoppiness fades a bit at end, though in
general holds its own; could be even sharper and zestier.

SEATTLEITE ALE   CT   0.7
(Helena, Montana)
Strong, forthright bready/yeasty taste with hint of flowery hops;
quickly becomes rather flat and less aromatic after initial scents
have dissipated; mildly roasted maltiness takes over, but overall
it stays benign and uncomplex; starts to taste like overripe cherries; texture turns distinctly watery; no staying power and not
well-made; a gimmicky beer without quality—or even a clever
gimmick.

SEPTANTE 5 MALT LIQUOR   CB   3.7
(Roubaix, France)
You know this is not a routine malt liquor on the first sip—it's

highly malted with a bitter, alcoholic taste; a hint of caramel tames the malt and alcohol, making the beer vertically rather than horizontally balanced; surprisingly unobtrusive with food; softens as it warms; segues into a touch of cloyingness; sweetness increases at the finish; ends better than it starts; I don't particularly care for the *bière de garde* style, as it has a more distinctive flavor profile than most so-called malt liquors, but I think this is a good example of it. Try with spicy pizzas or a garden salad with creamy dressing.

SEPTANTE ROUGE Ale   CB   2.2
(Roubaix, France)
Smoky taste reminiscent of smoked fish; silky texture; muddy color; distinctive but not distinguished, with a wine-like finish.

SEZOENS ALE   CB   3.0
(Bocholt, Belgium)
Rather fresh-smelling, with promise of pleasantness; crispness turns sweet with red meat; gives an impression of thinness, but is filling; daintiness remains on the tongue; finishing warmth at the back of the mouth; a summertime ale from Flanders with fresh, hoppy aroma; hearty dryness. A pleasant companion with light picnic fare such as cold chicken or turkey sandwiches.

SHAN SUI YEN SUM Pilsener   CT   2.5
(Utica, New York)
Definite aroma and taste of ginseng; bittersweet balance obscures the individuality of the hops and malt; needs non-spicy snack food; artificial-tasting fullness, the result, no doubt, of rice and/or corn adjuncts, makes this beer more American than Asian; indeed, it was brewed in the U.S. for a Hong Kong company; in the end, an average commercial American brew; finishes a bit sweet. Compatible with crackers and mild cheese.

SHANDY CARIB Lager   CB   0.2
(Trinidad, West Indies)
Overpowering ginger smell, albeit fresh and invigorating; taste packs a ginger wallop also; full and softly sweet; too strong in the mouth; tastes more like ginger ale than beer, but without the carbonation; this might go over better with non-beer drinkers; I had trouble finishing it, and it's not even a 12-ounce bottle; too syrupy; light-caramel color adds to the soda-pop feel; ugh.

SHEAF STOUT   CB   2.5
(Sydney, New South Wales, Australia)
Yeasty; immediately good aroma; looks like a good cup of coffee—strong, deep black, and silky smooth; burnt taste does not turn overly bitter; almost overpowering, needs to be cut with another, lighter beer; tough stuff—too much for one sitting; interestingly, it calms down with sweet foods; obviously a well-brewed

product that will be satisfying to those who like heavy, bitter beer; I personally don't care for it. Compatible with sweet desserts, Danish pastries, cinnamon buns.

SHIELDS CHANNEL ISLANDS WHEAT   MB/BP   1.7
(Ventura, California)
Weak, undistinguished, and bearing almost no relation to the advertised style; tentative sugary/molasses aroma; flat and unfizzy with no discernible ingredients, except for water; thin and lacking depth, though it gives fresh cinnamon twists a nice opportunity to show off their complexity, sweetness, and graininess; mild, thickish maltiness floats up midway through the bottle, but is ultimately bland and a non-player; no head, no Brussels lace—it just sits there without any particular character or merit; finishes with plain, mild, malty aroma, but remains basically one-dimensional.

SHIELDS STOUT   MB/BP   0.9
(Ventura, California)
Light and flat, with a vague hint of malty roastedness; the lack of aroma leaves you wondering about its existence; pallid and lifeless; no texture or taste, except for a distant sourness; good, deep-brown color with red tones is the closest it gets to a stout; some malt-hops interaction; overall, uninteresting, weak, and blah; a touch of roasted aroma at the end, as if to remind you what the style is supposed to be; a failure.

SHINER BOCK   CB   2.4
(Shiner, Texas)
Indistinct aroma; brownish-red color; hardly any head; not unpleasant mustiness at the back of the throat; somewhat flabby; satisfying warmth redeems it partially; seems to be on the verge of tasting good, but, in the end, disappoints; pedestrian with food.

SHINER PREMIUM Pilsener   CB   2.5
(Shiner, Texas)
Light, quickly fading taste; some passing hops and rice mouthfeel; sweet and mellow; thin but serviceable; taste and energy appear capable of holding up through several cans; give it time, and it will grow on you. An interesting companion to veal dishes and white bean salads.

SIAM ALE   CB   3.8
(Bangkok, Thailand)
Sweet, excellent mouthfeel; honey taste with mellow accompaniment; unfortunately, honey presence fades fast and is not replaced; a pleasant, emerging charcoal undertone; better at the beginning than at the end; a lovely, finely-tuned special brew; finishes spicy and with conviction; a beer this good should have an affinity for food but, alas, it does not.

SIERRA NEVADA BIGFOOT
BARLEYWINE STYLE ALE (annual)   **CB**   **0.2–1.3**
(Chico, California)
Fruity in taste and aroma, but also creamy and smooth; distinct
wineyness; highly hopped and alcoholic, producing a strong,
hearty flavor; rich, deep-red amber color and lush aroma reminiscent of apple cider, but tending toward perfumey; lacks balance; some cloyingness on the tongue; thick, creamy foam helps
moderate the strident bitterness—a good thing, too; fits the style
and, apparently, the taste of judges at the Great American Beer
Festival (it's a three-time Gold Medal winner)—but I couldn't
finish it; after five years in cold storage or under refrigeration,
the cloyingness should lessen and the ingredients should blend
(this style of ale is *intended* to improve with age).

SIERRA NEVADA CELEBRATION ALE
(annual)   **CB**   **2.3–3.9**
(Chico, California)
Vibrantly fresh, fruity aroma; flat, less aromatic taste brings a citrus tang to the roof of the mouth and is sidetracked by an astringent alcohol rawness; hops impart a pleasant bitterness;
comforting warmth and alcohol sharpness remain throughout; finishes with a yeasty freshness and a touch of fruity, alcoholic sweetness—in short, a true red ale, and a very decent one at that; Silver
Medal winner at the 1994 Great American Beer Festival. Good
with simply prepared red meats, beef pot pie, and meat loaf.

SIERRA NEVADA PALE ALE   **CB**   **3.2**
(Chico, California)
Musty, smoky; some bitter back-of-the-mouth taste and aftertaste; barley malt aroma is present, but not overwhelming; subdued fruitiness authenticates its ale lineage; hops are prominent,
which also confirms the style; lacks punch with strongly flavored
foods; in the end, not enough oomph; Gold Medal winner at the
1993 Great American Beer Festival. Best with lean fish, such as
red snapper, flounder, and halibut.

SIERRA NEVADA PALE BOCK   **CB**   **2.5**
(Chico, California)
Attenuated freshness; dull richness and body; clean; hint of floweriness keeps food in place; sharpness turns a bit edgy and freshness deflates; decent beginning, lackluster ending. Good with
unspicy Chinese dishes such as pork chow mein, vegetable fried
rice, and noodle soups.

SIERRA NEVADA PORTER   **CB**   **2.6**
(Chico, California)
Molasses aroma; very smooth; easy to swallow; has an enigmatic
quality; bitter first, sweeter afterwards. Not a particularly food-
friendly beer.

SIERRA NEVADA STOUT　　　　　CB　　　　　2.5
(Chico, California)
Restrained in taste, texture, and overall impression; dark, burnt-caramel taste eventually comes to the fore; soft and palatable in the mouth with food, but once food is swallowed, beer turns acrid and hard to savor; entirely handmade in the "old-world tradition," according to the label.

SIERRA NEVADA SUMMERFEST
(annual)　　　　　　　　　　CB　　　　　3.5-3.8
(Chico, California)
Fresh, fruity, and zesty with palate-cleansing initial taste and texture; simultaneously sweet and bitter; mustiness is also present; heavy yeastiness turns comfortingly sweet; heavy, quality head clings to the sides of the mug, putting a lid on the washed-out golden body; nicely pungent hoppiness takes over from the citrus fruitiness; mellows into a balanced, integrated brew; finishes with an ale thrust—warmish and slightly alcoholic; a quality product. Tasty with light summer fare such as cold pasta salads or tossed green salads.

SIGNATURE Lager　　　　　　　CB　　　　　1.8
(Made by Stroh's in Longview, Texas;
Detroit, Michigan)
Not distinctive for a so-called premium beer; flat; slight off-taste remains; some malt taste; too carbonated and not very flavorful; where—and what—are the ingredients?; has some strength and staying power; finishes too sweet. Silver Medal winner at the 1994 Great American Beer Festival.

SIMPATICO AMBER Lager　　　　CB　　　　　2.4
(Dubuque, Iowa)
Deep, fruity essence; crisp and sharp with some thick cloyingness at the back of the tongue; rather bland texture with underlay of malty warmth; in the end, spicy food overtakes any nuances that this beer may have; closes with a faux-caramel taste that is cool rather than warm; run-of-the-mill amber. A beer nuts and pretzels companion.

SIMPATICO GOLDEN LAGER　　　CB　　　　　1.2
(Dubuque, Iowa)
Light and artificial-tasting, apparently from a clear abundance of chemicals and adjuncts; flat; watery, and goes nowhere; cloudy, almost muddy, especially for a lager; sharp without redeeming flavor; finishes with a tart, honey flavor that belatedly raises its status.

SINGHA Lager　　　　　　　　CB　　　　　2.5
(Bangkok, Thailand)
Smooth at first, followed by a sour citrus taste that overwhelms

anything other than bland food; gentle and mildly tingly on the tongue; okay in a pinch. A match for pasta with a simple fresh tomato sauce.

SKOL CERVEJA PILSEN   CB   1.0
(Rio Claro, Brazil)

Fruity, a touch spunky, and almost fizzless; nicely configured Brussels lace remains throughout; milky haze obscures pale-blond body; obviously old and punchless, but some malt flavor remains; textureless and unaromatic.

SKOL HOLLAND PILSENER   CB   2.2
(Rotterdam, Holland)

Faint smokiness; no texture/fizziness; quite unpilsener-like; unassertive; bland, but pleasantly so; hint of honeyed fruitiness emerges at the finish; tea leaf-like sediment collects at the bottom; bland, bland, boring, blah.

SLAVAYANSKY Lager   CB   0.3
(Moscow, Russia)

This beer is so bad that the Russian waiter at first said I shouldn't have it, then claimed he didn't have any on hand; foolishly, I prevailed; tasteless and lacking effervescence, as if it had come straight from a water tap; fortunately, it was served warmish, so that the only identifiable characteristic—an almost palatable potato-like aroma—made itself known; I can only presume the vodka was of a higher quality.

SLEEMAN CREAM ALE   MB   3.0
(Guelph, Ontario, Canada)

Tastes like a soft lager; refreshing and mellow; exhibits no extremes in texture, aroma, or taste; good brew by itself. Or try it with a T-bone steak and baked potato.

SLEEMAN LAGER   MB   3.3
(Guelph, Ontario, Canada)

Hoppy with surprisingly invigorating adjuncts—a beer for the ballpark if there ever was one; spritzy with some body—designed to satisfy all comers; overall an easy-going brew for those who like it cold and with some pizzazz; refreshing and predictable at the same time; a convivial beer to share with friends; hint of greenness mars some of the good feelings; I liked it, though it is definitely not high-quality, just one with which to while away the time. Best with hot dogs and other ballpark foods.

SLEEMAN ORIGINAL DARK ALE   MB   2.3
(Guelph, Ontario, Canada)

A bit oxidized; mellow, mild toastedness becomes almost honey-like; weak, watery maltiness fades quickly, leaving a core of obvious quality in its wake; just as quickly, it becomes flat and uninteresting; mild, malty aroma; very accommodating sweetness evolves with foods; in the end, there is more promise than delivery; faintly bitter finish within a too watery context; try drinking this closer to the source. Okay with a tuna salad sandwich.

SMITH AND REILLY HONEST BEER
Pilsener CT 2.7
(Tumwater, Washington)
Variable initial tastes and texture, with an eventual strengthening of body and overall mouthfeel; hops reminiscent of a mildly bitter grassiness; the malt is plain and remains in the background; not quite bland, but not a challenge to your taste buds, either; a beer not out to offend anyone, while giving the impression there's something of substance in the bottle. Fine with raw vegetable snacks, chips and dip.

SNOWFLAKE Pilsener CB 2.3
(Shenyang, China)
Mellow and mild with a hint of carbonation; suggestion of sweetness at the beginning; smells like it's been sitting a little too long; while texture remains watery, mild hop sharpness is present; too light and gentle for spicy foods; rice flavor ultimately floats to the top as the beer warms; pale-golden color adds to light ambience of this pilsener; best enjoyed on its own or with a bowl of nuts.

SOL Pilsener CB 2.7
(Guadalajara, Mexico)
Light, some tang; first bottle or two creates excitement; a simplistic presentation of malt, hops, and yeast; a good common beer you can sip, and enjoy, for hours. Savor with spicy snacks such as Buffalo-style chicken wings, chili dogs, and nachos.

SOLANA BEACH BEACON
BITTER Ale BP 3.2
(Solana Beach, California)
Very hoppy, reflecting the complexity of several varieties of hops; subdued floweriness appropriate to the style; moderated acidity; I like this beer—direct and to the point; a good example of an American-made bitter. Good with pizza.

SOLANA BEACH PORT'S PORTER BP 2.8
(Solana Beach, California)
Smooth and laid back; understated roasted-malt taste; almost melts in your mouth; thick, foamy Brussels lace covers sides of the glass in sheets like a frosty curtain; nice balance; chewy and accommodating; roasted flavor fades much too quickly; color not quite dark enough for the style. Try with California-style pizzas or focaccia.

**SOLANA BEACH RIVERMOUTH
RASPBERRY Ale**   **BP**   **2.1**
(Solana Beach, California)

Flat; thankfully understated in its fruity sweetness; light and very much like quality soda pop, though less carbonated; hint of bitterness is useful against even the minimal fruitiness; generally weak and uncomplex; made with ripe, local raspberries—which should have been saved for something better, like sherbet, for example. Drink alone in place of dessert.

**SOLANA BEACH SUMMER
BLONDE WHEAT**   **BP**   **2.1**
(Solana Beach, California)

Slight honey taste with full, smooth texture; emerging bitterness signals hops; citrus sharpness is missing; no head and no Brussels lace; more amber than the usual cloudy blond wheat-style color; leaves slight musky, neutral aftertaste; rather undistinguished; unassuming and unmemorable.

SOULARD OUR SPECIAL LAGER   **MB**   **2.5**
(Cold Spring, Minnesota)

Soft on the palate without expected zest; not unsatisfying; unique root beer-like taste; flat texture; soft, gentle maltiness with a vague hint of mildly roasted caramel; rather trite and plain, fading further in the stretch; best alone, but would also go with a garden salad.

**SOUTH PACIFIC SPECIAL EXPORT
LAGER**   **CB**   **2.0**
(Papua, New Guinea)

Off-taste odor is off-putting; undistinguished and somewhat watery; sparkling crispness; texture gets more attention than the flat, somewhat bland taste; a hint of warmth and sweetness; predictable rather than changeable or complex; thickness lingers in the mouth; despite its pretty label it remains a below-par beer.

SOUTHWARK GOLD LAGER   **CB**   **2.3**
(Thebarton, South Australia, Australia)

Faintly sour, acrid flavor with intimations of citrus; aroma reminiscent of butter; goes poorly with light summer fare, revealing an essentially undemanding character; respectable head; gains bitterness toward the end, but not enough to make a difference; a middling beer with lots of burps in the bottle; best without food.

SOUTHWARK PREMIUM Pilsener   **CB**   **4.1**
(Adelaide, South Australia, Australia)

Nice and hoppy, almost fruity; smooth; sweet, then gently tart at the back of the tongue; some dull aftertaste, which subsides with food; more flavor and continuity than other Australian beers;

invigorating sharpness is predictable and continuous. Try with chicken teriyaki or mesquite-grilled meat and poultry.

SPANISH PEAKS BLACK DOG ALE   · CT   2.5
(New Ulm, Minnesota)
Fresh-tasting, but somewhat amateurish in execution; not fully developed, though initial aroma and first sip or two do suggest potential; hops eventually dominate; only a hint of fruitiness or yeastiness (more of latter than former) suggests this is ale; malt presence pops up as it warms; with work, it might become a tasty brew—but how long before we find out? Good with chicken fajitas, nachos, or guacamole and tortilla chips.

SPARTAN LAGER   CB   4.0
(Atalanti, Greece)
Fine-tasting, light, medium-bodied beer with even crispness; fresh-smelling, holding its aroma from start to finish; nice blend of flavor and sharpness; hops and malts relate well to each other, providing an easygoing, well-tuned interaction; rich and complex, Spartan is anything but. Try it with stuffed grape leaves, olives, figs, or hearty American soup classics like beef-barley.

SPATEN FRANZISKANER
HEFE-WEISSBIER   CB   2.6
(Munich, Germany)
Yeast bite on first sip; full-bodied, but light, lively, and fluffy with pervasive fizziness; very noisy (put your ear to the top of a pilsener glass and listen); spicy (clove) and dry; bottle-sedimented; clean and fresh-tasting; more like wake-up juice for breakfast than a partner for dinner; cloudy, pale color is typical of this beer style; too sweet; add a slice of lemon to the glass and enjoy on its own without food.

B E E R   F A C T

*S*paten, like all other Bavarian beers, adheres to the Reinheitsgebot, or German Pure Beer Law of 1516, which mandates that all beer be made only from barley malts, hops, and water. Yeast, now required, was not included in the original list, as the function of this important ingredient was not yet identified or understood. Today, many breweries, including an increasing number in the United States, voluntarily adhere to the 479-year-old guideline. To underscore the quality of their products, they often advertise this fact on the label.

SPATEN FRANZISKUS HELLER BOCK CB 3.1
(Munich, Germany)
Prickly and sharp; sweet, with an edge; clean and fresh-tasting; malty and a tad sour; wine-like alcohol is increasingly apparent at the finish; very serviceable, but not award-winning; malty finish. A good choice with a burger or cold cuts.

SPATEN MUNCHEN CLUB—WEISSE CB 3.5
(Munich, Germany)
Attractive, sweet aroma with pleasant fruitiness that, unfortunately, turns sour at the base of the throat; spritzy overlay tops off mellow smoothness underneath; moves around a great deal on the palate, providing interest at each sip; warm and comfortable with a slight tang at the end. Try this at brunch with waffles or pancakes.

BEER FACT

*S*paten, which means "spade" in German, was one of the first companies to apply scientific methods to brewing. The brewery still delivers some of its product in Munich by horse and wagon.

SPATEN MUNICH OPTIMATOR
DOPPELSPATEN BOCK CB 3.4
(Munich, Germany)
Sharp and pleasantly caramelized with full, burnt taste; soft and subtle; warm sweetness settles on the back of the tongue, while mild hoppiness attaches itself at the front of the tongue; smoothly malted, creamy, and consistently pleasant going down, though too much too soon produces syrupy accumulation in the mouth and stomach; good, slightly chewy example of strong German bock; too sweet to be rated higher. Compatible with veal and lamb dishes.

SPATEN OKTOBERFEST UR-MARZEN CB 2.8
(Munich, Germany)
Zestiness appears on first sip, along with a mild, rounded texture that fades away down the throat; pleasurable balance of hops, malt, and sweetness; flat texture; slight caramel flavor emerges with spicy Italian foods; head disappears quickly; sweet taste, but no texture in this beer. Scrumptious with salty snacks such as barbecue potato chips; also good with an Italian salami sandwich.

SPATEN PILS CB 2.5
(Munich, Germany)
Spritzy; distinct hoppiness floats to the back of the throat; puffy,

airy head steps aside as the body of this pale brew slides past; tightly controlled balance and complexity; makes a partially successful effort at Brussels lace; in the end, rather undistinguished. Compatible with grain dishes such as risotto, polenta, and couscous.

SPECIAL EXPORT Lager   **CB**   **3.4**
(brewed by Heileman in La Crosse,
Wisconsin)
This above-average Midwestern brew has a beguiling, complex flavor; characteristic fizziness provides textural balance, making it especially agreeable when blended with tomato juice (mixed half-and-half, or to taste); smoothly layered ingredients and some depth make for a good American beer. Compatible with most foods, though it tends toward sourness with highly spiced dishes.

> ### BEER FACT
>
> *S*pecial Export, like many other beers, is *kräusened*—a double fermentation process that naturally results in more carbonation, additional smoothness, and a richer, foamier head.

SPENCES PALE ALE   **CT**   **2.2**
(Chatsworth, California)
Bitter fruitiness; watery; hardly aromatic except for the initial whiff; settles into minimal fruitiness with a touch of hops at the back of the mouth; maintains a sour citrus taste that seems to blot out other taste qualities; flat texture; wispy head quickly settles into thin, gray line; yeast cloudiness muddies up color. Match with starchy foods to help absorb some of the sourness.

ST. IDES MALT LIQUOR   **CT**   **1.6**
(brewed by Heileman in San Antonio, Texas)
Syrupy, ginger-ale taste, but flatter in texture than a pancake; almost candy-like all over the mouth; continuous, mild, after-dinner liqueur mouthfeel. Serve as an *apéritif* or *digestif*, if at all.

ST. PAULI GIRL Pilsener   **CB**   **3.4**
(Bremen, Germany)
Fresh, tart, and sharp, with a hint of wateriness; very clear, light-blond color; tender mouthfeel; nicely contained hops mix well with rice and grain dishes; an unintrusive player with food; traditional and predictable with a dry finish. Try it with salty tortilla chips and spicy black bean dip.

ST. PAULI GIRL DARK Pilsener   **CB**   **3.5**
(Bremen, Germany)
Lightly toasted and lightly fizzy, with no apparent complexity; based on the color—thin yet rich brown, like Coca-Cola—you expect a more intense aroma and stronger taste; smoked meats sweeten the liquid and bring out the hoppiness; much fuller and sweeter at the end; more than one bottle is needed to fully appreciate what this popular pilsener has to offer; clearly well-made. A good match with smoked meats and salty snack foods.

ST. SEBASTIAAN CROCK ALE   **CB**   **2.6**
(Meer, Belgium)
Sharp with a surprising mellow undercurrent of warmth at the front of the mouth, but lacks depth at the back of the tongue; effervescence pricks the roof of the mouth and the throat; a magnificent, well-intact head on top of light-amber body enhances the overall effect; color holds unfulfilled promise—without seeing the label, it would be hard to know it's a Belgian brown ale; without food, it warms up a bit; lots of Brussels lace—it's from Belgium, after all; in the end, lacks the usual distinctiveness of an abbey-style brew. Match with fresh and/or dried fruit or brunch dishes such as waffles or French toast with syrup.

ST. SIXTUS ABBEY ALE   **AB**   **3.1**
(Watou, Belgium)
No question this contains alcohol; starts with creamy, soft palate; pleasant fruitiness; some vinegary odor; alcohol and hoppiness mellow toward the end; subdued tartness remains; a sheath of tiny bubbles coats the sides of the glass; some yeastiness emerges at the very bottom of the bottle as does an acidic component; dry finish; best alone, without food.

ST. STAN'S AMBER ALT   **MB**   **3.8**
(Modesto, California)
Cidery aroma, taste, and color; soft and smooth to the palate; citrus fruitiness gently turns into an appealing sweetness and draws out the flavor and nuances of food; remains soft and creamy throughout; somehow plain and tasty at the same time; very pleasant, simple, warm brew with staying power; no highs or lows; brewed with dark malts, adding to flavor intensity; "creamy head evokes its natural ingredients," according to the neck label, which also has other bits of interesting information; strongly recommended. Good with nearly any pork or lamb dish.

ST. STAN'S DARK ALT   MB   3.9
(Modesto, California)

Mild, burnt taste on first sip; fresh-tasting, dark, rich, chocolate color; thick body texture; very pleasant and rewarding; distinctively mellow and full-bodied. Quite nice with barbecued chicken or pork with a fruited sauce.

ST. STAN'S FEST BIER Alt   MB   3.5
(Modesto, California)

Pungent citrus fruitiness makes its mark on the roof of the mouth; less robust and less sweet than the other St. Stan's I've had, but simultaneously possesses a nice bite with mellowness; subdued alcohol presence; some muddiness and aftertaste, however, spoil the show at the end; final sips are cool and fruity. Try it with a bacon-wrapped filet mignon.

ST. STAN'S GRAFFITI WHEAT
(annual)   MB   1.9
(Modesto, California)

Brewed each summer to celebrate the Modesto Graffiti Festival; yeast all over the place: overwhelms the aroma, dulls the golden-yellow color, ruins the taste, making it rough and raw; no head; no zip; gradual, mild citrus aroma pushes its way through; increasing lemon taste with or without food; too fruity, too thick, and not thirst-quenching enough for this style; needs work.

STAG Lager   CB   2.1
(La Crosse, Wisconsin)

Typical light American lager, with a calm, unprovocative approach; transient tart sharpness distinguishes it a bit from the rest; overall, the hops, malt, and yeast are played down and successfully hidden; a certain textural crudeness is part of its beer-to-be-swilled charm; no surprises, nuances, or pretension, this is definitely a no-frills approach to brewing. Fine with a hot dog.

STALLION TEN EXTRA MALT LIQUOR   CT   0.7
(Utica, New York)

Bland with a hint of sourness; sends back a fishy smell when eaten with smoked salmon—an odd experience; much too accepting of the fish taste and smell, even though the salmon by itself didn't smell or taste fishy in the least; uninteresting and surprisingly disappointing; expensive for the usually less expensive, high-alcohol malt liquor category.

STAROPRAMEN Pilsener   **CB**   **3.9**
(Prague, Czechoslovakia)
Full-bodied, crisp, clean and flavorful; immediate, playful interaction of hops and malt; pervasive, smooth, grainy mouthfeel; clean aroma; delicate bitterness with no offensive aftertaste; direct, with few nuances; substantial, irregular Brussels lace; well-made and invigorating; finish is refreshingly hoppy, a credit to the style. Goes nicely with green vegetables or salads.

STEELER LAGER   **CB**   **0.5**
(Hamilton, Ontario, Canada)
Bleached, weak, prosaic; slight banana taste, suggesting too high fermentation temperatures or an inappropriate type of yeast strain.

STEELHEAD BOMBAY BOMBER IPA   **MB/BP**   **2.2**
(draft)
(Eugene, Oregon)
Clean-cut, citrus/grapefruit aroma suggests long-lasting taste; becomes tiresome and boring much too quickly; bitter toward the back of the mouth and soapy at the end of the glass; pale, apple-cider color continues the outdoorsy fruit character, but with no real gain in overall enjoyment; needs a lot more pizzazz and snap before I'd try it again.

STEELHEAD EXTRA PALE ALE   **MB**   **3.3**
(Blue Lake, California)
Strongly hopped on first sip with a lingering citrus punch as the liquid goes down; fruity and smooth; predictably even-tempered from start to finish; possesses a sharply defined, but restrained, cutting edge that bites nicely into red meat; not particularly complex, with each ingredient well-defined and offering its own separate note and balance; not as crisp as it should be for the style; leaves a slightly yeasty aftertaste and somewhat uneventful finish. Good with steak or roast beef and a baked potato.

STEENDONK WHITE ALE   **CB**   **3.9**
(Breendonk, Belgium)
Yeasty, flavorful, and fruity (kiwi?) with a clove theme; moderated sharpness keeps it from being too acidic; phosphorescent white paleness; sustains a high level of interest; assertive and charmingly wine-like with food; bottle-conditioned, there is sediment at the bottom of the bottle; exhibits a rare quality—it maintains its high overall standards in taste, texture, and aroma from start to finish; a gift from the hands of careful craftspeople. Try it with pasta or seafood.

STEFFL VIENNA LAGER   CB   2.1
(Linz, Austria)
Fruity hops taste from start to finish, though diminishes over time; odd, unexpected whitefish taste at the back of the mouth; thin; quite weak with food; not assertive at all.

STEGMAIER 1857 LAGER   CB   3.2
(Wilkes-Barre, Pennsylvania)
Fresh with a hint of fruitiness; dry and approachable with some aftertaste; clear and golden; aromatic hoppiness; comes close to typical lager style; good everyday beer with or without food; Gold Medal winner at the 1994 Great American Beer Festival. Appropriate with brunch.

BEER FACT

*S*tegmaier is produced by Lion, Inc., one of only a handful of independent regional brewers that remain in the U.S. Along with its own brands, it also does a lot of contract brewing for other companies.

STEGMAIER PORTER   CB   2.4
(Wilkes-Barre, Pennsylvania)
Roasted and mildly malty with matching aroma; bitterness creeps in—an acceptable nuance; smooth and perhaps too silky; appropriately dark; taste fades much too quickly, almost abruptly; too weak at the finish.

STEINHAUSER BIER Pilsener   CB   3.5
(Frankfurt, Germany)
Mild but attractive ginger perfume—almost nutty; smooth with soft, surrounding prickliness nicely balancing the warmth and maltiness of the beer; slightly thick, with a continuing nutty/honey taste; sturdy and consistent; cloudiness detracts from overall ambience; thin to non-existent head and thin Brussels lace; finishes gluey, thick, and honey-sweet. Good with broiled fish.

STEINLAGER Pilsener   CB   3.8
(Auckland, New Zealand)
Appealing and light with initial flatness; mildly dry; quickly mellows into balanced smooth-sharpness, especially when matched with a robust meal; since it comes in a large 25.4-ounce green bottle, there is more than enough to unhurriedly savor its limited but well-defined nuances; some aftertaste. Just right with roast beef and mashed potatoes.

BEER FACT

*G*reen bottles do not screen out fluorescent lighting or sunlight as well as brown bottles. Clear glass is worst of all. Even small amounts of exposure to light can damage the flavor and aroma of the beer. Remember: Always choose your bottle or six-pack from the darker areas of the cooler.

STELLA ARTOIS Pilsener   **CB**   **2.9**
(Leuven, Belgium)
Watery at first taste, but carbonation fills out the body after two to three sips; flavor remains a little flat; virtually no aroma; label proclaims, "Belgium's premium Beer." Versatile enough to go with a range of foods from poached eggs at brunch to seafood or steak.

STER ALE   **CB**   **3.1**
(Meer, Belgium)
Charming, quick hint of malt aroma followed by flat, bland taste; unlike many Belgian ales, this one is not overtly alcoholic, it is unfruity, unsweet, and unwine-like, thereby making it, in my opinion, an attractive companion with food; malt and yeast combine for solid grain texture with slightly warming sweetness; hazy reddish-brown color; gets a little stiffer toward the bottom of the bottle; never reveals much complexity or changing nuances; aroma continues to dominate taste. A good match with meat loaf.

STERLING Pilsener   **CT**   **1.5**
(Evansville, Indiana)
Rounded mouthfeel; bitter hop taste quickly disappears; light and wispy; bitterness evolves into an uncomplicated sweetness; bland, below-average beer; one redemption: water is fresh and invigorating; find the water source and forget the added brewing ingredients.

STIEGL COLUMBUS PILS   **CB**   **3.1**
(Salzburg, Austria)
Thick head atop thin, golden body with a hint of red; no effervescence to speak of—indeed, rather mild texture; fresh and dainty; turns smooth and comforting and gains a slight acidic taste with smoked fish; even-tempered and quite appealing; some thickish aftertaste; weak with spicy foods and beef; not zippy; predictable; balanced equitably between malt and hops. Good with plainly prepared fish.

STRATHCONA ALE   **MB**   **3.1**
(Edmonton, Alberta, Canada)
Flat, thin, and chocolatey; tangy and spicy; gains warmth with

barbecued foods; fruity ambience begins after a bite or two of food; serviceable and unpretentious in its green plastic 1.5-liter bottle; an increasingly likeable brew.

STRAUSS AMBER LAGER   BP   2.4
(San Diego, California)
Warm and soft, with malty mellowness; not much hops presence, adding to the one-note impression; no head; too cloying and not crisp enough for this copper-red brew; touch of roastedness adds class, if not style; aftertaste sticks to the roof of the mouth; essentially nondescript.

STROH'S Lager   CB   2.4
(Detroit, Michigan)
Stark and mildly malty; more substantive and flavorful than some American brews; brings a solid bite to spicy foods; noticeable textural punch—zingy and crisp; ruddy brown color is perfect, reminiscent of porter hue; good choice when more exotic beers are not available.

SUN LIK Pilsener   CB   3.5
(Hong Kong)
Attenuated sourness; surprisingly smooth with practically no fizziness or sharpness; weak with spicy foods; minimal balance of malt and hops, but essentially weak-kneed; some warmth pops out on occasion; smooth, grainy sweetness; immediate sweet/pungent aroma and crisp rice flavor emerge with pork and pasta dishes; taste fades quickly on the palate; feels dry on the roof of the mouth; worth having again.

SUN VALLEY GOLD LAGER   MB/BP   0.5
(Halley, Idaho)
Sour taste followed by flatness; the most striking thing about this beer is its creamy, very thick, long-lasting head; gains some complexity; thickness around the mouth and the tongue; they need to start over with this one.

SUN VALLEY HOLIDAY ALE (annual)   MB/BP   3.9
(Halley, Idaho)
Lovely, undulating, malted-barley aroma wafts upward and taste lazily coats the tongue; sweetness veers toward cloying but backs off into balanced fullness without much zest or tang; soothing, not texturally complex, but remains evenhanded and predictable; leaves thin lacework on the sides of the glass; appealing sipping beer with relatively high alcoholic content; also fits well with a grilled cheese sandwich, which actually enhances the beer's substance and taste complexity; as with any annual like this Christmas brew, character and quality may vary from year to year. Also, I tasted the last version that was brewed in Montana; the brewery is now located in Idaho.

SUN VALLEY WHITE CLOUD ALE   MB/BP   3.8
(Halley, Idaho)
Mildly creamy with moderated, fruity taste; cloudy, amber color
leans toward blond; hint of sharpness surrounds the liquid and
permeates the mouth; tart fruitiness is relatively subdued without food; as beer sits in the glass, the texture and taste spread
out, becoming even more integrated, smoother, and seamless; a
good ale for those who understand ale; nice malty finish. Goes
nicely with flavorful snacks such as barbecue potato chips or cold
shrimp with zippy cocktail sauce.

SUNTORY DRAFT Pilsener   CB   2.2
(Osaka, Japan)
Pale, yellow-gold color with fizzy texture preceding a rather mellow, unassuming character; undercurrent of almost indiscernible
tastelessness interrupted by some peripheral graininess; large quantities can be imbibed practically without realizing it; made with
corn filler; expensive, and not worth it.

SUNTORY GINJO DRAFT Pilsener   CB   2.6
(Osaka, Japan)
Very pale; rapidly rising bubbles clearly evident; modulated hoppiness with rice adjunct reminiscent of ballpark beer, but of significantly better quality; clean, fresh taste; remains pleasant with
food; gets a bit flat and fuzzy on the tongue toward the end; not
complex, and that fact makes it unexciting, too predictable; still,
it's drinkable with simple foods such as hamburgers and Sloppy
Joes.

SUNTORY GOLD DRAFT—
100% MALT BEER Pilsener   CB   3.3
(Osaka, Japan)
Thick and creamy with some sharpness at the back of the throat;
warm and rounded and mild; pleasant, easy to drink; gets finished
without you realizing it's gone. Try it with steak and a baked potato.

SUPER 49 MALT LIQUOR   CB   2.8
(Roubaix, France)
Muddy, undefined flavor on first sip, with an alcoholic taste;
honey-like mouthfeel; mellows out with peripheral fizziness with
hot foods; resonating yeastiness continues to play on the tongue
and sides of the mouth after food is finished; easily drinkable.
Serve with caviar, thick slices of glazed ham, or fruit tarts.

SUPERIOR Pilsener   CB   3.1
(Guadalajara, Mexico)
Good, smooth taste; circumscribed hoppiness, with a vague hint
of citrus; very satisfying; I generally drink this without food—it's
light, not filling, doesn't get you tipsy easily, and it's reminiscent
of old Mexico; toss in a slice of lime, and you'll swear you're there.

SWAN LAGER   CB   3.3
(Brisbane, Queensland, Australia)
Nicely smooth and immediately satisfying; light-bodied, with an easy-to-drink manner; the flavor is present, but not intrusive; a bit of sourness as meal progresses, along with mild bitterness; finishes relatively dry—a good thirst-quencher. Tasty with a seafood salad, oysters, or clams.

SWEET CHINA Lager   CB   0.2
(Guangzhou, China)
Immediate pineapple/hard candy aroma, followed by the same thing in the mouth; sweeter pineapple taste than fizzy-hoppy beer taste; far too frothy and sweet for most foods; more like soda pop than beer; label proclaims, "beer with natural pineapple juice"—true enough; but why draw attention to the fact? I didn't finish it.

SWEETHEART STOUT   CB   3.5
(Glasgow, Scotland)
Prominent and appealing taste of Concord grapes; rather flat, but smooth texture; clearly a "sweetheart" of a milk stout with very appealing, full, sugary sweetness and a distinguishing milky taste; nice deep-red to dark-brown color in the stout tradition; grapey finish with fermented aroma; very low alcohol content; all in all, this is one of the most unique beers I ever have had; classic milk stouts like this one have long been considered restoratives. Serve as a *digestif.*

SWINKELS Pilsener   CB   2.4
(Lieshout, Holland)
Calm, mild tasting—actually, hard to detect a taste, though there is a slight, pleasant, grainy flavor with salty snacks; interesting aroma; in short, a mixed bag. Fine with salted crackers, pretzels, black olives, and pistachios.

TABERNASH WEISS (draft)   BP   3.0
(Denver, Colorado)
Lemon and ginger—interesting, but is it beer? The answer is yes, with its floating yeast and circumscribed, but clearly evident, clove presence, giving it a ginger-alelike zip; not as sharp as it should be, but thirst-quenching nevertheless; cloudy and straw-colored; needs more body, but worth a try. A good match with marinated bean dishes.

TAIWAN BEER Lager   CB   1.8
(Taipei, Taiwan)
Immediate aroma is stale; minimal bubbly, crackly essence; quiet dullness at the back of the tongue; overall rounded taste with a hint of body; unassuming, rather run-of-the-mill; uneventful with food; presumably there are both malt and hops hidden some-

where amidst the slight fizziness; among the few English words on the label, other than the beer's name, are "Taiwan Tobacco and Wine Monopoly Bureau."

TAJ MAHAL LAGER   CB   3.1
(Calcutta, India)
Smooth and mini-bubbled with vague clove presence; intermittent hoppiness varies from sip to sip; the level of hoppiness stays true, steady, and predictable throughout—a good sign; flattened bitterness balances nicely with a late-blooming maltiness; thick, rocky head and thick chunks of Brussels lace stay from start to finish; slight alcohol presence; a moderate, serviceable beer with substance and guile. A good match with Indian food or fish and chips.

TAOS CERVEZA PRIMO Ale   CT   1.1
(Boulder, Colorado)
Soft, with hoppy alcohol taste that quickly stops; raw and unfinished; flat in taste; amateurishly made; doesn't go anywhere and is uninteresting getting there; rather unobtrusive, fortunately; meant to be an ale, this incarnation falls short; packs alcohol pinch (not punch); lacks complexity; finishes with a touch of warmth.

TECATE Pilsener   CB   3.0
(Monterrey, Mexico)
Popular south of the border, this strong-bodied brew is both gentle and rough on the palate; unvarying in its narrow-range malt-hop balance, it goes well with a variety of foods; each meal component responds differently to the unyielding taste and texture of the beer, while the beer itself stays composed and predictable; there are no extremes here, just a familiar strength that increases with time—alone or at mealtime, which could include Mexican salsas.

TELLURIDE Lager   CT   2.4
(Monroe, Wisconsin)
Bitter at the back of the tongue; sparkly, almost fizzy with a subdued, flat overlay; taste is middle-of-the-road, but texture raises the overall effect generously; fullness is captivating; interesting blend of Old-World ingredients and New-West taste; a bit watery with spicy or highly flavored foods.

TENNENT'S LAGER   CB   1.8
(Glasgow, Scotland)
Flat, bitter, and uninteresting; maltiness lurks in the background; broken patterns of white Brussels lace help the ambience; a bland, dulled, slightly malted brew; sweetish molasses finish—too little, too late. Match with hearty winter soups such as beef-barley.

T A P   T I P

Where's the Brewery?

*N*ot all beers are brewed where the company is located. A growing phenomenon is contract brewing, where individuals with a beer recipe contract with a functioning brewery to produce and package the beer. Often, the contract brewery is located many miles from the home company—even out of state. Thus, you get such anomalies as Telluride Lager and Black Hills Gold Label, both brewed in Monroe, Wisconsin, a major contract brewing location. Others are in Utica, New York (e.g., Portland Lager, Brooklyn Lager, Michael Shea's Irish Amber), Pittsburgh (half-a-dozen Samuel Adams styles—the brewery has also contracted with Utica on occasion), and Wilkes-Barre, Pennsylvania (e.g., Manhattan Gold, Nude Beer, Neuweiler Black and Tan). Pete's Wicked Ale and other Pete's brews are made in New Ulm, Minnesota, at the August Schell brewery. Pete's Brewing Company itself is based in Palo Alto, California.

Caveat emptor: Check the label to make certain the regional, handsomely packaged beer you think is made from the delicious local springwater is not in reality bottled across the country in some time-worn urban zone. The beer may be just as good, but it's always wise to know what you're getting.

TERKEN BIERE DE LUXE
MALT LIQUOR   CB   2.9
(Roubaix, France)

Immediate, pleasant, perfume odor quickly degenerates to sour; muddy fizziness with big head remains; warming softness; more complex taste—grainy and fruity—emerges with plain foods; alcohol is quite apparent with a meal, perhaps not surprising for a fermented French beverage; possesses ale characteristics but basically is a mixed style. Okay with a simple supper of meat loaf, mashed potatoes, and a green vegetable.

TERKEN BRUNE MALT LIQUOR   CB   2.5
(Roubaix, France)

Brewed in the brown ale-style—sweet, malty, and caramely with a mild texture; highly alcoholic and on the cloying side; much too sweet with food; minimal head; too much maltiness, not enough balancing hoppiness spoils the fun; they've probably been brewing this for centuries, or decades, at least, but I find it to be unfinished and uncertain, with no bond holding it together.

TEXAS COWBOY VIENNA LAGER
(draft) BP 0.5
(Dallas, Texas)
Cold and tasteless; when the wind is right, you get a faint odor of beer; vague hint of bitterness is a plus in this case, since its presence lets you know you're drinking something; some citrus taste creeps forward, but doesn't last long; this beer wasn't lagered (stored) long enough.

TEXAS PRIDE Pilsener CB 0.1
(San Antonio, Texas)
Green-tasting and sweet; raw and unintegrated; faint chemical, varnish taste; rather unappealing; unaccompanied by any food, it has no qualities, redeeming or otherwise; gave me a stomachache.

TGIF AMBER Lager CT 0.4
(Dubuque, Iowa)
Sweet, but not cloying; hint of seltzer-like spritziness in the nose and on the roof of the mouth; off-taste that is somewhat phenolic (medicinal); weak and unappetizing.

36.15 PECHEUR Lager CB 0.3
(Schiltigheim, France)
Mild skunkiness that dissipates rather quickly; fine spritz can't detract from the perfumed clash of not very complementary fruit and spice flavors (including cardamom, cinnamon, ginger, ginseng, kola, licorice, mango, myrrh, myrtle); aroma of myrrh is discernible, while no one flavor predominates; almost literally a boutique beer: really too cute for words (or for drinking); motto on label: *La Bière Amoureuse,* the beer for "intimate occasions." Interestingly, this concoction goes with toasted almonds.

33 EXPORT Lager CB 3.1
(Paris, France)
Mildly sour-sharp on back of mouth; integrates well with Indian dishes; allows spiciness to take over, but not overwhelmingly; understated, quickly disappearing taste; slightly cloying and watery; finish is warm, sweet, and quite comforting. Good with curries and spicy Indian dishes.

THOMAS COOPER ADELAIDE LAGER CB 2.4
(Leabrook, South Australia, Australia)
Crisp and musty on first sip, with hints of sourness and acidity; ebbs and flows as you drink it—changes from bittersweet to sharp and musty and back again; turns acridly sweet with food, playing second fiddle to it; a fair-to-middling beer.

THOMAS HARDY'S ALE—1989
(annual)   **CB**   **0.4**
(Dorchester, England)
Aroma of old yeast; fruity with alcoholic backdrop; sweetness turns to a dryness reminiscent of oak-aged sherry; unattractive overripeness with a hint of mustiness; some caramel remains when drunk alone after a hearty meal; its wine-like rosy-amber color and lack of head or lace suggest that this is a *digestif* rather than a more versatile beer; still, obviously has quality ingredients and substance; hint of redeeming warmth during last few sips—indeed, it can be imbibed only in small doses; though many people like this beer, I had trouble finishing it; high alcohol content makes it inappropriate with most foods—if you insist on trying this strong drink, do so before or after a meal; for highly individualized tastes only; I hope it's better after 25 years (see below).

B E E R   F A C T

*B*ecause of the continuing bottle fermentation (look for yeast sediment on the bottom), Thomas Hardy's Ale, named for the British poet and novelist, is one of the few beers that improves with age. Reputed to be England's strongest ale, it is produced in numbered, limited editions (mine was No. D11422), and is said to last for 25 years when maintained at 55°F. Technically a barley wine-style ale (big, full, complex, alcoholic, and fruity), its taste is apparently not the only thing that benefits from aging. The first bottles from the 1960s have been offered by collectors for $1,000. I hope that history is a good guide; I have stored eight bottles in my refrigerator, dating from 1988 and 1989.

THOMAS KEMPER HELLES BLUEBERRY
LAGER (draft)   **MB**   **2.4**
(Poulsbo, Washington)
Hard fizziness with the expected minimal fruit taste (thanks to the presence of real blueberry purée); dry, with a slightly musty aftertaste on the tongue, but not fruity/sweet at all; pale, faded blond color; no head; light and summery without being intrusive; flattens and gains in hoppiness, but essentially goes nowhere; finish is a mixed fruit/hop bag; drink this by itself, or with pastry for dessert.

THOMAS KEMPER HELLES LAGER   MB   2.1
(Poulsbo, Washington)
Mild, fruity sweetness thickens in the throat; pleasant creaminess accompanies a hint of sourness without food; apple-juice/vinegar taste; stale, flat texture without much carbonation; head stays upright and airy; too hoppy; coarseness is intrusive; integrated balance at the bottom of the bottle, but not enough to make up for the earlier deficits.

THOMAS KEMPER INTEGRALE
AMBER LAGER (draft)   MB   1.5
(Poulsbo, Washington)
Rather tasteless, with a compensating hit of hops; flat and unintegrated; not particularly fresh, even when imbibed less than eight miles from the brewery; chewy, caramel/malt mouthfeel appears, preceding a burst of citrus sharpness (tang) at midglass; no head, no Brussels lace; a disappointment.

THOMAS KEMPER PILSNER   MB   1.0
(Poulsbo, Washington)
Skunky and forms fur on the roof of the mouth; flat for a pilsener and uncomplicated; fades into thickish blandness with food; thick, but airy, head; too much will probably result in a stomachache.

THOMAS KEMPER ROLLING BAY
BOCK   MB   2.4
(Poulsbo, Washington)
Deep and abiding roasted-coffee flavor with a hint of yeastiness; sharp and increasingly controlled fruitiness; solid, flat Brussels lace sticks to the sides of the glass—not wispy or broken up; comes into its own as it warms at the middle of the bottle; tawny brown, as in bock style, but not very strong, unlike the bock style; remains sharp, puckery, and astringent; a bit too watery at the end; some residual alcohol.

THOMAS KEMPER WINTERBRAU Lager
(annual)   MB   1.2
(Poulsbo, Washington)
Mild spiciness, fruity, and a bit stale; tangy and mildly fizzy; begins to get full and mealy-mouthed as you drink it; this is a beer meant to be cute and seasonal, but instead is too general to be distinctive; gets tantalizing and seductive at the end, but by then it's too late; as a drinking companion put it: *feh*. Compatible with pepper-hot chicken dishes.

3 MONTS FLANDERS GOLDEN ALE   CB   3.3
(Saint-Sylvestre, France)
Overwhelmingly yeasty; full and sharp as it spreads all over your mouth; alcohol feel increases quickly and in quantity; heavy-duty; encompassing, rounded sweetness helps temper spicy foods; a lit-

tle cloying, with bitterness at the finish; some grittiness also at the end; pale color and underlying thinness are consistent. (Requires a corkscrew to open.) Match with spicy and/or highly-seasoned chicken dishes.

TIGER Lager   **CB**   **3.3**
(Singapore)
Unusually foamy; light and texturally quite satisfying, almost sensual; turns sweetish in tandem with some foods; subtle and even-handed from the tip of the tongue to the throat; so smooth and easy going down that its 23 ounces are finished before you're aware they're gone; not filling or otherwise intrusive; Asian equivalent of Miller or Bud; I found this hard to rate. Good with barbecued pork.

TIJUCA Pilsener   **CB**   **3.8**
(Belem, Brazil)
Very grainy and full; well-integrated; nice warmth; mild spritziness throughout; smooth and well-behaved; consistent, and assertive in interest; flavorful; you look forward to each sip. Especially good with Mexican food.

TIMMERMANS PECHE Lambic   **CB**   **3.3**
(Itterbeck, Belgium)
Slightly fruity; somewhat soft fizziness; peach aroma and hue; circumscribed sweetness, smell and looks bear out the promise; sadly, it quickly loses fizz; mild acidity makes it palatable if not exciting with some meats; sticks a bit to the sides of the mouth, but not cloying or cottony; cloudy, golden-peach color at the bottom; good choice for those desiring a little adventure. Match with veal scallops or chicken and dumplings.

TOBY Pilsener   **CT**   **2.2**
(Toronto, Ontario, Canada)
Rich, musty, hoppy aroma and taste; mild, tangy background on the flat of the tongue; light, rich amber color supports a long-lasting head with a foamy backbone and delicate Brussels lace; mild alcohol theme; thin and one-dimensional; leaves a furry thickness on the roof of the mouth; for those with very specialized tastes.

TORONTO LIGHT Pilsener   **CT**   **1.8**
(Guelph, Ontario, Canada)
Foamy crispness quickly fades to flatness on the tongue; a bit of zestiness at the very back of the throat; not quite bland, but not energetic, either; some hint of ingredients occasionally reaches the taste buds; not a bad beer, just a "nothing" beer; some hoppiness at the end.

TRAQUAIR HOUSE ALE MB 4.1
(Innerleithen, Scotland)
Warm and mellow, both in aroma and taste; tangible alcohol; smooth molasses feel; warming ambience with glowing, deep-amber color; no head to speak of; as it warms, the aroma, taste, and texture come together to make a full-bodied, complex ale in which no one ingredient, including the alcohol, dominates; fruitiness is downplayed; typical, hearty Scottish ale with prominent molasses presence; moderate chewiness adds to the fun; a good ale that deserves your attention. A fine match with smoked salmon or trout.

TRESTLES LAGER CT 1.0
(Dubuque, Iowa)
Ersatz taste quickly sinks into blandness; flowery/perfumey flavor emerges with shellfish; food spices up the beer, which is essentially flat; in the end, typical, unsatisfying, and safely generic; a below-par example of a contract brewery product.

TRIPLE TOISON D'OR ALE CB 2.5
(Mechelen, Belgium)
Very smooth, creamy texture; sturdy, fresh wine aroma; sharp sourness; overall, more attractive texture than taste; some muddiness to flavor and color; faint citric fruitiness doesn't help. Goes with shellfish.

TROIKA ORIGINAL RUSSIAN BEER
Lager CB 1.1
(Moscow, Russia)
Starchy, bitter, and old-tasting—not off to a flying start; unexciting and placidly hopped—keeping in the Russian beer tradition; light-straw color; no head to speak of, though it does display short-lasting, not particularly dainty, Brussels lace; integrity diminishes toward end, finishing wan, with a hint of dryness and hoppiness; bottle came with sediment which appeared to add a buttery taste (diacetyl)—not a good sign.

TROPICAL PILSENER CB 3.7
(Las Palmas, Canary Islands)
Sweetly pungent malt-grain taste; nice body; hint of sourness raises it above the predictable; moderated sweetness; texturally well-balanced and appropriately fizzy; an attractive beer with sweet-sour complexity. Try with Chinese and Japanese shrimp dishes.

TSINGTAO Pilsener CB 0.4
(Shanghai, China)
Flat and easily forgettable; ingredients are absent, or at least not discernible; tastes like water.

B E E R   F A C T

*B*eer was virtually unknown to the Chinese until the middle of the 19th century. The city of Tsingtao, which means "green island," was the site of China's first commercial lager brewing operation, started by Germans in 1897.

**TUBORG DELUXE DARK Lager   CB   1.1
(Portland, Oregon)**
Surprisingly thin and tasteless, with and without food; a rounded sharpness is this beer's main distinction; bland and flat—even the color has a faded, unattractive darkness; a beer this dull is difficult to finish.

**TUBORG LAGER   CB   2.4
(La Crosse, Wisconsin, et. al.)**
Sharp, bitter, and tingly; mild body; no head to speak of; in general, "thin" visual experience with opaque, dull-gold color; sharpness and bitterness abate, but fizziness remains; an obviously hoppy brew; label says "Export Quality," but brewed in the U.S. by Heileman; acceptable for those with accepting palates. Compatible with pork.

**TUCHER FESTBIER MARZEN (annual)   CB   2.0
(Nurnberg, Germany)**
Initially appealing sweetish/burnt taste quickly dissolves into watery, bland palate; starts with promise and ends with a yawn when sampled with food; mellows somewhat at the end, returning to its initial appeal.

**TUSKER MALT LAGER   CB   2.3
(Nairobi, Kenya)**
More aroma than flavor on initial sip; tasteless, like water, except for a back-of-the-mouth mustiness going down the throat; has freshness that turns boring; a touch of sweetness as it warms to room temperature; light but very hoppy. Does nothing for most foods. Okay with pizza.

**TUSKER PREMIUM LAGER   CB   4.3
(Nairobi, Kenya)**
Very pale color and thin, slightly lemony taste immediately cool you down in 100° weather; the water feels especially fresh, clean, and inviting; very thirst-quenching; faint hop bitterness is pleasantly balanced by mild maltiness; the ingredients don't intrude, but allow the overall freshness to predominate; light-bodied, fluffy (cottony), and very, very accommodating; dainty hop finish—a perfect hot-weather beer without food or other distractions.

T.W. FISHER'S FESTIVAL DARK ALE MB/BP 2.3
(Coeur d'Alene, Idaho)

Light; spritzy, and fruity; thin with essentially no head; rather "cold," remote taste; flat; mild hint of sour fruitiness appears with food; bland; cloudy, light-amber color does not enhance the attraction; somewhat watery at the end.

UB EXPORT LAGER CB 2.5
(Bangalore, India)

Immediate aroma is fresh and pungent with underlying metallic smell, none of which is long-lasting; primacy of bitterness with reasonable malt balance; texture becomes watery too soon for comfort; while texturally flat in general, it does maintain an active fizziness that goes well with poultry and salads; both hops and malts are more noticeable at the end of the bottle.

UMPQUA PERRY'S OLD ALE (draft) BP 2.4
(Roseburg, Oregon)

Fresh aroma; apple-cider taste, though somewhat hoppier; fairly rich and medium-bodied; malt overtakes the hops, ultimately making the beer more palatable; flinty malt aroma at the end helps integrate the maltiness on the tongue; vaguely fruity finish enhances the rating; needs to be more consistent to truly be a contender.

UNION PREMIUM Pilsener CB 2.3
(Ljubljana, the former Yugoslavia)

Sharp, but underpowered; fair amount of fizziness; initial honey taste subsides into sour dryness with food; thin and shallow; refreshing, but limited by flat, sour-honey taste; whiff of bruised Concord grapes, perhaps not surprising, as this comes from the wine-producing area of the country.

UPPER CANADA COLONIAL STOUT CB 2.3
(Toronto, Ontario, Canada)

A cherry roastedness wafts up as cap comes off the bottle; the taste, however, is slightly bitter, somewhat milky, and soft on the palate; aroma disappears fairly rapidly as does the initial intriguing complexity; moderated bitterness takes over; not as thick as it should be; diminished, deep-amber color; weak-textured and lacking backbone; finishes with coffee taste, burnt aroma, and overall blandness.

UPPER CANADA DARK ALE CB 3.2
(Toronto, Ontario, Canada)

Fruity tanginess on first sip, with an undercurrent of mustiness; dry and pointed; clean, fresh taste parallels the mustiness and offers a soothing complement to food; taste wanes as beer warms and becomes more of a background to the food; quite serviceable. Match with hearty pork dishes.

UPPER CANADA LAGER   CB   2.5
(Toronto, Ontario, Canada)

Extra-sharp with fading flavor; refreshing and cooling deep in the throat; eventual neutral taste is surprisingly invigorating against food; tall, thin pilsener glass seems to stretch and air out the beer, encouraging the coolness to blend and become evenly distributed; more a pretzels-and-nuts beer, or one to drink alone rather than with food.

UPPER CANADA LIGHT LAGER   CB   0.7
(Toronto, Ontario, Canada)

Typical, but subdued, lager taste; sharp but not prickly; flat and watery with food; plain and uninteresting—you quickly lose interest; too-full, hoppy aftertaste spoils any interest you might have had.

UPPER CANADA PALE ALE   CB   2.0
(Toronto, Ontario Canada)

Musty, malty aroma with soda-pop taste and texture—light-bodied and fizzy; remains flat-tasting and plain; sweetens unpleasantly on the roof of the mouth with food; light amber color with a hint of raspberry shading; some integration of malt and hops, but both are mild and uninvigorating; needs to be cranked up a notch or two to be worth a second try.

UPPER CANADA PUBLICAN'S
SPECIAL BITTER ALE   CB   2.2
(Toronto, Ontario, Canada)

Whiff of oxidation, followed by mild, increasingly strong bitterness; too much candy-coated taste; water too weak to support the strong input of the hops, although bitterness gradually decreases, paving the way for an appropriate balance as maltiness increases; light, thin copper color; understated boldness gives a hint of what this beer should be; malty aroma in the finish, but too placid. Pleasant accompaniment to a hero or submarine sandwich.

UPPER CANADA REBELLION
MALT LIQUOR   CB   3.8
(Toronto, Ontario, Canada)

Sweet roundness with fullness and warmth in the throat; lovely honey taste surrounds and subdues high-alcohol content and fits in seamlessly with food, as if the beer and food are one; not very complex, but predictable and evenhanded; with a little more zip, this could be a much better beer; as it is, it's a good choice for someone interested in something different, but not radically so; increased alcohol presence in the finish; light amber color; smooth and refined. Try with pork chops or breaded pork tenderloin.

UPPER CANADA TRUE BOCK   CB   3.7
(Toronto, Ontario, Canada)
Soft and warm-tasting, with pleasant hop aroma that encourages
you to sniff deeply; visually quite bubbly, but texturally not much
effervescence; hearty, full, complex flavor with mild, emerging
maltiness; gently flowing alcohol ambience; hint of wineyness in
the alcohol detracts somewhat; moderate amount of Brussels lace
provides an appealing backdrop to sparkling, red-amber color;
finishes with a pleasurable surprise—a light, malty, toasted aroma
atypical of bock. Be careful when you get out of your seat—you
know there's alcohol when you stand up; as the label notes, this
bock "is not for the faint of heart."

UPTOWN HONEY ALE   MB   0.8
(Youngstown, Ohio)
Sour; rather bland; elements are not integrated; slight, flat aftertaste; somewhat stale; weak, light-golden color further disappoints; not well-done.

VAIL ALE   CT   3.5
(Fort Mitchell, Kentucky)
Full and pleasantly sweet with a tang that is on same continuum
as guacamole and chips; not overly alcoholic; hint of fermented
cider; improves as it warms; predictable and readily handled by
newcomers yet with enough backbone for more experienced
drinkers; neither dry nor sweet. Also good with snack foods such
as cheese and crackers.

VAILIMA LAGER   MB   3.5
(Apia, Western Samoa)
Sharp and vaguely sour; off-taste background, but appealing in
any event; complexity of the ingredients makes this South Pacific offering interesting, though a little unpredictable; German-
strength hoppiness; well-integrated ingredients; becomes more
intriguing with food; nicely sweet, but not tacky or cloying, finish further encourages you to have another bottle of this brew
(at the outset, I wouldn't have expected to say that); grows more
pleasing as you drink it; label declares "brewed and bottled under German management.

VAILIMA LIGHT Pilsener   MB   2.1
(Apia, Western Samoa)
Prickly and fresh-tasting, with some sourness; quite light-bodied
and thin; aroma and texture predominate over the taste; some
hoppiness; dry, undistinguished finish.

BEER   FACT

Vailima, meaning "water in the hand," is a small mountain village in Western Samoa. According to legend, the wife of a man dying of thirst carried water from a nearby stream to him in the palms of her hands. It's not clear whether transplanted English novelist Robert Louis Stevenson used that story in any of his books. The writer spent the last years of his life in Vailima, where his house still stands. Neighbors called him Tusitala—"Teller of Tales."

VALENTINS KLARES WEIZENBIER   CB   2.3
(Heidelberg, Germany)
Quick, bubbly, thick head that with its airiness is hard to tell apart from the body; hint of green taste and sourness is all that greets the palate; only after several sips does sweet, wheat flavor surface; settles into routine fizz and strength with food; in the end, not all that interesting. Okay with a hamburger.

VICTORIA Pilsener   CB   0.0
(Mexico City, Mexico)
Thin, cranky, sour, and repellent—finally, a bad Mexican beer; green, without flavor—I didn't finish it; grossly overpriced; ties with Green Rooster (see page 129) as *numero uno* in the unpalatable class.

VIENNA LAGER   CT   2.5
(Milwaukee, Wisconsin)
Orange taste; rather undistinguished and a little off the mark; does nothing for food; hops try to push themselves into awareness; nothing terrible about this beer, just nothing to write home about.

VIKING LAGER   MB   2.2
(Victoria, British Columbia, Canada)
Fruity, highly carbonated combination with a fresh uninhibited taste; slightly filling without food; a bit of thickness disappears after the first few sips; in the end, rather routine with little distinction.

VONDEL DARK ALE   CB   0.3
(Dentergem, Belgium)
Fruity, malty, and soft, with an especially foamy head; sour citrus taste as the beer settles in; clearly a lot of alcohol in this drink;

much too sweet and alcoholic for food; too filling and slightly upsetting to my stomach; I found this hard to finish, indeed close to unpalatable; there is precious little to recommend it.

WARSTEINER Pilsener   **CB**   **3.9**
(Warstein, Germany)
Immediately distinctive; gentle, flowery hoppiness; solid, lingering taste that is nicely balanced between malts and hops; very responsive and complementary to food, remaining well-mannered and even-tasting all over the palate; improves in character as a meal progresses. Appropriate with spicy Thai food, hot Italian sausages, or salads with assertive dressings.

B E E R   F A C T

*I*n Germany, "premium" is the middle of five standard classifications based on price, not quality. There is no industry or government standard for the premium designation and as a result, no uniform relationship between what you pay and quality. American premium pilseners tend to offer lower adjunct levels than their non-premium—read: lower-priced—counterparts. Because standards are lacking for what is essentially advertising hyperbole, micro-breweries and brewpubs do not use "premium" in their labeling.

WARSTEINER PREMIUM VERUM
Pilsener   **CB**   **3.0**
(Warstein, Germany)
Foamy, creamy, small-bubbled head sets the stage for thin, golden sharpness underneath—but this prelude doesn't last long; hops are noticeable; light and frizzy in the middle; slight bitterness at the back of the mouth; holds its essence throughout, including heady, memorable, slightly flowery aroma; texture outweighs flavor; light by German standards; remains interesting, if not entirely attractive. Good with meat loaf, hot dogs, or wurst with sauerkraut.

WARTECK LAGER   **CB**   **3.2**
(Basel, Switzerland)
Smartly hopped and crisp on first sip, along with noticeable grainy taste; some acid undertones; maintains freshness throughout a meal; can be too assertive by itself, but just right for some foods;

dryness is pervasive; distinctive; appears to have relatively high alcohol content. Match with pork dishes.

WASATCH RASPBERRY WHEAT   MB/BP   2.8
(Park City, Utah)

It's got raspberry aroma and taste, alright—the instant the cap comes off the bottle; aroma is fuller and sweeter than the thin, somewhat harsh taste; refreshing, with a mild, yeasty sharpness that quenches thirst; uniform, sun-tea color is appropriately cloudy; raspberry aroma throughout is a pleasant treat each time you lift the glass to your lips; forceful hop backbone overpowers plain food; flavor intensity weakens about halfway through, allowing the yeast's citrus bitterness to emerge; there is a rigidity to the overall presentation; don't let this beer sit in the glass too long—drink it quickly before its energy and pizzazz are sapped (label calls this a malt beverage with raspberry juice concentrate). An interesting accompaniment to crêpes Suzette.

WASATCH SLICKROCK LAGER   MB/BP   2.7
(Park City, Utah)

Lazily fruity, with a tantalizing roughness and a quick, oxidized mouthfeel that disappears without a trace; imbalanced toward the hops, the taste is sharp and vibrant, though not overly flavorful; remains thick and fruity with food; cloudy, pale color supports pencil-thin, but well-designed head; bitterness mutes interplay of the ingredients; on the positive side, its harsh hop grittiness is a strong match for salty snacks; well made. Tasty with an Italian hero sandwich.

WASATCH STOUT   MB/BP   2.5
(Park City, Utah)

Fizzy and sharp; thin and bitter; stimulates the appetite, even after a big meal; bitterness combines with pungent roastedness and a lingering burnt taste on the roof of the mouth; ingredients never really integrate—they remain separate without coming together in a cohesive whole; fullness starts at the front of the mouth and disappears at the back; no head, no Brussels lace, just a deep brown sitting in the glass, awaiting some excitement; at the end, the roasted barley aroma is all but gone. Try with Indian food or rice dishes.

WASATCH WHEAT   MB/BP   0.3
(Park City, Utah)

Lemon-honey aroma with a distorted honey flavor that quickly turns ugly; musty, inconsistent, and then watery; eventually settles into a tea-like taste that lacks redeeming tannins and textural warmth; a baked-bread aroma shows itself briefly, offering the only sign of attractiveness; fruitiness never comes into full bloom, aroma never connects with the taste; unredeeming mild malt aroma at the end; hard to finish; inconsistent and unpredictable; poorly done; like a homebrew that failed; stay away.

WATNEY'S CREAM STOUT CB 3.9
(London, England)
Mellow, roasted palate with continued inviting ambience; restrained maltiness reflects its origins; beautiful dark-brown, almost black, color adds to the pleasure; retains strength with food; close to chocolatey in taste; rich roastedness and depth enhance spicy foods; versatile and sophisticated with several appealing faces, but with solid core; no bitterness, which it could have used; finish is a bit too watery. A good choice with hamburgers, roast beef, or Buffalo-style chicken wings.

WATNEY'S RED BARREL Lager CB 3.9
(London, England)
Lovely, mellow wine taste; touch of bitterness; surprisingly sweet aftertaste; extraordinarily smooth; a bit too light to be closer to perfection. Match with beef or pork stews, steak and kidney pie, and other hearty main dishes.

T A P   T I P

Dark and Tan

*A*Dark and Tan is the same as a Black and Tan (see page 132) but with Watney's Red Barrel Lager substituted for the Harp. A subtle, indirect, mildly burnt taste marks the first sips of the delectably deep-brown mixture; sheets of Brussels lace decorate the glass; dry, acceptably rough finish. Retains its burnt zest with a burger and fries.

WATNEY'S STINGO CREAM STOUT CB 3.5
(London, England)
Mellow and soft with dry-wine aroma; faint, palatable burnt taste; warm, with a hint of sweetness; doesn't really do justice to light or mildly flavored foods; a classic stout. Good with moderately sweet desserts such as a fruit tart or pound cake.

WEEPING RADISH BLACK RADISH
DARK LAGER MB/BP 2.2
(Manteo, North Carolina)
Mildly roasty with a pleasant aftertaste; vague, weak malt presence; pronounced, undifferentiated taste reminiscent of the brewer's amber and golden lagers; mild, burnt taste comes and goes quickly

at mid-bottle, then the beer resumes its plodding, unexciting course; not worth the effort. Serve with popcorn.

BEER FACT

Weeping Radish gets its name from the Bavarian vegetable favored by local clientele. Served sliced and salted with the beer, the resulting moisture makes it appear as if the radish is weeping.

WEEPING RADISH COROLLA
GOLDEN LAGER   MB/BP   2.7
(Manteo, North Carolina)
Immediate yeast aroma and taste—smells as if you just entered a bakery; bitter on the front of the tongue; quickly turns dry, in the manner of Champagne; light and airy; thick, creamy long-lasting head; Brussels lace covers sides of glass in curving sheets; a respectable, light, mildly bitter beer with staying power; a pleasant summer drink. Goes well with a mixed green salad or a French salade niçoise.

WEEPING RADISH FEST BEER
AMBER LAGER   MB/BP   2.1
(Manteo, North Carolina)
Hop-bitter and softly malty with gentle, very faint hint of toastedness; minor fizziness helps lessen the bitterness; predictable and uncomplex from start to finish; Brussels lace is bunched together rather than in pleasing patterns; unexciting; flavor diminishes by the end of the rather large bottle; disappointing; not worth trying with food.

WEIHENSTEPHAN EDEL—PILS   CB   2.6
(Freising, Germany)
Balanced malt and hop sweetness precedes faded, faintly bitter aftertaste; bold and crisp; gentles and mellows with food; light-golden color accurately reflects the lightness of this beer; not one of the brewery's better efforts. Goes with raw oysters or sushi.

WEIHENSTEPHAN EXPORT DUNKEL   CB   4.1
(Freising, Germany)
Smooth, long, malty swallow, with a splash-of-orange tang at the end; full-bodied and nicely modulated in both taste and texture; yeast fruitiness is a major player; well-balanced, temperate, but very flavorful; charming, mild roastedness on its own, or with hearty food; accommodating mellowness lingers on; a fine, comforting drinking partner that grows better after each sip. An accompaniment to lamb roasts and chops.

WEIHENSTEPHAN WEIZENBIER   **CB**   **3.8**
(Freising, Germany)
Faint, clove aroma turns into a strong, refreshing, sharp clove taste mixed in with crisp, full head of foam; dry and pleasantly tickly on the upper palate; firm, with evenly distributed ingredients; full-bodied and lush with subtle yeastiness; hazy, light-blond color is muted (label says: "crystal-clear"); a compelling tartness surfaces as the glass is drained; a very good representation of wheat beer from the self-described "Oldest Brewery in the World." A good match with roast beef.

WEINHARD'S LIGHT ALE—
IRISH STYLE   **CB**   **2.3**
(Portland, Oregon)
Very slight, flattened, fruity aroma, along with almost tasteless, bitter fizziness; you have to concentrate to experience the faint flavor; weak with food; some rounded fullness and a touch of sweetness follow through at the end; not unpleasant, just not interesting; a mass market beer that is better on its own than with a meal.

WEST END EXPORT LAGER   **CB**   **3.3**
(Thebarton, South Australia,
Australia)
Crisp, dry, and reasonably well-hopped; immediate impression of a substantial, quality lager, including a taste of bitterness alongside a sweetish character; attractive, full grains; agreeably balanced until the end, when hops begins to weaken; an enjoyable brew with a backbone. An excellent choice with grilled salmon or tuna steaks.

WESTMALLE TRAPPIST Ale   **AB**   **4.3**
(Abbey of Westmalle, Belgium)
Yeasty and fresh, with mouth-filling, rounded alcohol taste; gentle golden color; dainty texture, with substance and follow-through; a hint of fresh fruit is a delightful counterpoint; graduated upsurge of alcoholic potency continues at the end, underpinned by the gently swirling yeast performing its bottle-conditioned duty; a good example of the style—flavorful and well-balanced. Try it at brunch with ham and eggs.

WHITBREAD ALE (draft)   **CB**   **3.9**
(London/Sheffield, England)
Dark, sour, bitter taste remains yeasty; bracing aroma and full body; a little too sharp, but palatable; especially refreshing on tap, with thick, chewable head, topping off the body like cream froth on hot chocolate; bitter, firm in the mouth, and full-bodied; one of the better draft beers I have had. Tasty with black bean or vegetable soup accompanied by crusty bread.

WHITEFISH BROWN ALE (draft)　　　**BP**　　　　1.6
(Whitefish, Montana)
Genuine roasted taste is demanding on first sip, but fades fast;
fresh, malty initial aroma recalls the beach; in the meantime, taste
continues to diminish, flattening and weakening; the flavor changes
character, turning into a brew that tastes like roasty Kool-Aid;
weak and watery, with carbonation predominating at the end;
not offensive, but not pleasing, either. Food doesn't help this disappointing brew.

WIDMER ALT (draft)　　　　　**MB/BP**　　　　3.3
(Portland, Oregon)
Tart fruitiness with a gradual slide into compact fizziness; citrus
fruitiness is quite appropriate for food; pleasant sharpness merges
midway through the (large) glass; well-made, with good potential in its responsivity to a variety of foods, ranging from cold
cuts to shrimp salad.

TAP TIP

The Draft Difference

*N*aturally carbonated, usually unpasteurized
(pasteurization prolongs shelf life, but saps
the beer of flavor and charm), and a lot fresher
than the bottled variety, draft beer is a delight for the
senses. Generally, tapped beer has more character than
the same brand in a bottle. Compare the two and taste
for yourself. Because it is not pasteurized, draft is much
more perishable. The good part is that unpasteurized
beer allows more of the essence and complexity to
come through. That's why brewers prefer their customers to drink from the tap, rather than from a can
or bottle. An increasing number of breweries are now
marketing what they call draft beer in cans and bottles. It is just not the same. The fact is, once you try
freshly brewed draft beer, it's hard to enjoy anything
else, regardless of style, brand, or price.

WIDMER FESTBIER Lager (annual)　　**MB/BP**　　3.8
(Tigard, Oregon)
Slightly schizophrenic—strong caramel taste with surprisingly
thin body; some hint of chocolate; hoppy aroma balances nicely
with creamy smoothness; complex and charming; bitter hops
presence; good, continuing head; thick, clinging Brussels lace; an

interesting, satisfying interaction comes about with a ham and cheese soufflé—both the beer and food are improved.

WIDMER WEIZEN (draft)   MB/BP   2.0
(Portland, Oregon)

Dry and sour with a fragile body; no hint of clove; lemony taste lines the sides of the mouth, tangibly reducing any interest in having another glass; thirst-enhancing, rather than quenching; hoppy, but goes nowhere.

WILD BOAR SPECIAL AMBER Lager   CT   2.2
(Dubuque, Iowa)

Sweet, molasses presence, but texturally flat and uninteresting; core faithful to typical amber style; fades in the finish.

WILD GOOSE AMBER Ale   MB   2.6
(Cambridge, Maryland)

Mild, alluring caramel aroma and taste make for attractive opening; texturally full and very satisfying; simultaneously warm and bitter; strong caramel-popcorn aroma wafts up as the beer warms; decided caramel color; small, bubbly head emphasizes underlying thinness; eventually emerges mildly malty, like a good amber should; fades a bit in the end, with sour overtones; a step or two away from being a classy brew.

BEER FACT

*T*he term "amber" is often used in the United States by brewpubs and microbreweries to indicate the beer's color: copper, tawny, reddish-brown.

WILLAMETTE VALLEY NOR'WESTER
RYE ALE (draft)   BP   2.6
(Portland, Oregon)

Tart and bitter, with lemon/clove flavor; rye character is strong and unyielding, maintaining its strength and flavor to the extent that you can almost imagine rye seeds floating in the golden liquid; taste complexity slackens after several sips, leaving the bitterness to predominate; texture remains relatively smooth; clove presence returns at the end, in time to fall into step with the bitter aftertaste; an interesting brew that takes time getting used to. Try this alone with a twist of lemon or lime, or with salty snacks.

WIT White/Wheat   CT   3.1
(St. Paul, Minnesota)

Honey, lemony taste—sort of like cloudy, weak-colored but tasty tea; the gentle flavor ultimately becomes clear—orange peel and coriander; sweet musty aroma; naturally cloudy, the hazy hue settles between that of ale and wheat beer, with far less visual texture than wheat beer; ebb and flow of sweetness and tartness moves playfully over the tongue and the roof of the mouth; yeasty aroma is apparent at the end, as are clumps of yeast floating on the bottom of the glass (indicative of bottle-conditioning); interesting and light; satisfying without food, but hard to match *with* food; finishes with a slight thickness at the roof of the mouth that leaves you a little thirsty.

**WITKAP-PATER SINGEL ABBEY ALE   AB   4.0
(Ninove, Belgium)**
Fruity, clove taste along with lovely, soft texture resulting from a gentle fizziness; fluffy, thick, foamy head produces lasting, irregularly-shaped but attractive Brussels lace; bottle-conditioned and highly yeasty, as befits the style; light and fulfilling; head sits patiently and evenly on top of cloudy, straw-colored body; smooth bittersweetness glides down the throat leaving a faint clove aftertaste; combination of ingredients weakens somewhat at the end, allowing for a taste of the individual components, rather than the earlier blending; aroma keeps flavorful pace with the taste; well-made and lovely to look at; buy two, so you can taste and look longer. Try this with freshwater fish with delicate sauce, and make sure to drink it slightly warm.

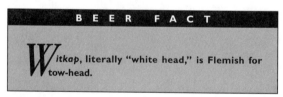

B E E R   F A C T

*W*itkap, literally "white head," is Flemish for tow-head.

**WOLFBRAU Pilsener   CB   3.3
(Osnabrück, Germany)**
Lemon-honey tea aroma is soothing, but flat; no head; tastes like fresh coffee grounds, but without the bitterness, making this very distinctive, if not outstanding; malt appears to be toasted; hops remain sweet with subterranean bite; interesting and different; cloudy, weak-tea appearance; I would drink this again, but perhaps with tea biscuits or crackers; finishes with a full honey sweetness; intriguing; worth the effort to locate.

**WOLFSBRAU AMBER LAGER   CB   2.5
(Calgary, Alberta, Canada)**
Warm, rosy upsurge with tickle of tiny bubbles at the back of the throat; simultaneously mildly sweet and sour with comforting, surprising heftiness; unassuming and appealing in a bland sort of way; benign balance of malt and hops. Fine with most types of sandwiches.

WRIGLEY RED Scottish Ale   CT   2.8
(brewed for Old Chicago in Boulder, Colorado)
Amber sweetness and toasted flavor; fresh-tasting and appropriately sweet; chewy and more integrated as you drink it; Gold Medal winner at the 1993 Great American Beer Festival. A perfect match for fish and chips.

WURZBURGER HOFBRAU
OCTOBERFEST Lager (annual)   CB   2.7
(Würzburg, Germany)
Medium-sharp texture and medium-caramel taste on first sip; settles into muted fruity/sweet balance; weak overall; somewhat thin-flavored for most foods; musty, demanding odor is too prominent; gets more ingratiating and full as it warms; a mixed bag, but worth trying.

WYNKOOP IRISH CREAM STOUT   MB/BP   3.0
(Denver, Colorado)
Romantic, delicate roasted flavor tantalizes on first sip, followed by smooth, fresh but uncomplicated taste; remains mellow with maltiness that unfortunately remains a bit too hidden and too flat texturally; could be thicker and more flavorful, but an intriguing example of an American-made cream stout.

WYNKOOP JED FEST Lager (annual)   MB/BP   3.7
(Denver, Colorado)
Fresh and thoroughly flavorful; retains fruitiness that is beguiling and a bit sweet; too sharp and sour with meats or heavy meals; maintains fresh, mildly fruity fragrance and taste; drink this before a meal or with light fare such as fish or chicken.

WYNKOOP SYMPOSIUM ALE   MB/BP   2.9
(Denver, Colorado)
Chocolatey, smooth, and fizzy—all at the same time; not as bitter as stout or porter; integrates and makes interesting a combination of not always compatible tastes and textures; good introduction to a different kind of beer. In order to fully experience the intricacies of this brew, an appropriate "background" food is called for, such as fresh salmon or trout.

XINGU BLACK BEER Stout/Lager   CB   4.5
(Cacador, Brazil)
Watery, caramel taste with complementary, nonintrusive aroma; not as thick or chewy as expected, but enough texture to please my palate; gets enticingly mellower and properly sweeter as more is imbibed; good blend of bitterness and sweetness; solid and enjoyable. Good with Buffalo-style chicken wings and other hot, spicy snacks.

B E E R   F A C T

Xingu is bottom-fermented like lager, but in all other respects (taste, texture, color), it resembles stout.

YEBISU ALL MALT Pilsener   CB   2.7
(Tokyo, Japan)
Fresh, but flat; slightly acidic; clearly malt beer, with dry ambience; mellow and smooth; nice, easy-going, sipping companion with which to pass the time while you wait for your meal; essentially no fizz; leaves some scrawny Brussels lace.

YEBISU STOUT DRAFT (bottle/can)   CB   2.4
(Tokyo, Japan)
Thick and light with minimal fizziness; overall impression of lightness; poorly balanced; pale-golden color. Try it with chicken.

B E E R   F A C T

The legendary 14th-century Japanese deity and prophet, Yebisu, is reputed to be the "bringer of good luck and prosperity."

YI KING Pilsener   CB   2.1
(Guangzhou, China)
Bland and flat with yeasty sharpness around the edges; thin body; no head; warms into mellowness at mid-bottle; too wine-like in taste; final swallow is more palatable than the first.

YOUNG'S LONDON PORTER   CB   3.2
(London, England)
Deep, rich, and dark; a typical porter: palatable bitterness, balanced texture, and moderated, sharp burnt taste; thins out a little bit at the end; traditional dry, weak-coffee flavor. Good with meat and potato meals.

YOUNG'S OATMEAL STOUT   CB   4.3
(London, England)
Appealing chocolate malt aroma on first sip; roasted flavor spreads out across the tongue; round and full-bodied; gets thicker, more chocolatey, and sweeter as it warms; brown-black color adds to the ambience; remains a medium-dry beer; easy to drink two to three bottles, with or without food; has substance and class. Good with steak and potatoes.

YOUNG'S OLD NICK Christmas Ale
(annual)   CB   3.9
(London, England)
Smooth, creamy, and voluptuous barley wine with deep, sweet, burnt taste—yummy; nice smoky-amber color; retains physically soft, warm texture throughout; unfortunately, a bit too mild for most foods. Savor as an *apéritif* or *digestif.*

YOUNG'S OLD NICK BARLEY WINE   CB   2.2
(London, England)
Made with soft water (as is true of most beers in England); ale yeasts interacts with malt to produce fruity (banana) esters; increasing alcohol warmth, but not as strongly alcoholic as other barley wines; flat on the tongue; unusually weak for the style; unsatisfying.

YOUNG'S RAM ROD Ale   CB   3.6
(London, England)
Dark and musty; sharp; hearty; rich malty presence; tingly on your tongue; strong flavor, aggressive in its strength. A good match with prime rib or roast beef.

YOUNG'S SPECIAL ALE   CB   3.0
(London, England)
Soft and creamy with mild pinprick of carbonation; fruity, flowery mouthfeel—more a physical than a taste sensation; some warmth, fullness and caramel candy sweetness emerges with food; this beer doesn't identify its intentions, resulting in some uncertainty about what to expect.

YOUNG'S WINTER ALE (annual)   CB   4.0–4.3
(London, England)
Pungent, chocolatey burnt-caramel taste with accompanying aroma; smooth; its complexity achieves a nice balance; gentle, medium head; retains warmth at the end; improves as you drink it; a tad too watery. Match with spicy foods.

YUCHAN Pilsener   CB   4.0
(Beijing, China)
Nice rice influence; malt and hops are secondary; very tasty, alone as well as with poultry; invigorating and appealing; helps work up the appetite; enjoyment is primary; try this, if you can find it. Not surprisingly, a good match with Chinese food, but also tasty with Western-style chicken and vegetable main courses.

YUENGLING LAGER   CB   3.4
(Pottsville, Pennsylvania)
Moderate-to-full body overlaid with thin fizziness; nice deep-amber color; pleasantly fresh-smelling; comforting warmth; evolves into palatable, workmanlike brew; retains softness and integrity as it goes. Serve with a hearty stew or shepherd's pie.

B E E R   F A C T

Yuengling, still family-owned, is America's oldest brewery. Operations began in 1829.

YUENGLING PORTER   CB   4.1
(Pottsville, Pennsylvania)
Airy; moderately bold, with slightly less body than it should have; pleasant, subdued, roasted flavor, especially in the finish; mellow, warm, and comforting; delightful and satisfying. Quite drinkable on its own, but also compatible with seafood.

YUENGLING TRADITIONAL LAGER   CB   3.3
(Pottsville, Pennsylvania)
Crisp and cold on the roof of the mouth, with quick malt rush; pleasant, somewhat prickly fizziness; malt flavor is sweet and well-balanced against the unobtrusive hops; smooth, yet with a certain roughness; slightly and nicely chewy; label proclaims, "Original Amber Beer." Good with spicy Chinese or Indian rice dishes.

ZAGORKA LAGER   CB   0.9
(Zagora, Bulgaria)
Sterile and flat on first sip; slightly rancid-tasting; so uncomplex as to be uniform in taste, texture, and lack of appeal; hint of fruitiness relieves, but doesn't excuse, tedium at the end.

ZEB O'BREEN'S IRISH ALE   CB   3.2
(Calgary, Alberta, Canada)
Hearty, fruity, and zesty with nice alcoholic punch; sweet maltiness; appropriately and unobtrusively carbonated; medium-full body; scalloped Brussels lace decorates the sides of the glass; develops hoppy sharpness about halfway through the pint; warm-amber color; entertaining, slow-sipping companion when you have time to spare at the bar.

ZHUJIANG Lager   CB   2.9
(Guangzhou, China)
Tart, slightly honey-flavored, and crisp; full and rounded with a solid core; soothing and mellow; feels silky around the edges; nice network of grains helps increasingly flat texture return some interest; roughly, rather than delicately, balanced; a lot of yin and yang in this brew, but in the end a bit too thickishly sweet. Compatible with seafood pastas.

ZIP CITY VIENNA AMBER Lager
(draft) BP 0.7
(New York, New York)
Fruity aroma, with hit of overly aggressive carbonation; sharp and flowery; slight skunkiness; neither toasted nor roasted, nor full-bodied lacks malt presence; too light in color and far too cloudy and milky—definitely not in the style; fizzy, long-lasting after-taste; not a good beer.

ZYWIEC FULL LIGHT Pilsener CB 1.5
(Zywiec, Poland)
Slightly cloying honey-like texture with matching aftertaste; bland; no fizziness—just flat throughout; slight sharpness comes along at mid-bottle; lacks depth and complexity; rather watery; finishes with some warmth; overall, unexciting and uninviting.

NON-ALCOHOLIC BREWS FOR THE DESIGNATED DRIVER

T here were skeptics in 1989 when major breweries like Budweiser and Miller jumped into the non-alcoholic beer market. But sales immediately shot skyward: The year after non-alcoholic brews were introduced as major players, total sales leaped 90%, representing 1% of all beer-industry sales. Those figures have changed little over the past several years, but there are now more players.

Truth be told, there is nothing new about non-alcoholic brews; they've been around commercially for at least 60 years (and, it is certain, for far longer than that—millennia, say— as even a brief historical review of home-brewing and cultural attitudes toward alcohol will reveal). Two leading European brands, Beck's Haake-Beck and Heineken's Buckler, have been available for more than a half-century.

In the United States, Cincinnati's Hudepohl Brewing Company introduced Pace Pilsner in 1983, marking the debut of the first non-alcoholic brew. At present, there are upwards of 40 on the market. Required by law to be labeled "brew," they contain no more than one-half of 1% alcohol by weight, which is the legal definition of non-alcoholic. Otherwise, the ingredients are the same as those found in beer.

I have rated some of the legally designated brews on the market. I have also included a type of non-alcoholic beverage not generally featured in this country. Malt beverages, popular in South America, contain no alcohol at all and can properly be enjoyed by designated drivers—or anyone else interested in beerlike flavor and complexity—without having to bother with the effects of fermentation. In fact, commercially produced non-alcoholic brews in this country must be identified as malt beverages on the label.

> **NOTE:** These brews are ranked in comparison to one another; the ratings should not be compared with those given to beers that contain alcohol.

BUCKLER   **CB**   **2.2**
(brewed by Heineken in Holland)
Tingly mouthfeel with fullness on the tongue and on the roof of the mouth; sharper and less sweet than many of the others; becomes one-dimensional and flat with spicy foods; turns bland and somewhat old-tasting on the palate; like weak tea at the end.

CLAUSTHALER   CB   3.8
(Frankfurt, Germany)
Sharp maltiness with suggestion of hop bitterness; flat and texturally uninvigorating; maintains flavor and integrates ingredients in a more unified package than the other brews; malty aroma is present even with strongly flavored or spicy foods; blond color with a hint of ruby; more filling and more beerlike than the others, though still far from the real thing; mildly hoppy finish adds to this brew's distinctiveness.

EXTRACTO DE MALTA MALT
BEVERAGE   CB   3.9
(Hamburg, Germany)
Rich, chocolatey flavor reminiscent of a malted or milk shake; pungent malty aroma with attenuated sweetness; accompanying bitterness is nicely tuned and balanced; flavor level is maintained with or without food; in the end, lacking fermentation, any oomph is overwhelmed by thick mouthfeel and soda-fountain ambience (syrupy viscosity); heavily hopped; comes within drinking distance of real beer.

FIRESTONE   CB   1.8
(Los Olivas, California)
Nicely balanced hop and malt character with onrushing crispness; while it maintains some backbone, it also exudes an off-putting harshness; malty aroma at the end, with a weak tea finish.

HAAKE BECK   CB   3.5
(Bremen, Germany)
Fresh and invigorating; honeyed-maltiness with a touch of hops doesn't allow sweetness to go too far; retains firmness and consistency missing from the other brews; maintains pleasantly beerlike presence with food; small bubbles make the head interfere with the taste of the light-golden body; fades a bit at the end.

HAMM'S NA   CB   2.5
(Milwaukee, Wisconsin)
Hoppy; some texture, but quickly surfacing flat taste on the roof of the mouth; faint sourness threads its way throughout; eventually tastes similar to a ballpark pilsener; tastes more like real Hamm's than any of the other brews taste like their alcoholic counterparts; a non-alcoholic brew with some pizzazz.

KALIBER   CB   2.8
(brewed in England for Guinness)
Tasty and highly malty; pleasantly attractive, clean, mid-range golden color; becomes very watery with most foods; mild, honey sweetness; emerging honey and malt integration suggests this brew should be imbibed alone or with relatively bland food; malt finish lingers on the roof of the mouth.

MALTINA   **CB**   **3.4**
(Lima, Peru)

Burnt-caramel taste is not unpleasant; deep, deep brown, almost black color; silky smooth and pleasantly sweet; solid textural ebb and flow; malt is restrained and slightly bitter; complements and surrounds food in a gentle cocoon of softness; sweetness has the potential to become overpowering after two or three glasses; thickens on the tongue; without fermentation, its potential is not reached.

MOLSON EXEL   **CB**   **3.3**
(Vancouver, British Columbia, Canada)

Grainy, almost coffee-flavored; fuller taste than other non-alcoholic brews; smells a little like soap; turns mildly sour, smooths out with smoked foods; matches up to some alcoholic beers with its projection of hop and malt taste and faint beer odor—as if there actually is a small portion of real beer in there somewhere, although I wouldn't seek it out in a bar or elsewhere; finishes with mild honey presence and appealing graininess; in general, Canada seems to produce better NA beers than does the U.S.

MORENITA MALTA   **CB**   **2.6**
(Osorno, Chile)

Soft, mushy, and on first several sips, tasteless; dark, brooding color; some warmth and presence emerge with spicy foods; plain, with a certain charm that makes you come back for more; neutral-tasting throughout; thickish at the end, with no carbonation.

MORENITA MALTA ESPECIAL   **CB**   **3.3**
(Concepción, Chile)

Softer and sweeter with a more chocolatey, auburn color than Morenita Malta; malts are ascendant here along with languid, almost syrupy texture; grows into some mild grittiness at the back of the mouth, while attractive, balmy sweetness remains in front; head is only a trifle creamier than the body; perhaps a tad too sweet for comfort with most foods; a filmy aftertaste remains in the mouth after drinking most of the unusually large bottle.

O'DOUL'S   **CB**   **3.1**
(brewed by Anheuser-Busch in
St. Louis, Missouri)

Quick pilsener feel without the usual accompanying spritzy texture; soft, foamy head is full of air, letting you get quickly to the pale-golden, light-tasting body; mild, faint hoppiness at the back of the throat reminds you that this is a "brew," not a beer; some flavor emerges with food, but it's essentially one-dimensional and not complex; possesses a core-taste solidity that others lack; Silver Medal winner at the 1993 Great American Beer Festival.

RAINIER PEAKS   CB   1.9
(Seattle, Washington)
Relatively characterless with a harsh texture and the barest suggestion of hops; smells more like beer than it tastes like beer; remains rough and intrusive in the mouth; medium-bodied with no complexity; thankfully, turns watery at the end.

RED BARON MALT BEVERAGE   CB   0.9
(Wilkes-Barre, Pennsylvania)
Cherry-flavored; very winelike in taste, texture, and mouthfeel; not fizzy at all; almost like liquid Jell-O, but not as sweet; clearly a before-dinner drink; not complex; simple and uninteresting.

SHARP'S   CB   0.8
**(brewed by Miller in
Milwaukee, Wisconsin)**
Fruity, vaguely citrus taste with minimum texture; no significant malt or hop presence; flavor goes flat early on, as does the head; more like a cross between lemon juice and fruit-flavored soda; cereal grain provides some sweetness; finish is watery and thin, without its previous hint of graininess; tastes and feels empty.

ST. PAULI   2.8
(Bremen, Germany)
Incredible, almost overpowering malt aroma quickly followed by pronounced honey taste; medium-bodied but very flat; honey flavor continues throughout, with no hops or, of course, alcoholic counterbalance; malt texture remains, especially at the back of the throat; lacks complexity; watery base with visible flecks of grain sprinkled throughout; in the end, taste is superior to the texture (none), color (wispy blond), and aroma (quickly fading).

TEXAS SELECT   CB   0.3
(San Antonio, Texas)
Very light, very weak, very uninteresting—and that's just the beginning; sour and unpleasantly musty; corn presence predominates resulting in an overwhelmingly pallid, grainy taste and ambience; degenerates into dirty-water mouthfeel with food; some feistiness, but the effort is not worth it.

UPPER CANADA POINT NINE   CB   2.9
(Toronto, Ontario, Canada)
Musty and very grainy-tasting, with honey overtones; subdued but pervasive hop presence; more full-bodied than other non-alcoholic beers, with a corresponding degree of complexity; substantial hop taste stays throughout, making up in strength and punch for the lowered alcohol content; aroma is sweeter and more pleasant than the taste, which retains a rough, unpolished mouthfeel; distinctive and curiously appealing—finishes with a malted milk or milk shake taste.

APPENDIXES

Beers by State: An
Alphabetical Listing

Beers by Country: An
Alphabetical Listing

Best Beers by Style

Best Beers for Novices

Try Something Different

Odd Beer Names

Visiting the Source: Microbreweries
and Brewpubs

Rating Notes

BEERS BY STATE: AN ALPHABETICAL LISTING

NAME	LOCATION	RATING	STYLE
ALASKA			
Alaskan Amber	Juneau	3.8	Alt
Alaskan Pale Ale	Juneau	1.0	Ale
ARIZONA			
Bandersnatch Big Horn Premium Ale	Tempe	3.4	Ale
Bandersnatch Edinbrew Seasonal Ale	Tempe	2.9	Ale
Bandersnatch Milk Stout	Tempe	4.0	Sto
Bandersnatch Pale Ale	Tempe	1.8	Ale
Bandersnatch Red Ale	Tempe	3.7	Ale
Bandersnatch Scottish Ale	Tempe	3.3	Ale
Barley's Fair Dinkum Amber Ale	Phoenix	2.4	Ale
Barley's IPA	Phoenix	2.3	IPA
Barley's Strangler Stout	Phoenix	2.9	Sto
Barley's Toby Stout	Phoenix	3.1	Sto
Barley's Trick Pale Ale	Phoenix	3.2	Ale
Cave Creek Chili Beer	Cave Creek	0.6	Spe
Coyote Springs Amber Ale	Phoenix	2.0	Ale
Coyote Springs Christmas Ale (annual)	Phoenix	2.5	Ale
Coyote Springs Forever Amber Ale	Phoenix	3.0	Ale
Coyote Springs Oatmeal Stout	Phoenix	1.2	Sto
Coyote Springs Pacific Northwest Pale Ale	Phoenix	2.9	Ale
Coyote Springs Vienna Pale Lager	Phoenix	1.0	Lag
Crazy Ed's Black Mountain Gold	Cave Creek	2.5	Lag
Gentle Ben's Big Horn Oatmeal Stout	Tucson	2.2	Sto
Gentle Ben's Catalina Kolsch Pale Ale	Tucson	2.0	Ale
Gentle Ben's Copperhead Ale	Tucson	0.6	Ale
Gentle Ben's Red Cat Amber	Tucson	2.3	Ale
Gentle Ben's T.J.'s Raspberry	Tucson	2.4	Ale
Hops Amber Ale	Scottsdale	2.4	Ale
Hops Bock	Scottsdale	3.1	Boc
Hops Pilsener	Scottsdale	3.2	Pil

NAME	LOCATION	RATING	STYLE
Hops Wheat	Scottsdale	2.3	Wht
San Francisco Cactus Lager	Tucson	1.0	Lag
San Francisco Wildcat Ale	Tucson	0.8	Ale
CALIFORNIA			
Alpine Village Hofbrau Lager	Torrance	2.3	Lag
Alpine Village Hofbrau Pilsener	Torrance	2.3	Pil
Anchor Liberty Ale	San Francisco	3.7	Ale
Anchor Old Foghorn Ale	San Francisco	3.4	Ale
Anchor Our Special Ale (annual)	San Francisco	2.5–4.0	Ale
Anchor Porter	San Francisco	4.0	Por
Anchor Steam	San Francisco	3.9	Ste
Anchor Wheat Draft	San Francisco	3.8	Wht
Anderson Valley Barney Flats Oatmeal Stout	Boonville	4.0	Sto
Anderson Valley Boont Amber Ale	Boonville	2.2	Ale
Anderson Valley Deep Enders Dark Porter	Boonville	3.8	Por
Anderson Valley High Rollers Wheat	Boonville	3.6	Wht
Anderson Valley Poleeko Gold Light Ale	Boonville	3.7	Ale
Belmont Long Beach Crude	Long Beach	2.1	Por
Belmont Long Beach Crude Nut Brown Ale	Long Beach	2.8	Ale
Belmont Marathon Ale	Long Beach	1.8	Ale
Belmont Pettifogger	Long Beach	3.4	Ale
Belmont Strawberry Blonde	Long Beach	2.2	Ale
Belmont Top Sail Ale	Long Beach	2.8	Ale
Brewski's Aztec Amber	San Diego	2.9	Lag
Brewski's Downtown Chestnut Brown Ale	San Diego	0.5	Ale
Brewski's Dry Honey Ale	San Diego	3.0	Ale
Brewski's Oatmeal Stout	San Diego	2.2	Sto
Brewski's Red Sails Ale	San Diego	2.8	Ale
Brewski's Two-Berry Ale	San Diego	1.7	Ale
Devil Mountain Devil's Brew Porter	Benicia	2.3	Por
Devil Mountain Gayle's Pale Ale	Benicia	2.4	Ale
Devil Mountain Ironhorse Alt	Benicia	2.8	Alt
Devil Mountain Ironhorse Stout	Benicia	2.6	Sto
Devil Mountain Railroad Ale	Benicia	3.6	Ale

NAME	LOCATION	RATING	STYLE
DILLON'S SIX SHOOTER RED ALE	CHATSWORTH	3.8	ALE
DILLON'S STRAIGHT SHOOTER PALE ALE	CHATSWORTH	2.3	ALE
DRAKE'S ALE	SAN LEANDRO	2.1	ALE
EMPEROR ALE	MODESTO	3.2	ALE
EXCALIBUR	CHICO	0.6	STO
GOLDEN PACIFIC CABLE CAR CLASSIC LAGER	EMERYVILLE	3.0	LAG
GOLDEN PACIFIC CASCADE WHOLE MALT	EMERYVILLE	2.5	LAG
GOLDEN PACIFIC GOLDEN BEAR DARK MALT LIQUOR	EMERYVILLE	3.3	MLT
GOLDEN PACIFIC GOLDEN GATE MALT LIQUOR	EMERYVILLE	3.1	MLT
GOLDEN PACIFIC THOUSAND OAKS LAGER	EMERYVILLE	3.0	LAG
HUMBOLDT GOLD RUSH EXTRA PALE ALE	ARCATA	2.3	ALE
HUMBOLDT RED NECTAR ALE	ARCATA	2.8	ALE
IVANHOE ALE	CHICO	0.1	ALE
JAMAICA BRAND RED ALE	BLUE LAKE	3.3	ALE
LA JOLLA PUMPHOUSE PORTER	LA JOLLA	0.0	POR
LIND RASPBERRY WHEAT	SAN LEANDRO	1.2	WHT
LOS GATOS OKTOBERFEST	LOS GATOS	0.1	ALE
LOST COAST DOWNTOWN BROWN ALE	EUREKA	3.2	ALE
LOST COAST STOUT	EUREKA	3.3	STO
MARIN OLD DIPSEA BARLEY WINE	LARKSPUR	3.0	ALE
MENDOCINO BLACK HAWK STOUT	HOPLAND	3.4	STO
MENDOCINO RED TAIL ALE	HOPLAND	2.5	ALE
MONTEREY KILLER WHALE AMBER ALE	MONTEREY	0.2	ALE
MONTEREY SEA LION STOUT	MONTEREY	0.0	STO
MOONLIGHT TWIST OF FATE BITTER ALE	WINDSOR	3.3	ALE
NORTH COAST OKTOBERFEST ALE (ANNUAL)	FORT BRAGG	0.8	ALE
NORTH COAST OLD NO. 38 STOUT	FORT BRAGG	3.1	STO
NORTH COAST RED SEAL ALE	FORT BRAGG	2.4	ALE
NORTH COAST SCRIMSHAW PILSENER	FORT BRAGG	3.1	PIL
NORTH COAST TRADITIONAL BOCK MALT LIQUOR	FORT BRAGG	2.8	BOC
OLD COLUMBIA AMBER LAGER	SAN DIEGO	2.9	LAG

NAME	LOCATION	RATING	STYLE
OLD COLUMBIA BLACK'S BEACH EXTRA DARK PORTER	SAN DIEGO	4.0	POR
OLD COLUMBIA DOWNTOWN AFTER DARK BROWN ALE	SAN DIEGO	3.3	ALE
OLD COLUMBIA GAS LAMP GOLD ALE	SAN DIEGO	2.7	ALE
OLD COLUMBIA PORT LOMA LIGHTHOUSE LIGHT LAGER	SAN DIEGO	1.1	LAG
OLD COLUMBIA RED TROLLEY ALE	SAN DIEGO	3.1	ALE
PACIFIC BEACH BLONDE	SAN DIEGO	1.6	WHT
PACIFIC BEACH MUNICH DARK LAGER	SAN DIEGO	1.5	LAG
PACIFIC BEACH OVER-THE-LINE STOUT	SAN DIEGO	2.7	ALE
PACIFIC BEACH STONEHENGE BROWN ALE	SAN DIEGO	2.7	ALE
PACIFIC BEACH SUNSET RED ALE	SAN DIEGO	2.5	ALE
PACIFIC HOP EXCHANGE GASLIGHT PALE ALE	NOVATO	2.5	ALE
PACIFIC HOP EXCHANGE '06 STOUT	NOVATO	2.3	STO
PRIMO	VAN NUYS	2.2	LAG
RHINO CHASERS AMBER ALE	CHATSWORTH	3.7	ALE
RHINO CHASERS AMERICAN ALE	CHATSWORTH	2.2	ALE
RHINO CHASERS LAGER	CHATSWORTH	3.7	LAG
SAMUEL ADAMS TRIPLE BOCK	CERES	4.7	BOC
SAN ANDRES EARTHQUAKE PALE ALE	HOLLISTER	3.0	ALE
SAN ANDRES KIT FOX AMBER	HOLLISTER	1.1	ALE
SAN ANDRES SEISMIC ALE	HOLLISTER	1.8	ALE
SAN RAFAEL AMBER ALE	NOVATO	2.4	ALE
SAN RAFAEL GOLDEN ALE	NOVATO	3.2	ALE
SAN RAFAEL TRADITIONAL ALE	NOVATO	0.4	ALE
SANTA CRUZ LIGHTHOUSE AMBER	SANTA CRUZ	1.1	LAG
SANTA CRUZ LIGHTHOUSE LAGER	SANTA CRUZ	0.6	LAG
SEABRIGHT BANTY ROOSTER IPA	SANTA CRUZ	2.4	IPA
SHIELDS CHANNEL ISLANDS WHEAT	VENTURA	1.7	WHT
SHIELDS STOUT	VENTURA	0.9	STO
SIERRA NEVADA BIGFOOT BARLEYWINE STYLE ALE (ANNUAL)	CHICO	0.2–1.3	ALE
SIERRA NEVADA CELEBRATION ALE (ANNUAL)	CHICO	2.3–3.9	ALE
SIERRA NEVADA PALE ALE	CHICO	3.2	ALE
SIERRA NEVADA PALE BOCK	CHICO	2.5	BOC
SIERRA NEVADA PORTER	CHICO	2.6	POR

NAME	LOCATION	RATING	STYLE
Sierra Nevada Stout	Chico	2.5	Sto
Sierra Nevada Summerfest (annual)	Chico	3.5–3.8	Lag
Solana Beach Beacon Bitter	Solana Beach	3.2	Ale
Solana Beach Port's Porter	Solana Beach	2.8	Por
Solana Beach Rivermouth Raspberry	Solana Beach	2.1	Ale
Solana Beach Summer Blonde Wheat	Solana Beach	2.1	Wht
Spences Pale Ale	Chatsworth	2.2	Ale
St. Stan's Amber Alt	Modesto	3.8	Alt
St. Stan's Dark Alt	Modesto	3.9	Alt
St. Stan's Fest Bier	Modesto	3.5	Alt
St. Stan's Graffiti Wheat (annual)	Modesto	1.9	Wht
Steelhead Extra Pale Ale	Blue Lake	3.3	Ale
Strauss Amber Lager	San Diego	2.4	Lag
COLORADO			
Aspen Silver City Ale	Boulder	2.4	Ale
Boulder Extra Pale Ale	Boulder	3.6	Ale
Boulder Porter	Boulder	2.7	Por
Boulder Stout	Boulder	2.2	Sto
Breckenridge Avalanche Amber	Breckenridge	0.4	Ale
Breckenridge India Pale Ale	Denver	2.4	Ale
Buffalo Gold Premium Ale	Boulder	3.7	Ale
Carver Amber Ale	Durango	2.5	Ale
Carver Anasazi Wheat	Durango	0.9	Wht
Carver Durango Dark	Durango	2.9	Sto
Carver Honey Pilsener	Durango	1.6	Pil
Carver IPA	Durango	2.1	Ipa
Carver Iron Horse Stout	Durango	2.6	Sto
Carver Raspberry Wheat	Durango	0.5	Wht
Coopersmith's Albert Damm Bitter Ale	Fort Collins	3.0	Ale
Coopersmith's Christmas Ale (annual)	Fort Collins	3.2	Ale
Coopersmith's Havel's Vienna Lager	Fort Collins	2.7	Lag
Coopersmith's Horsetooth Stout	Fort Collins	4.0	Sto
Coopersmith's Imperial Stout	Fort Collins	3.0	Sto
Coopersmith's Mac Scooter's	Fort Collins	0.3	Ale
Coopersmith's Mountain Avenue Wheat	Fort Collins	1.8	Wht

NAME	LOCATION	RATING	STYLE
COOPERSMITH'S NOT BROWN ALE	FORT COLLINS	2.7	ALE
COOPERSMITH'S POUDRE ALE	FORT COLLINS	2.4	ALE
COOPERSMITH'S PUNJABI INDIA PALE ALE	FORT COLLINS	3.8	IPA
COOPERSMITH'S SIGDA'S GREEN CHILE	FORT COLLINS	2.2	SPE
COORS	GOLDEN	1.4	PIL
COORS EISBOCK	GOLDEN	2.2	STO
COORS EXTRA GOLD	GOLDEN	1.8	PIL
COORS EXTRA GOLD DRAFT	GOLDEN	0.5	PIL
COORS WEIZENBIER	GOLDEN	2.9	WHT
COORS WINTERFEST (ANNUAL)	GOLDEN	1.5–3.1	LAG
CRESTED BUTTE RED LADY ALE	CRESTED BUTTE	2.3	ALE
DURANGO COLORFEST (ANNUAL)	DURANGO	3.5	LAG
DURANGO DARK	DURANGO	2.7	LAG
DURANGO WINTER ALE (ANNUAL)	DURANGO	3.2	ALE
HERMAN JOSEPH'S DRAFT	GOLDEN	2.6	LAG
HUBCAP RAZZLE DAZZLE BERRY	VAIL	1.0	WHT
IRONS HELLBENDER ALE	LAKEWOOD	2.3	ALE
JUDGE BALDWIN'S BROWN ALE	COLORADO SPRINGS	1.8	ALE
KEYSTONE	GOLDEN	0.9	PIL
KILLIAN'S RED ALE	GOLDEN	2.3	LAG
LEFT HAND MOTHERLODE GOLDEN ALE	LONGMONT	2.4	ALE
NEW BELGIUM FAT TIRE AMBER ALE	FORT COLLINS	3.9	ALE
ODELL'S DUNKEL WEIZEN BARLEY WINE	FORT COLLINS	3.5	WHT
ODELL'S 90 SHILLING ALE	FORT COLLINS	3.7	ALE
ROCKIES DRAFT	BOULDER	3.6	ALE
TABERNASH WEISS	DENVER	3.0	WHT
TAOS CERVEZA PRIMO	BOULDER	1.1	ALE
WRIGLEY RED	BOULDER	2.8	ALE
WYNKOOP IRISH CREAM STOUT	DENVER	3.0	STO
WYNKOOP JED FEST (ANNUAL)	DENVER	3.7	LAG
WYNKOOP SYMPOSIUM ALE	DENVER	2.9	ALE
CONNECTICUT			
HOBOKEN SPECIAL ALE	NEW HAVEN	2.8	ALE
NEW ENGLAND ATLANTIC AMBER	NORWALK	3.1	ALT
NEW ENGLAND HOLIDAY ALE (ANNUAL)	NORWALK	4.0	ALE
NEW HAVEN ELM CITY CONNECTICUT ALE	NEW HAVEN	2.9	ALE

NAME	LOCATION	RATING	STYLE
DELAWARE			
BLUE HEN	NEWARK	2.9	LAG
FLORIDA			
GATOR LAGER	AUBURNDALE	2.3	LAG
HAWAII			
DIAMOND HEAD DRY	HONOLULU	2.9	LAG
KO'OLAU LAGER	HONOLULU	3.1	LAG
MAUI LAGER	WAILUKU, MAUI	3.9	LAG
PALI HAWAIIAN	HONOLULU	1.0	LAG
IDAHO			
SUN VALLEY GOLD LAGER	HALLEY	0.5	LAG
SUN VALLEY HOLIDAY ALE (ANNUAL)	HALLEY	3.9	ALE
SUN VALLEY WHITE CLOUD ALE	HALLEY	3.8	ALE
T.W. FISHER'S FESTIVAL DARK ALE	COEUR D'ALENE	2.3	ALE
ILLINOIS			
CHICAGO'S BIG SHOULDERS PORTER	CHICAGO	4.0	POR
CHICAGO'S LEGACY LAGER	CHICAGO	2.1	LAG
CHICAGO'S LEGACY RED ALE	CHICAGO	1.8	ALE
GOOSE ISLAND DUNKEL WEIZEN BOCK	CHICAGO	2.2	BOC
OLD CHICAGO LAGER	CHICAGO	1.2	LAG
PAVICHEVICH BADERBRAU PILSENER	ELMHURST	2.3	PIL
INDIANA			
BALLANTINE INDIA PALE ALE	FORT WAYNE	3.8	IPA
BROAD RIPPLE EXTRA SPECIAL BITTER	INDIANAPOLIS	2.6	ALE
COOK'S GOLDBLUME	EVANSVILLE	0.5	LAG
INDIANAPOLIS DUESSELDORFER DRAFT ALE	INDIANAPOLIS	2.5	ALE
INDIANAPOLIS MAIN STREET PREMIUM LAGER	INDIANAPOLIS	3.1	LAG
GERST AMBER	EVANSVILLE	3.2	LAG
GRINGO EXTRA LAGER	EVANSVILLE	0.8	LAG
SCORPION MALT LIQUOR	EVANSVILLE	2.4	MLT
STERLING	EVANSVILLE	1.5	PIL
IOWA			
DALLAS COUNTY OLD DEPOT PALE ALE	ADEL	2.4	ALE
DARRYL'S PREMIUM LAGER	DUBUQUE	2.6	LAG
ERLANGER MARZEN BIER AMBER	DUBUQUE	2.8	LAG
MILLSTREAM LAGER	AMANA	3.8	LAG
MILLSTREAM SCHILD BRAU AMBER	AMANA	2.7	LAG
MILLSTREAM WHEAT	AMANA	0.3	WHT
RINCON DRY	DUBUQUE	2.3	PIL

NAME	LOCATION	RATING	STYLE
SIMPATICO AMBER	DUBUQUE	2.4	LAG
SIMPATICO GOLDEN LAGER	DUBUQUE	1.2	LAG
TGIF AMBER	DUBUQUE	0.4	LAG
TRESTLES LAGER	DUBUQUE	1.0	LAG
WILD BOAR SPECIAL AMBER	DUBUQUE	2.2	LAG
KANSAS			
FREE STATE OATMEAL STOUT	LAWRENCE	1.2	STO
KENTUCKY			
OLDENBERG PREMIUM VERUM	FORT MITCHELL	2.6	LAG
OLDENBERG WEISSE	FORT MITCHELL	3.9	WHT
VAIL ALE	FORT MITCHELL	3.5	ALE
LOUISIANA			
ABITA AMBER	ABITA SPRINGS	2.6	LAG
ABITA GOLDEN	ABITA SPRINGS	2.8	LAG
ABITA IRISH RED ALE	ABITA SPRINGS	2.0	ALE
ABITA TURBO DOG	ABITA SPRINGS	3.8	ALE
DIXIE	NEW ORLEANS	3.5	LAG
DIXIE BLACKENED VOODOO LAGER	NEW ORLEANS	2.4	LAG
DIXIE JAZZ AMBER LIGHT	NEW ORLEANS	2.0	PIL
MAINE			
GEARY'S PALE ALE	PORTLAND	2.4	ALE
HAMPSHIRE SPECIAL ALE (ANNUAL)	PORTLAND	2.4	ALE
MARYLAND			
SCHMIDT'S	BALTIMORE	2.4	LAG
WILD GOOSE AMBER	CAMBRIDGE	2.6	ALE
MASSACHUSETTS			
NORTHAMPTON OLD BROWN DOG ALE	NORTHAMPTON	3.3	ALE
SAMUEL ADAMS BOSTON STOCK ALE	BOSTON	2.6	ALE
SAMUEL ADAMS OCTOBERFEST	BOSTON	3.7	LAG
MICHIGAN			
ALTES GOLDEN LAGER	FRANKENMUTH	1.3	LAG
BULL ICE MALT LIQUOR	DETROIT	1.0	MLT
FRANKENMUTH DARK	FRANKENMUTH	3.1	LAG
FRANKENMUTH GERMAN-STYLE BOCK	FRANKENMUTH	2.4	BOC
FRANKENMUTH PILSENER	FRANKENMUTH	1.2	PIL
GOEBEL GOLDEN LAGER	DETROIT	2.1	LAG
OLD DETROIT AMBER ALE	FRANKENMUTH	3.8	ALE
OLD MILWAUKEE	DETROIT	0.8	LAG
PERRY'S MAJESTIC LAGER	FRANKENMUTH	2.8	LAG
PIELS DRAFT	DETROIT	1.0	PIL
RED BULL MALT LIQUOR	DETROIT	1.4	MLT
SCHAEFER	DETROIT	2.3	PIL

NAME	LOCATION	RATING	STYLE
SCHLITZ	DETROIT	1.8	LAG
SIGNATURE	DETROIT	1.8	LAG
STROH'S	DETROIT	2.4	LAG
MINNESOTA			
AUGSBURGER BOCK	ST. PAUL	2.5	BOC
AUGSBURGER DARK	ST. PAUL	2.2	LAG
AUGSBURGER GOLDEN	ST. PAUL	1.1	PIL
AUGSBURGER ROT LAGER	ST. PAUL	2.3	LAG
AUGUST SCHELL BOCK	NEW ULM	2.2	BOC
AUGUST SCHELL DEER BRAND	NEW ULM	3.8	LAG
AUGUST SCHELL EXPORT	NEW ULM	1.9	LAG
AUGUST SCHELL PILSNER	NEW ULM	2.8	PIL
AUGUST SCHELL WEISS	NEW ULM	3.2	WHT
AUGUST SCHELL WEIZEN	NEW ULM	3.3	WHT
BEVERLY HILLS HARVEST ALE	NEW ULM	0.4	ALE
COLD SPRING EXPORT	COLD SPRING	3.5	LAG
COLD SPRING SELECT STOCK	COLD SPRING	4.0	LAG
GARDEN ALLEY AMBER ALE	NEW ULM	0.1	ALE
GILA MONSTER	ST. PAUL	1.8	LAG
HECKLER BRAU PALE LAGER	NEW ULM	2.2	LAG
JUMPING COW AMBER ALE	NEW ULM	2.3	ALE
MINOTT'S BLACK STAR LAGER	ST. PAUL	2.7	LAG
OLD WEST AMBER	NEW ULM	2.2	LAG
PETE'S GOLD COAST LAGER	NEW ULM	3.2	LAG
PETE'S PACIFIC DRY	NEW ULM	3.3	LAG
PETE'S WICKED ALE	NEW ULM	3.8	ALE
PETE'S WICKED LAGER	ST. PAUL	2.9	LAG
PETE'S WICKED WINTER—BREW AMBER ALE (ANNUAL)	ST. PAUL	3.1	ALE
PIG'S EYE PILSNER	ST. PAUL	2.5	PIL
RHINO CHASERS WINTERFUL (ANNUAL)	ST. PAUL	2.5	ALE
SCHMALTZ'S ALT ALE	NEW ULM	3.3	ALE
SOULARD OUR SPECIAL LAGER	COLD SPRING	2.5	LAG
SPANISH PEAKS BLACK DOG ALE	NEW ULM	2.5	ALE
WIT	ST. PAUL	3.1	WHT
MISSOURI			
BOULEVARD "BULLY" PORTER	KANSAS CITY	3.8	POR
BUDWEISER	ST. LOUIS	1.1	PIL
BUSCH	ST. LOUIS	1.0	LAG
KING COBRA MALT LIQUOR	ST. LOUIS	2.2	MLT
MICHELOB DARK	ST. LOUIS	1.8	LAG
MICHELOB DRY	ST. LOUIS	2.1	LAG
SCHLAFLY HEFEWEIZEN	ST. LOUIS	1.1	WHT
SCHLAFLY OATMEAL STOUT	ST. LOUIS	4.0	STO

NAME	LOCATION	RATING	STYLE
SCHLAFLY PALE ALE	ST. LOUIS	2.5	ALE
SCHLAFLY PILS	ST. LOUIS	1.0	PIL
SCHLAFLY WHEAT	ST. LOUIS	1.6	WHT
MONTANA			
EUGENE ALE	HELENA	2.0	ALE
EUGENER-WEIZEN	HELENA	1.1	WHT
IDAHO CENTENNIAL PILSENER	HELENA	1.1	PIL
KESSLER LORELEI EXTRA PALE LAGER	HELENA	3.2	LAG
PACIFIC COAST LAGER	HELENA	2.4	LAG
SAINT NICK'S DARK ALE (ANNUAL)	HELENA	3.1	ALE
SEATTLEITE ALE	HELENA	0.7	ALE
NEW HAMPSHIRE			
PORTSMOUTH BLACK CAT STOUT	PORTSMOUTH	2.4	STO
NEW MEXICO			
ASSETS BLACK CHERRY ALE	ALBUQUERQUE	0.9	SPE
ASSETS DUKE CITY AMBER LAGER	ALBUQUERQUE	1.9	LAG
ASSETS HEFE WEIZEN	ALBUQUERQUE	2.2	WHT
ASSETS RIO GRANDE WHEAT	ALBUQUERQUE	1.2	WHT
ASSETS ROADRUNNER ALE	ALBUQUERQUE	1.0	ALE
ASSETS SANDIA STOUT	ALBUQUERQUE	2.5	STO
BLACK CLOUD PORTER	SANTA FE	2.6	POR
ESKE'S ALT BIER	TAOS	1.4	ALT
ESKE'S BOCK	TAOS	3.8	BOC
ESKE'S EL JEFE WEIZEN	TAOS	3.0	WHT
ESKE'S SMOKEHOUSE ALE	TAOS	2.2	ALE
ESKE'S SPECIAL BITTER	TAOS	3.5	ALE
ESKE'S TAOS GREEN CHILI	TAOS	2.7	SPE
LA CANADA PALE ALE	SANTA FE	0.9	ALE
RIO BRAVO BIG BOB'S BARLEYWINE	ALBUQUERQUE	2.6	ALE
RIO BRAVO ESTEBAN DARK PORTER	ALBUQUERQUE	4.1	POR
RIO BRAVO FRUIT ALE	ALBUQUERQUE	0.3	ALE
RIO BRAVO HIGH DESERT PALE ALE	ALBUQUERQUE	4.2	ALE
RIO BRAVO KURLY'S KOLSCH	ALBUQUERQUE	2.1	ALE
RIO BRAVO LARRY'S LAGER	ALBUQUERQUE	0.6	LAG
RIO BRAVO O'KEEFE DRY IRISH STOUT	ALBUQUERQUE	4.0	STO
RIO GRANDE OUTLAW LAGER	ALBUQUERQUE	2.8	LAG
SANTA FE CHICKEN KILLER BARLEY WINE	GALISTEO	1.3	ALE
SANTA FE FIESTA ALE	GALISTEO	1.5	ALE
SANTA FE OLD POJOAQUE PORTER	GALISTEO	3.5	POR
SANTA FE PALE ALE	GALISTEO	2.3	ALE

NAME	LOCATION	RATING	STYLE
NEW YORK			
BROOKLYN BROWN DARK ALE	UTICA	3.1	ALE
BROOKLYN LAGER	UTICA	2.3	LAG
BROOKLYN LAGER DRAFT	UTICA	3.6	LAG
BUFFALO BLIZZARD BOCK	BUFFALO	0.9	BOC
D'AGOSTINO PUB BEER	UTICA	2.2	LAG
DOCK STREET AMBER	UTICA	3.1	ALE
GENESEE	ROCHESTER	2.5	LAG
GENESEE CREAM ALE	ROCHESTER	2.7	ALE
GENESEE 12 HORSE ALE	ROCHESTER	3.4	ALE
GOLDEN HARPOON LAGER	UTICA	3.1	LAG
HARPOON ALE	UTICA	2.7	ALE
MANHATTAN BRITISH BITTER	NEW YORK	2.1	ALE
MANHATTAN EXTRA STOUT	NEW YORK	4.0	STO
MANHATTAN ROYAL AMBER	NEW YORK	3.2	LAG
MANHATTAN SPECIAL STOUT	NEW YORK	3.3	STO
MANHATTAN TAILSPIN BROWN ALE	NEW YORK	3.1	ALE
MANHATTAN WINTER WARMER (ANNUAL)	NEW YORK	3.8	ALE
MICHAEL SHEA'S IRISH AMBER	UTICA	3.0	LAG
NEW AMSTERDAM AMBER	UTICA	3.6	LAG
NEW AMSTERDAM NEW YORK ALE	UTICA	3.3	ALE
PORTLAND LAGER	UTICA	2.5	LAG
SAMUEL ADAMS CREAM STOUT	UTICA	2.3	STO
SARANAC ADIRONDACK WINTER SEASON'S BEST HOLIDAY AMBER (ANNUAL)	UTICA	3.4	LAG
SARANAC BLACK AND TAN	UTICA	3.8	STO/L
SARANAC 1888 LAGER	UTICA	2.2	LAG
SHAN SUI YEN SUM	UTICA	2.5	PIL
STALLION TEN EXTRA MALT LIQUOR	UTICA	0.7	MLT
ZIP CITY VIENNA AMBER	NEW YORK	0.7	LAG
NORTH CAROLINA			
DILWORTH ALBEMARLE ALE	CHARLOTTE	2.4	ALE
WEEPING RADISH BLACK RADISH DARK LAGER	MANTEO	2.2	LAG
WEEPING RADISH COROLLA GOLDEN LAGER	MANTEO	2.7	LAG
WEEPING RADISH FEST BEER AMBER LAGER	MANTEO	2.1	LAG
OHIO			
BANKS BEER	CINCINNATI	2.1	LAG
BRUIN PALE ALE	CINCINNATI	1.0	ALE
CHRISTIAN MOERLEIN BOCK	CINCINNATI	2.6	BOC

NAME	LOCATION	RATING	STYLE
CHRISTIAN MOERLEIN—			
CINCINNATI SELECT BEER	CINCINNATI	2.5	PIL.
CHRISTIAN MOERLEIN DOPPEL DARK	CINCINNATI	2.9	LAG
HOSTER WHITE TOP WHEAT	COLUMBUS	2.5	WHT
LITTLE KING'S CREAM ALE	CINCINNATI	2.0	ALE
UPTOWN HONEY ALE	YOUNGSTOWN	0.8	ALE
OREGON			
BRIDGEPORT BLUE HERON			
PALE ALE	PORTLAND	2.4	ALE
BRIDGEPORT OLD KNUCKLEHEAD			
BARLEY WINE STYLE ALE	PORTLAND	4.0	ALE
DESCHUTES BACHELOR BITTER	BEND	3.1	ALE
DESCHUTES BLACK BUTTE PORTER	BEND	3.7	POR
FULL SAIL BROWN ALE	HOOD RIVER	2.8	ALE
FULL SAIL GOLDEN ALE	HOOD RIVER	2.3	ALE
FULL SAIL WASSAIL WINTER			
ALE (ANNUAL)	HOOD RIVER	2.7	ALE
GOLDEN VALLEY RED THISTLE ALE	MCMINNVILLE	1.0	ALE
HENRY WEINHARD'S DARK	PORTLAND	2.3	LAG
MCMENAMINS BLACK RABBIT			
PORTER	PORTLAND	2.7	POR
MCMENAMINS FREUDIAN SIP ALE	PORTLAND	3.3	ALE
MCMENAMINS HAMMERHEAD			
AMBER ALE	PORTLAND	2.0	ALE
MCMENAMINS NEBRASKA BITTER	PORTLAND	2.9	ALE
MCMENAMINS RUBY			
RASPBERRY ALE	PORTLAND	3.0	ALE
MCMENAMINS TERMINATOR			
STOUT	PORTLAND	2.1	STO
MCTARNAHAN'S SCOTTISH ALE	PORTLAND	3.8	ALE
MIRROR POND PALE ALE	BEND	1.2	ALE
MULTNOMAH FIGUREHEAD			
EXTRA SPECIAL BITTER/PALE ALE	PORTLAND	2.0	ALE
PORTLAND ALE	PORTLAND	2.8	ALE
PORTLAND MT. HOOD BEER	PORTLAND	2.6	ALE
PORTLAND OREGON DRY HONEY	PORTLAND	1.5	ALE
PORTLAND PORTER	PORTLAND	4.0	POR
PORTLAND TIMBERLINE ALE	PORTLAND	2.6	ALE
ROGUE ALE	NEWPORT	3.1	ALE
ROGUE GOLDEN ALE	NEWPORT	2.4	ALE
ROGUE MAIERBOCK ALE	NEWPORT	3.9	BOC
ROGUE MEXICALI ALE	NEWPORT	2.5	ALE
ROGUE MOGUL ALE	NEWPORT	3.6	ALE
ROGUE NEW PORTER	NEWPORT	3.7	POR

NAME	LOCATION	RATING	STYLE
ROGUE OLD CRUSTACEAN			
BARLEY WINE	NEWPORT	3.6	ALE
ROGUE RED ALE	NEWPORT	4.4	ALE
ROGUE ROGUE-N-BERRY ALE	NEWPORT	3.1	ALE
ROGUE SHAKESPEARE STOUT	NEWPORT	4.8	STO
ROGUE SMOKE ALE	NEWPORT	2.0	SPE
ROGUE ST. ROGUE RED ALE	NEWPORT	3.0	ALE
SAMUEL ADAMS WINTER			
LAGER (ANNUAL)	PORTLAND	2.2–3.9	LAG
SAXER AMBER LAGER	LAKE OSWEGO	2.7	LAG
STEELHEAD BOMBAY BOMBER IPA	EUGENE	2.2	IPA
TUBORG DELUXE DARK	PORTLAND	1.1	LAG
UMPQUA PERRY'S OLD ALE	ROSEBURG	2.4	ALE
WEINHARD'S LIGHT ALE—			
IRISH STYLE	PORTLAND	2.3	ALE
WIDMER ALT	PORTLAND	3.3	ALT
WIDMER FESTBIER (ANNUAL)	TIGARD	3.8	SPE
WIDMER WEIZEN	PORTLAND	2.0	WHT
WILLAMETTE VALLEY NOR'WESTER			
RYE ALE	PORTLAND	2.6	ALE
PENNSYLVANIA			
ALLEGHENY PENN PILSENER	PITTSBURGH	3.7	PIL
BUNKERHILL LAGER	WILKES-BARRE	1.8	LAG
ESQUIRE EXTRA DRY	SMITHTON	0.9	LAG
LORD CHESTERFIELD ALE	POTTSVILLE	2.5	ALE
MANHATTAN GOLD	WILKES-BARRE	2.1	LAG
NEUWEILER BLACK AND TAN	WILKES-BARRE	2.5	POR/L
NUDE BEER	WILKES-BARRE	1.5	LAG
OLDE HEURICH MAERZEN	PITTSBURGH	2.6	LAG
PRIOR DOUBLE DARK	NORRISTOWN	3.7	BOC
RED FEATHER PALE ALE	CHAMBERSBURG	3.5	ALE
RHEINGOLD PREMIUM	PHILADELPHIA	1.1	PIL
ROLLING ROCK	LATROBE	3.6	LAG
ROLLING ROCK BOCK	LATROBE	3.5	BOC
SAMUEL ADAMS BREWHOUSE			
ORANGE CORIANDER WHEAT BEER	PHILADELPHIA	3.1	WHT
SAMUEL ADAMS CRANBERRY LAMBIC	PITTSBURGH	3.4	LAM
SAMUEL ADAMS CREAM STOUT	PITTSBURGH	2.3	STO
SAMUEL ADAMS DARK WHEAT	PITTSBURGH	2.7	WHT
SAMUEL ADAMS DOUBLE BOCK			
DARK LAGER	PITTSBURGH	3.7	LAG
SAMUEL ADAMS HONEY PORTER	LEHIGH VALLEY	3.3	POR
SAMUEL ADAMS OCTOBERFEST	PITTSBURGH	3.7	LAG
SAMUEL ADAMS WHEAT	PITTSBURGH	2.5	WHT

NAME	LOCATION	RATING	STYLE
STEGMAIER 1857 LAGER	WILKES-BARRE	3.2	LAG
STEGMAIER PORTER	WILKES-BARRE	2.4	POR
YUENGLING LAGER	POTTSVILLE	3.4	LAG
YUENGLING PORTER	POTTSVILLE	4.1	POR
YUENGLING TRADITIONAL LAGER	POTTSVILLE	3.3	LAG
RHODE ISLAND			
NARRAGANSETT	CRANSTON	3.0	LAG
PRIVATE STOCK MALT LIQUOR	CRANSTON	1.1	MLT
TENNESSEE			
BOHANNON MARKET STREET GOLDEN ALE	NASHVILLE	2.1	ALE
BOHANNON MARKET STREET OKTOBERFEST	NASHVILLE	0.3	LAG
TEXAS			
CELIS GOLDEN	AUSTIN	2.4	ALE
CELIS GRAND CRU	AUSTIN	2.4	ALE
CELIS PALE BOCK	AUSTIN	3.4	BOC
CELIS WHITE	AUSTIN	4.0	WHT
COLLIN COUNTY BLACK GOLD	PLANO	2.6	PIL
COLLIN COUNTY PURE GOLD	PLANO	3.0	PIL
DALLAS GOLD	DALLAS	1.0	PIL
DOUBLE EAGLE	ADDISON	1.4	LAG
FALSTAFF	SAN ANTONIO	2.3	LAG
JAX	SAN ANTONIO	3.0	PIL
KOSMOS RESERVE LAGER	SHINER	3.0	LAG
LONE STAR	SAN ANTONIO	3.1	LAG
LONE STAR NATURAL BOCK	SAN ANTONIO	2.0	BOC
OLYMPIA	SAN ANTONIO	2.1	PIL
PABST BLUE RIBBON DRAFT	SAN ANTONIO	2.1	LAG
PEARL LAGER	SAN ANTONIO	2.3	LAG
PECAN STREET	SHINER	2.5	LAG
PILSENER CLUB PREMIUM	SAN ANTONIO/GALVESTON	1.0	PIL
PROSPECTOR JOE'S SPECIAL DARK GOLDEN	SAN ANTONIO	2.9	LAG
RATTLESNAKE PREMIUM	SHINER	2.4	LAG
SHINER BOCK	SHINER	2.4	BOC
SHINER PREMIUM	SHINER	2.5	PIL
SIGNATURE	LONGVIEW	1.8	LAG
ST. IDES MALT LIQUOR	SAN ANTONIO	1.6	MLT
TEXAS COWBOY VIENNA LAGER	DALLAS	0.5	LAG
TEXAS PRIDE	SAN ANTONIO	0.1	PIL
UTAH			
WASATCH RASPBERRY WHEAT	PARK CITY	2.8	WHT
WASATCH SLICKROCK LAGER	PARK CITY	2.7	LAG

NAME	LOCATION	RATING	STYLE
WASATCH STOUT	PARK CITY	2.5	STO
WASATCH WHEAT	PARK CITY	0.3	WHT
VERMONT			
CATAMOUNT AMBER ALE	WHITE RIVER JUNCTION	0.2	ALE
CATAMOUNT CHRISTMAS ALE (ANNUAL)	WHITE RIVER JUNCTION	2.4	ALE
CATAMOUNT PORTER	WHITE RIVER JUNCTION	3.8	POR
GLENWALTER WEE HEAVY SCOTCH ALE	BURLINGTON	1.5	ALE
LE GARDE	WHITE RIVER JUNCTION	3.5	ALE
POST ROAD REAL ALE	WHITE RIVER JUNCTION	3.6	ALE
SARATOGA LAGER DORTMUNDER STYLE	WHITE RIVER JUNCTION	2.4	LAG
WASHINGTON			
ALBORZ ALE	SEATTLE	3.2	ALE
BIG TIME BHAGWANS BEST INDIA PALE ALE	SEATTLE	2.0	IPA
BIG TIME OLD WOOLY BARLEY WINE	SEATTLE	2.8	ALE
BLACK LABEL	SEATTLE, ET. AL.	2.1	LAG
BROWN DERBY	TUMWATER	0.3	PIL
EMERALD CITY ALE	SEATTLE	1.3	ALE
FISH EYE IPA	OLYMPIA	0.5	IPA
FITSPATRICK STOUT	SEATTLE	3.1	STO
GOLDEN CROWN PALE DRY	TUMWATER	0.1	LAG
GRANT'S CELTIC ALE	YAKIMA	3.1	ALE
GRANT'S IMPERIAL STOUT	YAKIMA	4.2	STO
GRANT'S INDIA PALE ALE	YAKIMA	3.6	ALE
GRANT'S SCOTTISH ALE	YAKIMA	2.0	ALE
GRANT'S SPICED ALE	YAKIMA	3.9	ALE
GRANT'S WEIS BEER	YAKIMA	2.8	WHT
HALE'S IPA	COLVILLE	4.4	IPA
HALE'S PALE ALE	COLVILLE	2.2	ALE
HART SPHINX STOUT	KALAMA	2.7	STO
HAZEL DELL RED ZONE PALE ALE	VANCOUVER	0.2	ALE
HENNESSEY'S LAGER	SEATTLE	1.8	LAG
JET CITY ALE	SEATTLE	2.4	ALE
LEAVENWORTH HODGSON'S IPA	LEAVENWORTH	2.5	IPA
MARITIME FLAGSHIP RED ALE	SEATTLE	3.0	ALE
MARITIME ISLANDER PALE ALE	SEATTLE	2.8	ALE
MARITIME NIGHTWATCH ALE	SEATTLE	3.0	ALE
MOSS BAY AMBER ALE	KIRKLAND	1.0	ALE
PACIFIC CREST ALE	KALAMA	1.1	ALE
PIKE PLACE PALE ALE	SEATTLE	3.6	ALE

NAME	LOCATION	RATING	STYLE
Pyramid Espresso Stout	Kalama	2.9	Sto
Pyramid Pale Ale	Kalama	2.5	Ale
Pyramid Snow Cap Ale (annual)	Kalama	2.5	Ale
Pyramid Wheaten Ale	Kalama	3.3	Ale
Rainier Ale	Seattle	3.6	Ale
Red Hook Ballard Bitter Pale Ale	Seattle	3.0	Ale
Red Hook Blackhook Porter	Seattle	4.0	Por
Red Hook ESB Ale	Seattle	3.1	Ale
Red Hook Wheat Hook Ale	Seattle	2.9	Ale
Red Hook Winterhook Christmas Ale (annual)	Seattle	3.6	Ale
Smith and Reilly Honest Beer	Tumwater	2.7	Pil
Thomas Kemper Helles Blueberry Lager	Poulsbo	2.4	Lag
Thomas Kemper Helles Lager	Poulsbo	2.1	Lag
Thomas Kemper Integrale Amber Lager	Poulsbo	1.5	Lag
Thomas Kemper Pilsner	Poulsbo	1.0	Pil
Thomas Kemper Rolling Bay Bock	Poulsbo	2.4	Boc
Thomas Kemper Winterbrau (annual)	Poulsbo	1.2	Lag
WISCONSIN			
Adler Brau Pilsner	Appleton	0.9	Pil
Amber—Vienna Style	Monroe	3.1	Lag
Augsburger Pilsener	Monroe	3.5	Pil
Berghoff	Monroe	2.9	Lag
Berghoff Bock	Monroe	2.4	Boc
Berghoff Dark	Monroe	3.3	Lag
Berghoff Dortmunder	Monroe	2.6	Lag
Big Apple Premium	Milwaukee	2.4	Pil
Black Hills Gold Label Lager	Monroe	2.7	Lag
Black Label	La Crosse	2.1	Lag
Braumeister Pilsener	Monroe	2.5	Pil
Buckhorn	Milwaukee	0.1	Pil
Capital Gartenbrau Dark	Middleton	3.2	Lag
Capital Gartenbrau Lager	Middleton	3.3	Lag
Capital Gartenbrau Oktoberfest	Middleton	2.5	Lag
Capital Gartenbrau Wild Rice	Middleton	2.4	Lag
Cherryland Cherry Rail Lager	Sturgeon Bay	2.9	Lag
Cherryland Golden Rail Lager	Sturgeon Bay	2.8	Lag
Cherryland Silver Rail Lager	Sturgeon Bay	2.2	Lag
Crazy Horse Malt Liquor	La Crosse	1.9	Mlt

NAME	LOCATION	RATING	STYLE
DEMPSEY'S ALE	MONROE	2.4	ALE
EAU CLAIRE ALL-MALT LAGER	EAU CLAIRE	3.7	LAG
FOECKING PREMIUM	MONROE	0.3	LAG
HAMM'S	MILWAUKEE	2.5	PIL
HARLEY-DAVIDSON HEAVY BEER (ANNUAL)	MONROE	2.4	PIL
ICEHOUSE ICE BEER MALT LIQUOR	MILWAUKEE	3.3	MLT
JAMES BOWIE KENTUCKY HILLS LTD. PILSNER	LA CROSSE	2.0	PIL
LEINENKUGEL'S ORIGINAL PREMIUM	CHIPPEWA FALLS	3.1	LAG
LEINENKUGELS RED LAGER	CHIPPEWA FALLS	2.1	LAG
LOWENBRAU	MILWAUKEE, ET. AL.	2.9	PIL
MAGNUM MALT LIQUOR	MILWAUKEE	1.4	MLT
MCSORLEY'S ALE	LA CROSSE	2.0	ALE
MICKEY'S MALT LIQUOR	LA CROSSE	3.1	MLT
MIDNIGHT DRAGON GOLD RESERVE ALE	LA CROSSE	1.5	ALE
MIDNIGHT DRAGON MALT LIQUOR	LA CROSSE	1.1	MLT
MIDNIGHT DRAGON ROYAL RESERVE LAGER	LA CROSSE	0.5	LAG
MILLER HIGH LIFE	MILWAUKEE	2.4	PIL
MILLER RESERVE BARLEY DRAFT	MILWAUKEE	2.6	LAG
MILLER RESERVE VELVET STOUT	MILWAUKEE	1.9	STO
MILWAUKEE 1851	LA CROSSE	0.4	PIL
NEW YORK HARBOR ALE	STEVENS POINT	1.9	ALE
OLDE ENGLISH 800	MILWAUKEE	2.9	MLT
POINT SPECIAL PREMIUM LAGER	STEVENS POINT	2.9	LAG
RED, WHITE AND BLUE SPECIAL LAGER	LA CROSSE	3.2	LAG
RHINELANDER	MONROE	2.4	LAG
SCHLITZ MALT LIQUOR	MILWAUKEE	1.3	MLT
SCHMIDT	LA CROSSE	2.2	LAG
SPECIAL EXPORT	LA CROSSE	3.4	LAG
STAG	LA CROSSE	2.1	LAG
TELLURIDE	MONROE	2.4	LAG
TUBORG LAGER	LA CROSSE	2.4	LAG
VIENNA LAGER	MILWAUKEE	2.5	LAG

BEERS BY COUNTRY: AN ALPHABETICAL LISTING

NAME	LOCATION	RATING	STYLE
ARGENTINA			
BIECKERT ESPECIAL	ANTARTIDA	4.2	PIL
CORDOBA-DORADA	CORDOBA	3.7	PIL
LEON DE ORO CERVEZA ESPECIAL	ANTARTIDA	3.8	LAG
PALERMO ESTRASBURGO	QUILMES	2.2	LAG
QUILMES CRISTAL	BUENOS AIRES	1.6	PIL
SAN CARLOS ESPECIAL	SAN CARLOS	2.3	PIL
SANTA FE RUBIA ESPECIAL	SANTA FE	3.9	LAG
SCHNEIDER CERVEZA RUBIA ESPECIAL	SANTA FE	2.5	LAG
AUSTRALIA			
AUSTRALIAN PREMIUM LAGER	BRISBANE, QUEENSLAND	1.9	LAG
BIG BARREL	LEABROOK, SOUTH AUSTRALIA	3.0	LAG
BOAGS PREMIUM LAGER	HOBART, TASMANIA	2.2	LAG
BROKEN HILL LAGER	THEBARTON/ADELAIDE, SOUTH AUSTRALIA	2.0	LAG
CASTLEMAINE XXXX LAGER	BRISBANE, QUEENSLAND	3.3	LAG
DOWN UNDER	PERTH, WESTERN AUSTRALIA	2.6	LAG
FOSTER'S LAGER	MELBOURNE, VICTORIA (ALSO CANADA)	3.4	LAG
FOSTER'S LIGHT LAGER	MELBOURNE, VICTORIA	3.2	LAG
KB AUSTRALIAN	SYDNEY, NEW SOUTH WALES	2.9	LAG
OLD AUSTRALIA STOUT	THEBARTON, SOUTH AUSTRALIA	3.8	STO
RAZOR EDGE LAGER	HOBART, TASMANIA	2.5	LAG
RED BACK MALTED WHEAT BEER	FREMANTLE, WESTERN AUSTRALIA	2.2	WHT
RESCHS PILSNER	SYDNEY, NEW SOUTH WALES	2.9	PIL
SHEAF STOUT	SYDNEY, NEW SOUTH WALES	2.5	STO
SOUTHWARK GOLD LAGER	THEBARTON, SOUTH AUSTRALIA	2.3	LAG
SOUTHWARK PREMIUM	ADELAIDE, SOUTH AUSTRALIA	4.1	PIL
SWAN LAGER	BRISBANE, QUEENSLAND	3.3	LAG
THOMAS COOPER ADELAIDE LAGER	LEABROOK, SOUTH AUSTRALIA	2.4	LAG
WEST END EXPORT LAGER	THEBARTON, SOUTH AUSTRALIA	3.3	LAG
AUSTRIA			
EDELWEISS DUNKEL DARK	SALZBURG	3.0	WHT
EDELWEISS HEFETRUB	SALZBURG	2.4	WHT

NAME	LOCATION	RATING	STYLE
EDELWEISS KRISTALLKLAR WEIZENBIER	SALZBURG	4.0	WHT
EGGENBERG URBOCK	SALZBURG/LINZ	2.3	BOC
GOSSER PALE	LEABEN GOSS	2.6	LAG
GOSSER STIFTSBRAU	GRAZ	3.5	LAG
OTTAKRINGER GOLD FASSL PILS	VIENNA	2.9	PIL
OTTAKRINGER GOLD FASSL VIENNA	VIENNA	2.5	LAG
PUNTIGAMER DARK MALT DRAFT	GRAZ	2.5	LAG
PUNTIGAMER PANTHER DRAFT	GRAZ	3.1	LAG
STEFFL VIENNA LAGER	LINZ	2.1	LAG
STIEGL COLUMBUS PILS	SALZBURG	3.1	PIL
BARBADOS			
BAJAN BEER	BRIDGETOWN	2.7	LAG
BELGIUM			
AFFLIGEM TRIPEL ABBEY	OPWIJK	3.6	ALE
ARTEVELDE ALE	MELLE/GHENT	4.1	ALE
BIOS COPPER ALE	ERTVELDE	1.4	ALE
BLANCHE DE BRUGES	BRUGES	3.9	WHT
BOON GUEUZE	LEMBEEK	2.2	LAM
BRIGAND BELGIAN ALE	INGELMUNSTER	3.8	ALE
CHIMAY PERES TRAPPISTES ALE—GRANDE RESERVE	CHIMAY ABBEY	2.5	ALE
CHIMAY PERES TRAPPISTES ALE—PREMIERE	CHIMAY ABBEY	4.7	ALE
CORSENDONK MONK'S BROWN ALE	SIGILLUM MONASTERY	3.8	ALE
CORSENDONK MONK'S PALE ALE	SIGILLUM MONASTERY	4.0	ALE
DENTERGEMS WHITE ALE	DENTERGEM	0.6	ALE
DOUGLAS SCOTCH BRAND ALE	ANTWERP	3.9	ALE
DUVEL	BREENDONK	2.9	ALE
GOUDEN CAROLUS ALE	MECHELEN	3.9	ALE
GRIMBERGEN DOUBLE ALE	WAARLOOS	4.0	ALE
HOEGAARDEN GRAND CRU ALE	HOEGAARDEN	0.9	ALE
HOEGAARDEN WHITE	HOEGAARDEN	2.6	WHT
KWAK	BUGGENHOUT	2.1	ALE
LEFFE BLOND ALE	LEFFE	3.1	ALE
LIEFMANS KRIEKBIER	OUDENAARDE	3.9	LAM
LINDEMANS KRIEK—LAMBIC	VLEZENBEEK	2.0	LAM

NAME	LOCATION	RATING	STYLE
LINDEMANS PECHE LAMBIC	VLEZENBEEK	1.3	LAM
LUCIFER	DENTERGEM	1.1	ALE/L
MAES PILS	WATERLOO	3.0	PIL
MAREDSOUS ABBEY ALE	DENEE	4.1	ALE
MARTIN'S PALE ALE	ANTWERP	3.5	ALE
MATEEN TRIPLE ALE	MELLE/GHENT	3.4	AB
ORVAL TRAPPIST ALE	FLORENVILLE	2.1	ALE
PALM ALE	BRUSSELS	3.2	ALE
PERTOTALE FARO LAMBIC	LEMBEEK	2.9	LAM
RIVA BLANCHE ALE	DENTERGEM	2.2	ALE
RODENBACH BELGIAN RED ALE	ROESELARE	2.9	ALE
RUBENS GOLD	KONTICH	3.0	ALE
SCALDIS NOEL ALE (ANNUAL)	PIPAIX	2.1	ALE
SEZOENS ALE	BOCHOLT	3.0	ALE
ST. SEBASTIAAN CROCK ALE	MEER	2.6	ALE
ST. SIXTUS ABBEY ALE	WATOU	3.1	ALE
STEENDONK WHITE ALE	BREENDONK	3.9	ALE
STELLA ARTOIS	LEUVEN	2.9	PIL
STER ALE	MEER	3.1	ALE
TIMMERMANS PECHE	ITTERBECK	3.3	LAM
TRIPLE TOISON D'OR ALE	MECHELEN	2.5	ALE
VONDEL DARK ALE	DENTERGEM	0.3	ALE
WESTMALLE TRAPPIST	ABBEY OF WESTMALLE	4.3	AB
WITKAP-PATER SINGEL ABBEY ALE	NINOVE	4.0	ALE
BELIZE			
CROWN LAGER	BELIZE CITY	2.3	LAG
BOLIVIA			
PACENA CENTENARIO	LA PAZ	2.6	PIL
BRAZIL			
ANTARCTICA	SAO PAULO	2.7	PIL
BRAHMA	RIO DE JANEIRO	3.8	PIL
BRAHMA CHOPP	RIO DE JANEIRO	3.7	PIL
KAISER	QUEIMADOS	0.8	PIL
SCHINCARIOL PILSEN	SCHINCARIOL	0.2	PIL
SKOL CERVEJA PILSEN	RIO CLARO	1.0	PIL
TIJUCA	BELEM	3.8	PIL
XINGU BLACK BEER	CACADOR	4.5	STO/L
BULGARIA			
ASTICA PREMIUM LAGER	HASKOWO	3.6	LAG
ZAGORKA LAGER	ZAGORA	0.9	LAG

NAME	LOCATION	RATING	STYLE
CANADA			
ALGONQUIN SPECIAL RESERVE ALE	FORMOSA, ONTARIO	2.9	ALE
ARCTIC BAY CLASSIC LAGER	VANCOUVER, BRITISH COLUMBIA	2.0	LAG
BEER	CALGARY, ALBERTA	1.0	LAG
BIG ROCK BITTER PALE ALE	CALGARY, ALBERTA	3.1	ALE
BIG ROCK BUZZARD BREATH ALE	CALGARY, ALBERTA	1.7	ALE
BIG ROCK COCK O' THE ROCK PORTER	CALGARY, ALBERTA	2.4	POR
BIG ROCK COLD COCK WINTER PORTER	CALGARY, ALBERTA	3.1	POR
BIG ROCK GRASSHOPPER WHEAT ALE	CALGARY, ALBERTA	2.5	ALE
BIG ROCK ROYAL COACHMAN DRY ALE	CALGARY, ALBERTA	3.9	ALE
BIG ROCK SPRINGBOK ALE	CALGARY, ALBERTA	2.1	ALE
BIG ROCK WARTHOG ALE	CALGARY, ALBERTA	2.5	ALE
BIG ROCK XO LAGER	CALGARY, ALBERTA	3.4	LAG
BRICK LAGER	WATERLOO, ONTARIO	3.1	LAG
BUCKERFIELD'S APPLETON BROWN ALE	VICTORIA, BRITISH COLUMBIA	3.3	ALE
BUCKERFIELD'S CYGNET ALE	VICTORIA, BRITISH COLUMBIA	2.0	ALE
BUCKERFIELD'S PANDORA PALE ALE	VICTORIA, BRITISH COLUMBIA	2.9	ALE
BUCKERFIELD'S SWANS OATMEAL STOUT	VICTORIA, BRITISH COLUMBIA	3.8	STO
CALGARY AMBER LAGER	TORONTO, ONTARIO	2.4	LAG
CANADA COUNTRY LAGER	VANCOUVER, BRITISH COLUMBIA	3.0	LAG
CANADIAN LAGER	VANCOUVER, BRITISH COLUMBIA	2.0	LAG
CLARK'S GREAT CANADIAN	VANCOUVER, BRITISH COLUMBIA	1.0	LAG
CLUB	TORONTO, ONTARIO, ET. AL.	2.7	LAG
DRUMMOND DRAFT LAGER	CALGARY, ALBERTA	2.4	LAG
DRUMMOND DRY	RED DEER, ALBERTA	0.8	LAG
DUFFY'S ALE	VANCOUVER, BRITISH COLUMBIA	4.1	ALE
F AND A	TORONTO, ONTARIO	3.1	LAG
FOSTER'S LAGER	TORONTO, ONTARIO (ALSO AUSTRALIA)	3.4	LAG
GLACIER BAY LAGER	TORONTO, ONTARIO	1.1	LAG
GRANVILLE ISLAND BOCK	VANCOUVER, BRITISH COLUMBIA	4.2	BOC
GRANVILLE ISLAND LAGER	VANCOUVER, BRITISH COLUMBIA	2.9	LAG
GRANVILLE ISLAND LORD GRANVILLE	VANCOUVER, BRITISH COLUMBIA	2.6	LAG
GRIZZLY	HAMILTON, ONTARIO	0.6	LAG

NAME	LOCATION	RATING	STYLE
HENNINGER MEISTER PILS	HAMILTON, ONTARIO	3.2	PIL
KEY DARK	VICTORIA, BRITISH COLUMBIA	1.2	LAG
KIRIN DRAFT	VANCOUVER, BRITISH COLUMBIA	3.9	PIL
KODIAK PREMIUM LAGER	SASKATOON, SASKATCHEWAN	2.5	LAG
KOKANEE GLACIER PILSENER	CRESTON, BRITISH COLUMBIA	3.4	PIL
LABATT CLASSIC	TORONTO, ONTARIO, ET. AL.	3.8	LAG
LABATT'S	VANCOUVER, BRITISH COLUMBIA	3.1	PIL
LABATT'S BLUE PILSENER	VANCOUVER, BRITISH COLUMBIA	3.1	PIL
LABATT'S 50 ALE	VANCOUVER, BRITISH COLUMBIA	3.7	ALE
LABATT'S VELVET CREAM STOUT	EDMONTON, ALBERTA	3.1	STO
LUCKY LAGER	VANCOUVER, BRITISH COLUMBIA	0.8	LAG
MCNALLY'S EXTRA ALE	CALGARY, ALBERTA	1.9	ALE
MILLER HIGHLIFE	TORONTO, ONTARIO	2.2	PIL
MOLSON BRADOR MALT LIQUOR	MONTREAL, BRITISH COLUMBIA, ET. AL.	2.7	MLT
MOLSON EXPORT ALE	MONTREAL, BRITISH COLUMBIA, ET. AL.	3.2	ALE
MOLSON GOLDEN	TORONTO, BRITISH COLUMBIA, ET. AL.	2.4	ALE
MOLSON ICE	VANCOUVER, BRITISH COLUMBIA	3.5	LAG
MOLSON SPECIAL DRY	TORONTO, ONTARIO	2.5	LAG
MOOSEHEAD CANADIAN LAGER	SAINT JOHN, NEW BRUNSWICK	1.4	LAG
MOUNTAIN CREST	TORONTO, ONTARIO	0.9	PIL
O'KEEFE ALE	TORONTO, ONTARIO	3.1	ALE
O'KEEFE'S EXTRA OLD STOCK MALT LIQUOR	VANCOUVER, BRITISH COLUMBIA	2.9	MLT
OKANAGAN SPRING PREMIUM LAGER	VERNON, BRITISH COLUMBIA	1.1	LAG
OKANAGAN SPRING ST. PATRICK STOUT	VERNON, BRITISH COLUMBIA	1.3	STO
OLD STYLE PILSNER	VANCOUVER, BRITISH COLUMBIA	2.4	PIL
OLD VIENNA	TORONTO, ONTARIO	3.0	LAG
PACIFIC DRAFT	VANCOUVER, BRITISH COLUMBIA	1.7	PIL
PASADENA LAGER NATURAL DRAFT	VANCOUVER, BRITISH COLUMBIA	1.0	LAG
RED BARON	WATERLOO, ONTARIO	2.3	LAG
RICKARD'S RED DRAUGHT ALE	CALGARY, ALBERTA, ET. AL.	2.5	ALE
SCHOONER LAGER	MONTREAL, QUEBEC	1.8	LAG
SLEEMAN CREAM ALE	GUELPH, ONTARIO	3.0	ALE
SLEEMAN LAGER	GUELPH, ONTARIO	3.3	LAG

NAME	LOCATION	RATING	STYLE
SLEEMAN ORIGINAL DARK ALE	GUELPH, ONTARIO	2.3	ALE
STEELER LAGER	HAMILTON, ONTARIO	0.5	LAG
STRATHCONA ALE	EDMONTON, ALBERTA	3.1	ALE
TOBY	TORONTO, ONTARIO	2.2	PIL
TORONTO LIGHT	GUELPH, ONTARIO	1.8	PIL
UPPER CANADA COLONIAL STOUT	TORONTO, ONTARIO	2.3	STO
UPPER CANADA DARK ALE	TORONTO, ONTARIO	3.2	ALE
UPPER CANADA LAGER	TORONTO, ONTARIO	2.5	LAG
UPPER CANADA LIGHT LAGER	TORONTO, ONTARIO	0.7	LAG
UPPER CANADA PALE ALE	TORONTO, ONTARIO	2.0	ALE
UPPER CANADA PUBLICAN'S SPECIAL BITTER ALE	TORONTO, ONTARIO	2.2	ALE
UPPER CANADA REBELLION MALT LIQUOR	TORONTO, ONTARIO	3.8	MLT
UPPER CANADA TRUE BOCK	TORONTO, ONTARIO	3.7	BOC
VIKING LAGER	VICTORIA, BRITISH COLUMBIA	2.2	LAG
WOLFSBRAU AMBER LAGER	CALGARY, ALBERTA	2.5	LAG
ZEB O'BREEN'S IRISH ALE	CALGARY, ALBERTA	3.2	ALE
CANARY ISLANDS			
TROPICAL PILSENER	LAS PALMAS	3.7	PIL
CHILE			
ANDES PILSENER	SANTIAGO	1.2	PIL
AUSTRAL POLAR PILSENER	PUNTA ARENAS	2.8	PIL
CRISTAL PILSENER	LIMACHE	1.3	PIL
DORADA PILSENER	TALCA	3.3	PIL
ESCUDO PILSENER	OSORNO	2.9	PIL
ESCUDO SCHOP	SANTIAGO	2.4	PIL
IMPERIAL PILSENER	PUNTA ARENAS	2.9	PIL
KUNSTMANN LAGER	VALDIVIA	2.7	LAG
LIMACHE CERVEZA TIPO CRUDA	LIMACHE	3.2	LAG
PAULANER PREMIUM LAGER	SANTIAGO	3.0	LAG
ROYAL GUARD CERVEZA— TIPO DORTMUND	SANTIAGO	2.5	LAG
ROYAL GUARD PILSENER	SANTIAGO	3.8	PIL
SCHOP OSCURO	OSORNO	3.4	PIL
CHINA			
CHANGLEE LAGER	SANSHUI	2.6	LAG
CHINA CLIPPER	GUANGZHOU	2.5	LAG
CHINA GOLD	GUANGZHOU	1.8	PIL
CHUNG HUA	GUANGZHOU	3.4	PIL
DOUBLE HAPPINESS	GUANGZHOU	2.3	LAG

NAME	LOCATION	RATING	STYLE
EMPERORS GOLD	GUANGZHOU	3.5	PIL
GENGHIS KHAN	GUANGZHOU	1.1	LAG
GOLDEN DRAGON	GUANGZHOU	3.1	PIL
GREAT WALL	HEBEI	2.9	LAG
HUA NAN	GUANGZHOU	3.8	LAG
JINDAO	QINGDAO	4.0	LAG
LONGXIANG	BEIJING	2.1	PIL
MON-LEI	BEIJING	2.6	LAG
NINE STAR	BEIJING	2.9	LAG
PANDA	SHANGHAI	3.5	PIL
SNOWFLAKE	SHENYANG	2.3	PIL
SWEET CHINA	GUANGZHOU	0.2	LAG
TSINGTAO	SHANGHAI	0.4	PIL
YI KING	GUANGZHOU	2.1	PIL
YUCHAN	BEIJING	4.0	PIL
ZHUJIANG	GUANGZHOU	2.9	LAG
COLOMBIA			
CERVEZA AGUILA	BARRANQUILLA	2.3	PIL
CLAUSEN EXPORT	BOGOTA	3.0	PIL
COSTA RICA			
HEINEKEN LAGER	SAN JOSE	2.7	LAG
IMPERIAL	SAN JOSE	1.3	LAG
CYPRUS			
KEO	LIMASSOL	3.1	LAG
CZECHOSLOVAKIA/CZECH REPUBLIC			
GAMBRINUS LAGER	PILSEN	2.9	LAG
KAREL IV LAGER	CZECH REPUBLIC	3.6	LAG
PILSNER URQUELL	PILSEN	3.5	PIL
RADEGAST ORIGINAL LAGER	NOSOVICE	3.1	LAG
STAROPRAMEN	PRAGUE	3.9	PIL
DENMARK			
BUUR BEER DELUXE	RANDERS	3.4	LAG
CARLSBERG	COPENHAGEN	3.3	LAG
CERES ROYAL EXPORT	ARTHUS	3.3	LAG
ELEPHANT MALT LIQUOR	COPENHAGEN	3.1	MLT
GIRAF MALT LIQUOR	ODENSE	2.3	MLT
GREEN ROOSTER	COPENHAGEN	0.0	LAG
DOMINICAN REPUBLIC			
PRESIDENTE PILSENER	SANTO DOMINGO	3.5	PIL
ECUADOR			
CLUB PREMIUM	QUITO	2.1	LAG
PILSENER	QUITO	4.0	PIL

NAME	LOCATION	RATING	STYLE
EL SALVADOR			
PILSENER OF EL SALVADOR	SAN SALVADOR	2.5	PIL
ENGLAND			
BASS PALE ALE	BURTON-ON-TRENT	3.8	ALE
BATEMAN'S DARK VICTORY ALE	WAINFLEET	3.8	ALE
BATEMAN'S XXXB ALE	WAINFLEET	3.7	ALE
BULLDOG	READING	3.3	ALE
CHESTER GOLDEN ALE	CHESHIRE	2.9	ALE
CHURCHILL AMBER	REDRUTH	3.3	LAG
CHURCHILL DRY	REDRUTH	2.3	LAG
CHURCHILL LAGER	REDRUTH	3.6	LAG
DOUBLE DIAMOND ALE	BURTON-ON-TRENT	2.5	ALE
FULLER'S E.S.B. EXPORT ALE	LONDON	2.5	ALE
FULLER'S LONDON PRIDE	LONDON	3.8	ALE
GREENALLS BITTER	WARRINGTON	2.4	ALE
GREENALL'S CHESHIRE ENGLISH PUB BEER	WARRINGTON	3.1	ALE
GURU LAGER	LONDON	2.2	LAG
IRISH BRIGADE	WARRINGTON	3.0	ALE
JOHN BULL	BURTON-ON-TRENT	2.9	ALE
JOHN COURAGE EXPORT	BRISTOL	2.8	ALE
JOHN PEEL	BLACKBURN	2.8	ALE
KINGPIN	MANSFIELD	1.0	LAG
LANDLORD STRONG PALE ALE	KEIGHLEY	2.9	ALE
LONDON LIGHT	LONDON	2.2	PIL
MACKESON TRIPLE XXX STOUT	LONDON	4.1	STO
MARKSMAN LAGER	MANSFIELD	3.3	LAG
NEWCASTLE BROWN ALE	NEWCASTLE-UPON-TYNE	2.0	ALE
NEWCASTLE BROWN ALE (DRAFT)	NEWCASTLE-UPON-TYNE	3.3	ALE
OLD PECULIER ALE	MASHAM	3.8	ALE
POPE'S "1880"	DORCHESTER	3.6	ALE
ROYAL OAK PALE ALE	DORCHESTER	4.4	ALE
RUDDLES BITTER	RUTLAND	1.4	ALE
RUDDLES COUNTRY ALE	RUTLAND	2.5	ALE
SAMUEL SMITH OATMEAL STOUT	TADCASTER	4.0	STO
SAMUEL SMITH TADCASTER TADDY PORTER	TADCASTER	3.7	POR
SAMUEL SMITH'S IMPERIAL STOUT	TADCASTER	4.0	STO

NAME	LOCATION	RATING	STYLE
SAMUEL SMITH'S LAGER	TADCASTER	4.0	LAG
SAMUEL SMITH'S NUT BROWN ALE	TADCASTER	3.4	ALE
SAMUEL SMITH'S OLD BREWERY PALE ALE	TADCASTER	3.0	ALE
SAMUEL SMITH'S WINTER WELCOME ALE (ANNUAL)	TADCASTER	2.3–3.8	ALE
THOMAS HARDY'S ALE 1989 (ANNUAL)	DORCHESTER	0.4	ALE
WATNEY'S CREAM STOUT	LONDON	3.9	STO
WATNEY'S RED BARREL	LONDON	3.9	LAG
WATNEY'S STINGO CREAM STOUT	LONDON	3.5	STO
WHITBREAD ALE	LONDON/SHEFFIELD	3.9	ALE
YOUNG'S LONDON PORTER	LONDON	3.2	POR
YOUNG'S OATMEAL STOUT	LONDON	4.3	STO
YOUNG'S OLD NICK (ANNUAL)	LONDON	3.9	ALE
YOUNG'S OLD NICK BARLEY WINE	LONDON	2.2	ALE
YOUNG'S RAM ROD	LONDON	3.6	ALE
YOUNG'S SPECIAL ALE	LONDON	3.0	ALE
YOUNG'S WINTER ALE (ANNUAL)	LONDON	4.0–4.3	ALE
ETHIOPIA			
ASMARA	ASMARA	2.1	LAG
FINLAND			
KOFF	HELSINKI	3.6	LAG
LAPIN KULTA	HELSINKI	2.2	LAG
FRANCE			
ADELSCOTT MALT LIQUOR	SCHILTIGHEIM	4.2	MLT
BRASSEURS BIERE DE PARIS	BONNEUIL	1.3	LAG
BRASSEURS GRAND CRU	BONNEUIL	3.5	LAG
BREUG LAGER	ROUBAIX	2.7	LAG
FISCHER D'ALSACE AMBER	SCHILTIGHEIM	3.2	MLT
JENLAIN FRENCH COUNTRY ALE	JENLAIN	2.3	ALE
KRONENBOURG PALE	STRASBOURG	3.1	LAG
LA BELLE STRASBOURGEOISE	SCHILTIGHEIM	2.9	LAG
SCHUTZ BIERE D'ALSACE PILS	SCHILTIGHEIM	2.4	PIL
SCHUTZENBERGER JUBILATOR	SCHILTIGHEIM	3.8	BOC
SEPTANTE 5 MALT LIQUOR	ROUBAIX	3.7	MLT
SEPTANTE ROUGE	ROUBAIX	2.2	ALE

NAME	LOCATION	RATING	STYLE
Super 49 Malt Liquor	Roubaix	2.8	Mlt
Terken Biere De Luxe Malt Liquor	Roubaix	2.9	Mlt
Terken Brune Malt Liquor	Roubaix	2.5	Mlt
36.15 Pecheur	Schiltigheim	0.3	Lag
33 Export	Paris	3.1	Lag
3 Monts Flanders Golden Ale	Saint -Sylvestre	3.3	Ale
GERMANY			
Aktien Jubilaums Pils	Kaufbeuren	2.8	Pil
Aktien St. Martin Dunkler Doppelbock	Kaufbeuren	2.8	Boc
Altenmunster Export	Marktoberdorf	2.0	Mlt
Altenmunster Malt Liquor	Marktoberdorf	2.4	Mlt
Arnold Pilsner	Bavaria	1.9	Pil
Ayinger Bavarian Wheat	Aying	2.9	Wht
Ayinger Celebrator Doppelbock	Aying	3.7	Boc
Ayinger Dunkles Ur-Weisse	Aying	4.0	Wht
Ayinger Jahrhundert Bier	Aying	2.9	Lag
Ayinger Maibock	Aying	2.0	Boc
Ayinger Oktoberfest— Marzen	Aying	3.9	Lag
Beck's	Bremen	3.1	Pil
Beck's Dark	Bremen	2.6	Pil
Beck's Oktoberfest (annual)	Bremen	3.7	Lag
Berliner Pils	Berlin	2.5	Pil
Berliner Ratskeller Lager	Berlin	2.2	Lag
Bitburger Pilsener	Bitburg	3.3	Pil
Broyhan Premium	Hannover	1.8	Lag
Cassel Schloss	Noerten-Hardenberg	2.5	Lag
Deininger Kristall Weizen	Hof	2.2	Wht
Dinkelacker	Stuttgart	2.9	Pil
Dinkelacker Dark	Stuttgart	3.4	Lag
Dortmunder Aktien Alt	Dortmund	1.2	Alt
Dortmunder Union Dark	Dortmund	0.1	Lag
Dortmunder Union Original	Dortmund	3.6	Pil

NAME	LOCATION	RATING	STYLE
DRESSLER	BREMEN	2.0	PIL
EDELWEISS LUXURY GRADE MALT LIQUOR	DRESDEN	1.4	MLT
EINBECKER UR-BOCK	EINBECK	3.0	BOC
EKU DARK HEFE WEISBIER	KULMBACH	3.8	WHT
EKU EDELBOCK	KULMBACH	3.7	BOC
EKU KULMBACHER PILS	KULMBACH	3.9	PIL
EKU KULMBACHER RUBIN	KULMBACH	1.9	LAG
EKU KULMINATOR URTYP HELL MALT LIQUOR	KULMBACH	0.2	MLT
ERDINGER WEISSBIER— DUNKEL	ERDING	4.0	WHT
ERDINGER WEISSBIER— HEFETRUB	ERDING	4.4	WHT
ERDINGER WEIZENBOCK	ERDING	3.8	WHT
ETTALER KLOSTER DUNKEL	ETTAL	4.5	LAG
FEST BIER	BAYREUTH	2.4	MLT
FIEDLERS BOCK IM STEIN	KOBLENZ	2.5	BOC
FIEDLERS PILS IM STEIN	KOBLENZ	2.3	PIL
FURSTENBERG	DONAUESCHINGEN	3.6	PIL
GRENZQUELL GERMAN PILSNER	HAMBURG	3.1	PIL
HACKER-PSCHORR DARK LAGER	MUNICH	2.5	LAG
HACKERBRAU EDELHELL MUNICH LAGER MALT LIQUOR	MUNICH	3.3	MLT
HENNINGER DARK	FRANKFURT	2.5	LAG
HENNINGER KAISER PILSENER	FRANKFURT	3.0	PIL
HENNINGER LIGHT PILSENER	FRANKFURT	1.9	PIL
HERRENBRAU PILSNER MALT LIQUOR	BAYREUTH	2.4	PIL
HERRENHAUSER PILSENER MALT LIQUOR	HANNOVER	1.2	PIL
HOFBRAU BAVARIA DARK RESERVE	KULMBACH	2.5	LAG
HOFBRAU BAVARIAN LIGHT RESERVE	KULMBACH	2.7	LAG
HOFBRAU MUNCHENER OKTOBERFEST (ANNUAL)	MUNICH	3.3	LAG
HOFBRAU ROYAL BAVARIAN LAGER	MUNICH	3.1	LAG

NAME	LOCATION	RATING	STYLE
HOLSTEN	HAMBURG	3.0	PIL
HOLSTEN DRY	HAMBURG	2.9	PIL
ISENBECK	HAMM	3.4	LAG
JULIUS ECHTER HEFE-WEISSBIER	WURZBURG	3.0	WHT
KAISER PILSENER	FRANKFURT	0.5	PIL
KAISERDOM EXTRA DRY	BAMBERG	3.9	LAG
KAISERDOM RAUCHBIER— SMOKED BAVARIAN DARK	BAMBERG	3.9	SPE
KAPUZINER WEIZEN KRISTALLKLAR	KULMBACH	3.1	WHT
KLOSTER SCHWARTZBIER— MONKSHOF	KULMBACH	2.9	LAG
KLOSTERBOCK MONKSHOF	KULMBACH	2.3	MLT
KRONEN CLASSIC ALL DARK	DORTMUND	2.1	LAG
KROPF DARK DRAFT	KASSEL	2.6	LAG
KROPF DRAFT	KASSEL	2.3	LAG
KROPF EDEL PILS	KASSEL	2.9	PIL
LANDSKRON PILS	RADEBERG	3.8	PIL
MAISEL'S HEFE WEISSE	BAYREUTH	4.0	WHT
MAISEL'S WEIZEN	BAYREUTH	2.0	WHT
MAISEL'S WEIZEN KRISTALL-KLAR	BAYREUTH	2.5	WHT
MAXIMATOR DARK DOPPELBOCK	MUNICH	3.5	BOC
OBERDORFER DARK HEFEWEIZEN	MARKTOBERDORF	3.1	WHT
PAULANER ALT MUNCHER DUNKEL	MUNICH	3.9	LAG
PAULANER HEFE-WEIZEN	MUNICH	2.9	WHT
PAULANER MUNCHEN NR. 1 LAGER	MUNICH	2.2	LAG
PAULANER OKTOBERFEST	MUNICH	3.8	LAG
PAULANER SALVATOR DOPPELBOCK	MUNICH	4.0	BOC
PINKUS HOME BREW MUNSTER ALT	MUNSTER	1.5	SPE
PINKUS HOME BREW UR PILS	MUNSTER	1.9	PIL
PINKUS HOME BREW WEIZEN	MUNSTER	1.3	WHT
PSCHORR-BRAU WEISSE	MUNICH	3.5	WHT
RED STAR SELECT	BERLIN	2.2	LAG
REICHELBRAU BAVARIAN DARK	KULMBACH	3.1	LAG

NAME	LOCATION	RATING	STYLE
RIEGELER SPEZIAL EXPORT	KAISERSTUHL	2.9	LAG
RITTERBRAU PALE	DORTMUND	4.0	LAG
SAILER PILS	MARKTOBERDORF	2.8	PIL
SCHULTHEISS BERLINER WEISSE	BERLIN	3.0	WHT
SCHULTHEISS GERMAN PILSENER	BERLIN	0.3	PIL
SCHWEIZERHOF-BRAU LAGER	MARKTOBERDORF	2.9	LAG
SPATEN FRANZISKANER HEFE-WEISSBIER	MUNICH	2.6	WHT
SPATEN FRANZISKUS HELLER BOCK	MUNICH	3.1	BOC
SPATEN MUNCHEN CLUB—WEISSE	MUNICH	3.5	WHT
SPATEN MUNICH OPTIMATOR DOPPELSPATEN BOCK	MUNICH	3.4	BOC
SPATEN OKTOBERFEST UR-MARZEN	MUNICH	2.8	BOC
SPATEN PILS	MUNICH	2.5	PIL
ST. PAULI GIRL	BREMEN	3.4	PIL
ST. PAULI GIRL DARK	BREMEN	3.5	PIL
STEINHAUSER BIER	FRANKFURT	3.5	PIL
TUCHER FESTBIER MARZEN (ANNUAL)	NURNBERG	2.0	LAG
VALENTINS KLARES WEIZENBIER	HEIDELBERG	2.3	WHT
WARSTEINER	WARSTEIN	3.9	PIL
WARSTEINER PREMIUM VERUM	WARSTEIN	3.0	PIL
WEIHENSTEPHAN EDEL—PILS	FREISING	2.6	PIL
WEIHENSTEPHAN EXPORT—DUNKEL	FREISING	4.1	LAG
WEIHENSTEPHAN WEIZENBIER	FREISING	3.8	WHT
WOLFBRAU	OSNABRUCK	3.3	PIL
WURZBURGER HOFBRAU OCTOBERFEST (ANNUAL)	WURZBURG	2.7	LAG
GREECE			
AEGEAN HELLAS	ATALANTI	4.2	LAG
ATHENIAN—THE GREEK BEER	ATHENS	0.8	LAG
SPARTAN LAGER	ATALANTI	4.0	LAG

NAME	LOCATION	RATING	STYLE
GUATEMALA			
CABRO EXTRA	GUATEMALA CITY	1.7	PIL
DURANGO	DEL SUR	0.8	PIL
MEDALLA DE ORO LAGER	GUATEMALA CITY	2.3	LAG
MONTE CARLO LAGER	GUATEMALA CITY	2.8	LAG
MOZA BOCK	GUATEMALA CITY	2.9	BOC
HAITI			
PRESTIGE STOUT	PORT-AU-PRINCE	4.0	STO
HOLLAND			
ALFA	SCHINNEN	3.1	PIL
BAVARIA LAGER	LIESHOUT	3.0	LAG
BRAND	LIMBURG	2.5	PIL
CHRISTOFFEL BIER LAGER	ROERMOND	2.5	LAG
GROLSCH	GROENLO	3.1	PIL
GROLSCH AUTUMN AMBER ALE	GROENLO	3.6	ALE
GROLSCH DARK LAGER	GROENLO	3.2	LAG
GROLSCH DRY DRAFT	GROENLO	3.0	PIL
HEINEKEN LAGER	AMSTERDAM	3.4	LAG
HEINEKEN SPECIAL DARK	AMSTERDAM	2.4	LAG
JOSEPH MEENS' HOLLAND PREMIUM	SCHINNEN	1.0	LAG
LA TRAPPE ALE	TILBURG	3.9	ALE
LEEUW PILSENER	LIMBURG	3.2	PIL
ORANJEBOOM PREMIUM LAGER	BREDA/ROTTERDAM	3.4	LAG
PETER'S BRAND PILSENER	AMERSFOORT	2.3	PIL
ROYAL BRAND	WYLRE	3.4	PIL
SKOL HOLLAND PILSENER	ROTTERDAM	2.2	PIL
SWINKELS	LIESHOUT	2.4	PIL
HONDURAS			
PORT ROYAL EXPORT	SAN PEDRO SULA	1.3	PIL
HONG KONG			
SUN LIK	HONG KONG	3.5	PIL
HUNGARY			
BORSOD PREMIUM	BOCSARLAPUJTO	2.5	PIL
INDIA			
COLTS BERG	BANGALORE	2.1	PIL
FLYING HORSE ROYAL LAGER	BANGALORE	2.7	LAG
GOA PILSNER DRY	GOA	2.9	PIL
GOLDEN EAGLE LAGER	MADRAS/TAMIL NADU	3.5	LAG
KALYANI BLACK LABEL PREMIUM LAGER	BANGALORE	3.5	LAG

NAME	LOCATION	RATING	STYLE
Kingfisher Lager	Bangalore	2.8	Lag
Taj Mahal Lager	Calcutta	3.1	Lag
UB Export Lager	Bangalore	2.5	Lag
INDONESIA			
Anker Pilsner	Djakarta	2.9	Pil
Bintang Pilsener	Surabaya	3.9	Pil
IRELAND			
Beamish Irish Cream Stout	Cork	3.2	Sto
Guinness Extra Stout	Dublin	3.8	Sto
Guinness Gold Lager	Dundalk	3.3	Lag
Guinness Pub Draught	Dublin	3.9	Sto
Harp	Dublin	3.5	Lag
Murphy's Irish Stout	Cork	2.5	Sto
Murphy's Stout	Cork	3.5	Sto
ISRAEL			
Maccabee	Netanya	2.2	Lag
ITALY			
Castello	San Giorgio di Nogaro	2.2	Pil
D'Aquino Italian Beer	Induno	2.3	Pil
Dreher Pilsener	Milan	2.1	Pil
McFarland Golden Fire	Milan	3.9	Ale
Messina Pilsener	Milan	4.1	Pil
Moretti Birra Friulana	Udine	1.3	Pil
Moretti La Rossa All Malt	Udine	3.1	Lag
Moretti La Rossa Doppiomalto	Udine	2.7	Lag
Peroni	Rome	3.1	Lag
Raffo	Rome	3.9	Pil
IVORY COAST			
Mamba	Abidjan	3.1	Mlt
JAMAICA			
Dragon Stout	Kingston	3.3	Sto
Red Stripe Lager	Kingston	2.2	Lag
JAPAN			
Asahi Draft	Tokyo	1.5	Pil
Asahi Super Dry Draft	Tokyo	2.9	Pil
Asahi Z Draft	Tokyo	3.7	Pil
Kirin Draft	Tokyo	2.3	Lag
Kirin Dry Draft	Tokyo	4.0	Pil
Kirin Ichiban Malt Liquor	Tokyo	4.0	Mlt
Kirin Lager	Tokyo	3.9	Lag
Sapporo Black Malt Liquor (NOT FOR EXPORT)	Tokyo	4.1	Mlt
Sapporo Black Malt Liquor	Tokyo	4.0	Mlt

NAME	LOCATION	RATING	STYLE
SAPPORO DRAFT	TOKYO	2.4	PIL
SAPPORO DRAFT DRY MALT LIQUOR	TOKYO	3.2	MLT
SUNTORY DRAFT	OSAKA	2.2	PIL
SUNTORY GINJO DRAFT	OSAKA	2.6	PIL
SUNTORY GOLD DRAFT— 100% MALT BEER	OSAKA	3.3	PIL
YEBISU ALL MALT	TOKYO	2.7	PIL
YEBISU STOUT DRAFT	TOKYO	2.4	STO
KENYA			
TUSKER MALT LAGER	NAIROBI	2.3	LAG
TUSKER PREMIUM LAGER	NAIROBI	4.3	LAG
KOREA			
CROWN	SEOUL	2.2	LAG
OB LAGER	SEOUL	2.5	LAG
LEBANON			
ALMAZA PILSENER	BEIRUT	3.9	PIL
LIBERIA			
MONROVIA CLUB BEER	MONROVIA	3.0	LAG
LUXEMBOURG			
DIEKIRCH	DIEKIRCH	2.9	PIL
MEXICO			
BARRIL CLARA	MEXICO CITY	3.8	PIL
BARRIL OSCURA	MEXICO CITY	4.0	PIL
BOHEMIA PILSENER	MONTERREY	1.7	PIL
BRISA	GUADALAJARA	2.8	LAG
CARTA BLANCA	MONTERREY	3.6	LAG
CHIHUAHUA	MONTERREY	2.7	LAG
CLARA ESTRELLA DORADO	GUADALAJARA	1.0	LAG
CORONA EXTRA	MEXICO CITY	1.5	PIL
DOS EQUIS CLARA—LAGER ESPECIAL	GUADALAJARA	3.2	LAG
HOMBRE	CIUDAD JUAREZ	2.9	LAG
HUSSONG'S CERVEZA CLARA	GUADALAJARA	3.4	PIL
INDIO OSCURA	MONTERREY	1.6	LAG
MODELO ESPECIAL	MEXICO CITY	2.9	LAG
MONTEZUMA DE BARRIL	MEXICO CITY	3.3	LAG
NAVIDAD CERVEZA COMMEMORATIVA (ANNUAL)	MONTERREY	0.1–3.4	LAG
NEGRA MODELO DARK ALE	MEXICO CITY	3.5	ALE
NOCHE BUENA (ANNUAL)	ORIZABA	2.4–3.3	LAG
PACIFICO CLARO	MAZATLAN	3.1	PIL
SOL	GUADALAJARA	2.7	PIL
SUPERIOR	GUADALAJARA	3.1	PIL

NAME	LOCATION	RATING	STYLE
TECATE	MONTERREY	3.0	PIL
VICTORIA	MEXICO CITY	0.0	PIL
NEW GUINEA			
SOUTH PACIFIC SPECIAL EXPORT LAGER	PAPUA	2.0	LAG
NEW ZEALAND			
KIWI LAGER	TIMARU	4.0	LAG
LEOPARD DELUXE	HASTINGS	3.0	PIL
NEW ZEALAND LAGER	AUCKLAND	2.4	LAG
STEINLAGER	AUCKLAND	3.8	PIL
NORWAY			
AASS AMBER	DRAMMEN	3.2	LAG
AASS BOCK	DRAMMEN	3.2	BOC
AASS JUBILEE	DRAMMEN	3.9	LAG
AASS JULE ØL	DRAMMEN	4.5	LAG
AASS PILSNER	DRAMMEN	2.9	PIL
AASS WINTER	DRAMMEN	2.3	LAG
FRYDENLUND	OSLO	2.9	PIL
HANSA DARK	BERGEN	4.1	PIL
HANSA LIGHT	BERGEN	2.6	PIL
MACK-OL ARCTIC BEER/PILSNER	TROMSØ	2.9	PIL
RINGNES EXPORT PALE	OSLO	4.0	PIL
RINGNES SPECIAL JUBILEE ALE	OSLO	2.7	ALE
PANAMA			
PANAMA CERVEZA ALLEMANA STYLE	PANAMA CITY	3.6	LAG
PERU			
CALLAO PILSEN	CALLAO	2.3	PIL
CRISTAL PREMIUM	CHICLAYO/LIMA	3.2	LAG
CUZCO	CUZCO	3.2	PIL
PHILIPPINES			
MANILA GOLD PALE PILSEN	CABUYAO	3.1	PIL
RED HORSE MALT LIQUOR	MANILA	3.2	MLT
SAN MIGUEL DARK	MANILA	4.4	PIL
SAN MIGUEL PALE PILSEN	MANILA	2.9	PIL
POLAND			
KRAKUS LIGHT	ZYWIEC	2.1	PIL
OKOCIM O.K. FULL LIGHT	WARSAW	2.2	PIL
OKOCIM O.K. PILS	WARSAW	0.3	PIL
ZYWIEC FULL LIGHT	ZYWIEC	1.5	PIL
PORTUGAL			
EUROPA	LISBON	3.1	LAG
SAGRES PREMIUM	LISBON	2.1	LAG

NAME	LOCATION	RATING	STYLE
PUERTO RICO			
INDIA	MAYAGUEZ	1.1	LAG
MEDALLA LIGHT	SAN JUAN	0.8	PIL
RUSSIA			
ADMEERAL TYEYSKOYE	MOSCOW	0.8	LAG
MOSCOVA	MOSCOW	1.9	LAG
SLAVAYANSKY	MOSCOW	0.3	LAG
TROIKA ORIGINAL RUSSIAN BEER	MOSCOW	1.1	LAG
SCOTLAND			
BELHAVEN SCOTTISH ALE	DUNBAR	4.0	ALE
GOLDEN PROMISE ALE	EDINBURGH	2.8	ALE
LORIMER'S SCOTTISH BEER	EDINBURGH	2.6	ALE
MACANDREW'S SCOTCH ALE	EDINBURGH	3.2	ALE
MCEWAN'S EXPORT INDIA PALE ALE	EDINBURGH	4.0	IPA
MCEWAN'S SCOTCH ALE	EDINBURGH	3.8	ALE
SWEETHEART STOUT	GLASGOW	3.5	STO
TENNENT'S LAGER	GLASGOW	1.8	LAG
TRAQUAIR HOUSE ALE	INNERLEITHEN	4.1	ALE
SINGAPORE			
ABC EXTRA STOUT	SINGAPORE	3.7	STO
ABC VERY SUPERIOR STOUT	SINGAPORE	3.6	STO
ANCHOR PILSENER	SINGAPORE	2.5	PIL
TIGER	SINGAPORE	3.3	LAG
SPAIN			
AGUILA IMPERIAL ALE	MADRID	3.8	ALE
AMBAR DOS ESPECIAL	ZARAGOZA	3.3	LAG
DAMM	BARCELONA/VALENCIA	3.8	PIL
SWEDEN			
PRIPPS LAGER	GOTHENBURG	2.9	LAG
SWITZERLAND			
CARDINAL LAGER	FRIBOURG	4.0	LAG
GLARNER LAGER	ZURICH	3.1	LAG
HOPFENPERLE	RHEINFELDEN	2.6	PIL
HOPFENPERLE SPECIAL	RHEINFELDEN	2.9	LAG
HURLIMANN SWISS DARK LAGER	ZURICH	2.4	LAG
LOWENBRAU ZURICH	ZURICH	3.0	PIL
SAMICHLAUS DARK (ANNUAL)	ZURICH	0.1	LAG
WARTECK LAGER	BASEL	3.2	LAG

NAME	LOCATION	RATING	STYLE
	TAHITI		
HINANO	PAPEETE	2.1	LAG
	TAIWAN		
CHINA LUXURY LAGER	TAIPEI	2.9	LAG
TAIWAN BEER	TAIPEI	1.8	LAG
	THAILAND		
AMARIT LAGER	BANGKOK	2.0	LAG
BANGKOK BEER	BANGKOK	1.6	PIL
SIAM ALE	BANGKOK	3.8	ALE
SINGHA	BANGKOK	2.5	LAG
	TOGO		
NGOMA MALT LIQUOR	LOME	2.1	MLT
NGOMA TOGO PILS	LOME	2.7	PIL
	TURKEY		
EFES	IZMIR	1.1	PIL
	UKRAINE		
RUSKI	KIEV	3.3	LAG
RUSSKOYE LAGER	KIEV	0.2	LAG
	VENEZUELA		
ANDES	CARACAS	2.6	LAG
POLAR	CARACAS	1.0	LAG
	VIET NAM		
HUE BEER	HUE	0.6	LAG
	WALES		
FELINFOEL DOUBLE DRAGON ALE	LLANELLI	4.1	ALE
FELINFOEL DRAGON ALE	LLANELLI	4.0	ALE
FELINFOEL HERCULES ALE	LLANELLI	4.0	ALE
FELINFOEL WELSH ALE	LLANELLI	3.9	ALE
FELINFOEL WELSH BITTER	LLANELLI	2.4	ALE
FELINFOEL WELSH PORTER	LLANELLI	1.8	POR
	WEST INDIES		
CARIBE	TRINIDAD	3.3	LAG
CARIB LAGER	TRINIDAD	2.5	LAG
ROYAL EXTRA STOUT	TRINIDAD	3.7	STO
SHANDY CARIB	TRINIDAD	0.2	LAG
	WESTERN SAMOA		
VAILIMA LAGER	APIA	3.5	LAG
VAILIMA LIGHT	APIA	2.1	PIL
	THE FORMER YUGOSLAVIA		
BELGRADE GOLD	BELGRADE	2.9	PIL
GOLDHORN CLUB	LASKO	3.4	PIL
KARLSBEER	KARLOVAC	3.2	PIL

NAME	LOCATION	RATING	STYLE
NEKTAR LIGHT	BANJA LUKA	1.4	PIL
NIKSICKO PIVO	NIKSIC	3.1	PIL
RED BREW-STER	LJUBLJANA	2.2	PIL
UNION PREMIUM	LJUBLJANA	2.3	PIL
ZAIRE			
NGOK' MALT LIQUOR	POINTE NOIRE	1.8	MLT

BEST BEERS BY STYLE

NAME	LOCATION	RATING
ALES		
CHIMAY PERES TRAPPISTES ALE—PREMIERE	BELGIUM, CHIMAY ABBEY	4.7
ROGUE RED ALE	USA, OREGON, NEWPORT	4.4
ROYAL OAK PALE ALE	ENGLAND, DORCHESTER	4.4
WESTMALLE TRAPPIST	BELGIUM, ABBEY OF WESTMALLE	4.3
RIO BRAVO HIGH DESERT PALE ALE	USA, NEW MEXICO, ALBUQUERQUE	4.2
ARTEVELDE ALE	BELGIUM, MELLE/GHENT	4.1
DUFFY'S ALE	CANADA, BRITISH COLUMBIA, VANCOUVER	4.1
FELINFOEL DOUBLE DRAGON ALE	WALES, LLANELLI	4.1
MAREDSOUS ABBEY ALE	BELGIUM, DENEE	4.1
TRAQUAIR HOUSE ALE	SCOTLAND, INNERLEITHEN	4.1
BELHAVEN SCOTTISH ALE	SCOTLAND, DUNBAR	4.0
BRIDGEPORT OLD KNUCKLEHEAD BARLEY WINE	USA, OREGON, PORTLAND	4.0
CELIS WHITE	USA, TEXAS, AUSTIN	4.0
CORSENDONK MONK'S PALE ALE	BELGIUM, SIGILLUM MONASTERY	4.0
FELINFOEL DRAGON ALE	WALES, LLANELLI	4.0
FELINFOEL HERCULES ALE	WALES, LLANELLI	4.0
GRIMBERGEN DOUBLE ALE	BELGIUM, WATERLOO	4.0
NEW ENGLAND HOLIDAY ALE (ANNUAL)	USA, CONNECTICUT, NORWALK	4.0
WITKAP-PATER SINGEL ABBEY ALE	BELGIUM, NINOVE	4.0
BIG ROCK ROYAL COACHMAN DRY ALE	CANADA, ALBERTA, CALGARY	3.9
DOUGLAS SCOTCH BRAND ALE	BELGIUM, ANTWERP	3.9
FELINFOEL WELSH ALE	WALES, LLANELLI	3.9
GOUDEN CAROLUS ALE	BELGIUM, MECHELEN	3.9
GRANT'S SPICED ALE	USA, WASHINGTON, YAKIMA	3.9
LA TRAPPE ALE	HOLLAND, TILBURG	3.9
MCFARLAND GOLDEN FIRE	ITALY, MILAN	3.9
NEW BELGIUM FAT TIRE AMBER ALE	USA, COLORADO, FORT COLLINS	3.9
SIERRA NEVADA CELEBRATION ALE '91 (ANNUAL)	USA, CALIFORNIA, CHICO	3.9
STEENDONK WHITE ALE	BELGIUM, BREENDONK	3.9

NAME	LOCATION	RATING
Sun Valley Holiday Ale (annual)	USA, Idaho, Halley	3.9
Whitbread Ale	England, London/Sheffield	3.9
Young's Old Nick (annual)	England, London	3.9
Abita Turbo Dog	USA, Louisiana, Abita Springs	3.8
Aguila Imperial Ale	Spain, Madrid	3.8
Bass Pale Ale	England, Burton-on-Trent	3.8
Bateman's Dark Victory Ale	England, Wainfleet	3.8
Brigand Belgian ale	Belgium, Ingelmunster	3.8
Corsendonk Monk's Brown Ale	Belgium, Sigillum Monastery	3.8
Dillon's Six Shooter Red Ale	USA, California, Chatsworth	3.8
Fuller's London Pride	England, London	3.8
Manhattan Winter Warmer	USA, New York, New York	3.8
McEwan's Scotch Ale	Scotland, Edinburgh	3.8
McTarnahan's Scottish Ale	USA, Oregon, Portland	3.8
Old Detroit Amber Ale	USA, Michigan, Frankenmuth	3.8
Old Peculier Ale	England, Masham	3.8
Pete's Wicked Ale	USA, Minnesota, New Ulm	3.8
Siam Ale	Thailand, Bangkok	3.8
Sun Valley White Cloud Ale	USA, Idaho, Halley	3.8
Anchor Liberty Ale	USA, California, San Francisco	3.7
Anderson Valley Poleeko Gold Light Ale	USA, California, Boonville	3.7
Bandersnatch Red Ale	USA, Arizona, Tempe	3.7
Bateman's XXXB Ale	England, Wainfleet	3.7
Buffalo Gold Premium Ale	USA, Colorado, Boulder	3.7
Labatt's 50 Ale	Canada, British Columbia, Vancouver	3.7
Odell's 90 Shilling Ale	USA, Colorado, Fort Collins	3.7
Rhino Chasers Amber Ale	USA, California, Chatsworth	3.7
Affligem Tripel Abbey	Belgium, Opwijk	3.6
Boulder Extra Pale Ale	USA, Colorado, Boulder	3.6
Devil Mountain Railroad Ale	USA, California, Benicia	3.6
Grant's India Pale Ale	USA, Washington, Yakima	3.6
Grolsch Autumn Amber Ale	Holland, Groenlo	3.6
Pike Place Pale Ale	USA, Washington, Seattle	3.6
Pope's "1880"	England, Dorchester	3.6
Post Road Real Ale	USA, Vermont, White River Junction	3.6

NAME	LOCATION	RATING
Rainier Ale	USA, Washington, Seattle	3.6
Red Hook Winterhook Christmas Ale (annual)	USA, Washington, Seattle	3.6
Rockies Draft	USA, Colorado, Boulder	3.6
Rogue Mogul Ale	USA, Oregon, Newport	3.6
Rogue Old Crustacean Barley Wine	USA, Oregon, Newport	3.6
Young's Ram Rod	England, London	3.6
Le Garde	USA, Vermont, White River Junction	3.5
Martin's Pale Ale	Belgium, Antwerp	3.5
Red Feather Pale Ale	USA, Pennsylvania, Chambersburg	3.5
Vail Ale	USA, Kentucky, Fort Mitchell	3.5
ALTS		
St. Stan's Dark Alt	USA, California, Modesto	3.9
Alaskan Amber	USA, Alaska, Juneau	3.8
St. Stan's Amber Alt	USA, California, Modesto	3.8
St. Stan's Fest Bier	USA, California, Modesto	3.5
BOCKS		
Samuel Adams Triple Bock	USA, California, Ceres	4.7
Granville Island Bock	Canada, British Columbia, Vancouver	4.2
Paulaner Salvator Doppelbock	Germany, Munich	4.0
Rogue Maierbock Ale	USA, Oregon, Newport	3.9
Schutzenberger Jubilator	France, Schiltigheim	3.8
Ayinger Celebrator Doppelbock	Germany, Aying	3.7
Eku Edelbock	Germany, Kulmbach	3.7
Prior Double Dark	USA, Pennsylvania, Norristown	3.7
Upper Canada True Bock	Canada, Ontario, Toronto	3.7
Maximator Dark	Germany, Munich	3.5
Rolling Rock Bock	USA, Pennsylvania, Latrobe	3.5
INDIA PALE ALES (IPA)		
Hale's IPA	USA, Washington, Colville	4.4
McEwan's Export India Pale Ale	Scotland, Edinburgh	4.0
Ballantine India Pale Ale	USA, Indiana, Fort Wayne	3.8
Coopersmith's Punjabi India Pale Ale	USA, Colorado, Fort Collins	3.8
LAGERS		
Aass Jule Øl	Norway, Drammen	4.5
Ettaler Kloster Dunkel	Germany, Ettal	4.5
Tusker Premium Lager	Kenya, Nairobi	4.3
Aegean Hellas	Greece, Atalanti	4.2

NAME	LOCATION	RATING
WEIHENSTEPHAN EXPORT DUNKEL	GERMANY, FREISING	4.1
CARDINAL LAGER	SWITZERLAND, FRIBOURG	4.0
COLD SPRING SELECT STOCK	USA, MINNESOTA, COLD SPRING	4.0
JINDAO	CHINA, QINGDAO	4.0
KIWI LAGER	NEW ZEALAND, TIMARU	4.0
RITTERBRAU PALE	GERMANY, DORTMUND	4.0
SAMUEL SMITH'S LAGER	ENGLAND, TADCASTER	4.0
SPARTAN LAGER	GREECE, ATALANTI	4.0
AASS JUBILEE	NORWAY, DRAMMEN	3.9
AYINGER OKTOBERFEST— MARZEN	GERMANY, AYING	3.9
KAISERDOM EXTRA DRY	GERMANY, BAMBERG	3.9
KIRIN LAGER	JAPAN, TOKYO	3.9
MAUI LAGER	USA, HAWAII, MAUI, WAILUKU	3.9
PAULANER ALT MUNCHER DUNKEL	GERMANY, MUNICH	3.9
SANTA FE RUBIA ESPECIAL	ARGENTINA, SANTA FE	3.9
WATNEY'S RED BARREL	ENGLAND, LONDON	3.9
AUGUST SCHELL DEER BRAND	USA, MINNESOTA, NEW ULM	3.8
HUA NAN	CHINA, GUANGZHOU	3.8
LABATT CLASSIC	CANADA, ONTARIO, TORONTO, ET. AL.	3.8
LEON DE ORO CERVEZA ESPECIAL	ARGENTINA, ANTARTIDA	3.8
MILLSTREAM LAGER	USA, IOWA, AMANA	3.8
PAULANER OKTOBERFEST	GERMANY, MUNICH	3.8
BECK'S OKTOBERFEST (ANNUAL)	GERMANY, BREMEN	3.7
EAU CLAIRE ALL-MALT LAGER	USA, WISCONSIN, EAU CLAIRE	3.7
RHINO CHASERS LAGER	USA, CALIFORNIA, CHATSWORTH	3.7
SAMUEL ADAMS DOUBLE BOCK DARK LAGER	USA, PENNSYLVANIA, PITTSBURGH	3.7
SAMUEL ADAMS OCTOBERFEST	USA, PENNSYLVANIA, PITTSBURGH	3.7
WYNKOOP JED FEST (ANNUAL)	USA, COLORADO, DENVER	3.7
ASTICA PREMIUM LAGER	BULGARIA, HASKOWO	3.6
BROOKLYN LAGER DRAFT	USA, NEW YORK, UTICA	3.6
CARTA BLANCA	MEXICO, MONTERREY	3.6
CHURCHILL LAGER	ENGLAND, REDRUTH	3.6
KAREL IV LAGER	CZECH REPUBLIC	3.6
KOFF	FINLAND, HELSINKI	3.6
NEW AMSTERDAM AMBER	USA, NEW YORK, UTICA	3.6
PANAMA CERVEZA ALLEMANA STYLE	PANAMA, PANAMA CITY	3.6
ROLLING ROCK	USA, PENNSYLVANIA, LATROBE	3.6

NAME	LOCATION	RATING
Brasseurs Grand Cru	France, Bonneuil	3.5
Cold Spring Export	USA, Minnesota, Cold Spring	3.5
Dixie	USA, Louisiana, New Orleans	3.5
Durango Colorfest (annual)	USA, Colorado, Durango	3.5
Golden Eagle Lager	India, Tamil Nadu, Madras	3.5
Gosser Stiftsbrau	Austria, Graz	3.5
Harp	Ireland, Dublin	3.5
Kalyani Black Label Premium Lager	India, Bangalore	3.5
Molson Ice	Canada, British Columbia, Vancouver	3.5
Vailima Lager	Western Samoa, Apia	3.5
LAMBICS		
Liefmans Kriekbier	Belgium, Oudenaarde	3.9
Samuel Adams Cranberry Lambic	USA, Pennsylvania, Pittsburgh	3.4
MALT LIQUORS		
Adelscott Malt Liquor	France, Schiltigheim	4.2
Sapporo Black Malt Liquor	Japan, Tokyo (not for export)	4.1
Kirin Ichiban Malt Liquor	Japan, Tokyo	4.0
Sapporo Black Malt Liquor	Japan, Tokyo	4.0
Upper Canada Rebellion Malt Liquor	Canada, Ontario, Toronto	3.8
Septante 5 Malt Liquor	France, Roubaix	3.7
NON-ALCOHOLIC		
Extracto De Malta Malt Beverage	Germany, Hamburg	3.9
Clausthaler	Germany, Frankfurt	3.8
Haake Beck	Germany, Bremen	3.5
PILSENERS		
San Miguel Dark	Philippines, Manila	4.4
Bieckert Especial	Argentina, Antartida	4.2
Hansa Dark	Norway, Bergen	4.1
Messina Pilsener	Italy, Milan	4.1
Southwark Premium	Australia, South Australia, Adelaide	4.1
Barril Oscura	Mexico, Mexico City	4.0
Kirin Dry Draft	Japan, Tokyo	4.0
Pilsener	Ecuador, Quito	4.0
Ringnes Export Pale	Norway, Oslo	4.0
Almaza Pilsener	Lebanon, Beirut	3.9
Bintang Pilsener	Indonesia, Surabaya	3.9
Eku Kulmbacher Pils	Germany, Kulmbach	3.9

NAME	LOCATION	RATING
KIRIN DRAFT	CANADA, BRITISH COLUMBIA, VANCOUVER	3.9
RAFFO	ITALY, ROME	3.9
STAROPRAMEN	CZECHOSLOVAKIA, PRAGUE	3.9
WARSTEINER	GERMANY, WARSTEIN	3.9
BARRIL CLARA	MEXICO, MEXICO CITY	3.8
BRAHMA	BRAZIL, RIO DE JANEIRO	3.8
DAMM	SPAIN, BARCELONA/VALENCIA	3.8
LANDSKRON PILS	GERMANY, RADEBERG	3.8
ROYAL GUARD PILSENER	CHILE, SANTIAGO	3.8
STEINLAGER	NEW ZEALAND, AUCKLAND	3.8
TIJUCA	BRAZIL, BELEM	3.8
ALLEGHENY PENN PILSENER	USA, PENNSYLVANIA, PITTSBURGH	3.7
ASAHI Z DRAFT	JAPAN, TOKYO	3.7
BRAHMA CHOPP	BRAZIL, RIO DE JANEIRO	3.7
CORDOBA-DORADA	ARGENTINA, CORDOBA	3.7
TROPICAL PILSENER	CANARY ISLANDS, LAS PALMAS	3.7
DORTMUNDER UNION ORIGINAL	GERMANY, DORTMUND	3.6
FURSTENBERG	GERMANY, DONAUESCHINGEN	3.6
AUGSBURGER PILSENER	USA, WISCONSIN, MONROE	3.5
EMPERORS GOLD	CHINA, GUANGZHOU	3.5
PANDA	CHINA, SHANGHAI	3.5
PILSNER URQUELL	CZECHOSLOVAKIA, PILSEN	3.5
PRESIDENTE PILSENER	DOMINICAN REPUBLIC, SANTO DOMINGO	3.5
ST. PAULI GIRL DARK	GERMANY, BREMEN	3.5
STEINHAUSER BIER	GERMANY, FRANKFURT	3.5
SUN LIK	HONG KONG	3.5
PORTERS		
RIO BRAVO ESTEBAN DARK PORTER	USA, NEW MEXICO, ALBUQUERQUE	4.1
YUENGLING PORTER	USA, PENNSYLVANIA, POTTSVILLE	4.1
ANCHOR PORTER	USA, CALIFORNIA, SAN FRANCISCO	4.0
CHICAGO'S BIG SHOULDERS PORTER	USA, ILLINOIS, CHICAGO	4.0
OLD COLUMBIA BLACK'S BEACH EXTRA DARK PORTER	USA, CALIFORNIA, SAN DIEGO	4.0
PORTLAND PORTER	USA, OREGON, PORTLAND	4.0
RED HOOK BLACKHOOK PORTER	USA, WASHINGTON, SEATTLE	4.0
ANDERSON VALLEY DEEP ENDERS DARK PORTER	USA, CALIFORNIA, BOONVILLE	3.8
BOULEVARD "BULLY" PORTER	USA, MISSOURI, KANSAS CITY	3.8
CATAMOUNT PORTER	USA, VERMONT, WHITE RIVER JUNCTION	3.8

NAME	LOCATION	RATING
DESCHUTES BLACK BUTTE PORTER	USA, OREGON, BEND	3.7
ROGUE NEW PORTER	USA, OREGON, NEWPORT	3.7
SAMUEL SMITH TADCASTER TADDY PORTER	ENGLAND, TADCASTER	3.7
SANTA FE OLD POJOAQUE PORTER	USA, NEW MEXICO, GALISTEO	3.5
SPECIALTY AND COMBINATION BEERS		
ANCHOR OUR SPECIAL ALE (ANNUAL)	USA, CALIFORNIA, SAN FRANCISCO	4.0
ANCHOR STEAM	USA, CALIFORNIA, SAN FRANCISCO	3.9
KAISERDOM RAUCHBIER— SMOKED BAVARIAN DARK	GERMANY, BAMBERG	3.9
SARANAC BLACK & TAN	USA, NEW YORK, UTICA	3.8
WIDMER FESTBIER (ANNUAL)	USA, OREGON, TIGARD	3.8
NEW AMSTERDAM AMBER	USA, NEW YORK, NEW YORK	3.6
STOUTS		
ROGUE SHAKESPEARE STOUT	USA, OREGON, NEWPORT	4.8
XINGU BLACK BEER	BRAZIL, CACADOR	4.5
YOUNG'S OATMEAL STOUT	ENGLAND, LONDON	4.3
GRANT'S IMPERIAL STOUT	USA, WASHINGTON, YAKIMA	4.2
MACKESON TRIPLE XXX STOUT	ENGLAND, LONDON	4.1
ANDERSON VALLEY BARNEY FLATS OATMEAL STOUT	USA, CALIFORNIA, BOONVILLE	4.0
BANDERSNATCH MILK STOUT	USA, ARIZONA, TEMPE	4.0
COOPERSMITH'S HORSETOOTH STOUT	USA, COLORADO, FORT COLLINS	4.0
MANHATTAN EXTRA STOUT	USA, NEW YORK, NEW YORK	4.0
PRESTIGE STOUT	HAITI, PORT-AU-PRINCE	4.0
RIO BRAVO O'KEEFE DRY IRISH STOUT	USA, NEW MEXICO, ALBUQUERQUE	4.0
SAMUEL SMITH'S IMPERIAL STOUT	ENGLAND, TADCASTER	4.0
SAMUEL SMITH OATMEAL STOUT	ENGLAND, TADCASTER	4.0
SCHLAFLY OATMEAL STOUT	USA, MISSOURI, ST. LOUIS	4.0
GUINNESS PUB DRAUGHT	IRELAND, DUBLIN	3.9
WATNEY'S CREAM STOUT	ENGLAND, LONDON	3.9
BUCKERFIELD'S SWANS OATMEAL STOUT	CANADA, BRITISH COLUMBIA, VICTORIA	3.8
GUINNESS EXTRA STOUT	IRELAND, DUBLIN	3.8
OLD AUSTRALIA STOUT	AUSTRALIA, SOUTH AUSTRALIA, THEBARTON	3.8
ABC EXTRA STOUT	SINGAPORE	3.7

NAME	LOCATION	RATING
ROYAL EXTRA STOUT	WEST INDIES, TRINIDAD	3.7
ABC VERY SUPERIOR STOUT	SINGAPORE	3.6
MURPHY'S STOUT	IRELAND, CORK	3.5
SWEETHEART STOUT	SCOTLAND, GLASGOW	3.5
WATNEY'S STINGO CREAM STOUT	ENGLAND, LONDON	3.5
WHEAT BEERS		
ERDINGER WEISSBIER HEFETRUB	GERMANY, ERDING	4.4
AYINGER DUNKLES UR-WEISSE	GERMANY, AYING	4.0
EDELWEISS KRISTALLKLAR WEIZENBIER	AUSTRIA, SALZBURG	4.0
ERDINGER WEISSBIER— DUNKEL	GERMANY, ERDING	4.0
MAISEL'S HEFE WEISSE	GERMANY, BAYREUTH	4.0
BLANCHE DE BRUGES	BELGIUM, BRUGES	3.9
OLDENBERG WEISSE	USA, KENTUCKY, FORT MITCHELL	3.9
ANCHOR WHEAT DRAFT	USA, CALIFORNIA, SAN FRANCISCO	3.8
EKU DARK HEFE WEISBIER	GERMANY, KULMBACH	3.8
ERDINGER WEIZENBOCK	GERMANY, ERDING	3.8
WEIHENSTEPHAN WEIZENBIER	GERMANY, FREISING	3.8
ANDERSON VALLEY HIGH ROLLERS WHEAT	USA, CALIFORNIA, BOONVILLE	3.6
ODELL'S DUNKEL WEIZEN BARLEY WINE	USA, COLORADO, FORT COLLINS	3.5
PSCHORR-BRAU WEISSE	GERMANY, MUNICH	3.5
SPATEN MUNCHEN CLUB— WEISSE	GERMANY, MUNICH	3.5

BEST BEERS
FOR NOVICES

S ome beers have characteristics that make them especially easy, and pleasurable, to enjoy. I have listed 18 of the best—from ale to weisse—for those interested in easing their way gently into the world of drinking beer with a brew likely to encourage a return for more—sort of a beer menu for the beginner. Of course, more knowledgeable drinkers, or the just plain curious, are welcome to sample these highly accommodating beers, too. (See The Rating Guide for each beer's qualities.)

NAME	RATING	COMMENTS
AUGUST SCHELL WEISS	3.2	POPULAR BRAND
BECK'S DARK	2.6	AVAILABLE MOST ANYWHERE
BRAHMA CHOPP	3.7	BRAZILIAN DRAFT IN A CAN
CHURCHILL LAGER	3.6	AVAILABLE IN LARGER CITIES
CORSENDONK MONK'S BROWN ALE	3.8	WORTH IT FOR THE COLOR ALONE
CUZCO	3.2	FIZZY AND FRUITY
GUINNESS GOLD LAGER	3.3	EASY TO LOCATE
HOFBRAU BAVARIA DARK RESERVE	2.5	FRIENDLY AND GENTLE
KALYANI BLACK LABEL PREMIUM LAGER	3.5	TART AND SHARP
KODIAK PREMIUM LAGER	2.5	NONTHREATENING
NORTH COAST SCRIMSHAW PILSENER	3.1	SOUTHERN CALIFORNIA FAVORITE
OLD PECULIER ALE	3.8	READILY AVAILABLE
RIO BRAVO BIG BOB'S BARLEYWINE	2.6	FRESH AND FRUITY
RUSKI	3.3	HAS MINI CULT FOLLOWING
SAMUEL ADAMS DARK WHEAT	2.7	BALANCED AND PREDICTABLE
SUNTORY GOLD DRAFT 100% MALT BEER	3.3	THICK AND CREAMY
VAIL ALE	3.5	KENTUCKY-BREWED
WYNCOOP SYMPOSIUM ALE	2.9	CHOCOLATE OVERTONES

TRY SOMETHING DIFFERENT

While each beer tries to create its own identity, there are several that incorporate brewing features that in my judgment make them truly stand out from the rest. The following are some of those you are likely to remember for a long time—regardless of how much, or how little, you enjoyed them.

NAME	RATING	COMMENTS
ANCHOR OUR SPECIAL ALE (U.S.)	4.0	TASTES LIKE A CHRISTMAS TREE
CHERRYLAND SILVER RAIL LAGER (U.S.)	2.9	JUICE IS IN THE TASTING
DUVEL (BELGIUM)	2.9	COMPLEXITY OF FRUITINESS/ ALCOHOL
KAISERDOM RAUCHBIER/SMOKED BAVARIAN DARK (GERMANY)	3.9	SMOKY LIQUID SAUSAGE
SAMUEL ADAMS TRIPLE BOCK (U.S.)	4.7	PORT-LIKE AND DENSELY FRUITY
SWEETHEART STOUT (SCOTLAND)	3.5	MILKY-GRAPE COMBINATION
THOMAS HARDY'S ALE (ENGLAND)	0.4	LOVE IT OR LOATHE IT; STRONG, FRUITY, AND RIPE

ODD
BEER NAMES

S ometimes what's *on* the label is more intriguing than what's *in* the bottle or can. Here are my favorite names, regardless of any other distinction (or lack of distinction).

NAME	RATING	COMMENTS
ABITA TURBO DOG (ABITA SPRINGS, LOUISIANA)	3.8	"I'M GOING TO WALK THE DOG"; CLASSIC EXCUSE FOR AFTER-DINNER BARHOPPING.
BEER (CALGARY, ALBERTA, CANADA)	1.0	THE ULTIMATE NO-FRILLS NAME.
BELMONT LONG BEACH CRUDE (LONG BEACH, CALIFORNIA)	2.1	THE SITE, AND SIGHT, OF THIS BEACHSIDE BREWPUB IS FAR FROM CRUDE.
BIG ROCK BUZZARD BREATH ALE (CALGARY, ALBERTA, CANADA)	1.7	UNFORTUNATELY, THE NAME ECHOES THE TASTE.
BIG ROCK COLD COCK WINTER PORTER (CALGARY, ALBERTA, CANADA)	3.1	BREWERY FOUNDED BY FORMER COMPANY LAWYER AND RANCHER.
BRIDGEPORT OLD KNUCKLEHEAD BARLEY WINE (PORTLAND, OREGON)	4.0	CARRIES A PUNCH THAT WILL WOBBLE YOU AT THE MEREST TOUCH.
BUFFALO BLIZZARD BOCK (BUFFALO, NEW YORK)	0.9	ODDLY, THIS BEER HAS SOME WARMTH.
COOPERSMITH'S HORSETOOTH STOUT (FORT COLLINS, COLORADO)	4.0	HORSETOOTH ROCK OVERLOOKS HORSETOOTH RESERVOIR IN FORT COLLINS.
COOPERSMITH'S NOT BROWN ALE (FORT COLLINS, COLORADO)	2.7	"NOT" IS NOT A TYPO. IT'S SIMPLY TELLING IT LIKE IT IS.
DIXIE BLACKENED VOODOO LAGER (NEW ORLEANS, LOUISIANA)	2.4	ONCE BANNED IN SOME PLACES.
FOECKING PREMIUM (MONROE, WISCONSIN)	0.3	PRONOUNCE THIS QUIETLY AND DISCREETLY TO YOURSELF.
GRINGO EXTRA LAGER (EVANSVILLE, INDIANA)	0.8	THE WORLD'S MOST POLITICALLY INCORRECT BEER.
HARLEY-DAVIDSON HEAVY BEER – '89 (MONROE, WISCONSIN)	2.4	PACKAGED TO RESEMBLE AN OIL CAN.

NAME	RATING	COMMENTS
HOMBRE (CIUDAD JUAREZ, MEXICO)	2.9	THE NAME, ONE OF MY FAVORITES, SAYS IT ALL.
HUBCAP RAZZLE DAZZLE BERRY WHEAT ALT (VAIL, COLORADO)	1.0	BOUTIQUE BEER FOR THE STARRY-EYED.
KING COBRA MALT LIQUOR (ST. LOUIS, MISSOURI)	2.2	MESMERIZING, WITH QUITE A BITE.
LANDLORD STRONG PALE ALE (KEIGHLEY, ENGLAND)	2.9	PROCLAIMED A "CHAMPIONSHIP WINNER" BY THOSE IN THE KNOW.
LEFT HAND MOTHERLODE GOLDEN ALE (LONGMONT, COLORADO)	2.4	SOMETIMES THE LEFT HAND *DOES* KNOW WHAT THE RIGHT IS DOING.
MCMENAMINS FREUDIAN SIP ALE (PORTLAND, OREGON)	3.3	CONSCIOUSLY AND UNCON-SCIOUSLY, THIS BEER IS EGO-ENHANCING.
MOONLIGHT TWIST OF FATE BITTER ALE (PETALUMA, CALIFORNIA)	3.3	OSTENSIBLY AN AFTER-HOURS BREWING OPERATION.
NEW BELGIUM FAT TIRE AMBER ALE (FORT COLLINS, COLORADO)	3.9	BREWERY OWNER IS A MOUNTAIN BIKE BUFF.
NUDE BEER (WILKES-BARRE, PENNSYLVANIA)	1.5	PHOTO ON THE LABEL SPORTS A REMOVABLE STRIP.
OLD PECULIER ALE (MASHAM, ENGLAND)	3.8	BREWERY LOCATION IS SITE OF OLD PARISH/CHURCH, OR "PECULIER."
PETE'S WICKED ALE (NEW ULM, MINNESOTA)	3.8	THAT'S PETE'S GRANDFATHER ON THE LABEL.
PIG'S EYE PILSNER (ST. PAUL, MINNESOTA)	2.5	HOW IT GOT ITS NAME IS NOT A PRETTY PICTURE (SEE LABEL FOR DETAILS).
RATTLESNAKE PREMIUM (SHINER, TEXAS)	2.4	NAME REFLECTS SLITHERING CRITTERS IN THE LONE STAR STATE.
RHINO CHASERS AMBER ALE (CHATSWORTH, CALIFORNIA)	3.7	BUY BREW, SAVE WILDLIFE—PROCEEDS EARMARKED FOR CONSERVATION.
RIO GRANDE OUTLAW LAGER (ALBUQUERQUE, NEW MEXICO)	2.8	A HEARTY BEER FOR THE GOOD GUYS, TOO.
ROGUE SHAKESPEARE STOUT (NEWPORT, OREGON)	4.8	WILD RIVER, FALSTAFF'S BARD, AND THE BEST BEER IN THE NORTHWEST.

NAME	RANK	COMMENTS
SAN ANDRES EARTHQUAKE PALE ALE (HOLLISTER, CALIFORNIA)	3.0	THE MICROBREWERY SERVES BEER OUT OF THE TAP FOR FIVE CENTS DURING EARTHQUAKES.
SUN LIK (HONG KONG)	3.5	COMPLEMENTS exotic cuisines, OR SO SERPENT ON THE LABEL BOASTS.
WEEPING RADISH BLACK RADISH DARK LAGER (MANTEO, NORTH CAROLINA)	2.2	THIS GERMAN vegetable "WEEPS" WHEN SLICED.
WRIGLEY RED (BOULDER, COLORADO)	2.8	NAMED FOR THE VENERABLE HOME OF THE CHICAGO CUBS BASEBALL TEAM.

VISITING THE SOURCE: MICROBREWERIES AND BREWPUBS

I t's a good idea to call before planning to visit a brewpub or microbrewery. Some establishments have seasonal hours, others may have changed their status from microbrewery to brewpub (or vice versa), and still others may have moved or gone out of business. Brewpubs serve beer-friendly food and, in some instances, also offer fresh beer on tap from other local brewpubs; microbreweries do not generally serve food.

Abita Brewing   (MB)
100 Leveson
Abita Springs, Louisiana
Phone: (504) 893-3143

Alaskan Brewing   (MB)
5429 Shaune Drive
Juneau, Alaska
Phone: (907) 780-5866

Algonquin Brewing   (MB)
One Old Brewery Lane
Formosa, Ontario, Canada
Phone: (519) 367-2995

**Allegheny Brewery &
Pub**   (MB/BP)
(Pennsylvania Brewing)
800 Vinial Street
Pittsburgh, Pennsylvania
Phone: (412) 237-9400

**Anderson Valley
Brewery**   (MB/PB)
14081 Highway 128
Boonville, California
Phone: (707) 895-2337

Angeles Brewing   (MB)
10009 Conoga Avenue
Chatsworth, California
Phone: (818) 407-0340

Appleton Brewing   (MB/BP)
(Adler Brau)
1004 S. Olde Oneida Street
Appleton, Wisconsin
Phone: (414) 731-3322

Arrowhead Brewing   (MB)
1667 Orchard Drive
Chambersburg, Pennsylvania
Phone: (717) 264-0101

Assets Grill & Brewing (BP)
6910 Montgomery N.E.
Albuquerque, New Mexico
Phone: (505) 889-6400

Bandersnatch Brewpub   (BP)
125 E. Fifth Avenue
Tempe, Arizona
Phone: (602) 966-4438

Belmont Brewing   (BP)
25 39th Place
Long Beach, California
Phone: (213) 433-3891

Big Time Brewing   (MB/BP)
4133 University Way N.E.
Seattle, Washington
Phone: (206) 545-4509

**Black Mountain
Brewery   (MB)**
Frontier Town
6245 E. Cave Creek Road
Cave Creek, Arizona
Phone: (602) 254-8594

Bohannon Brewing   (MB/BP)
134 Second Avenue N.
Nashville, Tennessee
Phone: (615) 242-8223

Boulevard Brewing   (MB)
2501 Southwest Boulevard
Kansas City, Missouri
Phone: (816) 474-7095

**Breckenridge Brewery
& Pub   (MB/BP)**
600 South Main
Breckenridge, Colorado
Phone: (303) 453-1550

**Breckenridge Brewery
& Pub   (MB/BP)**
2220 Blake Street
Denver, Colorado
Phone: (303) 297-3644

**Brewski's Gaslamp Pub,
Bistro & Brewery   (BP)**
310 Fifth Avenue
San Diego, California
Phone: (619) 231-7700

**Bridgeport Brewing &
Public House   (MB/BP)**
1313 N.W. Marshall
Portland, Oregon
Phone: (503) 241-7179

Broad Ripple Brewpub   (BP)
840 E. 65th Street
Indianapolis, Indiana
Phone: (317) 253-2739

Buffalo Brewing   (MB/BP)
1830 Abbott Road
Lackawanna, New York
Phone: (716) 828-0004

Capital Brewery   (MB)
7734 Terrace Avenue
Middleton, Wisconsin
Phone: (608) 836-7100

**Carver's Bakery Cafe
Brewery   (BP)**
1022 Main Street
Durango, Colorado
Phone: (303) 259-2545

Catamount Brewing   (MB)
58 S. Main Street
White River Junction,
    Vermont
Phone: (802) 296-2248

Celis Brewery   (MB)
2431 Forbes Drive
Austin, Texas
Phone: (512) 835-0884

Cherryland Brewing   (MB/BP)
341 N. Third Avenue
Sturgeon Bay, Wisconsin
Phone: (414) 743-1945

Chicago Brewing   (MB)
1830 N. Besly Court
Chicago, Illinois
Phone: (312) 252-2739

**CooperSmith's Pub
& Brewing   (BP)**
No. 5 Old Town Square
Fort Collins, Colorado
Phone: (303) 498-0483

**Coyote Springs Brewing
& Cafe**   **(BP)**
(formerly Barley's Brew Pub)
Town & Country Shopping
    Center (S.E. Corner of 20th
    and E. Camelback)
Phoenix, Arizona
Phone: (602) 468-0821

**Crested Butte
Brewing**   **(MB/BP)**
226 Elk Avenue
Crested Butte, Colorado
Phone: (303) 349-5026

D. L. Geary Brewing   **(MB)**
38 Evergreen Drive
Portland, Maine
Phone: (207) 878-2337

Dallas Brewing   **(MB)**
703 McKinney Avenue
Dallas, Texas
Phone (214) 871-7990

**Dallas County
Brewing**   **(MB/BP)**
301 S. 10th Street
Adel, Iowa
Phone: (515) 993-5064

**Deschutes Brewery
& Public House**   **(BP)**
1044 N.W. Bond Street
Bend, Oregon
Phone: (503) 382-9242

Devil Mountain Brewing (MB)
2283 Camel Road
Benicia, California
Phone: (707) 747-6961

Dilworth Brewing (MB/BP)
1301 East Boulevard
Charlotte, North Carolina
Phone: (704) 377-2739

Dock Street Brewing (MB/BP)
2 Logan Square
Philadelphia, Pennsylvania
Phone: (215) 496-0413

Durango Brewing   **(MB)**
3000 Main Street
Durango, Colorado
Phone: (303) 247-3396

Frankenmuth Brewery   **(MB)**
425 S. Main Street
Frankenmuth, Michigan
Phone: (517) 652-6183

Free State Brewing   **(BP)**
636 Massachusetts Street
Lawrence, Kansas
Phone: (913) 843-4555

Full Sail Brewery   **(MB/BP)**
506 Columbia Street
Hood River, Oregon
Phone: (503) 386-2281

Full Sail Brewery   **(MB/BP)**
0307 S.W. Montgomery
Portland, Oregon
Phone: (503) 222-5343

Gentle Ben's Brewing   **(BP)**
841 N. Tyndall
Tucson, Arizona
Phone: (602) 624-4177

Golden Pacific Brewing (MB)
5515 Doyle Street
Emeryville, California
Phone: (510) 547-8270

Goose Island Brewing   **(BP)**
1800 N. Clybourn
Chicago, Illinois
Phone: (312) 915-0071

Grant's Brewery Pub (MB/BP)
32 N. Front Street
Yakima, Washington
Phone: (509) 575-2922

**Granville Island
Brewing (MB)**
1441 Cartwright Street
Vancouver, British Columbia,
   Canada
Phone: (604) 688-9927

Hale's Ales (MB)
5634 E. Commerce Street
Spokane, Washington
Phone: (509) 534-7553

Hart Brewing (MB)
(Pyramid)
110 W. Marine Drive
Kalama, Washington
Phone: (206) 673-2121

Hazel Dell Brewpub
8513 N. E. Highway 99
Vancouver, Washington
Phone: (360) 576-0996

Hops! Bistro & Brewery
7000 E. Camelback Road
Scottsdale, Arizona
(602) 945-4677

Hoster Brewing (BP)
550 S. High Street
Columbus, Ohio
Phone: (614) 228-6066

**Hubcap Brewery &
Kitchen (MB/BP)**
143 East Meadow Drive
Vail, Colorado
Phone: (303) 476-5757

Humboldt Brewery (MB/BP)
856 10th Street
Arcata, California
Phone: (707) 826-2739

Indianapolis Brewing (MB)
3250 N. Post Road, #285
Indianapolis, Indiana
Phone: (317) 898-1235

Irons Brewing (MB)
12354 W. Alameda Parkway
Lakewood, Colorado
Phone: (303) 985-2337

Judge Baldwin's Brewing (BP)
Antlers Doubletree Hotel
4 S. Cascade
Colorado Springs, Colorado
Phone: (719) 473-5600

Kessler Brewery (MB)
1439 Harris Street
Helena, Montana
Phone: (406) 449-6214

La Jolla Brewing (MB/BP)
7536 Fay Avenue
La Jolla, California
Phone: (619) 456-2739

Leavenworth Brewing (BP)
636 Front Street
Leavenworth, Washington
Phone: (509) 548-4545

Left Hand Brewing (MB)
1265 Boston Avenue
Longmont, Colorado
Phone: (303) 772-0258

Lind Brewing (MB)
Westgate Mall
1933 Davis Street
San Leandro, California
Phone: (510) 562-0866

Los Gatos Brewing (BP)
130G N. Santa Cruz Avenue
Los Gatos, California
Phone: (408) 395-9929

Lost Coast Brewery   (MB/BP)
617 4th Street
Eureka, California
Phone: (707) 445-4480

Mad River Brewing   (MB)
195 Taylor Way
Blue Lake, California
Phone: (707) 668-4151

**Manhattan Brewing
Co.   (MB/BP)**
40–42 Thompson Street
New York, New York
Phone: (212) 925-1515

Marin Brewing   (MB/BP)
1809 Larkspur Landing
    Circle
Larkspur, California
Phone: (415) 461-4677

**Maritime Pacific
Brewing   (MB)**
1514 N.W. Leary Way
Seattle, Washington
Phone: (206) 782-6181

Mass. Bay Brewing   (MB)
306 Northern Avenue
Boston, Massachusetts
Phone: (617) 574-9551

McMenamin's   (BP)
432 N.W. 21st Street
Portland, Oregon
Phone: (503) 223-3184
(and other locations in
    Oregon and Washington)

Mendocino Brewing (MB/BP)
13351 South Highway 101
Hopland, California
Phone: (707) 744-1361

Millstream Brewing   (MB)
Lower Brewery Road
Amana, Iowa
Phone: (319) 662-3672

Monterey Brewing   (MB/BP)
638 Wave Street
Monterey, California
Phone: (408) 375-3634

Moonlight Brewing Co. (MB)
Windsor, California
Phone: (707) 528-2537
(not open to the public)

New Amsterdam   (MB)
257 Park Avenue South
New York, New York
Phone: (212) 473-1900

New Belgium Brewing   (MB)
350 Linden Street
Fort Collins, Colorado
Phone: (303) 221-0524

New England Brewing   (MB)
25 Commerce Street
Norwalk, Connecticut
Phone: (203) 866-1339

New Haven Brewing   (MB)
458 Grand Avenue
New Haven, Connecticut
Phone: (203) 772-2739

Niagara Falls Brewing   (MB)
6863 Lundy's Lane
Niagara Falls, Ontario,
    Canada
Phone: (905) 374-1166

**North Coast Brewing
Co.   (MB/BP)**
444 N. Main Street
Fort Bragg, California
Phone: (707) 964-2729

Northampton Brewery (BP)
11 Brewster Court
Northampton, Massachusetts
Phone: (413) 584-9903

NorthWestern Brewery (MB)
711 S.W. Ankeny
Portland, Oregon
Phone: (503) 226-2508

Odell Brewing (MB)
119 Lincoln Avenue
Fort Collins, Colorado
Phone: (303) 498-9070

**Okanagan Spring
Brewery** (MB)
2801 27th Avenue
Vernon, British Columbia,
  Canada
Phone: (604) 542-2337

Old Columbia Brewery (BP)
1157 Columbia Street
San Diego, California
Phone: (619) 234-2739

Oldenberg Brewery (MB/BP)
400 Buttermilk Pike and I-75
Fort Mitchell, Kentucky
Phone: (606) 341-2806

Pacific Beach Brewhouse (BP)
4475 Mission Boulevard
San Diego, California
Phone: (619) 274-2537

Pacific Coast Brewing (BP)
906 Washington Street
Oakland, California
Phone: (510) 836-2739

**Pacific Hop Exchange
Brewing** (MB)
158 Hamilton Drive
Novato, California
Phone: (415) 453-9675

Pavichevich Brewing (MB)
383 Romans Road
Elmhurst, Illinois
Phone: (708) 617-5252

Pike Place Brewery (MB)
1432 Western Avenue
Seattle, Washington
Phone: (206) 622-3373

Portland Brewing (MB/BP)
1339 N.W. Flanders Street
Portland, Oregon
Phone: (503) 222-7150

Portsmouth Brewing (BP)
56 Market Street
Portsmouth, New Hampshire
Phone: (603) 431-1115

Preston Brewery (BP)
Embudo, New Mexico
Phone: (505) 852-4707

**Rio Bravo Brewpub
and Restaurant** (BP)
515 Central N.W.
Albuquerque, New Mexico
Phone: (505) 242-6800

Rio Grande Brewing (MB)
3760 Hawkins, N.E.
Albuquerque, New Mexico
Phone: (505) 343-0903

Rockies Brewing (MB)
(formerly Boulder Beer Co.)
2880 Wilderness Place
Boulder, Colorado
Phone: (303) 444-8448

Rogue Brewery (MB/BP)
748 S.W. Bay Boulevard
Newport, Oregon
Phone: (503) 265-3188

Russell Brewery   **(MB)**
1242 Siler Road
Santa Fe, New Mexico
Phone: (505) 438-3138

San Andreas
Brewing   **(MB/BP)**
737 San Benito Street
Hollister, California
Phone: (408) 637-7074

San Rafael Brewery   **(MB/BP)**
7110 Redwood Boulevard
Novato, California
Phone: (415) 892-3474

Sangre de Cristo
Brewery   **(BP)**
106 Des Georges Lane
Taos, New Mexico
Phone: (505) 758-1517

Santa Cruz Brewing   **(MB/BP)**
516 Front Street
Santa Cruz, California
Phone: (408) 429-8838

Santa Fe Brewing   **(MB/BP)**
Galisteo, New Mexico
Phone: (505) 988-2340

Saxer Brewing   **(MB)**
5875 S.W. Lakeview Drive
Lake Oswego, Oregon
Phone: (503) 699-9524

Schlafly/St. Louis
Brewery   **(BP)**
2100 Locust Street
St. Louis, Missouri
Phone: (314) 241-2337

Seabright Brewery   **(BP)**
519 Seabright Avenue
Santa Cruz, California
Phone: (408) 426-2739

Shields Brewing   **(MB/BP)**
24 E. Santa Clara Street
Ventura, California
Phone: (805) 643-1807

Solana Beach Brewery   **(BP)**
135 N. Highway 101
Solana Beach, California
Phone: (619) 481-7332

Southern California
Brewing   **(MB)**
Alpine Village
833 W. Torrance Boulevard
Torrance, California
Phone: (213) 329-8881

Spanish Peaks
Brewing   **(MB/BP)**
120 N. 19th Avenue
Bozeman, Montana
Phone: (406) 585-2296

Sprecher Brewing   **(MB)**
730 W. Oregon Street
Milwaukee, Wisconsin
Phone: (414) 272-2337

St. Stan's Brewing   **(MB/BP)**
821 L Street
(Highway 132)
Modesto, California
Phone: (209) 524-4782

Steelhead Brewery
& Cafe   **(BP)**
199 E. 5th Street
Eugene, Oregon
Phone: (503) 686-2739

Sun Valley Brewing   **(MB/BP)**
202 N. Main
Halley, Idaho
Phone: (208) 788-5777

Swan's Brewpub/
Buckerfield Brewery (MB/BP)
506 Pandora Avenue
Victoria, British Columbia,
  Canada
Phone: (604) 361-3491

T.W. Fisher's—
A Brew Pub   (MB/PB)
204 N. Second Street
Coeur D'Alene, Idaho
Phone: (208) 664-2739

Tabernash Brewery   (BP)
205 Denargo Market
Denver, Colorado
Phone: (303) 293-2337

Thomas Kemper
Brewing   (MB)
22381 Foss Road N.E.
Poulsbo, Washington
Phone: (206) 697-1446

Umpqua Brewing   (BP)
328 S.E. Jackson Street
Roseburg, Oregon
Phone: (503) 672-0452

Wasatch Brewpub/
Schirf Brewing   (MB/BP)
250 Main Street
Park City, Utah
Phone: (801) 645-9500

Weeping Radish
Bavarian Restaurant
& Brewery   (MB/BP)
Highway 64E
Manteo, North Carolina
Phone: (919) 473-1157
(call for directions)

Whitefish Brewing   (MB)
P.O. Box 1949
Whitefish, Montana
Phone: (406) 862-2684
(call for directions)

Widmer Brewing   (MB/BP)
929 N. Russell Street
Portland, Oregon
Phone: (503) 221-0631

Widmer Brewing/
Heathman Bakery
& Pub   (MB/BP)
901 S.W. Salmon
Portland, Oregon
Phone: (503) 227-5700

Wild Goose Brewery   (MB)
20 Washington Street
Cambridge, Maryland
Phone: (410) 221-1121

Willamette Valley
Brewing   (MB/BP)
66 S.E. Morrison
Portland, Oregon
Phone: (503) 232-9771

Willett's Brewing   (BP)
(now Downtown Joe's
Brewery)
902 Main Street
Napa, California
Phone: (707) 258-2337

Woodland Brewing   (BP)
667 Dead Cat Alley
Woodland, California
Phone: (916) 661-2337

Wynkoop Brewing   (BP)
1634 18th Street
Denver, Colorado
Phone: (303) 297-2700

Zip City Brewing   (BP)
3 W. 18th Street
New York, New York
Phone: (212) 366-6333

RATING NOTES

BEER NAME	RATING

BEER NAME	RATING

BEER NAME	RATING